CLASSIC ELITE
knits

CLASSIC ELITE
knits

100 Gorgeous
Designs for
Every Occasion
from the Studios
of Classic Elite Yarns

The Taunton Press

ACKNOWLEDGMENTS

We thank the following people for their valuable contributions to this book: Jöelle Meier Rioux, Kristen TenDyke, Cecily Glowik; technical editors at Classic Elite Yarns; Carol Kaplan, Carolyn Ross; photographers; Patricia Chew; owner of Classic Elite Yarns; Pam Hoenig, Katie Benoit, Erica Sanders-Foege; editors at The Taunton Press

The Taunton Press
Inspiration for hands-on living®

The Taunton Press, Inc., 63 South Main Street, PO Box 5506, Newtown, CT 06470-5506
e-mail: tp@taunton.com

Editor: Erica Sanders-Foege
Copy Editor: Candace B. Levy
Indexer: Lynne Lipkind
Front Cover Design: Amy Bernard Russo
Interior Design & Layout: Susan Fazekas
Illustrations: Courtesy of Classic Elite Yarns
Photographer: Carol Kaplan, Carolyn Ross

Library of Congress Cataloging-in-Publication Data
Classic elite knits : 100 gorgeous designs for every occasion from the studios of Classic Elite Yarns / from the editors of Classic Elite Yarns.
    p. cm.
 Includes bibliographical references and index.
 ISBN 978-1-60085-010-3 (alk. paper)
 1. Knitting--Patterns. 2. Knitwear. I. Classic Elite Yarns (Firm)

TT825.C63234 2008
746.43'2041--dc22

                    2008001791

Printed in China
10 9 8 7 6 5 4 3 2 1

CONTENTS

Introduction

CLASSIC ELITE YARNS has long been a well-loved and well-respected leader in the hand-knitting industry. We strive to provide quality yarns composed of some of the finest fibers. When choosing pattern designs, we look at current fashion, while keeping in mind the elements that make for timeless garments. In this book, we have compiled the best of the designs we have presented over the past four years. We wanted to show how some of the most talented knitwear designers in the world use, what we believe to be, some of the world's finest yarns.

Not only did we search for the most intriguing designs for this collection but we also wanted to provide multiple patterns at every skill level. For the beginner knitter, this book will be an excellent source of patterns that will keep up with her as her skill level increases. The intermediate knitter will find many patterns that are comfortable as well as others that provide exciting new challenges. The 100 patterns here are sure to give the experienced knitter plenty to keep her knitting skills fine-tuned.

Included in this book are patterns for women, men, and children and an entire chapter of patterns devoted to accessories such as bags, purses, and scarves. Some of the acclaimed designers whose work is featured here are Melissa Leapman, Annie Modesitt, Michele Rose Orne, and Kathy Zimmerman. There are also patterns from new designers who are just beginning to showcase their wonderful talent for design. This mix of the new and the well known makes for a very exciting collection of garments.

We hope that this book provides you with many hours of fulfilling knitting and many compliments on the results!

ABOUT CLASSIC ELITE YARNS

Classic Elite Yarns had its origin in the late 1940s when Ernest Chew, the company's founder, became a partner in Warley Worsted Mills, an old-line textile-manufacturing mill in Lowell, Massachusetts. Under Chew's direction, Warley Worsted became a specialty yarn mill, producing fine mohair yarns for fabric manufacturers and yarn companies like Bernat.

In 1980, Classic Elite Yarns was created as a marketing division of the mill and catered to hand weavers and designers. In 1982 Classic Elite expanded its product line beyond mohairs to include cottons, silks, alpacas, wools, and natural fiber blends. The company then began presenting hand-knitting designs at national needlework shows and producing two annual collections—and the new company also began to make the pages of international fashion magazines.

Today Classic Elite, no longer in the manufacturing business, is owned, managed, and staffed primarily by women. The company now focuses on distributing fine hand-knitting yarns from international mills. In addition to providing exemplary customer service, Classic Elite's in-house staff also manages all pattern writing, technical editing, desktop publishing, and much of the designing for its collections. In 2001, Classic Elite added a luxury fiber division, which continues to provide handknitters with the world's finest cashmere yarns. Classic Elite still resides in an historic mill building on the banks of the Merrimack River in Lowell and prides itself on distributing fine hand-knitting yarns to the best yarn shops in America.

 # General Pattern Instructions

GAUGE

Obtaining the correct gauge is the single most important factor for a successful garment. Take time to save time; check your gauge. *To check gauge:* Knit a swatch at least 4" wide and long using the stitch pattern and needles recommended. Using the washing instructions on the yarn label, wash your swatch. This will tell you how your finished garment will behave after it has been washed. Measure the number of stitches over the 4" swatch. This should match the required gauge. If your gauge is smaller than what the pattern specifies, increase your needle size; if it is larger, decrease your needle size.

SIZING

Sizes ranging from Extra Small to Small, Medium, Large, 1X Large, and 2X Large are given for adult garments. Sizes ranging from 2 to 8 are given for children's garments and roughly correspond to a child's age, but please check your child's measurements against those of the finished sweater given in the pattern schematics.

To determine what size to knit, use a favorite sweater that fits well as a guide. Compare the measurements of your garment with the measurements given in the pattern and select the pattern size that most closely matches. Keep in mind that some sweaters are designed to fit snugly, whereas others are loose fitting. Instructions are for the smallest size, with changes for other sizes noted in parentheses.

BLOCKING

We recommend blocking all pieces to the measurements given before assembling.

SKILL LEVELS

BEGINNER: Projects for first-time knitters or crocheters using basic knit and purl/crochet stitches; minimal shaping.

EASY: Projects using basic stitches, repetitive stitch patterns, simple color changes, and simple shaping and finishing.

INTERMEDIATE: Projects with a variety of stitches, such as basic cables and lace and simple intarsia; use of double-pointed needles and knitting in the round techniques; mid-level shaping and finishing.

EXPERIENCED: Projects using advanced techniques and stitches, such as short rows, Fair Isle, more intricate intarsia, cables, lace patterns, and numerous color changes. Projects for crochet use intricate stitch patterns, techniques, and dimensions, such as nonrepeating patterns, fine threads, small hooks, detailed shaping, and refined finishing.

FELTING INSTRUCTIONS

Felting is a technique that transforms a flexible knitted fabric into a firm, slightly thicker fabric that can be molded to hold a new shape. Washing and agitating the knitted garment in hot water and cold rinse until the fibers interlock achieve this.

If you are following a pattern in this book and you use the same yarn in the same color as shown, you will get the desired results.

We recommend that you test felt your yarn by knitting a swatch and felting it before proceeding with your project.

Classic Elite cannot predict the effects of all washing machines, detergents, and local water conditions; you are felting at your own risk so please proceed cautiously with the process. It is easy to felt just a little more, but impossible to undo the effects of overfelting. Classic Elite cannot be responsible for finishing errors. Be sure to use a top-loading machine.

Steps to Successful Felting

1. PREPARE THE GARMENT

Weave in all ends. Place the knitted garment in a mesh bag or pillow cover and zip the case shut—this will help prevent clogging your machine with the fibers that come off in the washing process.

2. WASHING AND FELTING THE GARMENT

Place the mesh bag or pillow cover in the washer and add a very small amount of detergent (¼ cap). (Do not use detergent for delicates.) Set the washer on the hot water/cold rinse cycle and minimum size load, and wash the garment. Check the felting process every 1 minute to 2 minutes, depending on your machine, detergent, and local water conditions. If using the spin cycle to remove excess water, set it on the lowest setting—folds caused by the spin cycle are hard to remove.

3. FORMING THE GARMENTS

After the garments have finished washing, form as follows.

Hats: *Shape the crown:* Hold the turn-of-crown with one hand on each side, pull firmly in opposite directions; turn the hat 90 degrees and repeat around the hat. *Shape the sides:* With one hand, hold the turn-of-crown; with the other hand, hold the brim and stretch the rise. Continue this around the entire hat, taking special care to pull out the bottom edge of the hat, which has a tendency to curl up in the wash.

If possible, try the hat on the person who will be wearing it. If it is too tight, continue to pull it out until it is large enough. If it is too large, you can wash it again. If washing again, do not use detergent and use a shorter wash cycle.

Scarf: Place the scarf on a flat surface and pin to the schematic measurements.

Bag: Place the bag and pocket on a flat surface and pin to the schematic measurements.

4. DRYING THE GARMENTS

After you have finished forming the garments, let them air dry. Placing a hat over an appropriate size bowl or a balloon will help keep its shape while drying. It will take a day or two for the project to dry completely because of the thickness of the fabric.

ABBREVIATIONS

approx: approximately

beg: begin(ning)

bet: between

BO: bind off

C4B: slip 2 stitches to cable needle and hold in back; knit 2, knit 2 from cable needle

C4F: slip 2 stitches to cable needle and hold in front; knit 2, knit 2 from cable needle

C6B: slip 3 stitches to cable needle, hold in back; knit 3, knit 3 stitches from cable needle

CGF: slip 2 stitches to cable needle and hold in front; knit 3, knit 3 stitches from cable needle

CC: contrast color

ch: chain stitch

CO: cast on

cont: continue

cn: cable needle(s)

dc: double crochet

Ddec: double decrease—slip 2 stitches together as if to knit, knit 1, pass 2 slipped stitches over (p2sso) (2-stitch decrease)

dec: decrease

dpn: double-pointed needles

EOR: every other row

est: establish(ed)

foll: follows, following

Gtr st: Garter Stitch

inc: increase

k: knit

k1b: knit 1 stitch in row below

k1-f/b: knit into front and back of same stitch (1-stitch increase)

k2tog: knit 2 stitches together (1-stitch decrease)

k2tog-tbl: knit 2 stitches together through back loop (1-stitch decrease)

k3tog: knit 3 stitches together (2-stitch decrease)

k3tog-tbl: knit 3 stitches together through back loop (2-stitch decrease)

1/1 LC: slip 1 stitch to cable needle, hold in front, knit 1, knit 1 from cable needle

1/2 LC: slip 1 stitch to cable needle, hold in front, knit 2, knit 1 from cable needle

2/2 LC: slip 2 stitches to cable needle, hold in front, knit 2, knit 2 from cable needle (C4F)

LH: left hand

L1: lifted increase—increase 1 stitch by inserting tip of right-hand needle from top down into back of stitch on left-hand needle 1 row below; knit this stitch, then knit stitch on left-hand needle. (1-stitch increase)

m: meter(s)

m1 (M1L): make 1 stitch—insert left-hand needle, from front to back, under horizontal strand between stitch just worked and next stitch, knit through back loop (1-stitch increase)

m1k: make 1 stitch knitwise (1-stitch increase)

m1p: make 1 stitch purlwise (1-stitch increase)

M1R: insert left-hand needle, from back to front, under horizontal strand between stitch just worked and next stitch, knit through front loop (1-stitch increase)

MC: main color

meas: measure(s)

p: purl

p1b: purl 1 stitch in row below

p2tog: purl 2 stitches together (1-stitch decrease)

p2tog-tbl: purl 2 stitches together through back loop (1-stitch decrease)

p3tog: purl 3 stitches together (2-stitch decrease)

patt: pattern

pm(s): place marker(s)

psso: pass slipped stitch over

1/1 RC: slip 1 stitch to cable needle, hold in back, knit 1, knit 1 from cable needle

1/2 RC: slip 2 stitches to cable needle, hold in back, knit 1, slip next stitch on cable needle to left-hand needle, knit 1, knit 1 from cable needle

2/2 RC: slip 2 stitches to cable needle, hold in back, knit 2, knit 2 from cable needle (C4B)

rem: remain(ing)

rep: repeat

rev: reverse, reversing

Rev St st: Reverse Stockinette Stitch

RH: right hand

rnd: round

RS: right side

sc: single crochet

sep: separately

skp: slip 1, knit 1, pass slipped stitched over

sk2p: slip 1 stitch knitwise, from left-hand needle to right-hand needle; knit 2 together, pass slipped stitch over knit stitch created by knitting 2 together (2-stitch decrease)

sl: slip

sl1k: slip 1 stitch knitwise

sl1p: slip 1 stitch purlwise

ssk: slip, slip, knit—slip 2 sts, 1 at a time, knitwise to RH needle; retuen sts to LH needle in turned position and knit them tog tbl.

ssp: slip, slip, purl—slip 2 sts, 1 at a time, knitwise to RH needle; return to LH needle in turned position and purl them tog tbl.

st(s): stitch(es)

St st: Stockinette Stitch

3/3 RC: slip 3 stitches to cable needle, hold in back; knit 3; knit 3 from cable needle

T3B: slip 1 stitch to cable needle and hold in back; knit 2, purl 1 from cable needle

T3F: slip 2 stitches to cable needle and hold in front; purl 1, knit 2 from cable needle

tbl: through back loop

tog: together

tr: treble crochet

WS: wrong side

yb: yarn back

yd: yard(s)

yf: yarn forward

yo: yarnover

SUBSTITUTE YARNS

CEY Yarn	CEY Substitute
Wings	Renaissance/Inca Alpaca
Skye Tweed	Renaissance
	Bubbles
	Star
	Potpourri
Dazzle	Minnie
MarLa	Aspen
Tigress	Aspen
Two.Two	Duchess
Imagine	Miracle/Premiere
Vintage	Renaissance/Waterlily

■ STANDARD YARN WEIGHT SYSTEM

Yarn Weight Symbol and Category Name	Super Fine **1**	Fine **2**	Light **3**	Medium **4**	Bulky **5**	Super Bulky **6**
Types of yarn in category	Sock, fingering, baby	Sport, baby	DK, light worsted	Worsted, afghan, Aran	Chunky, craft, rug	Bulky, roving
Knit gauge range in stockinette st in 4"*	27–32 sts	23–26 sts	21–24 sts	16–20 sts	12–15 sts	6–11 sts
Recommended metric needle size	2.25–3.25 mm	3.25–3.75 mm	3.75–4.5 mm	4.5–5.5 mm	5.5–8 mm	8 mm and larger
Recommended U.S. needle size	1–3	3–5	5–7	7–9	9–11	11 and larger
Crochet gauge range in single crochet in 4"*	21–31 sts	16–20 sts	12–17 sts	11–14 sts	8–11 sts	5–9 sts
Recommended metric hook size	2.25–3.5 mm	3.5–4.5 mm	4.5–5.5 mm	5.5–6.5 mm	6.5–9 mm	9 mm and larger
Recommended U.S. hook size	B/1–E/4	E/4–7	7–I/9	I/9–K/10.5	K/10.5–M/13	M/13 and larger

*The information in this table reflects the most commonly used gauges and needle or hook sizes for the specific yarn categories.

WOMEN'S KNITS

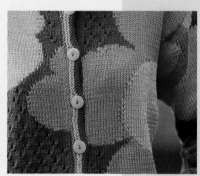

contents

PICOT V-NECK PULLOVER

SIZES
Small (Medium, Large, 1X Large)

FINISHED MEASUREMENTS
33½ (40, 46½, 53)"

Classic Elite Yarns
Bam Boo (100% bamboo, 50-g ball = approx 70 yd/64 m)
• 12 (14, 16, 18) balls 4947 Bluebird

Equivalent yarn
Worsted weight #4, 924 (1078, 1232, 1386) yd

Needles
• One pair size U.S. 6 (4 mm) or size to obtain gauge
• One 24" circular size U.S. 4 (3.5 mm) for neck finishing

Stitch holders

Stitch markers

GAUGE
22 sts and 28 rows = 4" in Stockinette Stitch, using larger needles.
Take time to save time, check your gauge.

PATTERN STITCHES

GARTER STITCH (GTR ST)
Knit every row.

CIRCULAR GARTER STITCH
Rnd 1: Purl.
Rnd 2: Knit.
Rep Rnds 1–2 for Circular Garter Stitch.

STOCKINETTE STITCH (ST ST)
Knit on RS, purl on WS.

FEATHER AND FAN LACE (MULTIPLE OF 18 STS + 2)
Row 1: (RS) Knit.
Row 2: Purl.
Row 3: K1 *k2tog 3 times, [yo, k1] 6 times, k2tog 3 times; rep from * across to last st, k1.
Row 4: Knit.
Repeat Rows 1–4 for Feather and Fan Lace.

PICOT EDGE BIND-OFF METHOD
*BO 2 sts, k2tog, BO 2 sts, sl st from RH needle back to LH needle, CO 3 sts, BO 3 sts; rep from * until all sts are bound off.

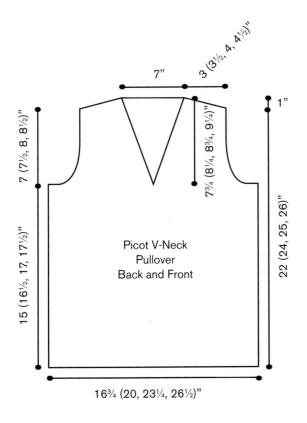

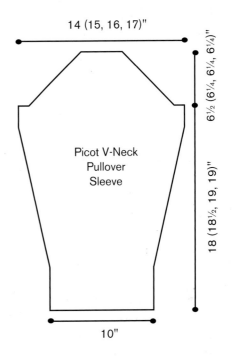

BACK

CO 92 (110, 128, 146) sts; work 4 rows in Gtr st, end WS row. Change to Feather and Fan Lace patt; work even until piece meas 7" from beg, end with Row 4. Change to Gtr st; work 4 rows even. Change to St st; work even until piece meas 15 (16½, 17, 17½)" from beg, end WS row. *Shape armholes:* (RS) BO 5 (8, 12, 15) sts at beg of next 2 rows, then dec 1 st each side EOR 5 (8, 11, 14) times—72 (78, 82, 88) sts rem. Work even until armhole meas 7 (7½, 8, 8½)" from beg of shaping, end WS row. *Shape shoulders:* BO 6 (7, 7, 8) sts at beg of next 4 rows, 5 (6, 8, 9) sts at beg of next 2 rows—38 sts rem. Place rem sts on holder for back neck.

FRONT

Work as for back until piece meas 15 (16½, 17, 17½)" from beg, and on last WS row divide for neck by working 46 (55, 64, 73) sts; join second ball of yarn, work to end. (RS) Working both sides at same time, shape armhole as for back—72 (78, 82, 88); and, at the same time, *shape neck:* (RS) Dec 1 st at each neck edge EOR 19 times—17 (20, 22, 25) sts rem. Work even until armhole meas same as back to shoulders, end WS row. *Shape shoulders* as for back.

SLEEVES

CO 56 sts; work 4 rows in Gtr st, end WS row. Change to Feather and Fan Lace patt; work even until piece meas 4" from beg, end WS row. Change to Gtr st; work 4 rows even. Change to St st, and *shape sleeve:* (RS) Inc 1 st each side this row, then every 10 (6, 6, 6) rows 5 (1, 11, 8) times, every 8 (8, 8, 4) rows 5 (11, 4, 10) times—78 (82, 88, 94) sts. Work even until piece meas 18 (18½, 19, 19)" from beg, end WS row. *Note:* This sleeve is designed to extend onto the hand. *Shape cap:* (RS) BO 5 (8, 11, 14) sts at beg of next 2 rows, then dec 1 st each side EOR 23 (22, 22, 22) times—22 sts rem. BO rem sts.

FINISHING

Block pieces to measurements. Sew shoulder seams. Set in sleeves; sew sleeve and side seams. *Neckband:* With RS facing, using circular needle, work 38 sts from holder for back neck, pick up and knit 43 (45, 48, 51) sts evenly along left front neck edge, 43 (45, 48, 51) sts evenly along right front neck edge; pm for beg of rnd—124 (128, 134, 140) sts. Work 3 rnds in Gtr st. BO all sts using Picot Edge Bind-Off Method.

BULKY RIDGE CARDIGAN

SIZES
Small (Medium, Large, 1X Large)

FINISHED MEASUREMENTS
36.5 (40.5, 44.5, 48.5)"

MATERIALS
Classic Elite Yarns

Bravo (40% rayon, 35% mohair, 13% silk, 6% wool, 6% nylon; 50-g hank = approx 48 yd/44 m)
• 14 (15, 16, 17) hanks 3744 Gold Vein

Equivalent yarn

Bulky weight #5, 672 (720, 768, 816) yd

Needles

• One pair size U.S. 11 (8 mm) or size to obtain gauge
• One pair size U.S. 10 (6 mm) for collar

GAUGE
12 sts and 16 rows = 4" in Reverse Stockinette Stitch, using larger needles. Take time to save time, check your gauge.

PATTERN STITCHES

REVERSE STOCKINETTE STITCH RIDGE (REV ST ST RIDGE)
Row 1: (RS) Knit.

Row 2: Purl.

Row 3: Knit.

Row 4: Purl.

Row 5: Purl.

Row 6: Knit.

Rep Rows 1–6 for Reverse Stockinette Stitch Ridge.

GARTER STITCH (GTR ST)
Knit every row.

STOCKINETTE STITCH (ST ST)
Knit on RS, purl on WS.

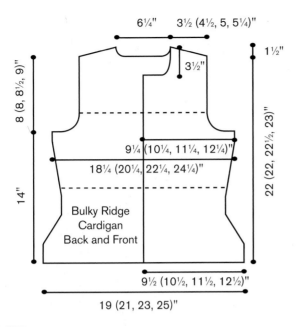

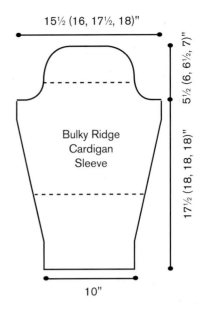

BACK

Using larger needles, CO 57 (63, 69, 75) sts; work in Rev St st Ridge until piece meas 2" from beg, end WS row. ***Shape waist:*** (RS) Dec 1 st each side this row, then every 4 rows 3 times—49 (55, 61, 67) sts rem. Work even until piece meas 6½" from beg, end WS row. ***Shape waist:*** (RS) Inc 1 st each side this row, then every 6 rows twice—55 (61, 67, 73) sts; and, at the same time, when piece meas 8" from beg, end WS row and change to Gtr st. Work even until piece meas 14" from beg, end WS row. ***Shape armholes:*** (RS) BO 2 (3, 4, 6) sts at beg of next 2 rows, then dec 1 st each side EOR 5 times—41 (45, 49, 51) sts rem; and, at the same time, when armhole meas 2" from beg of shaping, end WS row. Cont to shape armhole and change to St st; work even until armhole meas 8 (8, 8½, 9)" from beg of shaping, end WS row. ***Shape shoulders:*** (RS) BO 4 (4, 5, 5) sts at beg of next 4 rows, 3 (5, 5, 6) sts at beg of next 2 rows; and, at the same time, on first row of shoulder shaping, work to center 13 sts; join second ball of yarn, BO center sts, work to end. Working both sides at same time, at each neck edge BO 3 sts once.

LEFT FRONT

CO 29 (32, 35, 38) sts; work in Rev St st Ridge until piece meas 2" from beg, end WS row. ***Shape waist:*** (RS) Dec 1 st at beg of this row, then every 4 rows 3 times—25 (28, 31, 34) sts rem. Work even until piece meas 6½" from beg, end WS row. ***Shape waist:*** (RS) Inc 1 st at beg of this row, then every 6 rows twice—28 (31, 34, 37) sts; and, at the same time, when piece meas 8" from beg, end WS row and change to Gtr st. Work even until piece meas same as back to armhole, end WS row. ***Shape armhole*** as for back at beg of RS rows only—21 (23, 25, 26) sts rem; and, at the same time, when armhole meas

2" from beg, end WS row. Cont to shape armhole and change to St st; work even until armhole meas 5 (5, 5½, 6)" from beg of shaping, end RS row. ***Shape neck:*** (WS) BO 4 sts once, 3 sts once, then dec 1 st EOR 3 times—11 (13, 15, 16) sts rem for shoulder; and, **at the same time,** when armhole meas same as back to shoulder shaping, end WS row. ***Shape shoulder*** as for back at beg of RS rows only.

RIGHT FRONT

Work as for left front, rev all shaping.

SLEEVES

Using larger needles, CO 30 sts; work in Gtr st until piece meas 3" from beg, end WS row. ***Shape sleeve:*** (RS) Cont in Gtr st; inc 1 st each side this row, then every 6 rows 4 (4, 8, 6) times, every 8 (8, 4, 4) rows 3 (4, 2, 5) times—46 (48, 52, 54) sts; and, at the same time, when piece meas 10" from beg, end WS row. Cont to shape sleeve and change to Rev St st Ridge. Work even until piece meas 17½ (18, 18, 18)" from beg, end WS row. ***Shape cap:*** (RS) BO 2 (3, 4, 6) sts at beg of next 2 rows, then dec 1 st each side EOR 7 (8, 9, 10) times, BO 2 sts at beg of next 6 rows—16 (14, 14, 10) sts rem; and, at the same time, when cap meas 2" from beg of shaping, end WS row, and change to St st. BO rem sts.

FINISHING

Block pieces to measurements. Sew shoulder seams. Set in sleeves; sew sleeve and side seams. ***Collar:*** With RS facing, using smaller needles, pick up and knit 60 sts evenly around neck edge, beg and end at center front edges. Work in Gtr st until collar meas 4½" from pickup row. BO all sts loosely.

FIVE-RIB TURTLENECK

SIZES
Extra Small (Small, Medium, Large)

FINISHED MEASUREMENTS
34 (37, 40, 43)"

MATERIALS
Classic Elite Yarns

Bazic (100% superwash wool; 50-g ball = approx 65 yd/59 m)

• 14 (15, 16, 17) balls 2953 Magenta

Equivalent yarn

Worsted weight #4, 910 (975, 1040, 1105) yd

Needles

• One pair *each* size U.S. 8 (5 mm) and 9 (5.5 mm) or size to obtain gauge

• One 16" circular size U.S. 9 (5.5 mm) for neck finishing

Stitch holders

Stitch markers

GAUGE
16 sts and 23 rows = 4" in Stockinette Stitch, using larger needles. Take time to save time, check your gauge.

PATTERN STITCHES

STOCKINETTE STITCH (ST ST)
Knit on RS, purl on WS.

4 × 2 RIB (MULTIPLE OF 6 STS + 2)
Row 1: (RS) P2, *k4, p2; rep from * across.

Row 2: Knit the knit sts and purl the purl sts as they face you.

Rep Row 2 for 4 x 2 Rib.

BACK

Using larger needles, CO 68 (74, 80, 86) sts. Beg 4 × 2 Rib; work even for 6 rows, end WS row. Change to St st; (RS) work even until piece meas 16½ (16, 15½, 15)" from beg, end WS row. **Shape armholes:** (RS) BO 3 (4, 5, 6) sts at beg of next 2 rows—62 (66, 70, 74) sts rem. (RS) Dec 1 st each side EOR twice—58 (62, 66, 70) sts rem. Work even until armhole meas 7½ (8, 8½, 9)" from beg of shaping, end WS row. **Shape shoulders:** (RS) BO 14 (16, 18, 20) sts at beg of next 2 rows—30 sts rem for neck. Place rem sts on holder.

FRONT

Using larger needles, CO 74 (80, 86, 92) sts. Beg 4 × 2 Rib; work even for 6 rows, end WS row. **Est patt:** (RS) K21 (24, 24, 27) sts, pm; work center 32 (32, 38, 38) sts in 4 × 2 Rib, pm; k21 (24, 24, 27) sts. Cont as est, working sts each side of center panel in St st; work even until piece meas 16½ (16, 15½, 15)" from beg, end WS row. **Shape armholes:** (RS) BO 3 (4, 5, 6) sts at beg of next 2 rows—68 (72, 76, 80) sts rem. (RS) Dec 1 st each side EOR twice—64 (68, 72, 76) sts rem. Work even until armhole meas 5½ (6, 6½, 7)" from beg of shaping, end WS row; pm each side of center 22 sts. **Shape neck:** (RS) Work across to marker; place center sts on holder; join second ball of yarn and work to end—21 (23, 25, 27) sts rem each side. Working both sides at same time, at each neck edge, BO 2 sts once, then dec 1 st every row 5 times—14 (16, 18, 20) sts rem each side for shoulders. Work even until armhole meas 7½ (8, 8½, 9)" from beg of shaping. BO rem sts, in patt.

SLEEVES

Using smaller needles, CO 38 (38, 44, 44) sts. Beg 4 2 Rib; work even for 6 rows, end WS row. Change to larger needles and St st: (RS) Inc 4 (6, 4, 6) sts evenly across this row—42 (44, 48, 50) sts. Work 5 rows even, end WS row. **Shape sleeve:** (RS) Inc 1 st each side this row, then every 6 rows 3 (3, 4, 8) times, every 8 rows 5 (6, 5, 1) times—60 (64, 68, 70) sts. Work even until piece meas 14½ (14½, 14, 13)" from beg of St st, end WS row. **Shape cap:** (RS) BO 3 (4, 5, 6) sts at beg of next 2 rows, then dec 1 st each side EOR 5 (5, 8, 8) times—44 (46, 42, 42) sts rem. BO rem sts.

FINISHING

Block pieces to measurements. Sew shoulder seams. **Neckband:** With RS facing, using circular needle, beg at left shoulder, pick up and knit 13 sts along left front neck shaping, work 22 sts

from front neck holder in 4 × 2 Rib as est, pick up and knit 13 sts along right front neck shaping to shoulder, work 30 sts from back neck holder—78 sts. Maintaining est patt on sts from front holder, beg 4 × 2 Rib on rem sts; work even until band meas 5" from pickup row. BO all sts loosely in rib. Set in sleeves; sew sleeve and side seams.

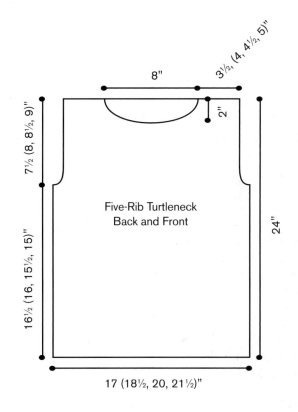

Five-Rib Turtleneck
Back and Front

8"

3½ (4, 4½, 5)"

2"

7½ (8, 8½, 9)"

24"

16½ (16, 15½, 15)"

17 (18½, 20, 21½)"

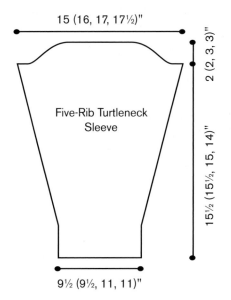

15 (16, 17, 17½)"

2 (2, 3, 3)"

Five-Rib Turtleneck
Sleeve

15½ (15½, 15, 14)"

9½ (9½, 11, 11)"

OPEN NECK CARDIGAN

SIZES
Small (Medium, Large, 1X Large)

FINISHED MEASUREMENTS
40 (44, 48, 52)"

MATERIALS
Classic Elite Yarns
Bubbles (50% cotton, 30% nylon, 20% acrylic; 50-g ball = approx 61 yd/55 m)
• 2 (14, 16, 17) balls Main Color (MC)—2432 Strawberry Soda
• 1 (1, 2, 2) balls Contrast Color (CC)—2485 Orange Fizz
Equivalent yarn
Bulky weight #5; MC: 732 (854, 976, 1037) yd; CC: 61 (61, 122, 122) yd
Needles
• One pair *each* size U.S. 8 (5 mm) and 10½ (6.5 mm) or size to obtain gauge
Five ⅞" buttons
Stitch markers

GAUGE
13 sts and 20 rows = 4" in Stockinette Stitch, using larger needles. Take time to save time, check your gauge.

PATTERN STITCHES
STOCKINETTE STITCH (ST ST)
Knit on RS, purl on WS.

2 × 2 RIB (MULTIPLE OF 4 STS)
Row 1: (WS) *P2, k2; rep from * across.
Row 2: Knit the knit sts and purl the purl sts as they face you.
Rep Row 2 for 2 x 2 Rib.

BACK
Using smaller needles and CC, CO 64 (72, 76, 84) sts. (WS) Beg 2 × 2 Rib; work 1 row even. Change to MC; work 2 rows; and, at the same time, inc 2 (0, 2, 0) sts evenly spaced on last row, end WS row—66 (72, 78, 84) sts. Change to larger needles and St st; work even until piece meas 11 (11½, 12, 12½)" from beg,

end WS row. ***Shape armholes:*** (RS) BO 5 (5, 6, 7) sts at beg of next 2 rows, 2 sts at beg of next 2 rows, then dec 1 st each side once—50 (56, 60, 64) sts rem. Work even until armhole meas 8 (8, 8½, 9)" from beg of shaping, end WS row; pm each side of center 22 (22, 24, 28) sts. ***Shape shoulders and neck:*** (RS) BO 7 (9, 9, 9) sts at beg of next 4 (2, 4, 4) rows, then 0 (8, 0, 0) sts

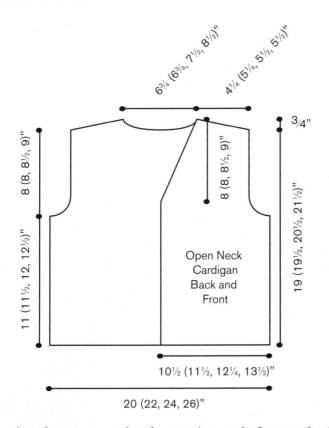

6¾ (6¾, 7½, 8½)"   4¼ (5¼, 5½, 5½)"

8 (8, 8½, 9)"

3/4"

8 (8, 8½, 9)"

11 (11½, 12, 12½)"

19 (19½, 20½, 21½)"

Open Neck
Cardigan
Back and
Front

10½ (11½, 12¼, 13½)"

20 (22, 24, 26)"

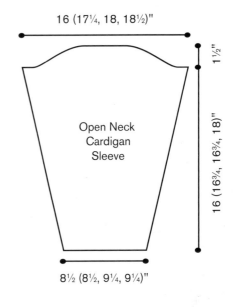

16 (17¼, 18, 18½)"

1½"

16 (16¾, 16¾, 18)"

Open Neck
Cardigan
Sleeve

8½ (8½, 9¼, 9¼)"

at beg of next 2 rows; and, **at the same time,** on the first row of shoulder shaping, work across to marker; join second ball of yarn and BO center 22 (22, 24, 28) sts, work to end. Working both sides at same time, complete shoulder shaping.

LEFT FRONT

Using smaller needles and CC, CO 32 (36, 40, 44) sts. (WS) Beg 2 × 2 Rib; work 1 row even. Change to MC; work 2 rows; and, at the same time, inc 2 (2, 0, 0) sts evenly spaced on last row, end WS row—34 (38, 40, 44) sts. Change to larger needles and St st; work as for back until armhole meas 1" from beg of shaping (extra decs are located in this section to shape armhole), end WS row. 26 (30, 32, 36) sts rem. *Shape neck:* (RS) At neck edge (end of RS rows), dec 1 st EOR 8 (10, 10, 13) times as foll: Work across to last 2 sts, ssk. Then dec 1 st every 4 rows 4 (3, 3, 3) times—14 (17, 18, 18) sts rem for shoulder. Work even until armhole meas same as back to shoulder shaping, end WS row. *Shape shoulder* as for back. Pm for 5 buttons, first 1¼" from lower edge, last 1" from beg of neck shaping, rem 3 evenly spaced bet.

RIGHT FRONT

Work as for left front, rev all shaping by working armhole and shoulder shaping at beg of WS rows, neck shaping at beg of RS rows as foll: K2tog, work to end, and at the same time, work buttonholes at beg of RS rows opposite markers on left front as foll: K2, [yo, k2tog] for buttonhole, knit to end.

SLEEVES

Using smaller needles and CC, CO 28 (28, 32, 32) sts. (WS) Beg 2 × 2 Rib; work 1 row even. Change to MC; work 2 rows even, end WS row. Change to larger needles and St st; and, at the same time, *shape sleeve:* (RS) Inc 1 st each side this row, then every 6 rows 11 (13, 12, 13) times—52 (56, 58, 60) sts. Work even until piece meas 16 (16¾, 16¾, 18)" from beg, end WS row. *Shape cap:* (RS) BO 5 (5, 6, 7) sts at beg of next 2 rows, 2 sts at beg of next 2 rows, then dec 1 st each side once—36 (40, 40, 40) sts rem. BO 3 sts at beg next 2 rows—30 (34, 34, 34) sts rem. BO rem sts.

COLLAR

Using larger needles and MC, CO 78 (78, 86, 94) sts. (WS) Beg 2 × 2 Rib, beg and end p2; work even until piece meas 3½" from beg, end RS row. Change to CC; work 1 row even. BO all sts in rib.

FINISHING

Block pieces to measurements. Sew shoulder seams. Set in sleeves; sew side and sleeve seams. Sew on collar. *Front edging:* With RS facing, using smaller needles and CC, pick up and knit 62 (66, 70, 74) sts along right front edge and collar edge. (WS) Work 1 row in 2 × 2 Rib, beg and end p2. BO all sts in rib. Work left front edge the same. Sew on buttons.

RISING STRIPES TURTLENECK

SIZES

Small (Medium, Large, 1X Large)

FINISHED MEASUREMENTS

33¼ (37¼, 41¼, 45¼)"

MATERIALS

Classic Elite Yarns

Desert (100% wool; 50-g ball = approx 110 yd/101 m)

• 10 (11, 12, 13) balls 2015 Lizard

Equivalent yarn

Worsted weight #4, 1100 (1210, 1320, 1430) yd

Needles

• One *each* 16" and 24" circular size U.S. 6 (4 mm) or size to obtain gauge

• One set double-pointed needles (dpn) size U.S. 6 (4 mm)

Stitch holders

Stitch markers (two different colors)

GAUGE

20 sts and 27 rows = 4" in Stockinette Stitch. Take time to save time, check your gauge.

NOTE

Body and sleeves are worked in the round to underarm; then they are worked back and forth to shoulders.

PATTERN STITCHES

STOCKINETTE STITCH (ST ST)

Knit on RS, purl on WS.

CIRCULAR STOCKINETTE STITCH

Knit every rnd.

CIRCULAR 1 × 1 RIB (MULTIPLE OF 2 STS)

Rnd 1: *K1, p1; rep from * around.

Rep Rnd 1 for Circular 1 x 1 Rib.

CIRCULAR 1 × 2 RIB (MULTIPLE OF 3 STS)

Rnd 1:*K1, p2; rep from * around.

Rep Rnd 1 for Circular 1 x 2 Rib.

CIRCULAR 1 × 3 RIB (MULTIPLE OF 4 STS)

Rnd 1:*K1, p3; rep from * around.

Rep Rnd 1 for Circular 1 x 3 Rib.

BODY

Using longer circular needle, CO 164 (184, 204, 224) sts. Join, being careful not to twist sts; pm for beg of rnd. Beg Circular 1 × 1 Rib: Work even for 5 rnds. Change to St st; work 55 (62, 68, 75) sts, inc 1; work 54 (60, 68, 74) sts, inc 1; work 55 (62, 68, 75) sts—166 (186, 206, 226) sts. Cont in St st, work 83 (93, 103, 113) sts, pm (different color from marker for beg of rnd), work to end. Work even until piece meas 2 (2½, 2½, 2 ½)" from beg. *Shape sides: Dec rnd:* *[Ssk, work around to 2 sts before marker, k2tog] twice—4 sts dec. Work 15 (11, 11, 13) rnds even. Rep from * 1 (2, 2, 2) times; work 1 more rnd even—158 (174, 194, 214) sts rem. *Shape sides: Inc rnd:* Inc 1 st before and after each marker, every 16 (12, 12, 14) rnds 2 (3, 3, 3) times—166 (186, 206, 226) sts. Work even until piece meas 14 (14½, 15, 15½)" from beg. Divide for front and back: BO 5 (7, 8, 7) sts, work across to marker, turn (back); place rem 83 (93, 103, 113) sts on holder for front.

BACK

Working in rows, on back sts only, (WS) BO 5 (7, 8, 7) sts, work to end—73 (79, 87, 99) sts rem. *Shape armholes:* (RS) Dec 1 st each side EOR 5 (6, 8, 9) times—63 (67, 71, 81) sts rem. Work even until armhole meas 4 (4½, 5, 5½)" from beg of shaping, end WS row; pm each side of center 35 (39, 39, 45) sts. *Shape neck:* (RS) Work across to marker; join second ball of yarn and BO center sts; work to end—14 (14, 16, 18) sts rem each shoulder. Working both sides at same time, work 1 row even, end WS row. (RS) At each neck edge, BO 2 sts EOR 2 (2, 3, 4) times, then dec 1 st EOR 3 times—7 sts rem each shoulder. Work even until armhole meas 7½ (8, 8½, 9)" from beg of shaping, end WS row. *Shape shoulders:* (RS) BO 4 sts at beg of next 2 rows, BO rem sts.

FRONT

Return front sts to needle; join yarn ready to work a RS row. BO 5 (7, 8, 7) sts at beg of next 2 rows—73 (79, 87, 99) sts rem. Work as for back.

SLEEVES

Using dpn, CO 42 (42, 46, 48) sts. Join, being careful not to twist sts; pm for beg of rnd. Beg Circular 1 × 1 Rib: Work even for 5 rnds. Change to St st; work even until piece meas 2 (2½, 2½, 2½)" from beg. *Shape sleeve:* Inc 1 st each side of marker this rnd, then every 0 (6, 6, 6) rnds 0 (7, 8, 11) times, every 8 rnds 11 (6, 6, 4) times, changing to shorter circular needle when desired—66 (70, 76, 80) sts. Work even until piece meas 17 (17½, 18, 18½)" from beg. Beg working in rows and *Shape*

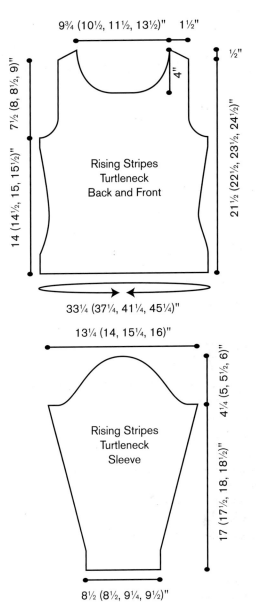

9¾ (10½, 11½, 13½)"   1½"

½"

4"

7½ (8, 8½, 9)"

21½ (22½, 23½, 24½)"

14 (14½, 15, 15½)"

Rising Stripes
Turtleneck
Back and Front

33¼ (37¼, 41¼, 45¼)"

13¼ (14, 15¼, 16)"

4¼ (5, 5½, 6)"

Rising Stripes
Turtleneck
Sleeve

17 (17½, 18, 18½)"

8½ (8½, 9¼, 9½)"

cap: (RS) BO 5 (7, 8, 7) sts at the beg of next 2 rows—56 (56, 60, 66) sts rem. (RS) Dec 1 st each side EOR 12 (14, 16, 18) times—32 (28, 28, 30) sts rem. BO 4 (3, 3, 3) sts at beg of next 4 rows—16 (16, 16, 18) sts rem. BO rem sts.

FINISHING

Block pieces to measurements. Sew shoulder seams. Set in sleeves. *Turtleneck:* With RS facing, using longer circular needle, pick up and knit 164 sts evenly around neck edge. Join; pm for beg of rnd. Beg Circular 1 × 3 Rib: Work even until piece meas 1½" from pickup rnd. *Shape neck:* *K1, p2tog, p1; rep from * around—123 sts rem. Beg Circular 1 × 2 Rib: Work even until piece meas 3" from pickup rnd. Change to shorter circular needle and *shape neck:* *K1, p2tog; rep from * around—82 sts rem. Beg Circular 1 × 1 Rib: Work even until piece meas 8" from pickup rnd. BO all sts loosely in rib.

AWRY CARDIGAN

SIZES

Extra Small (Small, Medium, Large, 1X Large)

FINISHED MEASUREMENTS

37 (40, 43, 46, 49)"

Note: Right front is designed to be 3" longer than left front.

MATERIALS

Classic Elite Yarns

Duchess (40% merino, 28% viscose, 10% cashmere, 7% angora, 15% nylon; 50-g ball = approx 75 yd/69 m)

12 (14, 16, 18, 20) balls 1025 Tawny Chestnut

Equivalent yarn

Bulky weight #5: 900 (1050, 1200, 1350, 1500) yd

Needles

• One pair *each* sizes U.S. 9 (5.5 mm) and 10½ (6.5 mm) or size to obtain gauge

• One 16" circular each size U.S. 9 (5.5 mm) and 10½ (6.5 mm)

• Two cable needles (cn)

Stitch markers

Three 1¾" toggle buttons

GAUGE

14 sts and 20 rows = 4" in Box Stitch, using larger needles; 17 sts = 3" in Trellis Cable, using larger needles; 16 sts and 20 rows = 4" in Swallow's Nest Stitch, after blocking, using larger needles. Take time to save time, check your gauge.

NOTES

• Sl markers every row.

• Work all inc and dec 1 st in from each edge.

PATTERN STITCHES

GARTER STITCH (GTR ST)

Knit every row.

2 × 2 RIB (MULTIPLE OF 4 STS + 2)

Row 1 (WS): P2, *k2, p2; rep from * across.

Row 2: Knit the knit sts and purl the purl sts as they face you.

Rep Row 2 for 2 x 2 Rib.

SWALLOW'S NEST STITCH (MULTIPLE OF 6 STS; 8-ROW REP)

See Chart A.

TRELLIS CABLE (MULTIPLE OF 16 STS; 8-ROW REP)

See Chart B.

BOX STITCH (MULTIPLE OF 4 STS + 2; 4-ROW REP)

See Chart C.

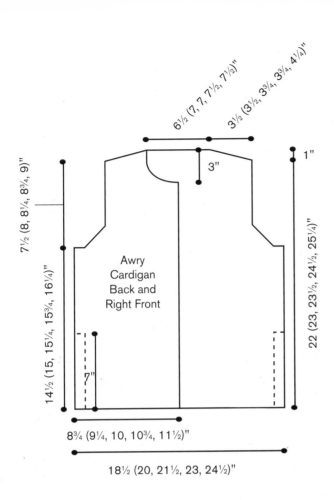

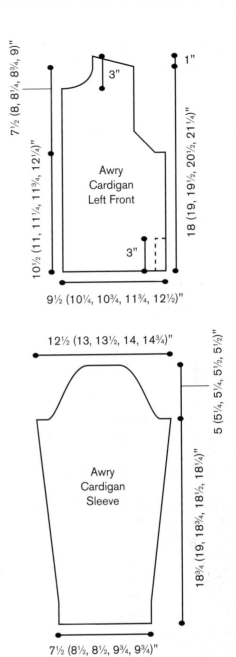

BACK

Using smaller needles, CO 74 (80, 86, 92, 98) sts. *Setup row:* (WS) Work 4 sts Gtr st, pm; k2, *p2, k4; rep from * to last 8 sts, p2, k2, pm; work 4 sts Gtr st. Keeping first and last 4 sts in Gtr st, for rem sts, knit the knit sts and purl the purl sts as they face you; work even for 8 more rows (9 rows completed), end WS row. Change to larger needles. *Set up patt:* (RS) Work 4 sts in Gtr st as est; beg with Row 1 of Chart A, work Swallow's Nest Stitch from Chart A across to last 4 sts, k4 in Gtr st as est. Work even as est for 26 more rows (27 rows of Chart A completed), end RS. (WS) Purl 1 row, removing markers. *Est patt:* (RS) Work 1 st in Gtr st; beg with Row 1 of Chart A for next 3 sts, then cont as est across to last 4 sts, work 3 sts from Chart A, 1 st Gtr st. Keeping first and last st in Gtr st and rem sts in Chart A as est, work even until piece meas 14½ (15, 15¼, 15¾, 16¼)" from beg, end WS. *Shape armholes:* (RS) Cont as est, BO 5 (5, 6, 6, 7) sts at beg of next 2 rows—64 (70, 74, 80, 84) sts rem. BO 2 sts at beg of next 0 (4, 6, 8, 8) rows, then dec 1 st each side EOR 5 (3, 2, 2, 2) times—54 (56, 58, 60, 64) sts rem. Work even until armhole meas 7½ (8, 8¼, 8¾, 9)" from beg of shaping, end WS.

Shape shoulders and neck: (RS) Cont as est, BO 4 (4, 5, 5, 5) sts at beg of next 2 rows, then 5 (5, 5, 5, 6) sts at beg of next 4 rows—26 (28, 28, 30, 30) sts rem for neck. BO rem sts in patt.

RIGHT FRONT

Using smaller needles, CO 39 (42, 45, 48, 51) sts. *Setup row:* (WS) Work 4 sts Gtr st, pm; k2, [p2, k4] 2 (3, 3, 4, 4) times, p2 (1, 2, 1, 2), k2 (0, 2, 0, 2), [k2, p2] 4 times, work 1 st Gtr st. Keeping first and last sts in Gtr st as est, work rem sts as foll: Knit the knit sts and purl the purl sts as they face you; work even for 8 more rows (9 rows completed), end WS row. Change to larger needles. *Set up patt:* (RS) Work 1 st Gtr st; beg with Row 1 of charts, work 16 sts Trellis Cable from Chart B, pm; work 18 (21, 24, 27, 30) sts Swallow's Nest Stitch using

Chart A, beg with st 1 (4, 1, 4, 1) of Chart A, pm; work 4 sts Gtr st. Work even as est for 26 more rows (27 rows of charts completed), end RS row. (WS) Work 1 st Gtr st, p3, remove marker, purl across to next marker, work 16 sts as est from Chart B, work 1 st Gtr st. *Est patt:* (RS) Work 1 st Gtr st, work Chart B across next16 sts , work Chart A across rem sts to last st, work 1 st Gtr st. Keeping first and last st in Gtr st and other

sts in charts as est, work even until piece meas 14½ (15, 15¼, 15¾, 16¼)" from beg, end RS. *Shape armhole:* (WS) BO 5 (5, 6, 6, 7) sts, work to end—34 (37, 39, 42, 44) sts rem. At armhole edge, BO 2 sts 0 (2, 3, 4, 4) times, then dec 1 st EOR 5 (3, 2, 2, 2) times—29 (30, 31, 32, 34) sts rem. Work even until armhole meas 5½ (6, 6¼, 6¾, 7)" from beg of shaping, end WS row. *Shape neck:* (RS) BO 10 sts, work to end—19 (20, 21, 22, 24) sts rem. At neck edge, BO 2 sts 0 (1, 1, 2, 2) times, then dec 1 st EOR 5 (4, 4, 3, 3) times—14 (14, 15, 15, 17) sts rem for shoulder. When piece meas same as back to shoulder shaping, end RS row. *Shape shoulder* as for back at beg of WS rows only.

LEFT FRONT

Using smaller needles, CO 39 (42, 45, 48, 51) sts. *Setup row:* (WS) Work 1 st Gtr st; k0 (3, 0, 3, 0), [p2, k4] 5 (5, 6, 6, 7) times; p2, k2, pm; work 4 sts Gtr st. Keeping first and last sts in Gtr st as est, for rem sts, knit the knit sts and purl the purl sts as they face you; work even for 8 more rows (9 rows completed), end WS row. Change to larger needles. *Set up patt:* (RS) Work 4 sts Gtr st; beg Row 1, st 1 of Chart A, work Swallow's Nest Stitch from Chart A across 34 (37, 40, 43, 46) sts, pm; work 1 st Gtr st. Work even as est for 10 more rows (11 rows of chart completed), end RS row. (WS) Work 1 st Gtr st, purl across to last 4 sts, remove marker, work Chart A across 3 sts, work 1 st Gtr st. *Est patt:* (RS) Work 1 st Gtr st; beg Row 1 of Chart A, work as est to last st, work 1 st Gtr st. Keeping first and last st in Gtr st and other sts in Chart A as est, work even until piece meas 10½ (11, 11¼, 11¾, 12¼)" from beg, end WS row. *Shape armhole:* (RS) BO 5 (5, 6, 6, 7) sts, work to end—34 (37, 39, 42, 44) sts rem. At armhole edge, BO 2 sts 0 (2, 3, 4, 4) times, then dec 1 st EOR 5 (3, 2, 2, 2) times—29 (30, 31, 32, 34) sts. Work even until armhole meas 5½ (6, 6¼, 6¾, 7)" from beg of shaping, end RS row. *Shape neck:* (WS) BO 7 (7, 8, 9, 9) sts, work to end—22 (23, 23, 23, 25) sts rem. At neck edge, BO 2 sts 3 (3, 2, 2, 2) times, then dec 1 st EOR 2 (3, 4, 4, 4) times—14 (14, 15, 15, 17) sts rem for shoulder. When piece meas same as back to shoulder shaping, end WS row. *Shape shoulder* as for back at beg of RS rows only.

SLEEVES

Using smaller needles, CO 26 (30, 30, 34, 34) sts. Beg 2 × 2 Rib; work even until piece meas 2" from beg, end WS row. Change to larger needles and Box Stitch (Chart C): (RS) Beg this row, inc 1 st each side every 8 rows 8 (2, 8, 4, 9) times, every 10 rows 1 (6, 1, 4, 0) times, working inc sts into Box Stitch—44 (46, 48, 50, 52) sts. Work even until piece meas 18¾ (19, 18¾, 18½,

18¼" from beg, end WS row. ***Shape cap:*** (RS) BO 5 (5, 6, 6, 7) sts at beg of next 2 rows—34 (36, 36, 38, 38) sts rem. (RS) Dec 1 st each end EOR 9 (11, 11, 13, 13) times, then BO 2 sts at beg of next 4 (2, 2, 0, 0) rows—8 (10, 10, 12, 12) sts rem. BO rem sts in patt.

FINISHING

Block lightly to measurements, if necessary, being careful not to flatten texture. Sew shoulder seams. ***Collar:*** With RS facing, using smaller circular needle, beg at right front neck, pick up and knit 10 sts across front neck, 14 (15, 15, 16, 16) sts along right front neck shaping, 26 (28, 28, 28, 28) sts across back neck, 14 (15, 15, 16, 16) sts along left front neck shaping, 8 (8, 8, 10, 10) sts across left front neck—72 (76, 76, 80, 80) sts. *Est patt:* (WS) 1 st Gtr st; beg 2 × 2 Rib, work across to last st, 1 st Gtr st. Keeping first and last st in Gtr st, and rem sts in 2 × 2 Rib, work even until collar meas 1½" from pickup row. Change to larger circular needle. Work even in 2 × 2 Rib as est for 5" more—collar meas 6½" from pickup row. BO all sts loosely in patt. ***Left front band:*** With RS facing, using smaller needles, beg at collar, pick up and knit 24 sts along collar, 68 (72, 76, 80, 84) sts along left front edge—92 (96, 100, 104, 108) sts. *Est patt:* (WS) 1 st Gtr st; beg 2 × 2 Rib, work across to last st, 1 st Gtr st. BO all sts loosely in patt. Pm for 3 buttons on left front band, first 2" from lower edge, last ½" below beg of neck shaping, rem 1 evenly spaced bet. ***Right front band:*** With RS facing, using smaller needles, beg at lower right front, pick up and knit, 80 (84, 88, 92, 96) sts along right front edge, then 24 sts along collar—104 (108, 112, 116, 120) sts. Est patt as for left front band; work even until band meas ¾" from pickup row, end WS row. *Next row:* (RS) Work buttonholes opposite markers on left front band as foll: [BO 2 sts] at each marker; and, on next row, CO 2 sts over BO sts. Work even until band meas 1½" from pickup row. BO all sts loosely in patt. Set in sleeves; sew side and sleeve seams. Sew buttons opposite buttonholes. Fold collar down.

Multiple of 6 sts; 8-row rep

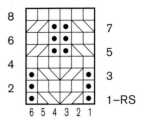

Multiple of 16 sts; 8-row rep

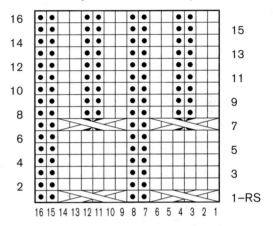

Multiple of 4 sts + 2; 4-row rep

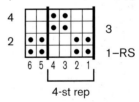

4-st rep

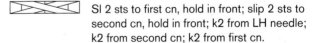

☐ Knit on RS, purl on WS.

● Purl on WS, knit on WS.

⬜ Sl 1 st to cn, hold in back, k1; k1 from cn.

⬜ Sl 1 st to cn, hold in front, k1; k1 from cn.

⬜ Sl 2 sts to first cn, hold in front; slip 2 sts to second cn, hold in front; k2 from LH needle; k2 from second cn; k2 from first cn.

⬜ Sl 2 sts to first cn, hold in front; slip 2 sts to second cn, hold in front; k2 from LH needle; p2 from second cn; k2 from first cn.

COLLARED CARDIGAN

SIZES

Small (Medium, Large, 1X Large)

FINISHED MEASUREMENTS

38 (40, 42, 44)"

MATERIALS

Classic Elite Yarns

Four Seasons (70% cotton, 30% wool; 50-g hank = approx 103 yd/94 m)

• 13 (14, 15, 16) hanks 7657 October Sky

Equivalent yarn

Worsted weight #4, 1339 (1442, 1545, 1648) yd

Needles

• One pair size U.S. 6 (4 mm) or size to obtain gauge

Five ¾" buttons

Stitch markers

GAUGE

19½ sts and 30 rows = 4" in Stockinette Stitch. Take time to save time, check your gauge.

PATTERN STITCHES

GARTER STITCH (GTR ST)

Knit every row.

GARTER RIDGE

Row 1: (RS) Knit.

Row 2: Purl.

Row 3: Knit.

Row 4: Knit.

Rep Rows 1–4 for Garter Ridge.

BACK

CO 92 (98, 102, 108) sts; work 5 rows Gtr st, end WS row. Change to Garter Ridge; (RS) work even until piece meas 1¾" from beg, end WS row. *Shape waist:* (RS) Dec 1 st each side this row, then every 12 rows 3 times—84 (90, 94, 100) sts rem. Work even until piece meas 6½" from beg, end WS row. *Shape waist:* (RS) Inc 1 st each side this row, then every 14 rows 3 times—92 (98, 102, 108) sts. Work even until piece meas 13½ (14, 14½, 15)" from beg, end WS row. *Shape armholes:* (RS) BO 5 (5, 6, 6) sts at beg of next 2 rows, then dec 1 st each side EOR 8 (9, 9, 11) times—66 (70, 72, 74) sts rem. Work even until armhole meas 7½ (8, 8, 8½)" from beg of shaping, end WS row. *Shape shoulders:* (RS) BO 7 sts at beg of the next 6 (6, 4, 4) rows, then 0 (0, 8, 8) sts beg next 2 rows—24 (28, 28, 30) sts rem for neck. BO rem sts.

LEFT FRONT

CO 49 (52, 55, 58) sts; work 5 rows Gtr st, end WS row. *Est patt:* (RS) Work 47 (50, 53, 56) sts in Garter Ridge, 2 sts in Gtr st. Work even until piece meas 1¾" from beg, end WS row. *Shape waist* as for back, working decs and incs at beg of RS rows only. Work even until piece meas same as back to armhole shaping, end WS row. *Shape armholes:* (RS) BO 5 (5, 6, 6) sts the beg of this row, then at armhole edge, dec 1 st EOR 8 (9, 9, 11) times—36 (38, 40, 41) sts. Work even until armhole meas 4½ (5, 5, 5½)" from beg of shaping, end RS row. *Shape neck:* (WS) BO 8 sts at beg of this row, then at neck edge dec 1 st EOR 7 (9, 10, 11) times—21 (21, 22, 22) sts rem. Work even until armhole meas 7½ (8, 8, 8½)" from beg of shaping, end WS row. *Shape shoulders* as for back at beg of RS rows only. Pm for 5 buttons, first 3 1/4" from lower edge, last 5½" from beg of neck shaping, rem 3 evenly spaced bet.

RIGHT FRONT

CO 49 (52, 55, 58) sts; work 5 rows in Gtr st, end WS row. *Est patt:* (RS) Work 2 sts in Gtr st, 47 (50, 53, 56) sts in Garter Ridge. Work as for left front, rev all shaping and working buttonholes opposite markers on left front as foll: Work 2 sts, [k2tog, yo], work to end.

SLEEVES

CO 44 (44, 48, 48) sts; work 5 rows in Gtr st, end WS row. Change to Garter Ridge; work even until piece meas 1¼" from beg, end WS row. *Shape sleeve:* (RS) Inc 1 st each side this row, then every 8 (6, 8, 6) rows 15 (12, 13, 12) times, every 10 rows 0 (4, 2, 5) times—76 (78, 80, 84) sts. Work even until piece meas 17½ (17½, 18, 18½)" from beg, end WS row. *Shape cap:*

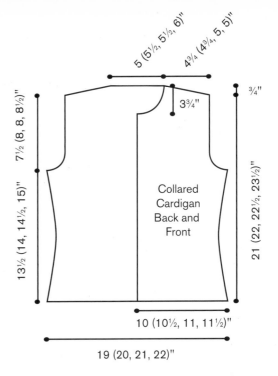

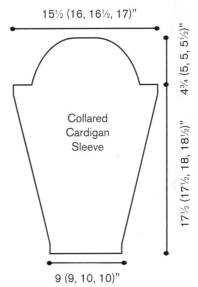

(RS) BO 5 (5, 6, 6) sts beg of next 2 rows, then dec 1 st each side EOR 8 (9, 9, 11) times—50 sts rem. BO 2 sts at beg of next 12 rows—26 sts rem. BO 3 sts at beg of next 4 rows—14 sts rem. BO rem sts.

FINISHING

Block pieces to measurements. Sew shoulder seams. Set in sleeves; sew sleeve and side seams. *Collar:* With RS facing, beg 2" from center front edge, pick up and knit 26 (30, 30, 31) sts evenly along right front neck edge, 24 (28, 28, 30) sts across back neck edge, 26 (30, 30, 31) sts along left front neck edge, end 2" from center front edge—76 (88, 88, 92) sts. *Est patt:* Work 2 sts in Gtr st, beg with Row 2, work 72 (84, 84, 88) sts in Garter Ridge, work 2 sts in Gtr st. Work even until collar meas 3" from pickup row, end RS row. BO all sts.

MOSAIC PATTERNED PULLOVER

SIZES
Small (Medium, Large, 1X Large)

FINISHED MEASUREMENTS
39½ (43, 47, 50)"

MATERIALS
Classic Elite Yarns

Inca Alpaca (100% alpaca; 50-g hank = approx 109 yd/100 m)
• 1 (2, 2, 2) hanks Color A—1198 Persimmon
• 1 (2, 2, 2) hanks Color B—1153 Damask Red
• 2 (2, 2, 3) hanks Color C—1183 Oriole
• 5 (6, 6, 7) hanks Color D—1107 Camacho Periwinkle
• 4 (4, 5, 5) hanks Color E—1129 Lincoln Blue
• 1 (1, 2, 2) hanks Color F—1124 Nuevo Blue Heather
• 1 hank all sizes Color G—1155 Harvest Bounty

Equivalent yarn

Light worsted weight #3 or worsted weight #4, Colors A and B: 109 (218, 218, 218) yd; Color C: 218 (218, 218, 327) yd; Color D: 545 (654, 654, 763) yd; Color E: 436 (436, 545, 545) yd; Color F: 109 (109, 218, 218) yd; Color G: 109 yd all sizes

Needles
• One pair *each* size U.S. 4 (3.5 mm), 5 (3.75 mm),
  and 7 (4.5 mm) or size to obtain gauge
• One 16" circular size U.S. 5 (3.75 mm) for neck finishing

Stitch holders

Stitch markers

GAUGE
24 sts and 25 rows = 4" in Stockinette Stitch color-work patterns, using largest needles. Take time to save time, check your gauge.

NOTE
Work V-neck dec 1 st in from neck edge.

SPECIAL TECHNIQUE

THREE-NEEDLE BIND-OFF METHOD
Sl sts from holders onto separate needles, with needles pointing in same direction and held parallel. The WS of garment pieces are held tog (to form ridge on outside of garment). With a third needle knit first st of front and back needles tog, *knit next st from each needle tog (2 sts on RH needle), BO 1 st; rep from * until all sts are bound off.

PATTERN STITCHES

1 × 1 RIB (MULTIPLE OF 2 STS + 1)
Row 1: (RS) P1, *k1, p1; rep from * across.
Row 2: (WS) Knit the knit sts and purl the purl sts as they face you.
Rep Row 2 for 1 x 1 Rib.

GARTER STITCH (GTR ST)
Knit every row.

STOCKINETTE STITCH (ST ST)
Knit on RS, purl on WS.

SMALL DIAMOND PATTERN (MULTIPLE OF 10 STS + 1)
See Chart A.

LARGE DIAMOND PATTERN:
(MULTIPLE OF 16 STS + 1; 22-ROW REP)
See Chart B

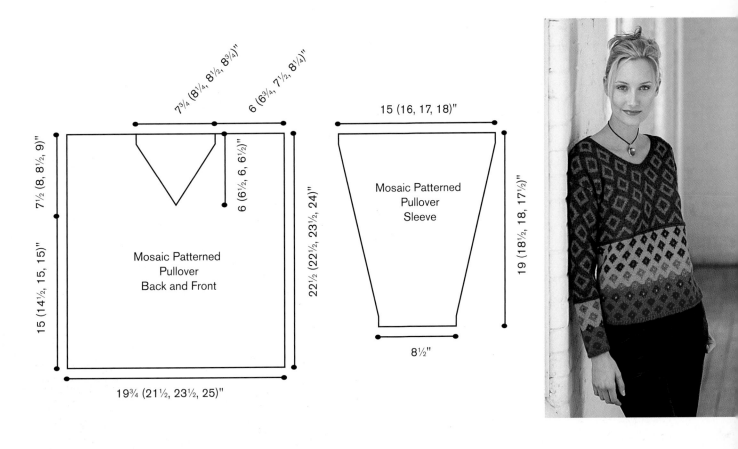

Mosaic Patterned
Pullover
Back and Front

Mosaic Patterned
Pullover
Sleeve

BACK

Using medium needles and Color G, CO 121 (131, 141, 151) sts. *Edging:* Work 1 (1, 3, 3) rows in Gtr st, end WS row. Change to 1 × 1 Rib and work 2 (2, 4, 4) rows, end WS row. Change to largest needles and Small Diamond patt (Chart A); work Rows 1–56, end WS row. Change to smallest needles and Color D; work 6 (6, 8, 10) rows in Gtr st, dec 2 (2, 0, 0) sts evenly across last WS row—119 (129, 141, 151) sts. Change to largest needles and Large Diamond patt (Chart B), beg and end where indicated for your size. Work 76 (76, 76, 78) rows, end WS row. *Shape shoulders and neck:* (RS) Work 36 (40, 45, 49) sts, BO center 47 (49, 51, 53) sts, work to end. Place sts on holder.

FRONT

Work as for back until 38 (36, 38, 38) rows of Large Diamond patt are complete, end WS row. *Shape V-neck:* (RS) Work 59 (64, 70, 75) sts and turn, place rem 60 (65, 71, 76) sts on holder. Working each side sep, at neck edge, dec 1 st every row 10 (12, 14, 14) times, then EOR 13 (12, 11, 12) times—36 (40, 45, 49) sts rem at shoulder. Work even until 77 (75, 77, 79) rows of Large Diamond patt are complete, end RS row. Place sts on holder. With RS facing, sl 60 (65, 71, 76) sts back to needle; join yarn and k2 tog, work to end—59 (64, 70, 75) sts. Complete to match first side.

SLEEVES

Using medium needles and Color G, CO 51 sts. Work edging as for back, end WS row. Change to largest needles and Small Diamond patt (Chart A); work even until piece meas 2" from beg, end WS row. *Shape sleeve:* Inc 1 st each side EOR 0 (0, 7, 14) times, every 4 rows 12 (23, 19, 15) times, every 6 rows 8 (0, 0, 0) times, working inc sts in patt as they become available—91 (97, 103, 109) sts; and, at the same time, when Row 35 of Small Diamond patt is complete, end RS row. *Next row:* (WS) Using Color C, purl 1 row. Change to smallest needles and Color D; work 6 rows in Gtr st, end WS row. Change to largest needles and Large Diamond patt (Chart B), beg and end where indicated for your size. Work even until piece meas 19 (18½, 18, 17½)" from beg, end WS row. BO all sts.

FINISHING

Block pieces to measurements. Join shoulder seams using Color D and Three-Needle Bind-Off Method. Meas 7½ (8, 8½, 9)" down from shoulder seam on back and front, pms. Sew sleeves bet markers; sew sleeve and side seams. *Neckband:* With RS facing, using circular needle and Color D, pick up and knit 121 (125, 129, 135) sts evenly around neck edge, pm for beg of rnd. Purl 1 rnd. BO all sts knitwise.

Multiple of 10 sts +1
Note: Chart shows 2 reps of patt

Multiple of 16 sts +1; 22-row rep
Note: Chart shows 2 reps of patt

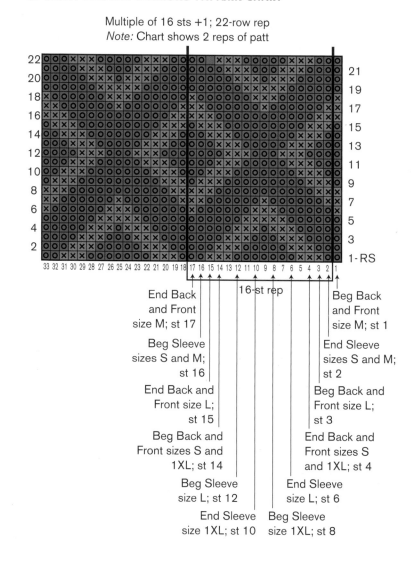

End Back
and Front
size M; st 17

16-st rep

Beg Back
and Front
size M; st 1

Beg Sleeve
sizes S and M;
st 16

End Sleeve
sizes S and M;
st 2

End Back and
Front size L;
st 15

Beg Back and
Front size L;
st 3

Beg Back and
Front sizes S and
1XL; st 14

End Back and
Front sizes S
and 1XL; st 4

Beg Sleeve
size L; st 12

End Sleeve
size L; st 6

End Sleeve
size 1XL; st 10

Beg Sleeve
size 1XL; st 8

10-st rep

End
all sizes;
st 11

Beg
all sizes;
st 1

▲ Color A–1198 Persimmon.

▣ Color B–1153 Damask Red.

■ Color C–1183 Oriole.

◉ Color D–1107 Camacho Periwinkle.

☒ Color E–1129 Lincoln Blue.

◆ Color F–1124 Nuevo Blue Heather.

DIAMOND COTTON CARDIGAN

SIZES

Extra Small (Small, Medium, Large, 1X Large)

FINISHED MEASUREMENTS

36 (37½, 39½, 41, 44)"

MATERIALS

Classic Elite Yarns

Provence (100% mercerized Egyptian cotton; 100-g hank = approx 205 yd/187 m)

• 5 (5, 6, 7, 8) hanks 2632 Summer Wheat

Equivalent yarn

Light worsted weight #3, 1025 (1025, 1230, 1435, 1640) yd

Needles

• One pair U.S. 7 (4.5 mm) or size to obtain gauge

• One 24" circular size U.S. 6 (4 mm)

Stitch markers

Two 1" buttons

GAUGE

20 sts and 27 rows = 4" in Diamond Pattern, using larger needles. Take time to save time, check your gauge.

NOTES

Work armhole and cap shaping as foll: (RS) Work 1 st, ssk, work to last 3 sts, k2tog, k1.

Work neck shaping on left front as foll: (RS) Work across row to last 2 sts, k2tog.

Work neck shaping on right front as foll: (RS) Ssk, work to end.

PATTERN STITCHES

STOCKINETTE STITCH (ST ST)

Knit on RS, purl on WS.

SEED STITCH (SEED ST) (OVER AN ODD NUMBER OF STS)

Row 1 (WS): P1 *k1, p1; rep from *.

Rep Row 1 for Seed st.

DIAMOND PATTERN (MULTIPLE OF 20 STS; 48-ROW REP)

See chart.

4 × 1 TWISTED STITCH RIB (MULTIPLE OF 5 STS + 4)

Row 1 (RS): P4, *k1b, p4; rep from *.

Row 2 (WS): Knit.

Rep Rows 1–2 for 4 × 1 Twisted Stitch Rib.

BACK

Using larger needles, CO 91 (95, 101, 105, 111) sts. Purl 1 row. *Est patt:* (RS) Work 2 sts in St st (edge sts), work 87 (91, 97, 101, 107) sts in Diamond Pattern from chart, beg and end where indicated for your size, work 2 sts in St st (edge sts). Work as est until piece meas 12½" from beg, end WS row. ***Shape armhole:*** (RS) BO 5 sts at beg of next 2 rows, then dec 1 st each side EOR 5 (5, 6, 5, 6) times—71 (75, 79, 85, 89) sts rem. Work even until armhole meas 7 (7½, 8¼, 8¾, 9¼)" from beg of shaping, end RS row. ***Shape neck and shoulders:*** (RS) Mark center 13 (15, 17, 19, 21) sts. BO 6 (7, 7, 8, 8) sts at beg of next 4 rows, 7 (6, 7, 7, 8) sts at beg of next 2 rows; and, **at the same time,** on the first row of shoulder shaping, work across to center 13 (15, 17, 19, 21) sts; join second ball of yarn, BO center sts, work to end. Working both sides at same time, at each neck edge BO 5 sts twice.

LEFT FRONT

Using larger needles, CO 46 (48, 50, 52, 56) sts. Purl 1 row. *Est patt:* (RS) Work 2 sts in St st (edge sts), work 43 (45, 47, 49, 53) sts in Diamond Pattern from chart, beg and end where indicated for your size, work 1 st in St st (edge st). Work as est until piece meas 12½" from beg, end WS row. ***Shape armhole*** as for back at beg of RS rows only; and, at the same time, ***shape V-neck:*** (RS) Dec 1 st at neck edge EOR 8 (9, 9, 9, 10) times, every 4 rows 9 (9, 9, 10, 11) times—19 (20, 21, 23, 24) sts rem for shoulder. Work even until armhole meas same as back to shoulder shaping, end WS row. ***Shape shoulder*** as for back at beg of RS rows only.

RIGHT FRONT

Work as for left front, rev patt placement and all shaping by working armhole and shoulder shaping at beg of WS rows and V-neck shaping at beg of RS rows only.

SLEEVE

Using larger needles, CO 38 (38, 43, 43, 48) sts. Purl WS row. *Est patt:* (RS) Work 2 sts in St st (edge sts), work 34 (34, 39, 39, 44) sts in Diamond Pattern from chart, beg and end where indicated for your size, work 2 sts in St st (edge sts). Work as est for 3 rows. ***Shape sleeve:*** (RS) Inc 1 st each side this row, then every 6 rows 6 (7, 7, 8, 8) times, every 8 rows 6 (7, 8, 9, 9) times—64 (68, 75, 79, 84) sts. Work even until piece meas 16½ (16½, 16½, 17, 17)" from beg, end WS row. *Note:* Trim at lower edge of sleeve will add 1" to the length. ***Shape cap:*** (RS) BO 5 sts at beg of next 2 rows, then dec 1 st each side EOR 14 (15, 18, 20, 22) times—26 (28, 29, 29, 30) sts. BO 2 sts at beg of next 4 rows—18 (20, 21, 21, 22) sts rem. BO rem sts.

FINISHING

Block pieces to measurements. ***Sleeve trim:*** With RS facing and smaller needles, pick up and knit 39 (39, 43, 43, 49) sts along CO edge of sleeve. Work in Seed st for 3 rows, end WS row. Change to St st; work 2 rows. BO all sts. Sew shoulder seams. Set in sleeves; sew sleeve and side seams. ***Lower edge trim:*** With RS facing, using circular needle, pick up and knit 183 (191, 201, 209, 223) sts along CO edge of garment. Work trim as for sleeve trim. ***Front band:*** With RS facing, using circular needle, beg at lower edge of right front, pick up and knit 64 sts along front edge to beg of V-neck shaping, pm, pick up and knit 41 (44, 48, 52, 57) sts along V-neck edge to shoulder, 37 (39, 41, 43, 45) sts along back neck, 41 (44, 48, 52, 57) sts along V-neck edge to beg of neck shaping on left front, 64 sts along front edge to lower edge. (WS) Working in Gtr st; work to marker on right front, BO 5 sts [buttonhole], work 13 sts, BO 5 sts [buttonhole], work to end. *Next row:* (RS) CO 5 sts over BO sts. Work 1 row even. BO all sts. Sew on buttons opposite buttonholes.

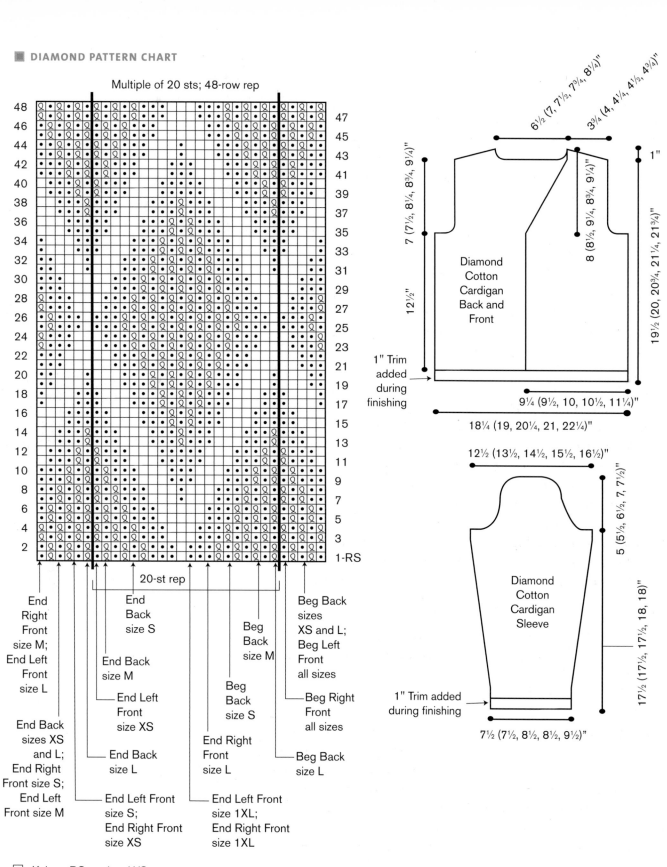

Multiple of 20 sts; 48-row rep

20-st rep

End Right Front size M; End Left Front size L

End Back sizes XS and L; End Right Front size S; End Left Front size M

End Back size M

End Left Front size S; End Right Front size XS

End Back size S

End Left Front size XS

End Back size L

Beg Back size M

Beg Back size S

End Right Front size L

End Left Front size 1XL; End Right Front size 1XL

Beg Back sizes XS and L; Beg Left Front all sizes

Beg Right Front all sizes

Beg Back size L

□ Knit on RS, purl on WS

• Purl on RS, knit on WS

Ｑ K1-tbl on RS, p1-tbl on WS

6½ (7, 7½, 7¾, 8¼)"   3¾ (4, 4¼, 4½, 4¾)"

1"

7 (7½, 8¼, 8¾, 9¼)"

8 (8½, 9¼, 8¾, 9¼)"

12½"

Diamond Cotton Cardigan Back and Front

19½ (20, 20¾, 21¼, 21¾)"

1" Trim added during finishing

9¼ (9½, 10, 10½, 11¼)"

18¼ (19, 20¼, 21, 22¼)"

12½ (13½, 14½, 15½, 16½)"

5 (5½, 6½, 7, 7½)"

Diamond Cotton Cardigan Sleeve

17½ (17½, 17½, 18, 18)"

1" Trim added during finishing

7½ (7½, 8½, 8½, 9½)"

BEADED SHELL

SIZES
Extra Small (Small, Medium, Large)

FINISHED MEASUREMENTS
34 (36, 38, 40)"

MATERIALS
Classic Elite Yarns

Flash (100% mercerized cotton, 50-g hank = .approx 93 yd/85 m)

• 7 (7, 8, 9) hanks 6189 Pink Tweed

Equivalent yarn

Worsted weight #4, 651 (651, 744, 837) yd

Needles

• One pair *each* size U.S. 5 (3.75 mm)
  and 7 (4.5 mm) or size to obtain gauge

• One 16" circular size U.S. 6 (4 mm) for neck finishing

• One crochet hook size U.S. G (4 mm) for armhole finishing

Stitch markers

20 9/16 " white tube-shaped beads

20 9/16" white diamond-shaped beads

Sewing needle and coordinating thread to attach beads

GAUGE
20 sts and 27 rows = 4" in Stockinette Stitch, using larger needles.
Take time to save time, check your gauge.

PATTERN STITCHES

GARTER STITCH (GTR ST)
Knit every row.

STOCKINETTE STITCH (ST ST)
Knit on RS, purl on WS.

CIRCULAR STOCKINETTE STITCH
Knit every rnd.

SINGLE CROCHET (SC)
Insert hook into edge st, yo hook and draw a loop through st,
yo hook and draw it through both loops on hook

BACK

Using smaller needles, CO 85 (90, 95, 100) sts; work in Gtr st until piece meas ½", end WS row. Change to larger needles and St st; work even until piece meas 13 (13½, 14, 14¾)" from beg, end WS row. **Shape armholes:** (RS) BO 5 sts at beg of next 2 rows—75 (80, 85, 90) sts rem. *Dec row:* (RS) *Work 2 sts, ssk, work in patt to last 4 sts, k2tog, work 2 sts. Work 1 row even. Rep from * 6 (7, 8, 9) times—61 (64, 67, 70) sts rem. Cont in patt est, work even until armhole meas 7 (7, 7½, 7¾)" from beg of shaping, end WS row. Mark center 31 (34, 37, 40) sts. **Shape shoulders and neck:** (RS) BO 3 sts at beg of next 4 rows, then 4 sts at beg of next 2 rows; and, **at the same time,** on first row of shoulder shaping, work to center marked sts; join second ball of yarn and BO center 31 (34, 37, 40) sts, work to end. Working both sides at same time, at each neck edge, BO 5 sts once.

FRONT

Work as for back until armhole meas 6 (6, 6½, 6¾)" from beg of shaping, end WS row. **Shape neck:** (RS) Work 20 (21, 22, 23) sts, join second ball of yarn and BO center 21 (22, 23, 24) sts, work to end. Working both sides at same time, at each neck edge, BO 3 (4, 5, 6) sts once, 2 sts 3 times, 1 st once—10 sts rem for shoulder; and, at the same time, when armhole meas same as back to shoulders, **shape shoulders** as for back.

FINISHING

Block pieces to measurements. Sew shoulder seams. Sew side seams. **Neckband:** With RS facing, using circular needle, pick up and knit 93 (98, 103, 108) sts evenly around neck edge; pm for beg of rnd. Work in St st until band meas 1½" from pickup row. BO all sts loosely. **Armhole edging:** With crochet hook and RS facing, work 1 rnd of sc around armhole edge. Sew beads to front of garment as desired or use photograph as guide for placement.

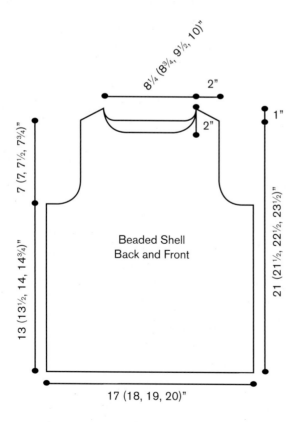

8¼ (8¾, 9½, 10)"

2"

1"

2"

7 (7, 7½, 7¾)"

13 (13½, 14, 14¾)"

21 (21½, 22½, 23½)"

Beaded Shell
Back and Front

17 (18, 19, 20)"

SLEEVELESS TEE

SIZES
Extra Small (Small, Medium, Large)

FINISHED MEASUREMENTS
31 (33, 35, 37)"

MATERIALS
Classic Elite Yarns

Classic Silk (50% cotton, 30% silk, 20% nylon; 50-g ball = approx 135 yd/123 m)

• 4 (5, 5, 5) balls 6947 Cobalt

Equivalent yarn

Light worsted weight #3; 540 (675, 675, 675) yd

Needles

• One *each* 29" circular size U.S. 5 (3.75 mm) and 7 (4.5 mm) or size to obtain gauge

• One 16" circular size U.S. 5 (3.75 mm) for neck and armhole finishing

• One set double-pointed needles (dpn) size U.S. 7 (4.5 mm) for gauge swatch

Large stitch holders

Stitch markers

GAUGE
20 sts and 30 rnds/rows = 4" in Stockinette Stitch using larger needles. Take time to save time, check your gauge.

Note: To measure gauge in the round: CO 30 sts and divide them evenly on 3 or 4 dpn. Join and work 30 rnds. BO all sts.

NOTES
Shell is worked in one piece to underarm.

Work neck decs 1 st in from neck edge.

PATTERN STITCHES

BROKEN RIB (MULTIPLE OF 2 STS)
Rnd 1: *K1, p1; rep from * around, end k1 if odd number of sts.

Rnd 2: Knit.

Rep Rnds 1–2 for Broken Rib.

STOCKINETTE STITCH (ST ST)
Knit on RS, purl on WS.

CIRCULAR STOCKINETTE STITCH
Knit every rnd.

BODY

Using smaller needles, CO 156 (164, 176, 184) sts; pm for beg of rnd and join, being careful not to twist sts. *Est patt:* P1 (seam st), work 77 (81, 87, 91) sts in Broken Rib, p1 (seam st), work 77 (81, 87, 91) sts in Broken Rib. Work 4 rnds even, end Rnd 1. Change to larger needles and *est patt:* P1 (seam st), work 77 (81, 87, 91) sts in St st, p1 (seam st), work 77 (81, 87, 91) sts in St st. Work even until piece meas 2¼ (2¼, 2¾, 2¾)" from beg. *Shape waist: Dec rnd:* P1 (seam st), k1, k2tog, work to 3 sts before seam st, k2tog-tbl, k1, p1 (seam st), k1, k2tog, work to 3 sts before end of rnd, k2tog-tbl, k1—4 sts dec'd. Rep dec rnd every 7 rnds 4 times—136 (144, 156, 164) sts rem. Work even until piece meas 8¼ (8¼, 8¾, 8¾)" from beg. *Shape waist: Inc rnd:* P1, k1, m1R, work to 1 st before seam st, m1L, k1, p1 (seam st), k1, m1R, work to 1 st before end of rnd, m1L, k1—4 sts inc'd. Rep inc rnd every 8 rnds 4 times—156 (164, 176, 184) sts. Work even until piece meas 14 (14, 14½, 14½)" from beg. *Divide for armholes:* BO 4 (4, 5, 5) sts at beg of next rnd for underarm; work until 71 (75, 79, 83) sts are on RH needle, place these sts on holder for front; BO next 7 (7, 9, 9) sts for underarm, work to end of rnd—74 (78, 83, 87) sts for back.

BACK

With WS facing, BO 3 (3, 4, 4) sts at beg of row for underarm, work to end—71 (75, 79, 83) sts rem. *Shape armhole: Dec row:* (RS) K1, k2tog, work to last 3 sts, k2tog-tbl, work to end. Rep dec row EOR 4 (4, 5, 5) times—61 (65, 67, 71) sts rem. Work even until armhole meas 7 (7½, 7½, 8)" from beg of shaping, end WS row. *Shape shoulders and neck:* BO 4 (5, 5, 6) sts at beg of next 4 (6, 6, 4) rows, then 5 (0, 0, 5) sts at beg of next 2 rows; and, **at the same time,** on first row of shoulder shaping, work to center 27 (27, 29, 29) sts, join second ball of yarn, BO center sts, work to end. Working both sides at same time, BO4 sts at each neck edge once.

FRONT

Place 71 (75, 79, 83) sts from front holder on needle. With WS facing, join yarn at underarm and work to end. *Shape armholes* as for back—61 (65, 67, 71) sts rem. Work even until armhole meas 4½ (5, 5, 5½)" from beg of shaping, end WS row. *Shape neck:* (RS) Work 23 (25, 25, 27) sts, join

second ball of yarn, BO center 15 (15, 17, 17) sts, work to end. Working both sides at same time, at each neck edge BO 3 sts once, then dec 1 st EOR 5 times, every 4 rows twice; and, **at the same time,** when piece meas same as back to shoulders *shape shoulders* as for back.

FINISHING

Block piece to measurements. Sew shoulder seams. *Neckband:* With RS facing, using smaller circular needle, pick up and knit 98 (98, 102, 102) sts evenly around neck edge, pm for beg of rnd. Work 3 rnds in Broken Rib. BO all sts knitwise. *Armhole bands:* With RS facing, using smaller circular needle, pick up and knit 82 (86, 86, 90) sts evenly around armhole edge, pm for beg of rnd. Work 3 rnds in Broken Rib. BO all sts knitwise.

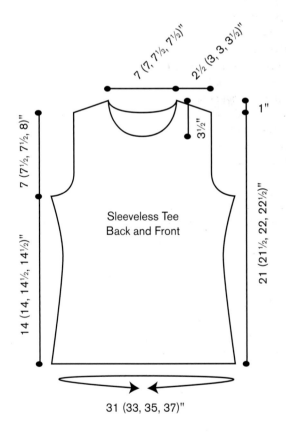

7 (7, 7½, 7½)" 2½ (3, 3, 3½)"

3½"

1"

7 (7½, 7½, 8)"

14 (14, 14½, 14½)"

Sleeveless Tee
Back and Front

21 (21½, 22, 22½)"

31 (33, 35, 37)"

FLOWER-SPRINKLED CARDIGAN

SIZES

Small (Medium, Large)

FINISHED MEASUREMENTS

39 (42, 45)"

MATERIALS

Classic Elite Yarns

Provence (100% mercerized Egyptian cotton, 100-g hank = approx 205 yd/187 m)

• 5 (6, 7) hanks Color A—2621 Herbal Sage
• 1 hank all sizes Color B—2609 Parchment
• 1 hank all sizes Color C—2673 Maize

Equivalent yarn

Light worsted weight #3 or worsted weight #4, Color A: 1025 (1230, 1435) yd; Colors B and C: 205 yd

Needles

• One pair size U.S. 7 (4.5 mm) or size to obtain gauge
• One crochet hook size U.S. F/5 (3.75 mm)

Four ³/₄" buttons

Tapestry needle

GAUGE

20 sts and 27 rows = 4" in Reverse Stockinette Stitch. Take time to save time, check your gauge.

NOTE

Work all incs and decs 1 st in from edge on each side.

PATTERN STITCHES

REVERSE STOCKINETTE STITCH (REV ST ST)

Purl on RS, knit on WS.

CHAIN (CH)

Make a sl knot on hook. Wrap yarn around hook and draw it through loop on hook to form first ch. Rep from this step as many times as instructed.

SINGLE CROCHET

Insert hook into st, yo and pull up a loop, yo and draw through both loops on hook.

PICOT EDGING FOR BODY

Work 4 sc, *ch 4, skip 1 st; work 4 sc; rep from * to end.

PICOT EDGING FOR SLEEVES

Work 3 sc, *ch 3, skip 1 st; work 3 sc; rep from * to end.

FRENCH KNOT

See diagram.

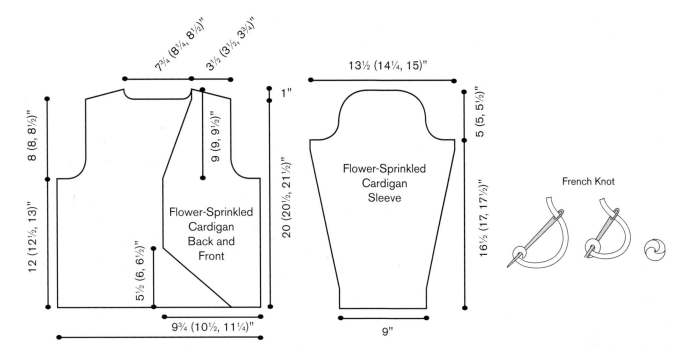

7¾ (8¼, 8½)"

3½ (3½, 3¾)"

8 (8, 8½)"

9 (9, 9½)"

1"

13½ (14¼, 15)"

5 (5, 5½)"

Flower-Sprinkled
Cardigan
Back and
Front

Flower-Sprinkled
Cardigan
Sleeve

French Knot

12 (12½, 13)"

20 (20½, 21½)"

16½ (17, 17½)"

5½ (6, 6½)"

9¾ (10½, 11¼)"

9"

BACK

Using Color A, CO 97 (105, 113) sts; work in Rev St st until piece meas 12 (12½, 13)" from beg, end WS row. *Shape armholes:* (RS) BO 5 sts at beg of next 2 rows, then dec 1 st each side EOR 7 (9, 11) times—73 (77, 81) sts rem. Work even until armhole meas 8 (8, 8½)" from beg of shaping, end WS row. *Shape shoulders and neck:* (RS) BO 6 sts at beg of next 6 (6, 4) rows, 0 (0, 7) sts at beg of next 0 (0, 2) rows; and, **at the same time,** on first row of shoulder shaping, work across to center 29 (33, 35) sts; join second ball of yarn, BO center sts, work to end. Working both sides at same time, at each neck edge, BO 4 sts once.

LEFT FRONT

Using Color A, CO 13 (15, 17) sts; beg with a purl row, work 1 row in Rev St st. *Next row:* (WS) CO 3 sts, work to end. Work 1 row even. Cont to CO at beg of every WS row as foll: 3 sts 3 (1, 0) times, 2 sts 9 (13, 15) times, then inc 1 st 5 (5, 6) times—48 (52, 56) sts. Work as est until piece meas 12 (12½, 13)" from beg, end WS row. *Shape armhole and V-neck:* (RS) BO 5 sts, work in patt to last 3 sts, p2tog-tbl, work to end. Work 1 row even. Cont to shape armhole as for back at beg of RS rows only; and, **at the same time, *shape V-neck:* At neck edge, dec 1 st EOR 7 (11, 11) times, then every 4 rows 10 (8, 9) times—18 (18, 19) sts rem for shoulder. Work even until armhole meas same as back to shoulders, end WS row. *Shape shoulders* as for back at beg of RS rows only.

RIGHT FRONT

Work as for left front, shaping center front by CO sts at end of WS rows and shaping V-neck at beg of RS rows, working V-neck decs as p2tog.

SLEEVES

Using Color A, CO 45 sts; work in Rev St st until piece meas 2" from beg, end RS row. *Shape sleeve:* (WS) Inc 1 st each side this row, then every 6 rows 0 (4, 11) times, every 8 rows 8 (8, 3) times, every 10 rows 2 (0, 0) times—67 (71, 75) sts. Work even until piece meas 16½ (17, 17½)" from beg, end WS row. *Shape cap:* (RS) BO 5 (5, 6) sts at beg of next 2 rows, then dec 1 st each side EOR 5 times, every 4 rows 4 (2, 2) times, EOR 3 (7, 8) times, every row 3 times—27 sts rem. BO 5 sts at beg of next 2 rows—17 sts rem. BO all rem sts.

FINISHING

Block pieces to measurements. Sew shoulder seams. Set in sleeves; sew sleeve and side seams. *Garment edging:* With RS facing, using crochet hook and beg at left side seam of back; work 1 row of sc around entire garment, then work Picot Edging for Body. Fasten off. Rep for sleeves beg at seam, working in Picot Edging for Sleeves. *Flowers:* Using crochet hook and Color B or C, *ch 6 sts, sl st to first ch; rep from * 4 times, sl st to beg ch. Fasten off. Make as many flowers as desired, the sweater shown has 17 flowers. Sew flowers to garment using photo as a guide or as desired. Using Color A, embroider French Knots into each flower center. Sew on 4 buttons, using loops of Picot Edging as buttonholes.

SEED AND DIAMOND PULLOVER

SIZES
Small (Medium, Large, 1X Large)

FINISHED MEASUREMENTS
38 (40, 46, 50)"

MATERIALS
Classic Elite Yarns

Four Seasons (70% cotton, 30% wool; 50-g hank = approx 103 yd/94 m)

• 11 (12, 13, 14) hanks 7616 Natural

Equivalent yarn

Worsted weight #4; 1133 (1236, 1339, 1442) yd

Needles

• One pair *each* size U.S. 5 (3.75 mm) and 7 (4.5 mm) or size to obtain gauge

• One 16" circular size U.S. 5 (3.75mm) for neck finishing

Stitch markers

GAUGE
20 sts and 28 rows = 4" in Stockinette Stitch and over Diamond Pattern after blocking, using larger needles. Take time to save time, check your gauge.

NOTE
Work all incs 1 st in from edge on each side.

PATTERN STITCHES

STOCKINETTE STITCH (ST ST)
Knit on RS, purl on WS.

CIRCULAR STOCKINETTE STITCH
Knit every rnd.

REVERSE STOCKINETTE STITCH (REV ST ST)
Purl on RS, knit on WS.

SEED STITCH (SEED ST) (MULTIPLE OF 2 STS)
Row 1: (RS) *P1, k1; rep from * across.

Row 2: (WS) *K1, p1; rep from * across.

Rep Rows 1–2 for Seed st.

2 × 2 RIB (MULTIPLE OF 4 STS)
Row 1: (RS) *K2, p2; rep from * across.

Row 2: (WS) *K2, p2; rep from * across.

Rep Rows 1–2 for 2 × 2 Rib.

DIAMOND PATTERN
(PANEL OF 13 STS; 10-ROW REP)

See chart.

CIRCULAR 1 × 1 RIB: (MULTIPLE OF 2 STS)
All rnds: *K1, p1; rep from * around.

BACK

Using smaller needles, CO 97 (101, 117, 127) sts. *Est patt:* (RS) Work 0 (2, 2, 1) sts in St st, work 2 sts in Rev St st, work 0 (0, 0, 4) sts in 2 × 2 Rib, work 13 sts in Diamond Pattern from chart, [work 8 (8, 12, 12) sts in 2 × 2 Rib, work 2 sts in St st, work 8 (8, 8, 10) sts in Seed st, work 8 (8, 12, 12) sts in 2 × 2 Rib, work 13 sts in Diamond Pattern] twice, work 0 (4, 4, 8) sts in

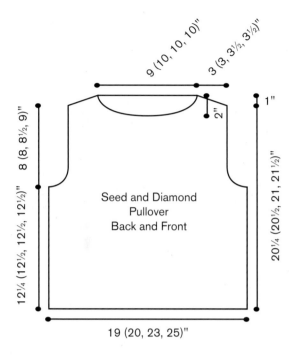

Seed and Diamond
Pullover
Back and Front

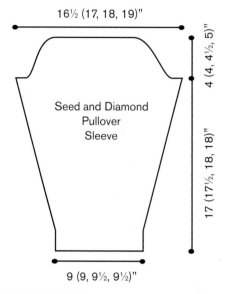

Seed and Diamond
Pullover
Sleeve

2×2 Rib, work 2 (2, 2, 1) sts in St st, work 2 (0, 0, 0) sts in Rev St st. Work as est until piece meas 1" from beg. Change to larger needles; work as est until piece meas 12¼ (12½, 12½, 12½)" from beg, end WS row. **Shape armholes:** (RS) BO 5 (5, 7, 10) sts at beg of next 2 rows, then dec 1 st each side EOR 5 (5, 8, 10) times—77 (81, 87, 87) sts rem. Work even until armhole meas 8 (8, 8½, 9)" from beg of shaping, end WS row. **Shape shoulders:** (RS) BO 6 (6, 7, 7) sts at beg of next 2 rows, then 5 (5, 6, 6) sts at beg of next 4 rows—45 (49, 49, 49) sts rem. BO rem sts.

FRONT

Work as for back until armhole meas 7 (7, 7½, 8)" from beg of shaping, end WS row—77 (81, 87, 87) sts. **Shape neck:** (RS) Work 31 (32, 35, 35) sts; join second ball of yarn, BO center 15 (17, 17, 17) sts, work to end. Working both sides at same time, at each neck edge, BO 4 sts 3 times, 2 (3, 3, 3) sts once, then dec 1 st EOR once; and, *at the same time,* when armhole meas same as back to shoulder shaping, **shape shoulders** as for back.

SLEEVES

Using smaller needles, CO 47 (47, 49, 49) sts. *Est patt:* (RS) Work 2 (2, 1, 1) sts in St st, work 6 (6, 8, 8) sts in Seed st, work 8 sts in 2×2 Rib, work 13 sts in Diamond Pattern from chart, work 8 sts in 2×2 Rib, work 2 sts in St st, work 6 (6, 8, 8) sts in Seed st, work 2 (2, 1, 1) sts in St st. Work as est until piece meas 2½" from beg, end WS row. Change to larger needles and **shape sleeve:** (RS) Inc 1 st each side this row, then every 4 rows 9 (13, 11, 15) times, every 6 rows 8 (6, 8, 7) times, working inc sts in 2×2 Rib—83 (87, 89, 95) sts. Work even until piece

DIAMOND PATTERN

Multiple panel of 13 sts; 10-row rep

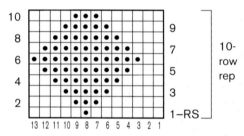

☐ Knit on RS, purl on WS.

⊡ Purl on RS, knit on WS.

meas 17 (17½, 18, 18)" from beg, end WS row. **Shape cap:** (RS) BO 5 (5, 7, 10) sts at beg of next 2 rows, then dec 1 st each side EOR 4 (8, 6, 5) times, then every 4 rows 3 (1, 2, 3) times—59 sts rem. Work even until cap meas 3½ (3½, 4, 4½)" from beg of shaping, end WS row. BO 6 sts at beg of next 6 rows—23 sts rem. BO rem sts.

FINISHING

Block pieces to measurements. Sew shoulder seams. Set in sleeves; sew sleeve and side seams. **Neckband:** With RS facing, using circular needle, pick up and knit 45 (51, 51, 51) sts evenly across back neck edge, 20 (21, 21, 21) sts along left neck edge, 15 (17, 17, 17) sts across front neck edge, 20 (21, 21, 21) sts along right neck edge, pm for beg of rnd—100 (110, 110, 110) sts. Work 2 rnds in 1×1 Rib, then 4 rnds in St st. BO all sts loosely.

ONE-BUTTON CARDIGAN

SIZES
Extra Small (Small, Medium, Large, 1X Large)

FINISHED MEASUREMENTS
34 (38, 42, 46, 50)"

MATERIALS
Classic Elite Yarns

Flash (100% mercerized marled cotton, 50-g hank = approx 93 yd/85 m)
• 14 (16, 17, 19, 21) hanks 6172 Gulf Green

Equivalent yarn

Worsted weight #4, 1302 (1488, 1581, 1767, 1953) yd

Needles
• One pair size U.S. 7 (4.5 mm) or size to obtain gauge

Stitch holders

One 2" button

One hook and eye fastener

GAUGE
20 sts and 32 rows = 4" in Moss Stitch. Take time to save time, check your gauge.

PATTERN STITCH

MOSS STITCH (MOSS ST) (MULTIPLE OF 2 STS + 1)
Row 1: (RS) Knit.
Row 2: P1, *k1, p1; rep from * across.
Row 3: Knit.
Row 4: K1, *p1, k1; rep from * across.
Rep Rows 1–4 for Moss Stitch

BACK

CO 85 (95, 105, 115, 125) sts; work in Moss st until piece meas 12½ (12½, 13, 14, 14½)" from beg, end WS row. **Shape armholes:** (RS) BO 6 (9, 14, 16, 20) sts at beg of next 2 rows—73 (77, 77, 83, 85) sts rem. Work even until armhole meas 7 1/2 (8, 8 1/2, 8 1/2, 9)" from shaping, end WS row. **Shape shoulders and neck:** (RS) BO 5 (6, 6, 7, 7) sts at beg of next 4 (6, 6, 6, 4) rows, then 6 (0, 0, 0, 8) sts at beg of next 2 rows; and, **at the same time,** on the first row of shoulder shaping, work across to center 33 sts; join second ball of yarn and BO center sts, work to end. Working both sides at same time, at each neck edge BO 4 sts once.

LEFT FRONT

CO 43 (47, 53, 57, 63) sts; work in Moss st until piece meas same as back to armhole, end WS row. **Shape armhole:** (RS) BO 6 (9, 14, 16, 20) sts at beg of this row—37 (38, 39, 41, 43) sts rem. Work even until armhole meas ½ (1, 1½, 1½, 2)" from shaping, end WS row. **Shape neck:** Dec row: (RS) Work across to last 6 sts, k2tog; work as est to end. Work 1 row even. Work dec row on this row, then EOR 2 (0, 2, 0, 2) times, every 4 rows 13 (14, 13, 14, 13) times—20 (22, 22, 25, 26) sts rem for shoulder. Work even until armhole meas same as back to shoulder shaping, end WS row. **Shape shoulder** as for back—4 sts rem. Place rem sts on holder for neckband.

RIGHT FRONT

Work as for left front, rev all shaping, until piece meas same as back to armhole, end RS row. **Shape armhole:** (WS) BO 6 (9, 14, 16, 20) sts at beg of this row—37 (38, 39, 41, 43) sts rem. Work even until armhole meas ½ (1, 1, 1½, 2)" from shaping, end WS row. **Shape neck:** Dec row: (RS) Work 4 sts as est, ssk, work as est to end. Work 1 row even. Rep dec row, then work dec row EOR 2 (0, 2, 0, 2) times, every 4 rows 13 (14, 13, 14, 13) times—20 (22, 22, 25, 26) sts rem for shoulder. Work even until armhole meas same as back to shoulder shaping, end RS row. **Shape shoulder** as for back at beg of WS rows—4 sts rem. BO rem sts.

SLEEVES

CO 45 (45, 45, 51, 51) sts; work in Moss st until piece meas 1" from beg, end WS row. **Shape sleeve:** (RS) Inc 1 st each side this row, then every 10 (10, 6, 10, 6) rows 14 (2, 6, 6, 6) times, every 8 rows 0 (15, 13, 10, 13) times, working inc sts in Moss st as they become available—75 (81, 85, 85, 91) sts. Work even until piece meas 20¼ (20¾, 21, 21¼, 21½)" from beg. BO all sts.

FINISHING

Block pieces to measurements. Sew left shoulder seam, beg at armhole edge to holder. **Neckband:** Return 4 sts on holder for neckband to needle, rejoin yarn to WS; work in patt as est, until neckband meas same as back neck opening when slightly stretched. BO all sts. Sew neckband to back neck opening. Sew right shoulder seam, including BO edges of neckband. Set in sleeves; sew sleeve and side seams. Sew hook and eye fastener at beg of V-neck shaping. Sew button to right front over hook and eye.

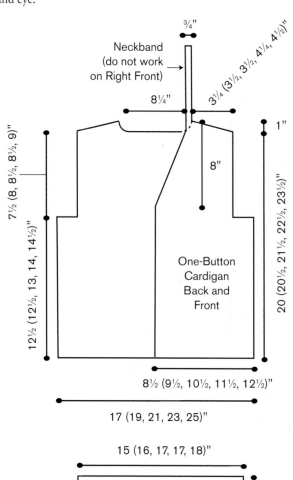

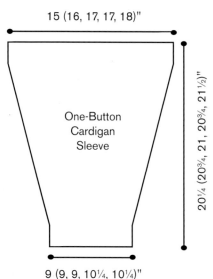

CHIC BOLERO

SIZES

Small (Medium, Large, 1X Large)

FINISHED MEASUREMENTS

38½ (41,43, 45½)"

MATERIALS

Classic Elite Yarns

Lush (50% angora, 50% wool;
50-g hank = approx 123 yd/112 m)

• 7 (8, 8, 9) hanks 4468 Madder

Equivalent yarn

Worsted weight #4, 861 (984, 984, 1107) yd

Needles

• One pair *each* size U.S. 6 (4 mm) and 8 (5 mm)
  or size to obtain gauge

Stitch markers

GAUGE

20 sts and 26 rows = 4" in Stockinette Stitch,
using larger needles. Take time to save time,
check your gauge.

PATTERN STITCHES

2 x 4 RIB (MULTIPLE OF 6 STS)

Row 1: (RS) *K1, p4, k1; rep from * across.

Row 2: *P1, k4, p1; rep from * across.

Rep Rows 1–2 for 2 x 4 Rib.

STOCKINETTE STITCH (ST ST)

Knit on RS, purl on WS.

BACK

Using larger needles, CO 96 (102, 108, 114) sts. *Est patt:* (RS) P2, k1 work in 2 × 4 Rib to last 3 sts, k1, p2. Work in est patt until piece meas 1" from beg, end WS row. Change to St st; (RS) work even until piece meas 6 (6¼, 6½, 6¾)" from beg; end WS row. *Shape armholes:* (RS) BO 6 sts at the beg of the next 2 rows, then dec 1 st each side EOR 2 (4, 5, 6) times, every row 8 (8, 8, 9) times—64 (66, 70, 72) sts rem. Work even until armhole meas 7¼ (7¾, 8¼, 8¾)" from beg of shaping, end WS row; pm each side of center 32 (34, 36, 36) sts. *Shape neck:* (RS) Work across to marker, join second ball of yarn and BO center sts, work to end. Work 1 row even. *Shape shoulders and neck:* (RS) BO 6 (6, 6, 7) sts at beg of next 4 (4, 2, 4) rows, then 0 (0, 7, 0) sts at beg of next 2 rows; and, **at the same time,** at each neck edge dec 1 st every row 4 times.

LEFT FRONT

Using larger needles, CO 46 (48, 50, 54) sts. *Est patt:* P1 (2, 0, 2), k1, work in 2 × 4 Rib to last 2 (3, 1, 3) sts, k1, p1 (2, 0, 2). Work as est until piece meas 1" from beg, end WS row. Change to St st; (RS) work even until piece meas same as back to underarm, end WS row. *Shape armhole:* (RS) BO 6 sts at beg of next row. Work 1 row even. (RS) At armhole edge, dec 1 st EOR 2 (4, 5, 6) times, then every row 8 (8, 8, 9) times— 30 (30, 31, 33) sts rem. Work even until armhole meas 4 (4½, 5, 5½)" from beg of shaping, end RS row. *Shape neck:* (WS) At neck edge, BO 4 sts once, then dec 1 st every row 12 (12, 12, 14) times, EOR 2 (2, 2, 1) times—12 (12, 13, 14) sts rem each shoulder. Work even until armhole meas 7½ (8, 8½, 9)" from beg of shaping, end WS row. Shape shoulder as for back at beg of RS rows only.

RIGHT FRONT

Work as for left front, working armhole and shoulder shaping at beg of WS rows and neck shaping at beg of RS rows.

SLEEVES

Using smaller needles, CO 48 sts; work in 2 × 4 Rib until piece meas 3" from beg, end WS row. Change to larger needles and St st; work 2 rows even, end WS row. *Shape sleeve:* (RS) Inc 1 st each side this row, then every 8 (8, 6, 6) rows 5 (3, 15, 12) times, every 6 (6, 0, 4) rows 7 (10, 0, 5) times—74 (76, 80, 84) sts. Work even until piece meas 18 (18¼, 18¾, 19)" from beg, end WS row. *Shape cap:* (RS) BO 6 sts at beg of next 2 rows— 62 (64, 68, 72) sts rem. Dec 1 st each side EOR 2 (4, 5, 6) times, then every row 23 (22, 23, 24) times—12 sts rem. BO rem sts.

FINISHING

Block pieces to measurements. Sew shoulder seams. Set in sleeves; sew side and sleeve seams. *Front bands:* With RS facing, using smaller needles, and beg at lower edge of right front, pick up and knit 54 (60, 66, 66) sts to beg of neck shaping. Beg Row 2 of 2 × 4 Rib, work even until front band meas ½" from pickup row. BO all sts loosely in rib. Rep for left front, beg at neck shaping and working to lower edge. *Neckband:* With RS facing, using smaller needles, pick up and knit 108 (108, 114, 114) sts evenly around neck shaping, including front bands. Work as for front bands.

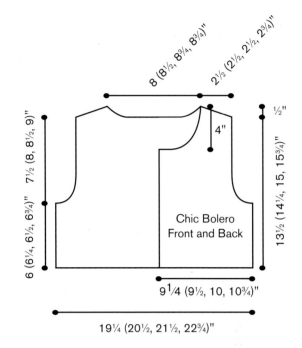

8 (8½, 8¾, 8¾)"

2½ (2½, 2½, 2¾)"

½"

4"

7½ (8, 8½, 9)"

13½ (14¼, 15, 15¾)"

6 (6¼, 6½, 6¾)"

Chic Bolero Front and Back

9¼ (9½, 10, 10¾)"

19¼ (20½, 21½, 22¾)"

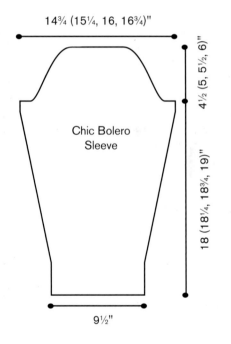

14¾ (15¼, 16, 16¾)"

4½ (5, 5½, 6)"

Chic Bolero Sleeve

18 (18¼, 18¾, 19)"

9½"

BRIOCHE RIB AND CABLE SWEATER

SIZES
Small (Medium, Large, 1X Large)

FINISHED MEASUREMENTS
36 (40, 44, 49)"

MATERIALS
Classic Elite Yarns
Four Seasons (70% cotton, 30% wool; 50-g hank = approx 103 yd/94 m)
• 8 (9, 10, 11) hanks 7655 Orange Peel
Equivalent yarn
Worsted weight #4, 824 (927, 1030, 1133) yd
Needles
• One pair size U.S. 7 (4.5 mm) or size to obtain gauge
• One 16" circular size U.S. 5 (3.75 mm) for neck edging
• One cable needle (cn)
Stitch markers
Stitch holders

GAUGE
19 sts and 27 rows = 4" in Reverse Stockinette Stitch, using larger needles; 12 sts = 2" in cable from Chart C, using larger needles; 24 sts = 3 ¾" in cables from Charts A and B, using larger needles. Take time to save time, check your gauge.

PATTERN STITCHES

CABLES
See Charts A (multiple of 24 sts; 8-row rep), B (multiple of 24 sts; 8-row rep), and C (multiple of 12 sts; 14-row rep).

REVERSE STOCKINETTE STITCH (REV ST ST)
Purl on RS, knit on WS.

BRIOCHE RIB (MULTIPLE OF 3 STS + 2)
Row 1: (RS) *P2, k1 in row below (k1b); rep from * across to last 2 sts, p2.
Row 2: K2, *p1, k2; rep from * across.
Rep Rows 1–2 for Brioche Rib.

CIRCULAR BRIOCHE RIB (MULTIPLE OF 3 STS)
Rnds 1 and 3: *K1b, p2; rep from * around.
Rnds 2 and 4: *K1, p2; rep from * around.
Rep Rnds 1–4 for Circular Brioche Rib.

BACK

CO 108 (120, 132, 144) sts. *Setup row:* (WS) [K2, p1] 3 (5, 7, 9) times, k3; pm; *p12; pm; k3, [p1, k2] twice, p6, [k2, p1] twice, k3; pm; rep from * once, p12, pm; k3, [p1, k2] 3 (5, 7, 9) times. *Est patt:* (RS) Work 11 (17, 23, 29) sts Brioche Rib, 1 st in Rev St st, 12 sts from Chart C, 24 sts from Chart A, 12 sts from Chart C, 24 sts from Chart B, 12 sts from Chart C, 1 st in Rev St st, 11 (17, 23, 29) sts Brioche Rib. Work as est until piece meas 4¾ (5, 5¼, 5¼)" from beg of work, end RS row. *Shape waist:* (WS) Dec 1 st before and after each Chart C—102 (114, 126, 138) sts rem. Work as est for 7 rows, end RS row. *Shape waist:* (WS) Inc 1 st before and after Chart C—108 (120, 132, 144) sts. Cont in patt as est until piece meas 11½ (12, 12½, 13)" from beg, end WS row. *Shape armholes:* (RS) BO 10 (11, 12, 13) sts at beg of next 2 rows—88 (98, 108, 118)

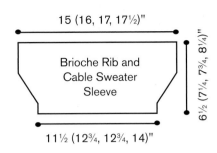

15 (16, 17, 17½)"

6½ (7¼, 7¾, 8¼)"

Brioche Rib and
Cable Sweater
Sleeve

11½ (12¾, 12¾, 14)"

sts rem. Work even until piece meas 7½ (8, 8½, 8 ¾)" from
shaping, end WS row. **Shape shoulders and neck:** (RS) BO
9 (11, 12, 13) sts at beg of next 4 rows, 9 (10, 11, 14) sts at
beg of next 2 rows; and, **at the same time,** on the first row of
shoulder shaping, work across to center 22 sts; join second
ball of yarn, BO center sts, work to end. Working both sides at
same time, at each neck edge BO 3 (3, 4, 4) sts twice.

FRONT

Work as for back until armhole meas 5½ (6, 6½, 6¾)" from
shaping, end WS row—88 (98, 108, 118) sts. **Shape neck:** (RS)
Work 37 (42, 47, 52) sts, join second ball of yarn, BO center
14 sts, work to end. BO 3 sts at each neck edge once, then
2 sts 2 (2, 3, 3) times, then 1 st 3 times—27 (32, 35, 40) sts rem
each shoulder. Work even until armhole meas same as back to
shoulder shaping. **Shape shoulders** as for back.

SLEEVES

CO 70 (76, 76, 82) sts. **Setup row:** (WS) [K2, p1] 1 (2, 2, 3)
times, k2; pm; k3, [p1, k2] twice, p6, [k2, p1] twice, k3; pm;
p12; pm; k3, [p1, k2] twice, p6, [k2, p1] twice, k3; pm; k2, [p1,
k2] 1 (2, 2, 3) times. **Est patt:** (RS) Work 5 (8, 8, 11) sts Brioche
Rib, 24 sts from Chart A, 12 sts from Chart C, 24 sts from
Chart B; 5 (8, 8, 11) sts in Brioche Rib. Work as est until piece
meas 1" from beg, end RS row. **Shape sleeve:** Inc 1 st each side
this row, then EOR 2 (2, 4, 0) times, then every 4 rows 3 (4,
5, 7) times, working inc sts in Rev St st—82 (90, 96, 98) sts.
Work even until piece meas 6½ (7¼, 7¾, 8¼)" from beg. BO
all sts loosely in patt.

FINISHING

Block pieces to measurements. Sew shoulder seams. Set in
sleeves; sew sleeve and side seams. **Neckband:** With RS facing,
using smaller circular needle, beg at left shoulder, pick up and
knit 46 sts evenly around front neck edge, 38 (38, 41, 41) sts
along back neck, pm for beg of rnd—84 (84, 87, 87) sts. Work
Circular Brioche Rib until band meas 1" from pickup row. BO
all sts in patt, working knit sts as k1b.

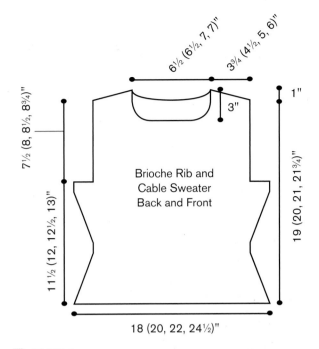

6½ (6½, 7, 7)"   3¾ (4½, 5, 6)"

7½ (8, 8½, 8¾)"

3"

1"

Brioche Rib and
Cable Sweater
Back and Front

11½ (12, 12½, 13)"

19 (20, 21, 21¾)"

18 (20, 22, 24½)"

■ CHART A

Multiple of 24 sts; 8-row rep

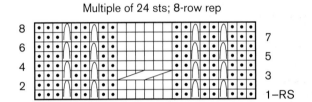

■ CHART B

Multiple of 24 sts; 8-row rep

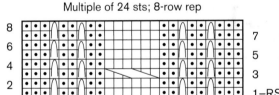

■ CHART C

Multiple of 12 sts; 14-row rep

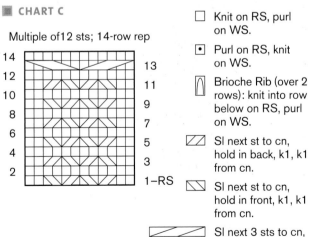

☐ Knit on RS, purl
on WS.

⊡ Purl on RS, knit
on WS.

⋔ Brioche Rib (over 2
rows): knit into row
below on RS, purl
on WS.

▨ Sl next st to cn,
hold in back, k1, k1
from cn.

▧ Sl next st to cn,
hold in front, k1, k1
from cn.

▱ Sl next 3 sts to cn,
hold in back, k3,
k3 from cn.

▱ Sl next 3 sts to cn,
hold in front, k3
from cn.

COLOR BLOCK AND CABLE CARDIGAN

SIZES

Extra Small (Small, Medium, Large, 1X Large, 2X Large)

FINISHED MEASUREMENTS

34 (37½, 42, 45½, 50, 53½)"

MATERIALS

Classic Elite Yarns

Inca Marl (100% alpaca; 50-g hank = approx 109 yd/100 m)

• 6 (6, 7, 8, 8, 9) hanks Main Color (MC) 1193 Great Lake

Inca Alpaca (100% alpaca; 50-g hank = approx 109 yd/100 m)

• 4 (4, 5, 5, 6, 7) hanks Contrast Color (CC) 1107 Camacho Periwinkle

Equivalent yarn

Worsted weight #4, MC: 654 (654, 763, 872, 872, 981) yd; CC: 436 (436, 545, 545, 654, 763) yd

Needles

• One pair *each* size U.S. 6 (4 mm) and 7 (4.5 mm) or size to obtain gauge

• One cable needle (cn)

Stitch holders

Stitch markers

Five ⅜" buttons

GAUGE

20 sts and 28 rows = 4" in Stockinette Stitch, using larger needles; 10 sts = approx 1½" in Snake Cable after light blocking, using larger needles. Take time to save time, check your gauge.

PATTERN STITCHES

STOCKINETTE STITCH (ST ST)

Knit on RS, purl on WS.

1 × 1 RIB (MULTIPLE OF 2 STS + 1)

Row 1: (RS) K1, *p1, k1; rep from * across.

Row 2: Knit the knit sts and purl the purl sts as they face you.

Rep Row 2 for 1 x 1 Rib.

SNAKE CABLE (MULTIPLE OF 10 STS; 20-ROW REP)

See chart.

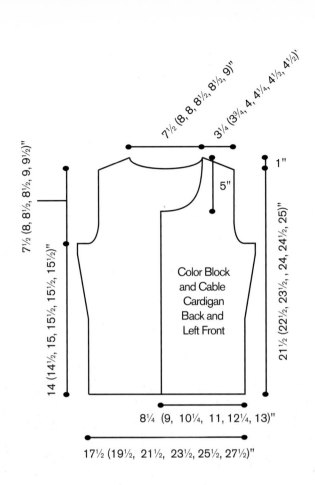

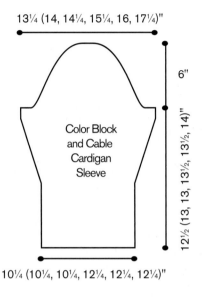

BACK

Using larger needles and CC, CO 98 (110, 122, 134, 146, 158) sts. *Est patt:* (RS) Work [k2, 10 sts Snake Cable from chart] 8 (9, 10, 11, 12, 13) times, k2. Work even as est for 52 rows, end WS row (Row 12 of chart). *Shape sides: Dec row:* (RS) K3, *k2tog, k4, ssk, k4; rep from * across end last rep, k3—82 (92, 102, 112, 122, 132) sts rem. Knit 1 WS row (Garter Ridge). Change to MC and St st: (RS) Work even for 12 rows, end WS row. *Shape sides: Inc row:* (RS) Inc 1 st each side this row, then every 12 rows twice—88 (98, 108, 118, 128, 138) sts. Work even until piece meas 14 (14½, 15, 15½, 15½, 15½)" from beg, end WS row. *Shape armholes:* (RS) BO 5 (6, 6, 7, 8, 8) sts at beg of next 2 rows, 0 (0, 2, 3, 5, 8) sts at beg of next 2 rows, then dec 1 st each side EOR 4 (5, 6, 6, 7, 8) times—70 (76, 80, 86, 88, 90) sts rem. Work even until armhole meas 7½ (8, 8½, 8½, 9, 9½)" from beg of shaping, end WS row. *Shape shoulders and neck:* (RS) BO 5 (6, 7, 7, 8, 8) sts at beg of next 4 rows, 6 (6, 6, 8, 7, 7) sts at beg of next 2 rows; and, **at the same time,** on the first row of shoulder shaping, work across to center 30 (32, 32, 34, 34, 36) sts; join second ball of yarn, BO center sts, work to end. Working both sides at same time, at each neck edge BO 4 sts once.

LEFT FRONT

Using larger needles and CC, CO 47 (50, 59, 62, 71, 74) sts. *Est patt:* (RS) Work [k2, 10 sts Snake Cable from chart] 3 (4, 4, 5, 5, 6) times, end k2, work sts 1–9 of Snake Cable chart 1 (0, 1, 0, 1, 0) times. Work even as est for 52 rows, end WS row (Row 12 of chart). *Shape side: Dec row:* (RS) K1 (3, 1, 3, 1, 3), k2tog (k0, k2tog, k0, k2tog, k0) *k2tog, k4, ssk, k4; rep from * across end last rep, k0 (3, 0, 3, 0, 3)—38 (42, 48, 52, 58, 62) sts rem. Knit 1 WS row (Garter Ridge). Change to MC and St st: (RS) Work even for 12 rows, end WS row. *Shape side: Inc row:* (RS) Inc 1 st this row, then every 12 rows 2 times—41 (45, 51, 55, 61, 65) sts. Work even until piece meas 14 (14½, 15, 15½, 15½, 15½)" from beg, end WS row. *Shape armhole* as for back at beg of RS rows only—32 (34, 37, 39, 41, 41) sts rem. Work even until armhole meas 3½ (4, 4½, 4½, 5, 5½)" from beg of shaping, end RS row. *Shape neck:* (WS) At neck edge, BO 4 (4, 5, 5, 6, 6) sts once, 3 sts once, 2 sts once, then dec 1 st EOR 7 times—16 (18, 20, 22, 23, 23) sts rem. Work even until armhole meas same as back to shoulder shaping, end WS row. *Shape shoulders* as for back at beg of RS rows only.

RIGHT FRONT

Using larger needles and CC, CO 47 (50, 59, 62, 71, 74) sts.
Est patt: (RS) Work sts 2–10 Snake Cable from chart 1 (0, 1, 0, 1, 0) times, k2, work [10 sts Snake Cable from chart, k2] 3 (4, 4, 5, 5, 6) times. Work even as est for 52 rows, end WS row (Row 12 of chart). *Dec row:* (RS) K0 (3, 0, 3, 0, 3), *k2tog, k4, ssk, k4; rep from * across end last rep k1 (3, 1, 3, 1, 3), k2tog (k0, k2tog, k0, k2tog, k0)—38 (42, 48, 52, 58, 62) sts rem. Knit 1 WS row (Garter Ridge). Change to MC and St st: Work as for left front, rev all shaping by working side shaping at end of RS rows, armhole and shoulder shaping at beg of WS rows, and neck shaping at beg of RS rows.

SLEEVES

Using larger needles and CC, CO 62 (62, 62, 74, 74, 74) sts.
Est patt: (RS) Work [k2, 10 sts Snake Cable from chart] 5 (5, 5, 6, 6, 6) times, k2. Work even as est for 42 rows, end WS row (Row 2 of Snake Cable chart). *Dec row:* (RS) K3, *k2tog, k4, ssk, k4; rep from * across, end last rep, k3—52 (52, 52, 62, 62, 62) sts rem. Knit 1 WS row (Garter Ridge). Change to MC and St st: (RS) Work even for 2 rows, end WS row. **Shape sleeve:** (RS) *Note:* To make seaming neater, work all incs 2 sts in from each edge. Inc 1 st each side this row, then every 6 (5, 4, 6, 5, 4) rows 6 (8, 9, 6, 8, 11) times, working inc sts in St st as they become available—66 (70, 72, 76, 80, 86) sts. Work even until piece meas 12½ (13, 13, 13½, 13½, 14)" from beg, end WS row. **Shape cap:** (RS) BO 5 (6, 6, 7, 8, 8) sts at beg of next 2 rows, 0 (0, 2, 3, 4, 7) sts at beg of next 2 rows—56 (58, 56, 56, 56, 56) sts rem. Dec 1 st each side EOR 17 (17, 16, 16, 16, 16) times—22 (24, 24, 24, 24, 24) sts rem. BO 3 sts at beg of next 4 rows—10 (12, 12, 12, 12, 12). BO rem sts.

FINISHING

Block pieces to measurements. Sew shoulder seams. Set in sleeves; sew side and sleeve seams. **Button band:** Using smaller needles and MC, CO 7 sts. Beg 1 × 1 Rib; work even until piece meas same as left front from lower edge to beg of neck shaping slightly stretched. Place sts on holder. Sew band in place. Pm for 5 buttonholes on right front, first 2" from lower edge, last 1½" from beg of neck shaping, rem 3 evenly spaced

bet. **Buttonhole band:** Work as for button band; and, **at the same time,** work buttonholes opposite markers as foll: [yo, k2tog] at each marker. Sew bands in place. **Neckband:** With RS facing, using smaller needles and MC, work 6 sts from right front band holder as est in 1 × 1 Rib, [work last 2 sts tog (seam st)], pick up and knit 105 (107, 109, 111, 113, 115) sts evenly around neck edge, work 6 sts from left front band holder as est [work seam st tog with adjoining st]—115 (117, 119, 121, 123, 125) sts. Work in 1 × 1 Rib for 1½". BO all sts loosely in rib.

■ SNAKE CABLE CHART

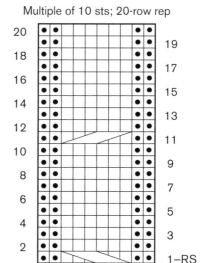

Multiple of 10 sts; 20-row rep

☐ Knit on RS, purl on WS.

⊡ Purl on RS, Knit on WS.

Sl 3 sts to cn, hold in front, k3, k3 from cn.

Sl 3 sts to cn, hold in back, k3, k3 from cn.

COLLARED MOHAIR JACKET

SIZES

Extra Small (Small, Medium, Large)

FINISHED MEASUREMENTS

35 (37, 39, 41)"

MATERIALS

Classic Elite yarns

La Gran (76½% mohair, 17½% wool, 6% nylon;
42-g ball = approx 90 yd/82 m)

• 9 (10, 11, 12) balls 6511 Seashell

Equivalent yarn

Worsted weight #4; 810 (900, 990, 1080) yd

Needles

• One pair *each* size U.S. 7 (4.5 mm) and
  9 (5.5 mm) or size to obtain gauge

Split ring stitch markers

Stitch holders

Five ⅞" buttons

GAUGE

16 sts and 22 rows = 4" in Stockinette
Stitch, using larger needles. Take time to
save time, check your gauge.

NOTE

Work sleeve incs and decs 2 sts in from
edge on each side.

SPECIAL TECHNIQUES

WRAP AND TURN

Bring yarn to front of work, sl 1p onto
RH needle, bring yarn to back of work,
sl same st back to LH needle, then turn
work.

HIDE WRAPS

On knit row: Pick up wrap from front with RH
needle and knit tog with st it wraps.

On purl row: Pick up wrap tbl with RH needle and
purl tog with st it wraps.

PATTERN STITCHES

**SEED STITCH (SEED ST)
(MULTIPLE OF 2 STS + 1)**

Row 1: (RS) *K1, p1; rep from * across to last st, k1.

Row 2: Knit the purl sts and purl the knit sts
as they face you.

Rep Row 2 for Seed st.

STOCKINETTE STITCH (ST ST)

Knit on RS, purl on WS.

BACK

Using smaller needles, CO 65 (69, 73, 77) sts. Beg Seed st; work
even until piece meas 1" from beg, inc 1 st across last (WS)
row—66 (70, 74, 78) sts. Change to larger needles and St st;
(RS) work even for 10 rows (piece meas 2¾" from beg), end
WS row. Counting in from each side, pms on st 16 (17, 18, 19).
Shape waist: Dec row: (RS) Work to within 1 st of first marker;
remove marker, k3tog, return marker to resulting st, work
to within 1 st of second marker, remove marker, k3tog-tbl,
return marker to resulting st, work to end. Rep dec row every
8 rows twice, end RS row—54 (58, 62, 66) sts rem. Work even
for 11 rows, end WS row. *Shape waist: Inc row:* (RS) *Work
to marked st, m1, k1, m1; rep from * once, work to end. Rep
inc row every 8 rows 3 times, end RS row—70 (74, 78, 82) sts.
Remove markers. Work even until piece meas 14" from beg,

end WS row. *Shape armholes:* (RS) BO 3 sts at beg of next
2 rows—64 (68, 72, 76) sts rem. Working all decs 2 sts in
from edge, dec 1 st each side every row 3 times, EOR 3 (4, 5, 6)
times—52 (54, 56, 58) sts rem. Work even until armhole meas
7½ (8, 8½, 9)" from beg of shaping, end WS row; pm each
side of center 20 (22, 22, 24) sts. *Shape shoulders and neck:*
(RS) BO 5 sts at beg of next 2 (2, 4, 4) rows, 4 sts at beg of next
4 (4, 2, 2) rows; and, **at the same time,** on first row of shoulder
shaping, work across to marker; join a second ball of yarn and
BO center sts, work to end. Working both sides at same time,
at each neck edge BO 3 sts once.

LEFT FRONT

Using smaller needles, CO 39 (41, 43, 45) sts. Beg Seed st; work
even until piece meas 1" from beg, end WS row. Change to

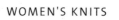

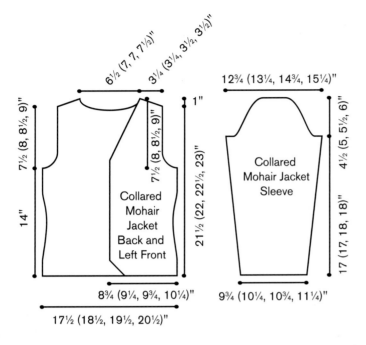

Collared Mohair Jacket Back and Left Front

6½ (7, 7, 7½)"

3¼ (3¼, 3½, 3½)"

7½ (8, 8½, 9)"

14"

7½ (8, 8½, 9)"

21½ (22, 22½, 23)"

1"

8¾ (9¼, 9¾, 10¼)"

17½ (18½, 19½, 20½)"

Collared Mohair Jacket Sleeve

12¾ (13¼, 14¾, 15¼)"

4½ (5, 5½, 6)"

17 (17, 18, 18)"

9¾ (10¼, 10¾, 11¼)"

larger needles and St st; (RS) work to last 6 sts, sl 6 sts to holder for button band—33 (35, 37, 39) sts rem. Work 1 row even, end WS row. **Shape center front:** as foll: *Row 1:* (RS) Work 30 (32, 34, 36) sts, Wrap and Turn. *Rows 2, 4, and 6:* Work even. *Row 3:* Work 28 (30, 32, 34) sts, Wrap and Turn. *Row 5:* Work 26 (28, 30, 32) sts, Wrap and Turn. *Row 7:* Work 24 (26, 28, 30) sts, Wrap and Turn. *Row 8:* Rep Row 2. Counting in from side edge, pm on st 16 (17, 18, 19). **Shape waist:** *Row 9:* Work to within 1 st of marker, remove marker, k3tog, return marker to resulting st, work until 20 (22, 24, 26) sts are on RH needle, Wrap and Turn—31 (33, 35, 37) sts rem. *Rows 10, 12, and 14:* Rep Row 2. *Row 11:* Work 18 (20, 22, 24) sts, Wrap and Turn. *Row 13:* Work 16 (18, 20, 22) sts, Wrap and Turn. *Row 15:* Work across all sts; and, **at the same time,** Hide Wraps. *Row 16:* Rep Row 2. *Next row: Dec row:* (RS) Work to within 1 st of marked st, k3tog, work to end. Work 7 rows even, end WS row. (RS) Rep dec row—27 (29, 31, 33) sts rem. Work 11 rows even, end WS row. **Shape waist:** *Inc row:* (RS) *Work to marker, m1, k1, m1, work to end. Rep inc row every 8 rows 3 times—35 (37, 39, 41) sts. Remove markers. Work even until piece meas 14" from beg, end WS row. **Shape armhole and V-neck:** (RS) At armhole edge, BO 3 sts, work across to last 4 sts, k2tog, work to end. Work 1 row even. Working all decs (armhole and neck) 2 sts in from each edge, at armhole edge, dec 1 st every row 3 times, EOR 3 (4, 5, 6) times; and, **at the same time,** at neck edge dec 1 st EOR 4 (4, 2, 3) times, every 4 rows 8 (9, 11, 11) times—13 (13, 14, 14) sts rem for shoulder. And, **at the same time,** when armhole meas same as back to shoulder shaping, end WS row. **Shape shoulder:** As for back at beg of RS rows only.

RIGHT FRONT

Using smaller needles, CO 39 (41, 43, 45) sts. Beg Seed st; work even until piece meas 1" from beg, end WS row. (RS) Work 6 sts and place on holder for buttonhole band; change to larger needles and St st; work to end of row. **Shape center front:** (WS) Work 30 (32, 34, 36) sts, Wrap and Turn. Complete to match left front; beg waist shaping at side edge on Row 9 and Hide Wraps on a WS row. Rev all shaping by working armhole and shoulder shaping at beg of WS rows, and neck shaping at beg of RS rows as foll: K2, ssk, work to end.

SLEEVES

Using larger needles, CO 39 (41, 43, 45) sts. Beg Seed st; work even until piece meas 2" from beg. Change to smaller needles and St st; (RS) work even until piece meas 4" from beg, end WS row. Change to larger needles and **shape sleeve:** (RS) Inc 1 st each side this row, then every 10 rows 0 (0, 2, 2) times, every 12 rows 0 (0, 5, 5) times, every 14 rows 5 (5, 0, 0) times— 51 (53, 59, 61) sts. Work even until piece meas 17 (17, 18, 18)" from beg, end WS row. **Shape cap:** (RS) BO 3 sts at beg of next 2 rows. Dec 1 st each side every row 3 times, EOR 2 (2, 2, 3) times, every 4 rows 3 (4, 2, 3) times, EOR 0 (0, 5, 4) times, every row 5 times—19 sts rem. BO rem sts.

FINISHING

Block pieces to measurements. Sew shoulder seams. **Button band and collar:** With RS facing, sl 6 sts from left front holder onto smaller needles, join yarn: Work 1 st in St st (edge st), work rem 5 sts in Seed st. Cont in Seed st until band meas same as front to beg of neck shaping when slightly stretched, end WS row. Sew band in place. Cont in patt as est; and, **at the same time, shape collar:** (RS) *Work 1 st, m1, k1-f/b, work to end—8 sts. Work 3 rows even. Rep from * 3 times, end WS row—14 sts. *Inc row:* (RS) *Work 1 st, k1-f/b, work to end— 15 sts. Work 3 rows even. Rep from * 4 times, sewing band in place as you go along, end WS row—19 sts. Work 1 row even. *Next row:* (WS) BO 11 sts, work to end—8 sts rem. *Next row:* (RS) Work 8 sts, turn and CO 11 sts—19 sts. Cont without shaping until collar fits along V-neck shaping and across to center of back neck, end WS row. BO all sts. Pm for 5 buttons, first 1¼" from lower edge, last at beg of V-neck shaping, rem 3 evenly spaced bet. **Buttonhole band and collar:** Work as for button band, working buttonholes opposite markers as foll: (RS) Work 2 sts, yo, work 2 sts tog, work to end. Complete to match left collar, rev all shaping. Sew collar seam; sew collar along back neck shaping. Set in sleeves; sew side and sleeve seams, rev seam at lower edge 2" for cuff. Sew on buttons.

ROLL-NECK PULLOVER

SIZES
Small (Medium, Large, 1X Large, 2X Large)

FINISHED MEASUREMENTS
36 (40, 44, 48, 52)"

MATERIALS
Classic Elite Yarns

MarL La (100% wool; 100-g hank = approx 57 yd/52 m)

• 10 (11, 12, 13, 15) hanks 8527 Crazy Copper

Equivalent yarn

Super bulky weight #6; 570 (627, 684, 741, 855) yd

Needles

• One pair size U.S. 17 (12.75 mm) or size to obtain gauge

• One 16" circular size U.S. 17 (12.75 mm) for neck finishing

Stitch holders

Stitch markers

GAUGE
8 sts and 14 rows = 4" in Stockinette Stitch. Take time to save time, check your gauge.

PATTERN STITCHES

STOCKINETTE STITCH (ST ST)
Knit on RS, purl on WS.

CIRCULAR STOCKINETTE STITCH
Knit every rnd.

2 × 2 RIB (MULTIPLE OF 4 STS + 2)
Row 1: (RS) K2, *p2, k2; rep from * across.

Row 2: Purl the purl sts and knit the knit sts as they face you.

Rep Row 2 for 2 x 2 Rib.

BACK

CO 36 (40, 44, 48, 52) sts; purl 2 rows, end WS row. Change to St st; work even until piece meas 14" from beg, end WS row. **Shape armholes:** (RS) BO 2 (2, 3, 4, 4) sts at beg of next 2 rows, then dec 1 st each side EOR 2 (3, 3, 3, 4) times—28 (30, 32, 34, 36) sts rem. Work even until armhole meas 7½ (8, 8½, 9, 9½)" from beg, end WS row. **Shape shoulders:** (RS) BO 3 (3, 4, 4, 5) sts at beg of next 4 (2, 4, 2, 4) rows, 0 (4, 0, 5, 0) sts at beg of next 2 rows—16 sts rem. Place rem sts on holder for neck.

FRONT

Work as for back until armhole meas 5 (5½, 6, 6½, 7)" from beg of shaping, end WS row—28 (30, 32, 34, 36) sts rem. **Shape neck:** (RS) Work 12 (13, 14, 15, 16) sts, join second ball of yarn, work center 4 sts and place on holder for neck, work to end. Working both sides at same time, at each neck edge BO 3 sts once, then dec 1 st EOR 3 times—6 (7, 8, 9, 10) sts rem each shoulder. Work even until armhole meas same as back to shoulders, end WS row. **Shape shoulders** as for back.

SLEEVES

CO 20 sts; work 2" in 2 × 2 Rib, end WS row. **Shape sleeve:** Inc 1 st each side this row, then every 12 (10, 8, 6, 6) rows 4 (5, 6, 7, 8) times, working inc sts in patt as they become available—30 (32, 34, 36, 38) sts; and, **at the same time,** work 2 × 2 Rib until piece meas 7" from beg, end WS row. Change to St st; work even until piece meas 9" from beg, end RS row. Knit 1 row, purl 2 rows, end WS row. Change to St st; work even until piece meas 17½ (18, 18, 18, 18)" from beg, end WS row. **Shape cap:** (RS) BO 2 (2, 3, 4, 4) sts at beg of next 2 rows, then dec 1 st each side EOR 5 (6, 6, 6, 7) times—16 sts rem. BO 2 sts at beg of next 4 rows—8 sts rem. BO rem sts.

FINISHING

Block pieces to measurements. Sew shoulder seams. Set in sleeves; sew sleeve and side seams. **Neckband:** With RS facing, using circular needle, work 16 sts from holder for back neck, pick up and knit 10 sts around left neck edge, work 4 sts from holder for neck, 10 sts around right neck edge, pm for beg of rnd—40 sts. Purl 2 rnds, then change to St st; work even until band meas 3½" from pickup row. BO all sts purlwise.

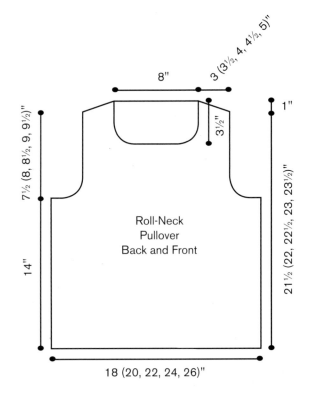

8"

3 (3½, 4, 4½, 5)"

1"

3½"

7½ (8, 8½, 9, 9½)"

14"

21½ (22, 22½, 23, 23½)"

Roll-Neck
Pullover
Back and Front

18 (20, 22, 24, 26)"

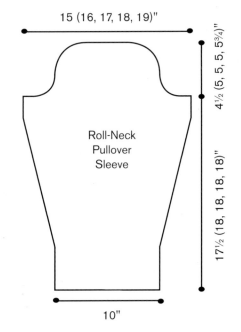

15 (16, 17, 18, 19)"

4½ (5, 5, 5, 5¾)"

17½ (18, 18, 18, 18)"

Roll-Neck
Pullover
Sleeve

10"

KIMONO COAT

SIZES
Small (Medium, Large, 1X Large, 2X Large)

FINISHED MEASUREMENTS
36 (40, 44, 48, 51)"

MATERIALS
Classic Elite Yarns

Lush (50% angora, 50% wool; 50-g hank = approx 123 yd/112 m)

• 12 (13, 14, 15, 17) hanks 4450 Gulf Stream

Equivalent yarn

Worsted weight #4, 1476 (1599, 1722, 1845, 2091) yd

Needles

• One pair *each* size U.S. 6 (4 mm) and 8 (5 mm) or size to obtain gauge

• One crochet hook any size for closures

• Two cable needles (cn)

Stitch markers

Stitch holder

Six 1" buttons

GAUGE
18 sts and 26 rows = 4" in Reverse Stockinette Stitch, using larger needles; 22 sts = 3¼" in Outlined Diamond Cable (Charts B and D), using larger needles; 10 sts = 1½" in Rope Cable (Charts A and C), using larger needles; 6 sts = 1" in Bamboo Stitch, using larger needles. Take time to save time, check your gauge.

NOTE
If there are not enough sts to complete a patt rep, work in St st until enough sts are present.

PATTERN STITCHES

STOCKINETTE STITCH (ST ST)
Knit on RS, purl on WS.

REVERSE STOCKINETTE STITCH (REV ST ST)
Purl on RS, knit on WS.

GARTER STITCH (GTR ST)
Knit every row.

BAMBOO STITCH (BAMBOO ST) (MULTIPLE OF 2 STS)
Row 1: (RS) *Yo, k2, pass yo over k2; rep from * across.

Row 2: Purl.

Rep Rows 1–2 for Bamboo Stitch.

ROPE CABLE (MULTIPLE OF 10 STS; 6-ROW REP)
See Charts A and C.

OUTLINED DIAMOND CABLE
(MULTIPLE OF 22 STS; 20-ROW REP)
See Charts B and D.

WELT (ANY NUMBER OF STS)
Row 1 (WS): Knit

Rows 2–3: Purl

Row 4: Knit

Rep Rows 1–4 for Welt.

CHAIN (CH)
Make a sl knot on hook. Wrap yarn around hook and draw it through loop on hook to form first ch. Rep from this step as many times as instructed.

BACK

Using smaller needles, CO 112 (120, 128, 136, 144) sts. *Setup row:* (WS) K0 (1, 1, 0, 0); p2 (1, 2, 0, 0); [k2, p2] 0 (1, 0, 0, 1) time, [k2, p1, k2, p2] 1 (1, 2, 3, 3) times, k2; pm; *p1, k2, p4, k2, p1; pm; k2, p2, k2, p1, k2, p4, k2, p1, k2, p2, k2; pm; p1, k2, p4, k2, p1; pm*; k2, p2, k2; pm; rep bet *s once, k2, [p2, k2, p1, k2] 1 (1, 2, 3, 3) times; [p2, k2] 0 (1, 0, 0, 1) time, p2 (1, 2, 0, 0); k0 (1, 1, 0, 0). Work sts as they appear, knit the knit sts, purl the purl sts as they face you, for 9 more rows, end RS row. Change to larger needles and *Foundation row:* (WS) Work 1 st in Gtr st (edge st), p8 (12, 16, 20, 24), k2; *p1, k2, p4, k2, p1, k6, p1, k2, p4, k2, p1, k6, p1, k2, p4, k2, p1*; k2, p2, k2; rep bet *s once; k2, p 8 (12, 16, 20, 24), work 1 st in Gtr st (edge st). *Est patt:* (RS) Work 1 st in Gtr st (edge st); 8 (12, 16, 20, 24) sts in Bamboo st; p2; 10 sts of Rope Cable Right (Chart A); 22 sts of Outlined Diamond Cable Right (Chart B); 10 sts of Rope Cable Right; p2, k2, p2; 10 sts of Rope Cable Left (Chart C); 22 sts of Outlined Diamond Cable Left (Chart D); 10 sts of Rope Cable Left; p2; 8 (12, 16, 20, 24) sts in Bamboo st; 1 st in Gtr st (edge st). Work even as est until piece meas 13¾ (13¾, 13¾, 13¾, 14)" from beg, end WS row. *Shape armholes:* (RS) BO 9 (12, 12, 14, 14) sts at beg of next 2 rows—94 (96, 104, 108, 116) sts. Work even until piece meas 8¼ (8½, 8¾, 9, 9)" from beg of shaping, end WS row. *Shape shoulders and neck:* (RS) BO 8 (9, 9, 10, 11) sts at beg of next 4 rows, 9 (8, 10, 10, 11) sts at beg of next 2 rows; and, **at the same time,** on the first row of shoulder shaping, work across to center 28 (28, 28, 28, 30) sts; join second ball of yarn, BO center sts, work to end. Working both sides at same time, BO 4 (4, 5, 5, 5) sts at each neck edge twice.

LEFT FRONT

Using smaller needles, CO 54 (58, 62, 66, 70) sts. *Setup row:* (WS) Work 1 st in Gtr st (edge st); p1, k2, p4, k2, p1; pm; k2, p2, k2, p1, k2, p4, k2, p1, k2, p2, k2; pm; p1, k2, p4, k2, p1; pm; k2, [p2, k2, p1, k2] 1 (1, 2, 3, 3) times; pm; [p2, k2] 0 (1, 0, 0, 1); p 2 (1, 2, 0, 0); k 0 (1, 1, 0, 0). Work sts as they appear, knit the knit sts and purl the purl sts as they face you, for 9 more rows, end RS row. Change to larger needles and *Foundation row:* (WS) Work 1 st in Gtr st (edge st), p1, k2, p4, k2, p1, k6, p1, k2, p4, k2, p1, k6, p1, k2, p4, k2, p1, k2, p8 (12, 16, 20, 24) sts, 1 st in Gtr st (edge st). *Est patt:* (RS) Work 1 st in Gtr st (edge st); 8 (12, 16, 20, 24) sts in Bamboo st; p2; 10 sts of Rope Cable Right (Chart A); 22 sts of Outlined Diamond Cable Right (Chart B); 10 sts of Rope Cable Right (Chart A); 1 st in Gtr st (edge st). Work as est until piece meas 13¾ (13¾, 13¾, 13¾, 14)" from beg, end WS row. *Shape armhole:* (RS) BO 9 (12, 12, 14, 14) sts at beg of this row—45 (46, 50, 52, 56) sts.

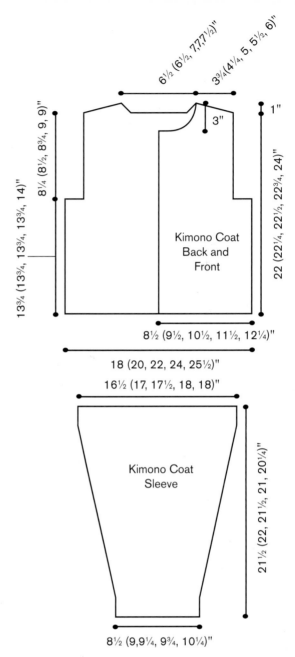

Kimono Coat
Back and
Front

6½ (6½, 7, 7, 7½)"

3¾ (4¼, 5, 5½, 6)"

3"

1"

8¼ (8½, 8¾, 9, 9)"

22 (22¼, 22½, 22¾, 24)"

13¾ (13¾, 13¾, 13¾, 14)"

8½ (9½, 10½, 11½, 12¼)"

18 (20, 22, 24, 25½)"

16½ (17, 17½, 18, 18)"

Kimono Coat
Sleeve

21½ (22, 21½, 21, 20¼)"

8½ (9,9¼, 9¾, 10¼)"

Work even as est until armhole meas 6¼ (6½, 6¾, 7, 7)" from shaping, end RS row. *Shape neck:* (WS) Work 10 (10, 11, 11, 11) sts and place on holder, work to end. At neck edge, BO 3 sts 1 (1, 1, 1, 2) times, 2 sts 2 (2, 3, 3, 2) times, then 1 st 3 (3, 2, 2, 2) times—25 (26, 28, 30, 33) sts rem. Work even as est until piece meas same as back to shoulder shaping, end WS row. *Shape shoulders* as for back at beg of RS rows only.

RIGHT FRONT

Using smaller needles, CO 54 (58, 62, 66, 70) sts. *Setup row:* (WS) K0 (1, 1, 0, 0); p2 (1, 2, 0, 0); [k2, p2] 0 (1, 0, 0, 1), [k2, p1, k2, p2] 1 (1, 2, 3, 3) times, k2; pm; p1, k2, p4, k2, p1; pm; k2, p2, k2, p1, k2, p4, k2, p1, k2, p2, k2; pm; p1, k2, p4, k2, p1; pm; work 1 st in Gtr st (edge st). Work sts as they appear, knit the knit sts and purl the purl sts as they face you, for 9 more

■ CHART A: ROPE CABLE RIGHT

Multiple of 10 sts; 6-row rep

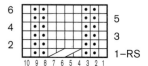

■ CHART B: OUTLINED DIAMOND CABLE RIGHT

Multiple of 22 sts; 20-row rep

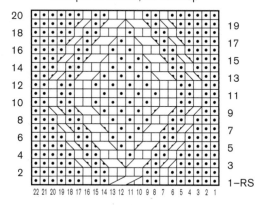

■ CHART C: ROPE CABLE LEFT

Multiple of 10 sts; 6-row rep

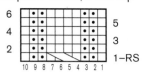

■ CHART D OUTLINED DIAMOND CABLE LEFT

Multiple of 22 sts, 20-row rep

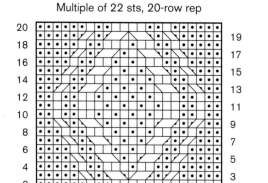

☐ Knit on RS, purl on WS.

⊡ Purl on RS, knit on WS.

▧ Sl 1 st to cn, hold in back, k1, p1 from cn.

◩ Sl 1 st to cn, hold in front, p1, k1 from cn.

▧ Sl 1 st to cn, hold in back, k2, k1 from cn.

◩ Sl 2 sts to cn, hold in front, k1, k2 from cn.

▧ Sl 1 st to cn, hold in back, k2, p1 from cn.

◩ Sl 2 sts to cn, hold in front, p1, k2 from cn.

▧ Sl 2 sts to cn, hold in back, k2, k2 from cn.

◩ Sl 2 sts to cn, hold in front, k2, k2 from cn.

FINISHING

Block pieces to measurements. Sew shoulder seams. Set in sleeves; sew sleeve and side seams. *Neckband:* With RS facing, using smaller needles, work 10 (10, 11, 11, 11) sts from holder for right front neck, pick up and knit 15 sts around right front neck edge, 48 (48, 52, 52, 54) sts across back neck edge, 15 sts around left front neck edge, work 10 (10, 11, 11, 11) sts from holder for left front neck—98 (98, 104, 104, 106) sts. *Est patt:* (WS) Work 1 st in Gtr st (edge st), 96 (96, 102, 102, 104) sts in Welt patt, 1 st in Gtr st (edge st). Work even until neckband meas 1" from pickup row. BO all sts loosely. *Left front button band:* With RS facing, using smaller needles, pick up and knit 99 (101, 103, 105, 106) sts evenly across left front edge (do *not* pick up neckband sts). *Est patt:* (WS) Work 1 st in Gtr st, 97 (99, 101, 103, 104) sts in Welt patt, 1 st in Gtr st (edge st). Work even until button band meas 1" from pickup row. BO all sts loosely. *Right front button band:* Work as for left front button band. Sew 3 buttons on left front, first 13" from lower edge of garment, last 1" below neck edge, rem 1 button evenly spaced bet. Rep on right front. *Closures (make 3):* Using crochet hook, work ch st cord until piece meas 6" from beg, sl st to beg. Sew closures to right front, forming two loops, one for each button (see photo).

rows, end RS row. Change to larger needles and *Foundation row:* (WS) Work 1 st in Gtr st (edge st), p8 (12, 16, 20, 24), k2, p1, k2, p4, k2, p1, k6, p1, k2, p4, k2, p1, k6, p1, k2, p4, k2, p1; work 1 st in Gtr st (edge st). *Est patt:* (RS) Work 1 st in Gtr st (edge st); work 10 sts of Rope Cable Left (Chart C); 22 sts of Outlined Diamond Cable Left (Chart D); 10 sts of Rope Cable Left; p2; 8 (12, 16, 20, 24) sts in Bamboo st; 1 st in Gtr st (edge st). Work as for left front, rev all shaping by working armhole and shoulder shaping at beg of WS rows, and neck shaping at beg of RS rows.

SLEEVES

Using smaller needles, CO 38 (40, 42, 44, 46) sts. Work 18 rows in Welt patt, end RS row. Change to larger needles. Purl 1 row. *Est patt:* (RS) Work 1 st in Gtr st (edge st), 36 (38, 40, 42, 44) sts in Bamboo st, 1 st in Gtr st (edge st). Work 1 row even as est. *Shape sleeve:* (RS) Inc 1 st each side every 4 rows 0 (0, 2, 8, 7) times, every 6 rows 16 (18, 16, 11, 11) times, then every 8 rows 2 (0, 0, 0, 0) times, working all inc sts in Bamboo st— 74 (76, 78, 82, 82) sts. Work even until piece meas 21½ (22, 21½, 21½, 20¼)". BO all sts loosely in patt.

MULTI-LENGTH MOHAIR CARDIGAN

SIZES

Extra Small (Small, Medium, Large)

FINISHED MEASUREMENTS

• Chest: 32 (36, 40, 44)", buttoned

• Length: 22 (22½, 23, 23½)" {24 (24½, 25, 25½)" }

Note: Changes for longer cardigan are shown in braces { }; if only one set of numbers is given, it applies to both lengths.

MATERIALS

Classic Elite Yarns

La Gran (76½% mohair, 17½% wool, 6% nylon; 42-g ball = approx 90 yd/82 m)

• 9 (9, 10, 10) {9 (10, 11, 11)} balls 6513 Black

Equivalent yarn

Worsted weight #4, 810 (810, 900, 900) {810 (900, 990, 990)} yd

Needles

• One pair *each* size U.S. 6 (4 mm) and 8 (5 mm) or size to obtain gauge

Nine (9, 10, 10) {12 (12, 13, 13)} ⅜" buttons

Two small stitch holders

Stitch markers

GAUGE

17 sts and 24 rows = 4" in Stockinette Stitch, using larger needles. Take time to save time, check your gauge.

SPECIAL TECHNIQUE

FULLY FASHIONED SHAPING

Inc: (RS) K2, m1, work across to last 2 sts, m1, k2.

Dec: (RS) K1, ssk, work across to last 3 sts, k2tog, k1.

Dec: (WS) P1, p2tog, work across to last 3 sts, ssp, p1.

PATTERN STITCHES

STOCKINETTE STITCH (ST ST)

Knit on RS, purl on WS.

1 × 1 RIB (MULTIPLE OF 2 STS)

Row 1: *K1, p1; rep from * across.

Row 2: Knit the knit sts and purl the purl sts as they face you.

Rep Row 2 for 1 x 1 Rib.

BACK

Using larger needles, CO 70 (78, 86, 96) sts. Beg 1 × 1 Rib; work even until piece meas 3" from beg, end WS row. Change to St st; {(RS) work even for 2", end WS row}. *Shape waist:* (RS) Beg this row, dec 1 st each side every 6 rows 3 (3, 1, 0) times, every 4 rows 2 (2, 5, 6) times, then EOR 0 (0, 0, 1) time—60 (68, 74, 82) sts rem. Work even until piece meas 9½ (9¾, 9¾, 9¾)" {11½ (11¾, 11¾, 11¾)"} from beg, end WS row. (RS) Inc 1 st each side EOR 0 (1, 3, 5) times, then every 4 rows 5 (4, 3, 2) times—70 (78, 86, 96) sts. Work even until piece meas 13" {15"} from beg, end WS row. *Shape armholes:* (RS) BO 2 (3, 4, 5) sts at beg of next 2 rows—66 (72, 78, 86) sts rem. (RS) Dec 1 st each side every row 0 (0, 2, 3) times, EOR 2 (5, 4, 7) times, then every 4 rows 3 (2, 3, 2) times—56 (58, 60, 62) sts rem. Work even until armhole meas 7½ (8, 8½, 9)" from beg of shaping, end WS row; pm each side of center 24 sts. *Shape neck:* (RS) Work across to marker; join second ball of yarn and BO 24 sts; work to end—16 (17, 18, 19) sts rem each side for shoulders. Working both sides at same time, at each neck edge, dec 1 st once—15 (16, 17, 18) sts rem each side. Work even until

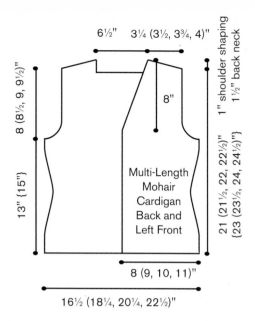

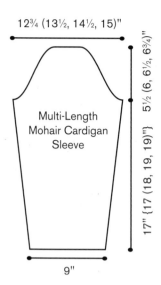

armhole meas 8 (8½, 9, 9½)" from beg of shaping, end WS row. **Shape shoulders:** (RS) BO 5 (5, 6, 6) sts at beg of next 4 rows, then 5 (6, 5, 6) sts at beg of next 2 rows.

LEFT FRONT

Using larger needles, CO 38 (42, 46, 52) sts. Beg 1 × 1 Rib; work even until piece meas 3" from beg, end RS row. **Front band:** (WS) Work across first 6 sts, place on holder for front band. Change to St st; m1, work to end—33 (37, 41, 47) sts rem. {Work even for 2", end WS row.} **Shape waist:** (RS) At armhole edge, dec 1 st every 6 rows 3 (3, 1, 0) times, every 4 rows 2 (2, 5, 6) times, then EOR 0 (0, 0, 1) time—28 (32, 35, 40) sts rem. Work even until piece meas 9½ (9¾, 9¾, 9¾)" {11½ (11¾, 11¾, 11¾)"} from beg, end WS row. (RS) At armhole edge, inc 1 st EOR 0 (1, 3, 5) times, then every 4 rows 5 (4, 3, 2) times—33 (37, 41, 47) sts. Work even until piece meas 13" {15"} from beg, end WS row. **Shape armhole:** (RS) BO 2 (3, 4, 5) sts, work to end—31 (34, 37, 42) sts rem. Work 1 row even. (RS) At armhole edge dec 1 st every row 0 (0, 2, 3) times, EOR 2 (5, 4, 7) times, then every 4 rows 3 (2, 3, 2) times, and **at the same time,** when armhole meas 1 (1½, 2, 2½)" from beg of shaping, end WS row. **Shape neck:** (RS) Dec 1 st at neck edge EOR 1 (1, 1, 2) times, then every 4 rows 10 times as foll: Work across to last 3 sts, k2tog, k1—15 (16, 17, 18) sts rem for shoulder. Work even until piece meas same as back to shoulder shaping, end WS row. **Shape shoulder:** (RS) At armhole edge, BO 5 (5, 6, 6) sts twice, then 5 (6, 5, 6) sts once.

RIGHT FRONT

Using larger needles, CO 38 (42, 46, 52) sts. Beg 1 × 1 Rib; work even until piece meas 1½" from beg, end WS row. **Buttonhole row:** (RS) K1, p1, [yo, p2tog] for buttonhole, work to end. On next row, work yo in patt. Work even as est until

piece meas 3" from beg, end WS row. **Front band:** (RS) Work first 6 sts and place on holder for front band; change to St st; m1, work to end—33 (37, 41, 47) sts rem. {Work even for 2", end WS row.} **Shape side, armhole neck, and shoulder:** As for left front, rev all shaping.

SLEEVES

Using smaller needles, CO 40 sts. Beg 1 × 1 Rib; work even until piece meas 3" from beg, end WS row. Change to larger needles and St st; (RS) inc 1 st each side every 6 rows 0 (0, 5, 9) times, every 8 rows 0 (6, 6, 3) times, every 10 rows 3 (3, 0, 0) times, then every 12 rows 4 (0, 0, 0) times—54 (58, 62, 64) sts. Work even until piece meas 17 (18, 19, 19)" from beg, end WS row. **Shape cap:** (RS) BO 2 (3, 4, 5) sts at beg of next 2 rows, then dec 1 st each side EOR 10 (12, 14, 17) times, every row 6 (5, 4, 1) times—18 sts rem. BO 2 sts at beg of next 4 rows—10 sts rem. BO rem sts.

FINISHING

Block pieces to measurements, if necessary. Sew shoulder seams. **Button band:** Place 6 sts from left front holder onto smaller needles, ready to work a RS row. K1-f/b of first st, work rem 5 sts as est—7 sts. Work even in 1 × 1 Rib until band, slightly stretched, will reach center of back neck. Place sts on holder. Pm for 9 (9, 10, 10) {12 (12, 13, 13)} buttons along band; first is already worked in lower band of right front, last 1¼" from neck shaping, rem buttons evenly spaced bet. **Buttonhole band:** Place 6 sts from right front holder onto smaller needles, ready to work a WS row. P1-f/b of first st, work to end as est. Cont as for button band, working buttonholes opposite markers as for first buttonhole on right front. Sew bands into place and graft tog at center back neck. Set in sleeves; sew side and sleeve seams. Sew buttons opposite buttonholes.

RIBBED SHELL

{ SKILL LEVEL: INTERMEDIATE }

SIZES
Small (Medium, Large, 1X Large)

FINISHED MEASUREMENTS
36 (38, 40, 44)"

MATERIALS
Classic Elite Yarns
Potpourri (100% nylon; 50-g ball = approx 86 yd/79 m)
• 7 (7, 8, 9) balls 7258 Sunset Red
Equivalent yarn
Worsted weight #4 ribbon yarn, 602 (602, 688, 774) yd
Needles
• One pair size U.S. 10 (6 mm) or size to obtain gauge
• One crochet hook size U.S. G/6 (4 mm)

GAUGE
20 sts and 24 rows = 4" in 2 × 2 Rib. Take time to save time, check your gauge.

PATTERN STITCHES

2 × 2 RIB (MULTIPLE OF 4 STS + 2)
Row 1: K2, *p2, k2; rep from * across.
Row 2: Knit the knit sts and purl the purl sts as they face you.
Rep Row 2 for 2 x 2 Rib.

GARTER RIDGE LACE STITCH (MULTIPLE OF 2 STS)
Rows 1–4: Knit.
Row 5: K1,*yo, k2tog; rep from * to last st, k1.
Row 6: Purl.
Rep Rows 1–6 for Garter Ridge Lace Stitch.

SINGLE CROCHET (SC)
Insert hook in indicated st, yo and pull up a loop; yo and draw through both loops on hook.

BACK AND FRONT (BOTH ALIKE)

Using larger needles, CO 90 (94, 102, 110) sts; work 2 × 2 Rib until piece meas 13½ (14, 14, 14)" from beg, end WS row. **Shape armholes:** (RS) BO 6 (6, 7, 7) sts at beg of next 2 rows, then dec 1 st each side EOR 6 (6, 7, 10) times—66 (70, 72, 76) sts rem; and, **at the same time,** when armhole meas 1" from beg of shaping, change to Garter Ridge Lace Stitch. Work even until armhole meas approx 5½" from beg of shaping, end on Row 4 of Garter Ridge Lace Stitch. **Shape neck:** (RS) Work 15 (15, 16, 18) sts; join second ball of yarn and BO center 36 (40, 40, 40) sts, work to end. Working both sides at same time, at each neck edge dec 1 st EOR 3 (3, 4, 6) times—12 sts rem each shoulder. Work even until armhole meas 6½ (7, 7½, 8)" from beg of shaping, end WS row. BO rem sts.

FINISHING

Block pieces to measurements. Sew shoulder and side seams. **Armhole finishing:** Attach yarn at side seam, using crochet hook; work 1 sc in every other st on armhole BO and in EOR around armhole edge; join with a sl st in top of first sc and fasten off.

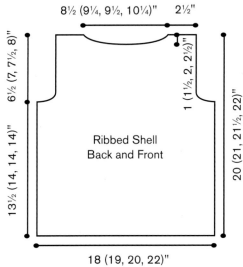

8½ (9¼, 9½, 10¼)" 2½"

6½ (7, 7½, 8)"

1 (1½, 2, 2½)"

13½ (14, 14, 14)"

Ribbed Shell
Back and Front

20 (21, 21½, 22)"

18 (19, 20, 22)"

SLIP-STITCH COLOR-BLOCK SWEATER

SIZES

Small (Medium, Large, 1X Large, 2X Large)

FINISHED MEASUREMENTS

37½ (42, 44½, 49, 53½)"

MATERIALS

Classic Elite Yarns

Duchess (40% merino wool, 28% viscose, 10% cashmere, 7% angora, 15% nylon; 50-g ball = approx 75 yd/69 m)

• 6 (6, 7, 8, 9) balls Main Color (MC)—1095 Privileged Plum

Princess (40% merino wool, 28% viscose, 10% cashmere, 7% angora, 15% nylon; 50-g ball = approx 150 yd/137 m)

• 2 (2, 3, 4, 5) balls Contrast Color A (CCA)—3495 Privileged Plum

• 1 ball all sizes Contrast Color B (CCB)—3432 Majesty's Magenta

• 1 ball all sizes Contrast Color C (CCC)—3458 Royal Red

• 1 ball all sizes Contrast Color D (CCD)—3485 Milord's Madder

• 1 ball all sizes Contrast Color E (CCE)—3468 Orange Attitude

Equivalent yarn

Bulky weight #5, MC: 450 (450, 525, 600, 675) yd

Worsted weight #4, CCA: 300 (300, 450, 600, 750) yd; CCB, CCC, CCD, and CCE: 150 yd all sizes

Needles

• One pair *each* sizes U.S. 7 (4.5 mm) and 8 (5 mm) or size to obtain gauge

GAUGE

14 sts and 28 rows = 4" in Slip Stitch Pattern, using larger needles. Take time to save time; check your gauge.

NOTE

At color changes, carry color to where it is next needed, rather than cutting.

PATTERN STITCHES

REVERSE STOCKINETTE STITCH (REV ST ST)

Purl on RS, knit on WS.

SLIP STITCH PATTERN (SL ST PATT) (MULTIPLE OF 2 STS)

Row 1: (RS) Using MC, k1 st (edge st), *k1, yf, sl 1p, yb; rep from * across to last st, k1 (edge st).

Row 2: Using MC, purl.

Row 3: Using CCs as established by color chart, k1, *yf, sl 1p, yb, k1; rep from * to last st, k1 (edge st).

Row 4: Using CCs as established by color chart, purl.

COLOR WORK

See chart.

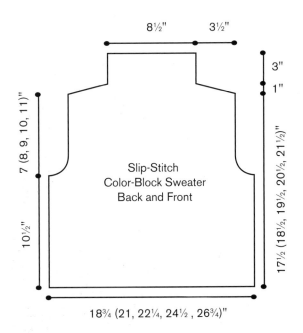

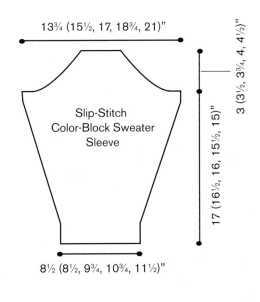

BACK AND FRONT (BOTH ALIKE)

Using smaller needles and CCA, CO 66 (74, 78, 86, 94) sts; work 4 rows in Rev St st, end WS row. Change to larger needles, MC, and Sl st patt; work 2 rows, end WS row. Cont with Sl st patt, beg with Row 3, and est color patt from Color Chart, beg and end where indicated for your size. Work even as est until piece meas 10½" from beg, end with Row 2 of Sl st patt. *Shape armholes:* (RS) BO 3 (4, 6, 8, 10) sts at beg of next 2 rows, then dec 1 st each side EOR 3 (6, 6, 8, 10) times—54 sts rem. Work even until armhole meas 7 (8, 9, 10, 11)" from beg of shaping, end WS row. *Shape shoulders:* BO 3 sts at beg of next 8 rows—30 sts rem. *Funnel neck:* Work even until neck meas 3" from shoulder shaping. Change to Rev St st; work 4 rows. BO rem sts.

SLEEVES

Note: For sleeves, work Sl st patt in MC only; do *not* use Color Work Chart.

Using smaller needles and CCA, CO 30 (30, 34, 38, 40) sts; work 4 rows in Rev St st, end WS row. Change to larger needles, MC, and Sl st patt; work 4 rows. *Shape sleeve:* (RS) Inc 1 st each side this row, then every 8 (8, 8, 6, 6) rows 8 (11, 12, 13, 16) times—48 (54, 60, 66, 74) sts. Work even until piece meas 17 (16½, 16, 15½, 15)" from beg, end WS row. *Shape cap:* BO 3 (4, 6, 8, 10) sts at beg of next 2 rows, then dec 1 st each side EOR 10 (11, 12, 13, 15) times—22 (24, 24, 24, 24) sts rem. BO 2 (3, 3, 3, 3) sts beg next 2 rows—18 sts rem. BO rem sts.

FINISHING

Block pieces to measurements. Sew neck and shoulder seams. Set in sleeves; sew side and sleeve seams.

■ CCA–3495 Privileged Plum.
⊞ CCB–3432 Majesty's Magenta.
✖ CCC–3458 Royal Red.
◉ CCD–3485 Milord's Madder.
☐ CCE–3468 Orange Attitude.

(work in SI st patt)

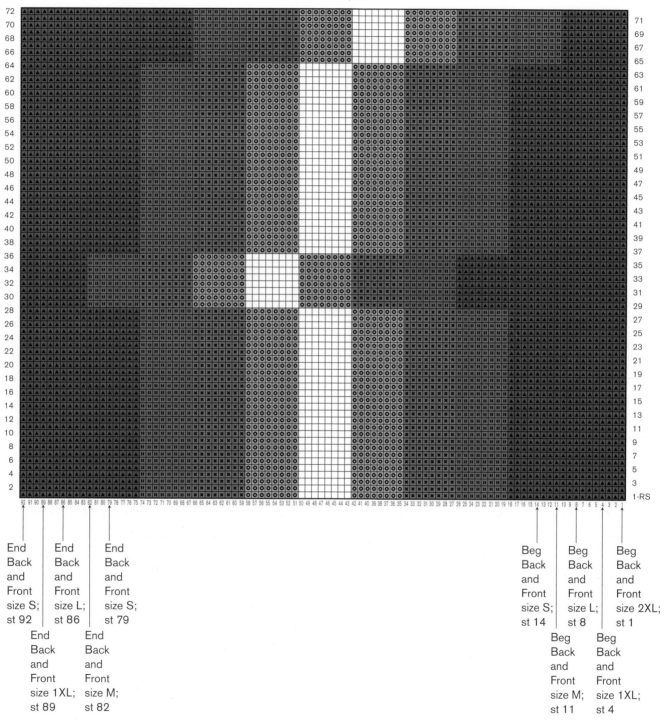

End
Back
and
Front
size S;
st 92

End
Back
and
Front
size 1XL;
st 89

End
Back
and
Front
size L;
st 86

End
Back
and
Front
size M;
st 82

End
Back
and
Front
size S;
st 79

Beg
Back
and
Front
size S;
st 14

Beg
Back
and
Front
size M;
st 11

Beg
Back
and
Front
size L;
st 8

Beg
Back
and
Front
size 1XL;
st 4

Beg
Back
and
Front
size 2XL;
st 1

CONSIDERABLE CABLE COAT

SIZES
Small (Medium, Large, 1X Large)

FINISHED MEASUREMENTS
42 (44, 46, 48)"

MATERIALS
Classic Elite Yarns
MarL La (100% wool; 100-g hank = approx 57 yd/52 m)
• 10 (11, 12, 13) hanks 8558 Seeing Reds
Equivalent yarn
Super bulky weight #6, 570 (627, 684, 741) yd
Needles
• One 29" circular size U.S. 17 (12.75 mm) or size to obtain gauge
• Two cable needles (cn)
Two stitch holders
Stitch markers
One 1¾" x 1½" rectangular button

GAUGE
8 sts and 10 rows = 4" in Reverse Stockinette Stitch.
Take time to save time, check your gauge.

PATTERN STITCHES

REVERSE STOCKINETTE STITCH (REV ST ST)
Purl on RS, knit on WS.

FRONT PANEL (MULTIPLE OF 12 STS; 16-ROW REP)
See Chart A.

SLEEVE CABLE (MULTIPLE OF 4 STS; 8-ROW REP)
See Chart B.

BACK

CO 40 (42, 44, 46) sts. Beg Rev St st; work even until piece meas 15 (15, 16, 16)" from beg, end WS row. **Shape armholes:** (RS) BO 2 sts at beg of next 2 rows—36 (38, 40, 42) sts rem. (RS) Dec 1 st each side EOR 3 times—30 (32, 34, 36) sts rem. Work even until armhole meas 9 (9½, 10, 10½)" from beg of shaping, end WS row; pm each side of center 10 sts. **Shape**

neck: Work across to marker; join second ball of yarn and BO center sts; work to end—10 (11, 12, 13) sts each shoulder. Working both sides at same time, at each neck edge dec 1 st once—9 (10, 11, 12) sts rem each shoulder. BO rem sts.

LEFT FRONT

CO 22 (23, 24, 25) sts. *Setup row:* (RS) P6 (7, 8, 9), k2, p2,

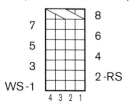

Multiple of 4 sts; 8-row rep

Multiple of 12 sts; 16-row rep

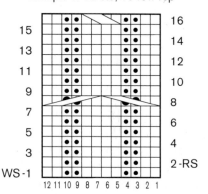

Schematic measurements for Back and Left Front:

5"   4½ (5, 5½, 6)"

9 (9½, 10, 10½)"

15 (15, 16, 16)"

Considerable Cable Coat Back and Left Front

24 (24½, 26, 26½)"

11 (11½, 12, 12½)"

20 (21, 22, 23)"

Sleeve measurements:

16 (17, 18, 19)"

5½ (6½, 7, 8)"

Considerable Cable Coat Sleeve

19"

10"

☐ Knit on RS, purl on WS.

⊡ Purl on RS, knit on WS.

Sl 2 sts to cn, hold in front, k2; k2 from cn.

Sl 2 k sts to first cn, hold in front; sl 2 p sts to second cn, hold in front; k2 sts from LH needle; p2 from second cn; k2 from first cn.

Sl 2 k sts to first cn, hold in back; sl 2 p sts to second cn, hold in back; k2 sts from LH needle; p2 from second cn; k2 from first cn.

k4, p2, k2; pm for front band, p1, k3. *Est patt:* (WS) K2, p1, k1 (front band), work 12 sts of Front Panel (Chart A: Front Panel), knit to end. (RS) P6 (7, 8, 9), work 12 sts of Front Panel, p1, k3. Work even as est until piece meas 15 (15, 16, 16)" from beg, end WS row. **Shape armhole:** (RS) BO 2 sts, work to end—20 (21, 22, 23) sts rem. At armhole edge, dec 1 st EOR 3 times—17 (18, 19, 20) sts rem. Work even as est until armhole meas 6½ (7, 7½, 8)" from beg of shaping; cont as est, but discontinue turning cables. Work even until armhole meas 9 (9 ½, 10, 10½)" from beg of shaping, end WS row. *Note:* Front neck shaping shown in schematic will be achieved only by binding off as instructed. **Shape shoulder and neck:** (RS) BO across to last 3 sts, and **at the same time,** k2tog or p2tog in patt across 12 sts of Front Panel as foll: (RS) P1 ([p1, BO] across to Front Panel for Medium, Large, and 1X Large), k2tog, BO, p2tog, BO, k2tog, BO, k2tog, BO, p2tog, BO, k2tog, BO; p1, BO, k1, BO, k2; place rem 3 sts on holder for neckband.

RIGHT FRONT

CO 22 (23, 24, 25) sts. *Setup row:* (RS) K3, p1, pm for front band; k2, p2, k4, p2, k2, p6 (7, 8, 9). Work as for left front, rev all shaping by working armhole, shoulder, and neck shaping at beg of WS rows. Replace k2tog with p2tog, and p2tog with k2tog.

SLEEVES

CO 20 sts. *Est patt:* (WS) Work in Rev St st across to center 4 sts, work 4 sts of Sleeve Cable (Chart B: Sleeve Cable), work

in Rev St st to end.
Shape sleeve: (RS) Inc 1 st each side this row, then every 8 (7, 6, 5) rows 5 (6, 7, 8) times—32 (34, 36, 38) sts. Work even until piece meas 19" from beg, end WS row.
Shape cap: (RS) BO 2 sts at the beg of next 2 rows, then dec 1 st each side EOR 3 (4, 5, 6) times—22 sts rem. BO 2 sts at the beg of next 8 rows— 6 sts rem. BO rem sts.

FINISHING

Block pieces to measurements. Sew shoulder seams. Set in sleeves; sew sleeve and side seams. **Neckband:** Place sts from left front holder on needle; cont in est patt until piece meas length to center back neck. BO all sts. Work sts from right front holder as for left front. Join center back seam. *Note:* Sts may be left live and joined with Three-Needle Bind-Off Method (see p. 24), if desired. Sew band to back neck. Sew on button (see photo) and sl bet sts on opposite side.

LACE CABLE PULLOVER

SIZES
Extra Small (Small, Medium, Large, 1X Large)

FINISHED MEASUREMENTS
32 (36½, 41, 45½, 50)"

MATERIALS
Classic Elite Yarns

Premiere (50% pima cotton, 50% tencel; 50-g hank = approx 108 yd/99 m)

• 9 (10, 11, 12, 14) hanks 5220 Icy Blue

Equivalent yarn

Light worsted weight #3, 972 (1080, 1188, 1296, 1512) yd

Needles

• One pair *each* size U.S. 5 (3.75 mm) and 6 (4 mm) or size to obtain gauge

• One 16" circular size U.S. 5 (3.75 mm) for neck finishing

• One cable needle (cn)

Stitch markers

GAUGE
21 sts and 28 rows = 4" in Flat Rib, using larger needles; 47 sts = 7¼" in Lace Cable, using larger needles. Take time to save time, check your gauge.

PATTERN STITCHES

STOCKINETTE STITCH (ST ST)
Knit on RS, purl on WS.

CIRCULAR STOCKINETTE STITCH
Knit every rnd.

1 x 1 RIB (OVER AN ODD NUMBER OF STS)
Row 1: (RS) K1, *p1, k1; rep from * across.

Row 2: Knit the knit sts and purl the purl sts as they face you.

Rep Row 2 for 1 x 1 Rib.

FLAT RIB (MULTIPLE OF 6 STS + 5)
Row 1: (RS) Knit.

Row 2: P5, *k1, p5; rep from * across.

Rep Rows 1–2 for Flat Rib.

LACE CABLE (PANEL OF 47 STS; 40-ROW REP)
See chart.

Multiple of 47 sts; 40-row rep

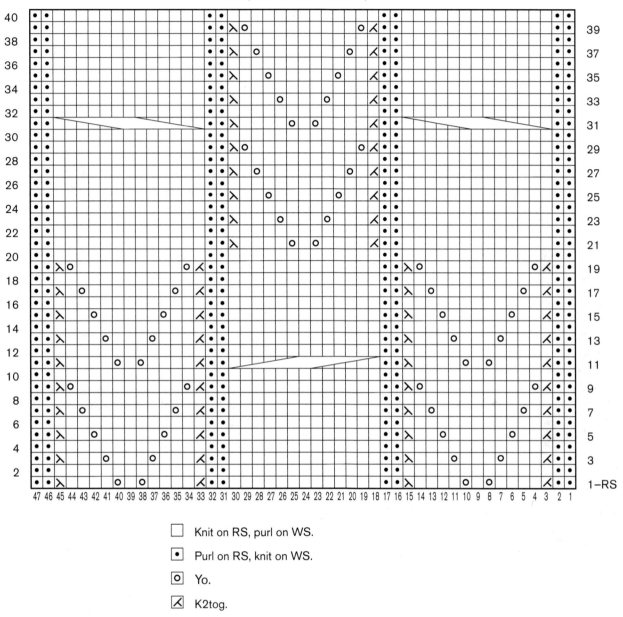

☐ Knit on RS, purl on WS.

▪ Purl on RS, knit on WS.

◎ Yo.

╱ K2tog.

╲ Ssk.

⟋ Sl 6 sts to cn, hold in back, k7, k6 from cn.

⟍ Sl 7 sts to cn, hold in front, k6, k7 from cn.

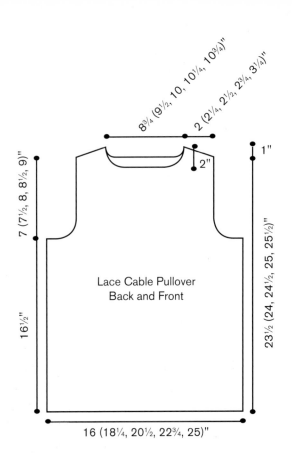

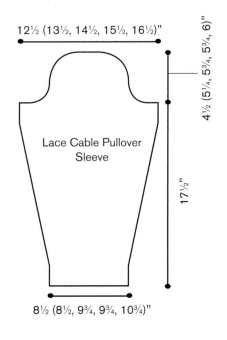

Lace Cable Pullover
Back and Front

Lace Cable Pullover
Sleeve

BACK

Using smaller needles, CO 97 (109, 121, 133, 145) sts. Work
1 × 1 Rib until piece meas ½" from beg, end RS row. Purl next
row, dec 4 sts evenly spaced across row—93 (105, 117, 129,
141) sts rem. Change to larger needles and *est patt:* (RS) Work
23 (29, 35, 41, 47) sts in Flat Rib patt, 47 sts in Lace Cable
(from chart), 23 (29, 35, 41, 47) sts in Flat Rib patt. Work as est
until piece meas 16½" from beg, end WS row. *Shape armholes:*
(RS) BO 4 (5, 6, 8, 10) sts at the beg of next 2 rows, then dec
1 st each side EOR 4 (6, 8, 10, 11) times—77 (83, 89, 93, 99) sts
rem. Work even until armhole meas 7 (7½, 8, 8½, 9)" from beg
of shaping, end WS row. *Shape shoulders and neck:* (RS) BO
4 (4, 5, 5, 6) sts at beg of next 4 rows, 3 (4, 4, 5, 5) sts at beg of
next 2 rows; and, **at the same time,** on the first row of shoulder
shaping, work to center 31 (35, 37, 39, 41) sts, join second ball
of yarn, BO center sts, work to end. Working both sides at same
time, at each neck edge, BO 6 sts twice.

FRONT

Work as for back until armhole meas 6 (6½, 7, 7½, 8)" from
beg of shaping, end WS row—77 (83, 89, 93, 99) sts rem.
Shape neck: (RS) Work 23 (24, 25, 28, 29) sts, join second
ball of yarn, BO center 31 (35, 37, 39, 41) sts, work to end.
Working both sides at same time, at each neck edge BO 3 sts
4 times—11 (12, 14, 15, 17) sts rem each shoulder. Work even

until armhole meas same as back to shoulder shaping, end WS
row. *Shape shoulders* as for back.

SLEEVES

Using smaller needles, CO 49 (49, 55, 55, 61) sts. Work in 1 × 1
Rib until piece meas ½" from beg, end RS row. Purl next row,
dec 4 sts evenly across—45 (45, 51, 51, 57) sts rem. Change to
larger needles and *est patt:* (RS) Work 2 sts in St st (edge sts),
41 (41, 47, 47, 53) sts in Flat Rib patt, 2 sts in St st (edge sts).
Work 9 (5, 5, 3, 3) rows even. *Shape sleeve:* (RS) Maintaining
edge sts, inc 1 st each side this row, then every 10 (8, 8, 8, 8)
rows 9 (12, 12, 14, 14) times—65 (71, 77, 81, 87) sts. Work
even until piece meas 17½" from beg, end WS row. *Shape cap:*
(RS) BO 4 (5, 6, 8, 10) sts at the beg of next 2 rows, then dec
1 st each side EOR 13 (15, 17, 17, 18) times—31 sts rem. BO
2 sts at beg of next 2 rows, 3 sts at beg of next 2 rows—21 sts
rem. BO rem sts.

FINISHING

Block pieces to measurements. Sew shoulder seams. Set in
sleeves; sew sleeve and side seams. *Neckband:* With RS facing,
using circular needle, pick up and knit 63 (65, 67, 69, 71)
sts evenly along back neck edge, 69 (73, 75, 79, 81) sts evenly
along front neck edge; pm for beg of rnd—132 (138, 142,
148, 152) sts. Purl 1 rnd. Work 3 rnds in St st. BO all sts.

LARGE FLOWER PATTERN CARDIGAN

Note: See p. 170 for matching Children's sweater.

SIZES

Small (Medium, Large, 1X Large)

FINISHED MEASUREMENTS

36 (40, 44, 48)"

MATERIALS

Classic Elite Yarns

Provence (100% mercerized Egyptian cotton; 100-g hank = approx 205 yd/187 m)

- 3 (3, 4, 4) hanks Main Color (MC)—2627 French Red
- 2 hanks all sizes Color A—2619 Zinnia Flower
- 2 hanks all sizes Color B—2630 Peony Pink
- 1 hanks all sizes Color C—2625 Rosa Rugosa

Equivalent yarn

Light worsted weight #3 or worsted weight #4, MC: 615 (615, 820, 820) yd; Colors A and B: 410 yd all sizes; Color C: 205 yd all sizes

Needles

- One pair *each* size U.S. 4 (3.5 mm) and 6 (4 mm) or size to obtain gauge

Six 1" buttons (three orange, three hot pink)

GAUGE

20 sts and 28 rows = 4" in Stockinette Stitch, using larger needles. Take time to save time, check your gauge.

PATTERN STITCHES

GARTER STITCH (GTR ST)

Knit every row.

FLOWER PATTERN

See chart.

BACK

Using smaller needles and MC, CO 90 (100, 110, 120) sts; beg Gtr st. Work 1 row. Change to Color A; work 2 rows. Change to Color C; work 2 rows. Change to Color B; work 2 rows, end WS row. Change to larger needles and beg working Flower Pattern (see chart), beg and end where indicated for your size. Work as est until piece meas 12½ (13½, 14, 14½)" from beg, end WS row. *Shape armholes:* (RS) BO 5 sts at beg of next 2 rows, then dec 1 st each side EOR 5 times—70 (80, 90, 100) sts rem. Work as est until armhole meas 7½ (7½, 8, 8½)" from beg of shaping, end WS row. *Shape neck:* (RS) Work 17 (21, 25, 29) sts, join second ball of yarn, BO center 36 (38, 40, 42) sts, work

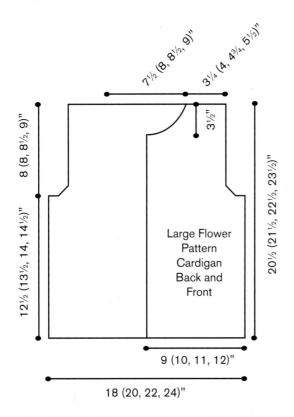

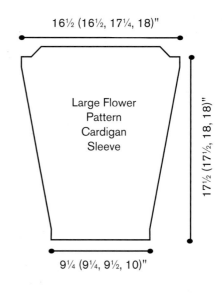

to end. Working both sides at same time, at each neck edge, dec 1 st once—16 (20, 24, 28) sts rem each shoulder. Work even until armhole meas 8 (8, 8½, 9)" from beg. BO rem sts.

LEFT FRONT

Using smaller needles and MC, CO 45 (50, 55, 60) sts; beg Gtr st. Work 1 row. Change to Color A; work 2 rows. Change to Color C; work 2 rows. Change to Color B; work 2 rows, end WS row. Change to larger needles and beg working Flower Pattern (see chart), beg and end where indicated for your size. Work as est until piece meas 12½ (13½, 14, 14½)" from beg, end WS row. *Shape armhole:* (RS) BO 5 sts at beg of this row, work to end. Dec 1 st at armhole edge EOR 5 times—35 (40, 45, 50) sts rem. Work as est until armhole meas 4½ (4½, 5, 5½)" from beg of shaping, end RS row. *Shape neck:* (WS) At neck edge, BO 6 (7, 7, 8) sts once, 4 sts once, 3 sts 1 (1, 2, 2) times, 2 sts 2 (2, 1, 1) time, 1 st twice—16 (20, 24, 28) sts rem. Work even until piece meas same as back to shoulders, end WS row. BO all sts.

RIGHT FRONT

Work as for left front, rev all shaping and placing Flower Pattern as indicated on chart.

SLEEVES

Using smaller needles and MC, CO 46 (46, 48, 50) sts; beg Gtr st. Work 1 row. Change to Color A; work 2 rows. Change to Color C; work 2 rows. Change to Color B; work 2 rows, end

WS row. Change to larger needles and beg working Flower Pattern (see chart), beg and end where indicated for your size; and, **at the same time,** inc 1 st each side every 6 rows 18 times, then every 4 rows 0 (0, 1, 2) times—82 (82, 86, 90) sts. Work even until piece meas 17½ (17½, 18, 18)" from beg, end WS row. *Shape cap:* (RS) BO 5 sts at beg of next 2 rows, then dec 1 st each size EOR 5 times—62 (62, 66, 70) sts rem. BO rem sts.

FINISHING

Block pieces to measurements. Sew shoulder seams. Set in sleeves; sew side and sleeve seams. *Neckband:* With RS facing, using smaller needles and Color B, pick up and knit 86 (90, 94, 98) sts evenly around neck edge. Work in Gtr st. Using Color B, work 1 row. Change to Color C; work 2 rows. Change to Color A; work 2 rows. Change to MC; work 1 row. BO all sts. *Button band:* With RS facing, using smaller needles and Color B, pick up and knit 100 (104, 109, 114) sts evenly along left front center edge. Work in Gtr st; using Color B, work 1 row. Change to Color C; work 2 rows. Change to Color A; work 2 rows. Change to MC; work 1 row. BO all sts. *Buttonhole band:* With RS facing, using smaller needle and Color B, pick up and knit 100 (104, 109, 114) sts evenly across right front center edge. Work in Gtr st; work 1 row. Change to Color C; work 2 rows, end WS row. Change to Color A and work button-hole row as foll: K7 (6, 6, 6), *BO 4 sts, k13 (14, 15, 16); rep from * 4 times, BO 4 sts, work to end. *Next row:* Work in Gtr st and CO 4 sts over BO sts of previous row. Change to MC; work 1 row. BO all sts. Sew buttons opposite buttonholes.

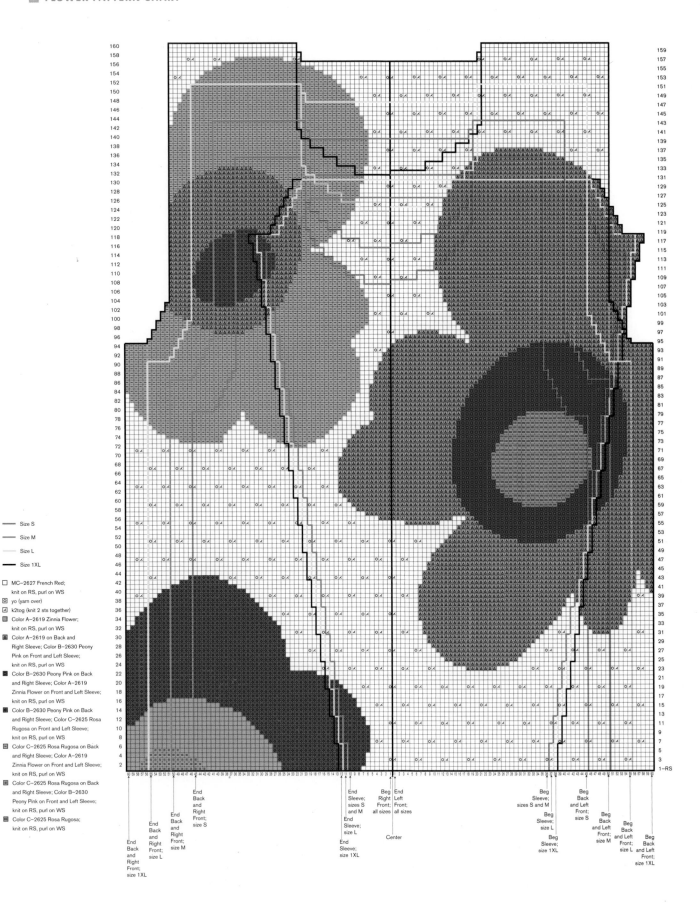

□ MC–2627 French Red;
knit on RS, purl on WS

◎ yo (yarn over)

◢ k2tog (knit 2 sts together)

▨ Color A–2619 Zinnia Flower;
knit on RS, purl on WS

▲ Color A–2619 on Back and
Right Sleeve; Color B–2630 Peony
Pink on Front and Left Sleeve;
knit on RS, purl on WS

■ Color B–2630 Peony Pink on Back
and Right Sleeve; Color A–2619
Zinnia Flower on Front and Left Sleeve;
knit on RS, purl on WS

■ Color B–2630 Peony Pink on Back
and Right Sleeve; Color C–2625 Rosa
Rugosa on Front and Left Sleeve;
knit on RS, purl on WS

▣ Color C–2625 Rosa Rugosa on Back
and Right Sleeve; Color A–2619
Zinnia Flower on Front and Left Sleeve;
knit on RS, purl on WS

▨ Color C–2625 Rosa Rugosa on Back
and Right Sleeve; Color B–2630
Peony Pink on Front and Left Sleeve;
knit on RS, purl on WS

▩ Color C–2625 Rosa Rugosa;
knit on RS, purl on WS

— Size S
— Size M
— Size L
— Size 1XL

SEED STITCH BLAZER

SIZES
Small (Medium, Large, 1X Large)

FINISHED MEASUREMENTS
36 (40½, 45½, 50½)"

MATERIALS
Classic Elite Yarns
Skye Tweed (100% wool; 50-g hank = approx 110 yd)
• 14 (15, 17, 18) hanks 1235 Spring Green
Equivalent yarn
Worsted weight #4, 1540 (1650, 1870, 1980) yd
Needles
• One pair size U.S. 6 (4 mm)
• One 29" circular size U.S .6 (4 mm) or size to obtain gauge
• One cable needle (cn)
Stitch markers
Stitch holders
Three ¾" buttons

GAUGE
19½ sts and 35 rows = 4" in Seed Stitch. Take time to save time, check your gauge.

NOTES
Jacket is worked in one piece to underarms, then fronts and back are worked sep to shoulders.

Garment is worked back and forth on a circular needle to accommodate large number of sts.

Buttonholes are worked at same time as garment. Work buttonholes on RS rows as foll: Work 3 sts, BO 2 sts, work to end. (WS) CO 2 sts over BO sts to complete buttonhole.

Sl markers on every row.

PATTERN STITCHES

SEED STITCH (SEED ST) (MULTIPLE OF 2 STS)
Row 1: (RS) *K1, p1; rep from * across.
Row 2: Purl the knit sts and knit the purl sts as they face you.
Rep Row 2 for Seed Stitch

ARAN MOTIF (PANEL OF 14 STS; 22-ROW REP)
See chart.

BODY

Small flap: (make 4) CO 24 (24, 28, 28) sts. Beg Seed st; work even until piece meas 3½" from beg, end RS row. *Medium flap:* (make 2) CO 28 (34, 36, 42) sts; work as for small flap. *Large flap:* (make 1) CO 48 (58, 62, 74) sts; work as for small flap. *Join flaps:* With WS facing, using circular needle; work as est across 28 (34, 36, 42) sts of medium flap, pm, [24 (24, 28, 28) sts of small flap, pm] twice, 48 (58, 62, 74) sts of large flap, pm, [24 (24, 28, 28) sts of small flap, pm] twice, 28 (34, 36, 42) sts of medium flap—200 (222, 246, 270) sts. Work 2 rows even, end WS row. *Est Aran Motif:* (RS) *Work to 7 sts before marker, work 14 sts of Aran Motif (see chart) across next 7 sts and across 7 sts after marker; rep from * 5 times, work to end. Work 1 row as est—206 (228, 252, 276) sts. Work as est until Row 22 of Aran Motif is complete; and, **at the same time,** work first button-hole in right front on Row 9 (9, 13, 13) of chart, end WS row—182 (204, 228, 252) sts. (RS) Dec 1 st in each Aran Motif to maintain Seed st as originally est—176 (198, 222, 246) sts rem. Remove markers. Cont in Seed st; and, **at the same time,** work 2 rem buttonholes spaced 16 (16, 18, 18) rows apart. Work even until piece meas 14½ (14, 14½, 14)" from beg, end WS row. Divide for armholes and *shape lapels:* (RS) K1-f/b, work 40 (47, 53, 58) sts and place on holder [right front], BO next 8 (10, 12, 16) sts, work 78 (82, 90, 96) sts and place on holder [back], BO next 8 (10, 12, 16) sts, work 40 (47, 53, 58) sts, k1-f/b [left front]—42 (49, 55, 60) sts for left front.

LEFT FRONT

(WS) Cont on left front sts only; work 1 row even. *Shape armholes:* (RS) At armhole edge, BO 2 sts 1 (1, 2, 3) times, then dec 1 st every 4 rows once; and, **at the same time,** cont to *shape lapel* at end of RS row, every 10 rows 4 times—43 (50, 54, 57) sts. Work even until armhole meas 5½ (6, 6½, 7)" from beg of shaping, end RS row. *Shape neck:* (WS) At neck edge, BO 19 (19, 25, 25) sts once, 2 sts 1 (4, 3, 4) times, 1 st 1 (0, 0, 0) time—21 (23, 23, 24) sts rem for shoulder. Work even until armhole meas 8 (8½, 9, 9½)" from beg of shaping, end WS row. *Shape shoulder:* At beg of RS rows only, BO 4 (5, 5, 5) sts 4 (3, 3, 4) times, 5 (4, 4, 4) sts 1 (2, 2, 1) times.

BACK

With WS facing, return 78 (82, 90, 96) sts for back to needle; rejoin yarn. Work 1 row even. *Shape armholes:* (RS) BO 2 sts at beg of next 2 (2, 4, 6) rows, then dec 1 st each side every 4 rows once—72 (76, 80, 82) sts rem. Work even until arm-hole meas 8 (8½, 9, 9½)" from beg of shaping, end WS row. *Shape shoulders:* (RS) BO 4 (5, 5, 5) sts at beg of next 8 (6, 6, 8) rows, then 5 (4, 4, 4) sts at beg of next 2 (4, 4, 2) rows—30 (30, 34, 34) sts rem for neck. Place rem sts on holder.

RIGHT FRONT

With WS facing, return 42 (49, 55, 60) sts for right front to needle; rejoin yarn. Work as for left front, rev all shaping by working armhole and shoulder shaping at beg of WS rows, and neck and lapel shaping at beg of RS rows.

SLEEVES

Right flap: CO 24 sts. Beg Seed st; work even until piece meas 3½" from beg, end RS row. Break yarn and leave sts on holder. *Left flap:* CO 24 sts; work as for right flap, end RS row. Do not break yarn. *Join flaps:* With WS facing work 24 sts of left flap, then 24 sts of right flap—48 sts. Work 2 rows even, end WS row. *Est Aran Motif:* (RS) Work 17 sts in patt, pm, work 14 sts of Aran Motif (see chart), pm, 17 sts in patt. *Shape sleeve:* Inc 1 st each side every 4 rows 0 (0, 0, 7) times, every 6 rows 5 (10, 19, 14) times, then every 8 rows 10 (7, 0, 0) times—78 (82, 86, 90) sts; and, **at the same time,** when Row 22 of Aran Motif is complete, end WS row. (RS) Work to 1 st before second marker, work 2 sts tog to maintain Seed st as originally est. Remove markers. Work even until piece meas 17 (17½, 17½, 17½)" from beg, end WS row. *Shape cap:* (RS) BO 4 (5, 6, 8) sts at beg of next 2 rows, 2 sts at beg of next 2 (4, 4, 4) rows, then dec 1 st each side EOR 2 (2, 2, 0) times, every 4 rows 8 (7, 8, 10) times—46 sts rem. Work even until cap meas 4¾ (4¾, 5¼, 5¾)" from beg of shaping, end WS row. (RS) BO 2 sts at beg of next 2 rows, 3 sts at beg of next 2 rows, 4 sts at beg of next 4 rows, then 5 sts at beg of next 2 rows—10 sts rem. BO rem sts.

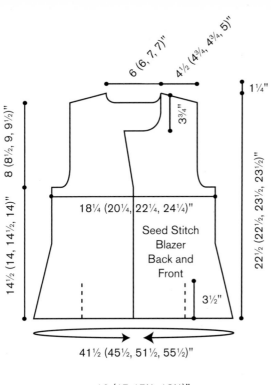

6 (6, 7, 7)"

4½ (4¾, 4¾, 5)"

1¼"

3¾"

8 (8½, 9, 9½)"

14½ (14, 14½, 14)"

18¼ (20¼, 22¼, 24¼)"

Seed Stitch Blazer Back and Front

22½ (22½, 23½, 23½)"

3½"

41½ (45½, 51½, 55½)"

16 (17, 17½, 18½)"

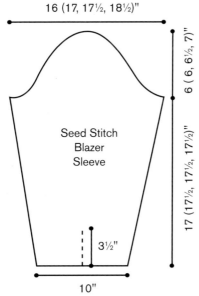

6 (6, 6½, 7)"

17 (17½, 17½, 17½)"

Seed Stitch Blazer Sleeve

3½"

10"

■ **ARAN MOTIF CHART**

(14 st panel; 22 rows)

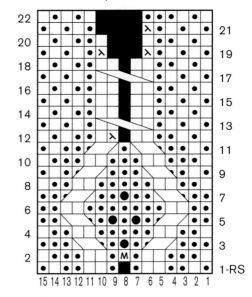

☐ Knit on RS, purl on WS

• Purl on RS, knit on WS

■ No st

Ⓜ Make 1 – Increase 1 st

● Bobble: K into front, back and front of st, turn, p3, turn, k3, turn, p3, turn, double dec

λ K2tog on RS, p2tog on WS

 Sl 1 st to cn, hold in back; k2; p1 from cn

Sl 2 st to cn, hold in front; p1; k2 from cn

Sl 2 sts to cn, hold in front; k2; k2 from cn

FINISHING

Block pieces to measurements. Sew shoulder seams. Set in sleeves; sew sleeve seams. *Collar:* With RS facing, using circular needle, beg at right front neck edge, pick up and knit 24 (24, 28, 28) sts along neck edge, work 30 (30, 34, 34) sts for back neck as est from holder, pick up and knit 24 (24, 28, 28) sts along left front neck edge—78 (78, 90, 90) sts. Beg Seed st and *shape collar:* (RS) Inc 1 st each side every 4 rows 2 (2, 3, 3) times—82 (82, 96, 96) sts. Work even until collar meas 1 (1, 1½, 1½)" from pickup row, end WS row. (RS) Inc 6 (6, 8, 8) sts evenly across next 2 rows—94 (94, 112, 112) sts. Cont as est, inc 1 st each side every 4 rows 3 (3, 4, 4) times—100 (100, 120, 120) sts. Work even until collar meas 2½ (2½, 3, 3)" from pickup row. BO all sts in patt. Sew edge of collar neatly to BO edge of lapel.

EVERYDAY PULLOVER

Note: See p. 197 for matching shawl.

{ SKILL LEVEL: INTERMEDIATE }

SIZES

Extra Small (Small, Medium, Large)

FINISHED MEASUREMENTS

33 (35, 37, 39)"

MATERIALS

Classic Elite Yarns

Princess (40% merino wool, 28% viscose, 10% cashmere, 7% angora, 15% nylon; 50-g ball = approx 150 yd/137 m)

• 6 (6, 7, 7) balls 3468 Orange Attitude

Equivalent yarn

Worsted weight #4, 900 (900, 1050, 1050) yd

Needles

• One pair *each* size U.S. 5 (3.75 mm) and 7 (4.5 mm) or size to obtain gauge

• One 16" circular size U.S. 4 (3.5 mm) for neck finishing

Stitch markers

GAUGE

20 sts and 29 rows = 4" in Stockinette Stitch, using larger needles. Take time to save time, check your gauge.

NOTE

Work all decs and incs for waist shaping and sleeves 3 sts in from each side.

PATTERN STITCHES

1 x 1 RIB (ODD NUMBER OF STS)

Row 1: (RS) P1, *k1, p1; rep from * across.

Row 2: Knit the knit sts and purl the purl sts as they face you.

Rep Row 2 for 1 x 1 Rib.

CIRCULAR 1 x 1 RIB (EVEN NUMBER OF STS)

All rnds: *P1, k1; rep from * around.

STOCKINETTE STITCH (ST ST)

Knit on RS, purl on WS.

BACK

Using smaller needles, CO 83 (87, 93, 97) sts; knit 1 WS row. Work 2 rows 1 × 1 Rib, end WS row. Change to larger needles and St st; work even until piece meas 1½ (2, 2½, 2½)" from beg, end WS row. ***Shape waist:*** (RS) Dec 1 st each side this row, then every 8 rows 4 times—63 (77, 83, 87) sts. Work even until piece meas 8 (8½, 9, 9½)" from beg, end WS row. ***Shape waist:*** (RS) Inc 1 st at each side this row, then every 6 rows 4 times—83 (87, 93, 97) sts. Work even until piece meas 12½ (13½, 14, 14½)" from beg, end WS row. ***Shape armholes:*** (RS) BO 4 (4, 5, 5) sts at beg of next 2 rows, then dec 1 st each side EOR 5 (6, 6, 7) times—65 (67, 71, 73) sts. Work even until armhole meas 6½ (7, 7, 7½)" from beg of shaping, end WS row. ***Shape neck:*** (RS) Work 22 (22, 23, 23) sts, join second ball of yarn, BO center 21 (23, 25, 27) sts, work to end. Working both sides at same time, at each neck edge, BO 4 sts twice—14 (14, 15, 15) sts rem each shoulder. Work even until armhole meas 7½ (8, 8, 8½)" from beg of shaping, end WS row. ***Shape shoulders:*** (RS) BO 5 sts at beg of next 4 (4, 6, 6) rows, 4 sts at beg of next 2 (2, 0, 0) rows.

FRONT

Work as for back until armhole meas 4 (4½, 4½, 5)" from beg of armhole shaping, end WS row—65 (67, 71, 73) sts. ***Shape neck:*** (RS) Work 21 (21, 22, 22) sts, join second ball of yarn, BO center 23 (25, 27, 29) sts, work to end. Working both sides at same time, at each neck edge, dec 1 st EOR 4 times, every 4 rows 3 times—14 (14, 15, 15) sts rem each shoulder. Work even until armhole meas same as back to shoulder shaping, end WS row. ***Shape shoulders*** as for back.

SLEEVES

Using smaller needles, CO 45 (47, 49, 49) sts; knit 1 WS row. Work 2 rows in 1 × 1 Rib, end WS row. Change to larger needles and St st; work even until piece meas 4" from beg, end WS row. ***Shape sleeve:*** (RS) Inc 1 st each side this row, then every 8 rows 0 (0, 0, 8) times, every 10 rows 9 (9, 9, 3) times—65 (67, 69, 73) sts. Work even until piece meas 17½ (18, 18, 18½)" from beg, end WS row. ***Shape cap:*** (RS) BO 4 (4, 5, 5) sts at beg of next 2 rows, then dec 1 st each side every row 5 (3, 3, 3) times, EOR 4 (6, 6, 6) times, every 4 rows 2 times, EOR 6 (7, 7, 9) times—23 sts. Work 1 row even. BO 4 sts at beg of next 2 rows—15 sts. BO rem sts.

FINISHING

Block pieces to measurements. Sew shoulder seams. Set in sleeves; sew sleeve and side seams. ***Neckband:*** With RS facing, using circular needle, pick up and knit 114 (118, 122, 126) sts evenly around neck edge; pm for beg of rnd. Purl 1 rnd then work 2 rnds in 1 × 1 Rib. BO all sts purlwise.

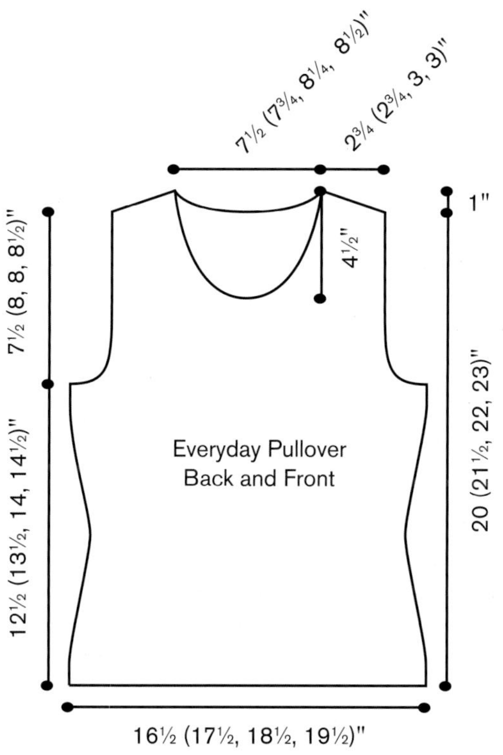

7½ (7¾, 8¼, 8½)"
2¾ (2¾, 3, 3)"
1"
4½"
7½ (8, 8, 8½)"
12½ (13½, 14, 14½)"
Everyday Pullover
Back and Front
20 (21½, 22, 23)"
16½ (17½, 18½, 19½)"

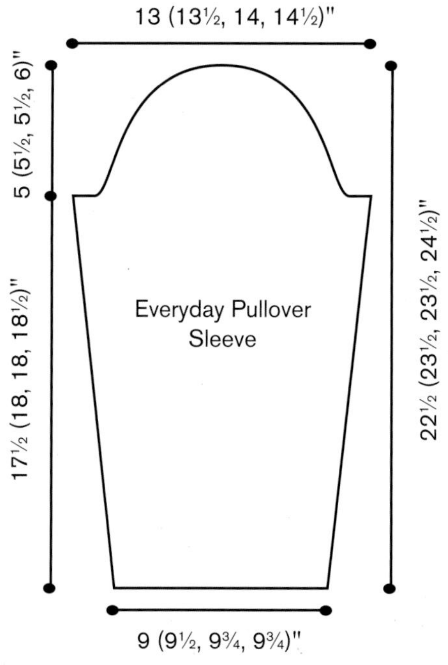

13 (13½, 14, 14½)"
5 (5½, 5½, 6)"
17½ (18, 18, 18½)"
Everyday Pullover
Sleeve
22½ (23½, 23½, 24½)"
9 (9½, 9¾, 9¾)"

MULTI-CABLE MOCK TURTLENECK

Note: See p. 188 for matching Children's sweater.

SIZES
Small (Medium, Large, 1X Large)

FINISHED MEASUREMENTS
37 (39, 43, 47)"

MATERIALS
Classic Elite Yarns

Skye Tweed (100% wool; 50-g ball = approx 112 yd/103 m)

• 13 (14, 15, 16) balls 1208 Skye Blue

Equivalent yarn

Light worsted weight #3, 1456 (1568, 1680, 1792) yd

Needles

• One pair *each* U.S. size 4 (3.5 mm) and 6 (4 mm) or size to obtain gauge

• One 16" circular U.S. size 6 (4 mm) for neck

• One cable needle (cn)

Stitch holders

Stitch markers

GAUGE
16 sts and 24 rows = 4" in Stockinette Stitch using larger needles; 22 sts and 24 rows = 4" in Left O-Cable, Left Eyelet, V-Cable, Right Eyelet, and Right O-Cable combination, using larger needles. Take time to save time, check your gauge.

PATTERN STITCHES

TWISTED RIB (MULTIPLE OF 6 STS + 3)
Row 1: (RS) [K1-tbl] 3 times, *p3, [K1-tbl] 3 times; rep from * across.

Row 2: *[P1-tbl] 3 times, k3; rep from * across to last 3 sts, [P1-tbl] 3 times.

Rep Rows 1–2 for Twisted Rib.

STOCKINETTE STITCH (ST ST)
Knit on RS, purl on WS.

REVERSE STOCKINETTE STITCH (REV ST ST)
Purl on RS, knit on WS.

LEFT O-CABLE (MULTIPLE OF 6 STS; 4-ROW REP)
See Left O-Cable Chart A.

RIGHT O-CABLE (MULTIPLE OF 6 STS; 4-ROW REP)
See Right O-Cable Chart B.

V-CABLE (MULTIPLE OF 26 STS; 12-ROW REP)
See V-Cable Chart C.

LEFT EYELET (MULTIPLE OF 13 STS; 10-ROW REP)
See Left Eyelet Chart D.

RIGHT EYELET (MULTIPLE OF 13 STS; 10-ROW REP)
See Right Eyelet Chart E.

CABLED RIB (MULTIPLE OF 6 STS)
Rnds 1 and 3: *P2, k4; rep from * around.

Rnd 2: *P2, sl 1 st to cn, hold in back, k1, k1 from cn; sl 1 st to cn, hold in front, k1, k1 from cn; rep from * around.

Rnd 4: *P2, sl 1 to cn, hold in front, k1, k1 from cn; sl 1 st to cn, hold in back, k1, k1 from cn; rep from * around.

Rep Rnds 1–4 for Cabled Rib.

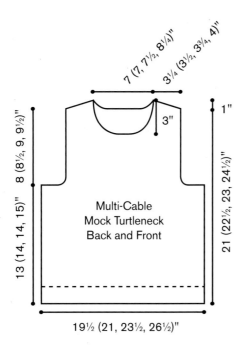

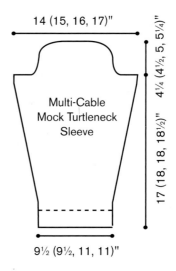

BACK

Using smaller needles, CO 93 (99, 111, 123) sts; work in Twisted Rib until piece meas 2" from beg, end WS row. Change to larger needles and purl 1 row, inc 9 (9, 7, 7) sts evenly across—102 (108, 118, 130) sts. *Est patt:* (WS) Work 7 (10, 15, 21) sts in St st, 18 sts in Chart A: Left O-Cable, 13 sts in Chart D: Left Eyelet, 26 sts in Chart C: V-Cable, 13 sts in Chart E: Right Eyelet, 18 sts in Chart B: Right O-Cable, 7 (10, 15, 21) sts in St st. Work as est until piece meas 13 (14, 14, 15)" from beg, end WS row. *Shape armholes:* (RS) BO 10 (12, 14, 15) sts at beg of next 2 rows, then dec 1 st each side EOR 4 (4, 4, 5) times—74 (76, 82, 90) sts rem. Work even until armhole meas 8 (8½, 9, 9½)" from beg of shaping, end WS row. *Shape shoulders and neck:* (RS) BO 6 (6, 7, 7) sts at beg of next 6 (4, 4, 4) rows, 0 (7, 6, 8) sts at beg of next 2 rows; and, **at the same time**, on the first row of shoulder shaping, work across to center 32 (32, 36, 40) sts, join second ball of yarn, work center sts and place on holder for neck, work to end. Working both sides at same time, at each neck edge, dec 1 st EOR 3 times.

FRONT

Work as for back until armhole meas 6 (6½, 7, 7½)" from beg of shaping, end WS row—74 (76, 82, 90) sts rem. *Shape neck:* Work 21 (22, 23, 26) sts, join second ball of yarn, work center 32 (32, 36, 38) sts and place on holder for neck, work to end. Working both sides at same time, at each neck edge, dec 1 st EOR 3 (3, 3, 4) times—18 (19, 20, 22) sts rem each shoulder. Work even until armhole meas same as back to shoulders, end WS row. *Shape shoulders* as for back.

SLEEVES

Using smaller needles, CO 51 (51, 57, 57) sts; work in Twisted Rib until piece meas 2½" from beg, end WS row. Change to larger needles and purl 1 row, inc 1 st on this row—52 (52, 58, 58) sts. *Est patt:* (WS) Work 1 (1, 4, 4) sts in St st, 12 sts in Chart A: Left O-Cable, 26 sts in Chart C: V-Cable, 12 sts Chart B: Right O-Cable, 1 (1, 4, 4) sts in St st. Work as est until piece meas 3" from beg, end WS row. *Shape sleeve:* (RS) Inc 1 st at each side on this row, then every 8 rows 0 (7, 2, 11) times, every 10 rows 8 (3, 7, 0) times, working inc sts in St st—70 (74, 78, 82) sts. Work even until piece meas 17 (18, 18, 18½)" from beg, end WS row. *Shape cap:* (RS) BO 10 (12, 14, 15) sts at beg of next 2 rows, then dec 1 st at each side EOR 8 (9, 10, 11) times—34 (32, 30, 30) sts rem. BO 2 sts at beg of next 8 rows—18 (16, 14, 14) sts rem. BO rem sts.

FINISHING

Block pieces to measurements. Sew shoulder seams. Set in sleeves; sew sleeve and side seams. *Neckband:* With RS facing, using circular needle, work 32 (32, 36, 40) sts from holder for back neck, pick up and knit 13 (13, 12, 12) sts along left neck edge, work 32 (32, 36, 38) sts from holder for front neck, pick up and knit 13 (13, 12, 12) sts along right neck edge, pm for beg of rnd—90 (90, 96, 102) sts. Purl 1 rnd. Change to Cabled Rib patt; work even until band meas 3" from pickup row, end with Rnd 4. BO all sts loosely in patt.

Multiple of 6 sts; 4-row rep

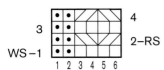

Multiple of 6 sts; 4-row rep

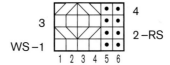

CHART C: V-CABLE

Multiple of 26 sts; 12-row rep

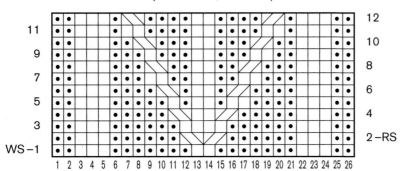

CHART D: LEFT EYELET

Multiple of 13 sts; 10-row rep

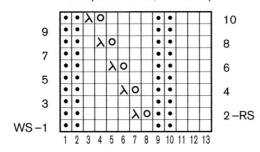

CHART E: RIGHT EYELET

Multiple of 13 sts; 10-row rep

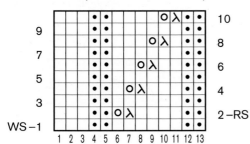

Note: Odd-numbered rows are WS rows, even-numbered rows are RS.

☐	Knit on RS, purl on WS.
●	Purl on RS, knit on WS.
O	Yo.
λ	Ssk.
⅄	K2tog.
⟋	Sl 1 st to cn, hold in front, k1, k1 from cn.
⟋	Sl 1 st to cn, hold in back, k1, k1 from cn.

MEANDERING CARDIGAN

SIZES

Small (Medium, Large)

FINISHED MEASUREMENTS

37½ (39¼ , 40½)"

MATERIALS

Classic Elite Yarns

Inca Alpaca (100% alpaca; 50-g hank = approx 109 yd/100 m)

• 4 (5, 6) hanks Color A—1105 Begonia

Inca Marl (100% alpaca; 50-g hank = approx 109 yd/100 m)

• 5 (6, 7) hanks Color B—1188 Coral Spice

Equivalent yarn

Worsted weight #4, Color A: 436 (545, 763) yd; Color B: 545 (654, 763) yd

Needles

• One pair size U.S. 6 (4 mm) or size to obtain gauge

Five ¾" buttons

Bobbins (optional)

GAUGE

22 sts and 28 rows = 4" in Stockinette Stitch intarsia pattern. Take time to save time, check your gauge.

NOTES

Garment is worked from the charts using intarsia St st. Use a separate ball of yarn for each color.

Zigzag Pattern is random and will not match at the side seams.

PATTERN STITCHES

GARTER STITCH (GTR ST)

Knit every row.

STOCKINETTE STITCH (ST ST)

Knit on RS, purl on WS.

ZIGZAG PATTERN

See charts.

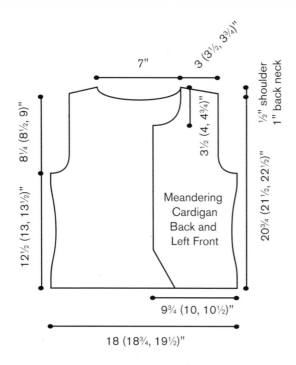

7"

3 (3½, 3¾)"

½" shoulder
1" back neck

3½ (4, 4¾)"

8¼ (8½, 9)"

12½ (13, 13½)"

20¾ (21½, 22½)"

Meandering
Cardigan
Back and
Left Front

9¾ (10, 10½)"

18 (18¾, 19½)"

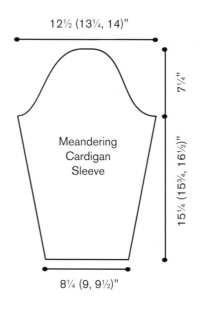

12½ (13¼, 14)"

7¼"

15¼ (15¾, 16½)"

Meandering
Cardigan
Sleeve

8¼ (9, 9½)"

■ **ZIGZAG PATTERN:SLEEVE CHART**   ■ **ZIGZAG PATTERN: FRONT CHART**

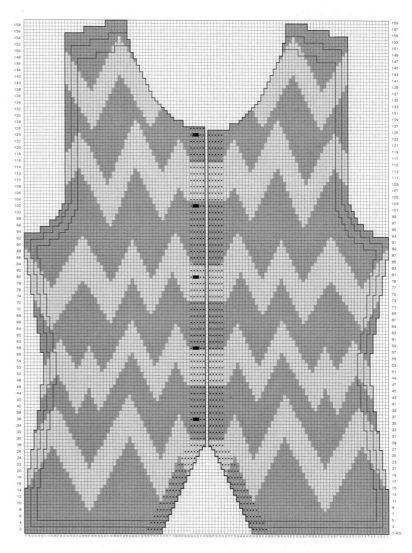

BACK

Using Color A, CO 99 (103, 107) sts. Beg Gtr st; work even for 4 rows, end WS row. Change to St st and chart; using separate balls of color for each section, adding or removing balls of color as necessary. *Shape sides, armholes, and neck:* As shown on chart.

RIGHT FRONT

Using Color A, CO 42 (43, 44) sts. Work as for back; and, **at the same time,** *make front band:* Work 5 sts at center front in Gtr st for front band until beg of neck shaping, working buttonholes where indicated on chart by BO sts on RS row and CO sts on next WS row; and, **at the same time,** *shape lower front:* (RS) Where indicated on chart, K5, yo, work to end.

LEFT FRONT

Work as for right front, rev shaping; and, **at the same time,** *front band:* Work 5 sts at center front in Gtr st for front band until beg of neck shaping; work inc at lower front before working 5 band sts.

SLEEVES

Using Color A, CO 45 (49, 53) sts. Beg Gtr st; work even for 6 rows, end WS row. Change to St st and chart; using separate balls of color for each section, adding or removing balls of color as necessary. *Shape sleeve and cap:* As shown on chart.

FINISHING

Block pieces to measurements. Sew shoulder seams. Set in sleeves; sew sleeve and side seams. *Neckband:* Using Color A, pick up and knit 97 (105, 113) sts evenly around neck shaping. Beg Gtr st; work even for 3 rows. BO all sts loosely. Sew buttons opposite buttonholes.

▢ ZIGZAG PATTERN: BACK CHART

——— Size Small

——— Size Medium

——— Size Large

☐ Color A – 1105 Begonia
as instructed in pattern

▨ Color B – 1188 Coral Spice
as instructed in pattern

⊡ Purl on RS, knit on WS

GARTER-STITCH COLOR-BLOCK CARDIGAN

SIZES
Small (Medium, Large, 1X Large)

FINISHED MEASUREMENTS
34 (38, 42, 46)"

MATERIALS
Classic Elite Yarns

Wings (55% alpaca, 23% silk, 22% wool; 50-g hank = approx 109 yd/100 m)

- 9 (10, 12, 13) hanks Main Color (MC)—2398 September Sunset
- 1 (2, 2, 2) hanks Contrast Color (CC)—2330 Ipswich Pink

Equivalent yarn

Worsted weight #4, MC: 981 (1090, 1308, 1417) yd; CC: 109 (218, 218, 218) yd

Needles

- One pair *each* size U.S. 7 (4.5 mm) and 8 (5 mm) or size to obtain gauge

Stitch markers

One 18" separating zipper to match MC

GAUGE
18 sts and 36 rows = 4" in Garter Stitch, using larger needles. Take time to save time, check your gauge.

PATTERN STITCHES

GARTER STITCH (GTR ST)
Knit every row.

LEFT FRONT ZIPPER EDGING
Row 1: K3.

Row 2: Sl 1p, p2.

Rep Rows 1–2 for Left Front Zipper Edging.

RIGHT FRONT ZIPPER EDGING
Row 1: (RS) Sl 1k, k2.

Row 2: P3.

Rep Rows 1–2 for Right Front Zipper Edging.

BACK

Using MC and larger needles, CO 77 (86, 95, 104) sts; work in Gtr st until piece meas 13" from beg, end WS row. **Shape armholes:** (RS) BO 5 sts at beg of next 2 rows, then dec 1 st each side EOR 4 (6, 9, 11) times—59 (64, 67, 72) sts rem; and, **at the same time,** when armhole meas 2" from beg of shaping, end WS row and change to CC. Work even until armhole meas 8 (8½ , 9, 9½)" from beg of shaping, end WS row. BO all sts.

LEFT FRONT

Using MC and larger needles, CO 38 (43, 47, 52) sts. *Est patt:* (RS) Work 35 (40, 44, 49) sts in Gtr st, work 3 sts in Front Left Zipper Edging. Work even as est until piece meas 13" from beg, end WS row. **Shape armhole:** (RS) BO 5 sts at beg of this row, then dec 1 st at armhole edge EOR 4 (6, 9, 11) times—29 (32, 33, 36) sts rem; and, **at the same time,** when armhole meas 2" from beg of shaping, end WS row and change to CC. Work even until armhole meas 6" from beg of shaping, end RS row. **Shape neck:** (WS) At neck edge, BO 8 (9, 8, 9) sts once, 3 sts once, 2 sts once, then dec 1 st once—15 (17, 19, 21) sts rem. Work even until armhole meas same as back to shoulders, end WS row. BO all sts.

RIGHT FRONT

Using MC and larger needles, CO 38 (43, 47, 52) sts. *Est patt:* (RS) Work 3 sts in Right Front Zipper Edging, 35 (40, 44, 49) sts in Gtr st. Work as for left front, rev all shaping by working armhole shaping at beg of WS rows and neck shaping at beg of RS rows.

SLEEVES

Using MC and larger needles, CO 45 sts; work even in Gtr st until piece meas 2½" from beg, end WS row. **Shape sleeve:** (RS) Inc 1 st each side this row, then every 14 (12, 10, 8) rows 8 (10, 13, 15) times—63 (67, 73, 77) sts. Work even until piece meas 18" from beg, end WS row. **Shape cap:** (RS) BO 5 sts at beg of next 2 rows, then dec 1 st EOR 10 (12, 17, 19) times, every 4 rows 6 (6, 4, 4) times—21 sts rem. BO 3 sts at beg of next 2 rows—15 sts rem. BO rem sts.

FINISHING

Block pieces to measurements on back, meas 3¼ (3¾, 4¼, 4¾)" in from each armhole edge and pms for neck edge. Sew each shoulder seam bet armhole edge and marker. Set in sleeves; sew sleeve and side seams. **Collar:** With WS facing, using MC and smaller needles, pick up and knit 60 (66, 70, 74) sts evenly around neck edge, beg after Zipper Edging

and end before Zipper Edging; and, **at the same time,** pm at each shoulder seam. Work 2 rows in Gtr st, end WS of collar. **Shape collar:** (RS) Dec 1 st, before first marker and after second marker this row, then EOR 5 times—48 (54, 58, 62) sts rem. Change to larger needles and shape collar: Inc 1 st each side this row, then EOR 11 (12, 12, 12) times—72 (80, 84, 88) sts. Work 2 rows even. **Scalloped Edge Bind-Off:** *BO 4 sts at beg of row, work to end; rep from * until all sts have been bound off. Sew in zipper.

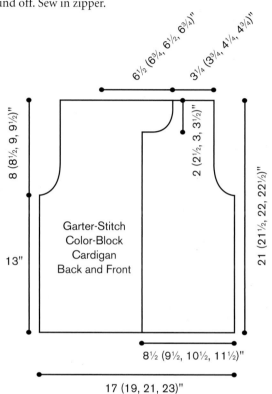

6½ (6¾, 6½, 6¾)"   3¼ (3¾, 4¼, 4¾)"

8 (8½, 9, 9½)"

2 (2½, 3, 3½)"

21 (21½, 22, 22½)"

13"

Garter-Stitch Color-Block Cardigan Back and Front

8½ (9½, 10½, 11½)"

17 (19, 21, 23)"

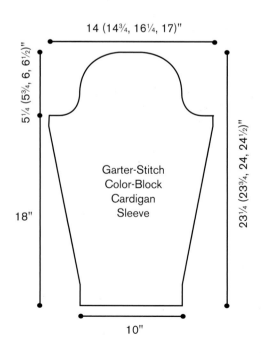

14 (14¾, 16¼, 17)"

5¼ (5¾, 6, 6½)"

23¼ (23¾, 24, 24½)"

18"

Garter-Stitch Color-Block Cardigan Sleeve

10"

MOSAIC CABLE PULLOVER

SIZES

Small (Medium, Large, 1X Large)

FINISHED MEASUREMENTS

36 (40, 46, 51)"

MATERIALS

Classic Elite Yarn

Wool Bam Boo (50% wool, 50% bamboo; 50-g ball = approx 118 yd/108 m)

• 13 (14, 15, 16) balls 1681 Celery

Equivalent yarn

Light worsted weight #3; 1534 (1652, 1770, 1888) yd

Needles

• One pair *each* sizes U.S. 4 (3.5 mm) and 6 (4 mm) or size to obtain gauge

• One 16" circular size U.S. 4 (3.5 mm)

• One cable needle (cn)

Stitch holders

Stitch markers

GAUGE

22 sts and 30 rows = 4" in Reverse Stockinette Stitch, using larger needles; 18 sts = 2" in Diamond Cable, using larger needles; 84 sts = 13½" in cable from Chart B, using larger needles; 9 sts = 1¼" in 3 x 6 Rib, usiing larger needles. Take time to save time, check your gauge. *Note:* Row gauge is important

NOTES

Sl markers every row.

Work all incs and decs 1 st in from each edge.

PATTERN STITCHES

REVERSE STOCKINETTE STITCH (REV ST ST)

Purl on RS, knit on WS.

CABLES

See Charts A (multiple of 18 sts; work 1x), B (multiple of 84 sts), and C (multiple of 18 sts; 22-row rep).

3 x 6 RIB (MULTIPLE OF 9 STS):

Row 1: (RS) *K3, p6; rep from * across.

Row 2: Knit the knit sts and purl the purl sts as they face you.

Rep Row 2 for 3 x 6 Rib.

CIRCULAR 3 x 3 RIB (MULTIPLE OF 6 STS)

Rnd 1: *K3, p3; rep from * around.

Rep Rnd 1 for 3 x 3 Rib.

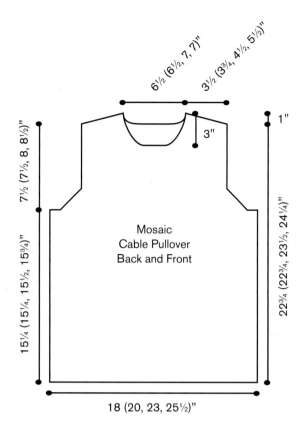

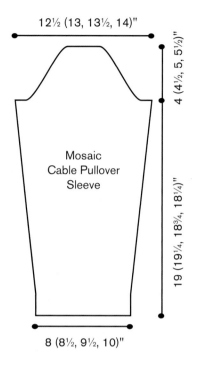

BACK

Using larger needles, CO 134 (152, 170, 188) sts. *Foundation row:* (WS) K4, p3, [k6, p3] 6 (7, 8, 9) times, k3, p6, k3, [p3, k6] 6 (7, 8, 9) times, p3, k4. *Setup row:* (RS) P4, k3, [p6, k3] 5 (6, 7, 8) times, p6, pm; work 18 sts from Chart A (beg with Row 1) over center, pm; [p6, k3] 6 (7, 8, 9) times, p4. Work even as est, working Rows 1–6 of Chart A 1 (1, 2, 3) times, then Rows 7–34 once; rep Rows 13–34 until 66 (66, 72, 78) rows completed, end (WS) Row 22 of Chart A, remove markers. *Est patt:* (RS) Work as est across 25 (34, 43, 52) sts, pm; work 84 sts from Chart B (beg with Row 1) across center, pm; work to end as est. Work even until 114 (114, 116, 118) total rows worked—piece meas 15¼ (15¼, 15½, 15¾)" from beg, end WS row. *Shape armholes:* (RS) BO 5 (7, 8, 9) sts at beg next 2 rows—124 (138, 154, 170) sts rem. BO 2 sts at beg next 4 (16, 16, 18) rows, then dec 1 st each side EOR 6 (0, 1, 1) times—104 (106, 120, 132) sts rem. Work even until 106 rows of Chart B worked, end WS row. *Shape neck and shoulders:* (RS) Shape neck as shown on Chart B for your size by working across to center 26, (26, 30, 30) sts, place center sts on holder for back neck, join second ball of yarn and work to end. Working both sides at same time, at each neck edge, BO 5 sts twice; and, **at the same time,** beg first row of neck shaping, BO 10 (10, 12, 14) sts each shoulder edge twice, then 9 (10, 11, 13) sts once.

FRONT

Work as for back until 90 rows of Chart B have been worked, end WS row. *Shape neck:* (RS) Shape neck as shown on Chart B; work across to center 20 (20, 24, 24) sts, place center sts on holder for front neck; join second ball of yarn and work to end. BO 3 sts at each neck edge once, 2 sts 3 times, then 1 st 4 times—29 (30, 35, 41) sts rem for shoulders; and, **at the same time,** beg Row 107 of Chart B, *shape shoulders* as for back.

RIGHT SLEEVE

Using smaller needles, CO 60 (66, 72, 78) sts. *Foundation row:* (WS) K3 (0, 0, 3), p3 (0, 3, 3), [k6, p3] 2 (3, 3, 3) times, k3, p6, k3, [p3, k6] 2 (3, 3, 3) times, p3 (0, 3, 3), k3 (0, 0, 3). *Setup row:* (RS) P3 (0, 0, 3), k3 (0, 3, 3), p6, work in 3 × 6 Rib as est across 18 sts, pm; work 18 sts from Chart C (beg with Row 1) over center, pm; work in 3 × 6 Rib as est across 18 sts, p6, k 3 (0, 3, 3), p 3 (0, 0, 3). Work even as est until 12 rows of Chart C completed, end WS row. Change to larger needles and *shape sleeve:* (RS) Inc 1 st each side every 6 rows 7 (2, 0, 0) times, every 8 rows 10 (14, 15, 12) times, then every 10 rows 0 (0, 0, 2) times—94 (98, 102, 106) sts. Work even until piece meas 19 (19¼, 18¾, 18¼), end WS row. *Shape cap:* (RS) BO 5 (7, 8, 9) sts at beg next 2 rows—84 (84, 86, 88) sts rem. BO 2 sts at beg next 20 (16, 16, 14)" rows, 1 st at beg next 6 (12, 16, 24) rows, 2 sts at beg next 4 (4, 2, 0) rows, then 4 sts at beg next 2 rows. BO rem 22 (24, 26, 28) sts in patt.

Multiple of 18 sts; 22-row rep

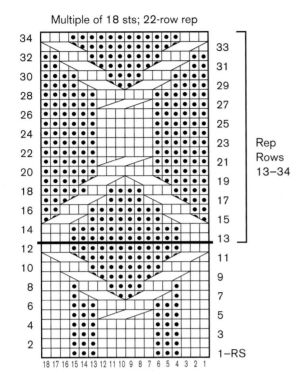

Rep Rows 13–34

Multiple of 18 sts; 22-row rep

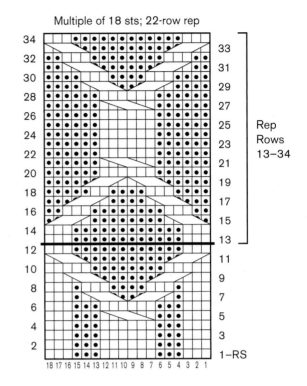

Rep Rows 13–34

LEFT SLEEVE

Work as for right sleeve, working center sts from Chart A instead of Chart C.

FINISHING

Sew shoulder seams. **Neck:** With RS facing, using circular needle, beg at left shoulder seam, pick up and knit 18 sts along left front neck shaping, p0 (0, 3, 3), k3, p3, pm, 3/3RC, pm, p3, k3, p 0 (0, 3, 3) across 18 (18, 24, 24) sts on holder for front neck; pick up and knit 18 sts along right front neck shaping, pick up and knit 11 (11, 12, 12) sts along back neck, k1 (1, 0, 0), p3 (3, 0, 0), [k3, p3] 1 (1, 2, 2) times, pm, 3/3 RC, [p3, k3] 1 (1, 2, 2) times, p3 (3, 0, 0), k1 (1, 0, 0) across 26 (26, 30, 30) sts on holder for back neck, pick up and knit 11 (11, 12, 12) sts along rem of back neck, pm for beg of rnd—102 (102, 114, 114) sts. *Rnd 1:* P0 (0, 3, 3), work in 3 × 3 Rib to first marker, k6; beg p3, work in 3 × 3 Rib to second marker, k6, cont in 3 × 3 Rib to end of rnd. *Rnds 2–5:* Rep Rnd 1. *Rnd 6:* P0 (0, 3, 3), work as est to first marker, 3/3RC; work as est to second marker, 3/3RC; cont in 3 × 3 rib to end of rnd. Rep Rnds 1–6 once, then work Rnds 1–5 once more. *Next rnd:* BO all sts in patt as for Rnd 6, dec 3 sts at each cable as foll: Sl 3 sts to cn and hold in back, [knit tog 1 st from LH needle with 1 st from cn] 3 times. Set in sleeves. Sew side and sleeve seams. Block lightly to measurements.

☐ Knit on RS, purl on WS.

◉ Purl on RS, knit on WS.

Sl 1 st to cn, hold in back, k3; p1 from cn.

Sl 3 sts to cn, hold in front, p1; k3 from cn.

Sl 2 sts to cn, hold in back, k3; p2 from cn.

Sl 3 sts to cn, hold in front, p2; k3 from cn

Sl 2 sts to cn, hold in back, k3; (k1, p1) from cn.

Sl 2 sts to cn, hold in back, k3; (p1, k1) from cn.

Sl 3 sts to cn, hold in front, (k1, p1); k3 from cn.

Sl 3 sts to cn, hold in front, (p1, k1); k3 from cn.

Sl 3 sts to cn, hold in back, k3; k3 from cn.

Sl 3 sts to cn, hold in front, k3; k3 from cn.

Sl 3 sts to cn, hold in back, k3; (k1, p1, k1) from cn.

Sl 3 sts to cn, hold in back, k3; (p1, k1, p1) from cn.

Sl 3 sts to cn, hold in front, (p1, k1, p1); k3 from cn.

Sl 3 sts to cn, hold in front, p1, k1, p1); k3 from cn.

━━ Place sts on holder (all sizes).

── Back neck shaping (sizes S and M).

── Front neck shaping (sizes S and M).

── Back neck shaping (sizes L and 1XL).

── Front neck shaping (sizes L and 1XL).

Note: Shoulder Shaping is not shown on Charts; see text for Shoulder Shaping.

Multiple of 84 sts; 112-row rep

EMBROIDERED CARDIGAN

SIZES

Small (Medium, Large, 1X Large)

FINISHED MEASUREMENTS

37½ (40, 42, 44½)"

MATERIALS

Classic Elite Yarns

Princess (40% merino, 28% viscose, 10% cashmere, 7% angora, 15% nylon; 50-g ball = approx 150 yd/137 m)

• (8, 9, 9) balls 1085 Milord's Madder

Equivalent yarn

Worsted weight #4, 1050 (1200, 1350, 1350) yd

Needles

• One pair size U.S. 6 (4 mm) or size to obtain gauge
• One crochet hook size U.S. F/5 (3.75 mm)

Sewing needle, thread, tapestry needle

Eight (9, 9, 9) ½" buttons

GAUGE

21 sts and 30 rows = 4" in Stockinette Stitch. Take time to save time, check your gauge.

PATTERN STITCHES

STOCKINETTE STITCH (ST ST)

Knit on RS, purl on WS.

1 × 1 RIB (MULTIPLE OF 2 STS)

Row 1: *K1, p1; rep from * across.
Row 2: Knit the knit sts and purl the purl sts as they face you.
Rep Row 2 for 1 x 1 Rib.

CHAIN (CH)

Beg by making a sl knot on hook. Wrap yarn around hook (yo) and draw it through loop on hook to form first ch. Rep this step as many times as instructed. (Loop on hook is never included when counting number of chs.)

SLIP STITCH (SL ST)

Insert hook in indicated st, yo, and draw through both st and loop on hook.

SINGLE CROCHET (SC)

Insert hook in indicated st, yo, and pull up a loop; yo and draw through both loops on hook.

BACK

CO 100 (106, 112, 118) sts. Beg 1 × 1 Rib; work even until piece meas 2" from beg, end WS row. Change to St st; (RS) work even for 1", end WS row. *Shape waist:* (RS) Dec 1 st each side this row, then every 4 rows 3 times—92 (98, 104, 110) sts rem. Work even for 1", end WS row. *Shape waist:* (RS) Inc 1 st each side this row, then every 6 rows 3 times—100 (106, 112, 118) sts. Work even until piece meas 13 (13½, 14, 14½)" from beg, end WS row. *Shape armholes:* (RS) BO 5 (5, 6, 7) sts at beg of next 2 rows—90 (96, 100, 104) sts rem. Dec 1 st each side every row 4 times—82 (88, 92, 96) sts rem. Dec 1 st each side EOR 4 times—74 (80, 84, 88) sts rem. Work even until armhole meas 7 (7½, 8, 8½)" from beg of shaping, end WS row; pm each side of center 38 sts. *Shape neck:* (RS) Work across to marker; join second ball of yarn and BO center sts; work to end—18 (21, 23, 25) sts rem each side. Working both sides at same time, at each neck edge, dec 1 st every row twice, end WS row—16 (19, 21, 23) sts rem each side for shoulder. *Shape shoulders:* (RS) BO 5 (6, 7, 8) sts at beg of next 4 rows. BO rem sts.

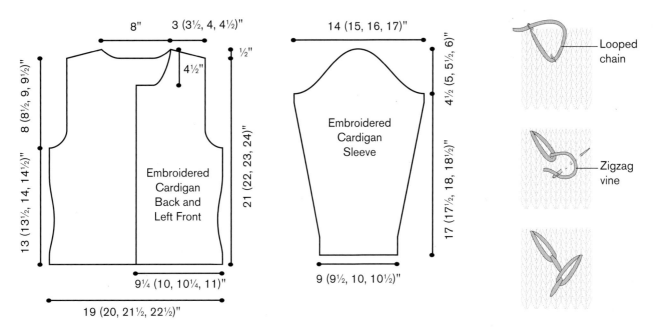

8"

3 (3½, 4, 4½)"

½"

4½"

8 (8½, 9, 9½)"

13 (13½, 14, 14½)"

Embroidered
Cardigan
Back and
Left Front

21 (22, 23, 24)"

9¼ (10, 10¼, 11)"

19 (20, 21½, 22½)"

14 (15, 16, 17)"

4½ (5, 5½, 6)"

Embroidered
Cardigan
Sleeve

17 (17½, 18, 18½)"

9 (9½, 10, 10½)"

Looped
chain

Zigzag
vine

LEFT FRONT

CO 48 (52, 54, 58) sts. Beg 1 × 1 Rib; work even until piece meas 2" from beg, end WS row. Change to St st; (RS) work even for 1", end WS row. *Shape waist:* (RS) Dec 1 st at beg of this row, then every 4 rows 3 times—44 (48, 50, 54) sts rem. Work even for 1", end WS row. *Shape waist:* (RS) Inc 1 st at beg of this row, then every 6 rows 3 times—48 (52, 54, 58) sts. Work even until piece meas 13 (13½, 14, 14½)" from beg, end WS row. *Shape armhole:* (RS) BO 5 (5, 6, 7) sts once—43 (47, 48, 51) sts rem. At armhole edge, dec 1 st every row 4 times—39 (43, 44, 47) sts rem. Dec 1 st EOR 4 times—35 (39, 40, 43) sts rem. Work even until armhole meas 4 (4½, 5, 5½)" from beg of shaping, end RS row. *Shape neck:* (WS) At neck edge, BO 8 (9, 8, 9) sts once—27 (30, 32, 34) sts rem. Dec 1 st at neck edge EOR 11 times—16 (19, 21, 23) sts rem for shoulder. Work even until piece meas same as back to shoulder shaping, end WS row. *Shape shoulder* as for back at beg of RS rows only.

RIGHT FRONT

Work as for left front rev all shaping by working armhole and shoulder shaping at beg of WS rows and neck shaping at beg of RS rows.

SLEEVES

CO 48 (50, 52, 56) sts. Beg 1 × 1 Rib; work even until piece meas 1 1/2" from beg, end WS row. Change to St st; (RS) work even for 1", end WS row. *Shape sleeve:* (RS) Inc 1 st each side this row, then every 6 rows 12 (13, 15, 16) times—74 (78, 84, 90) sts. Work even until piece meas 17 (17½, 18, 18½)" from beg, end WS row. *Shape cap:* (RS) BO 5 (5, 6, 7) sts at beg of next 2 rows—64 (68, 72, 76) sts rem. Dec 1 st each side

every row 4 times—56 (60, 64, 68) sts rem. Dec 1 st each side EOR 11 (13, 14, 16) times—34 (34, 36, 36) sts rem. Dec 1 st each side every row 4 times—26 (26, 28, 28) sts rem. BO 4 sts at the beg of next 2 rows—18 (18, 20, 20) sts rem. BO rem sts.

FINISHING

Block pieces to measurements. Sew shoulder seams. Set in sleeves; sew side and sleeve seams. *Button band: Row 1:* With RS facing, using crochet hook, beg at left front neck edge, join yarn with a sl st; ch 1, sc in EOR along center front, inserting hook in half of st along edge; turn. *Row 2:* Ch 1, sc in each sc across; turn. *Row 3:* Work as Row 2. Fasten off. *Buttonhole band: Row 1:* With RS facing, using crochet hook, beg at lower edge of right front, join yarn with a sl st; work as for button band. *Row 2:* Ch 1, sc in each sc across; turn. *Row 3:* Ch 1, sc in next 3 sc, ch 2, skip 2 sc, *sc in next 5 sc, ch 2, skip 2 sc; rep from * until less than 2" left of row, sc in rem sts; turn. *Row 4:* Ch 1, sc in each st, work 2 sc in each ch-2 space. Fasten off. *Crochet edging:* With RS facing, beg at upper corner of buttonhole band, join yarn with a sl st; ch 1, work 1 row sc evenly around neckline. Fasten off. With RS facing, beg at lower corner of buttonhole band, join yarn with a sl st; *ch 4, sl st in third ch from hook, ch 1, skip 2 sts, sc in next st; rep along center right front, around neck shaping and down center left front, adjusting spacing at upper corners of front bands so that you sc in corners. Fasten off. *Embroidery:* Using tapestry needle and one strand of yarn, embroider the Chained Feather patt as shown, stitching down each side of front sections, beg at upper edge, 1 st away from center front crochet bands. Work looped ch over 2 sts and 2 rows of knitting; work zigzag vine over 1 st and 2 rows of knitting—see photo and illustrations. Sew on buttons.

POLKA DOT CARDIGANS

SIZES

Woman's Small (Medium, Large, 1X Large) {Child's 2 (4, 6, 8)}

FINISHED MEASUREMENTS

35 (39½, 44½, 49)" {24½ (27, 30, 33)"}

Note: Woman's directions are given first, and Child's directions appear in braces { }. If only one number is given, it applies to all sizes.

MATERIALS

Classic Elite Yarns

Princess (40% merino wool, 28% viscose, 10% cashmere, 7% angora, 15% nylon; 50-g ball = approx 150 yd/137 m)

• 6 (7, 8, 9) balls 3497 Lady Leaf {4 (4, 5, 6) balls 3431 Top Turq}

Equivalent yarn

Worsted weight #4, 900 (1050, 1200, 1350) yd {600 (600, 750, 900) yd}

Needles

• One pair *each* sizes U.S. 6 (4 mm) and 7 (4.5 mm) or size to obtain gauge

Seven {5} ¾" buttons

GAUGE

20 sts and 28 rows = 4" in Stockinette Stitch, using larger needles. Take time to save time, check your gauge.

PATTERN STITCHES:

GARTER STITCH (GTR ST)

Knit every row.

STOCKINETTE STITCH (ST ST)

Knit on RS, purl on WS.

CHEVRON (MULTIPLE OF 12 STS; 16-ROW REP)

See Chevron Chart.

POLKA DOT (MULTIPLE OF 12 STS; 20-ROW REP)

See Polka Dot Chart.

BACK

Using larger needles, CO 87 (99, 111, 123) {61 (67, 75, 83)} sts; work 4 rows in Gtr st, end WS row. Change to St st; work 4 rows, end WS row. *Est patt:* (RS) Work 1 {0} st in St st (edge st), 85 (97, 109, 121) {61 (67, 75, 83)} sts in Chevron (Chart), beg and end where indicated for your size, 1 {0} st in St st (edge st). Work as est until Row 16 of Chevron Chart is complete. Change to St st; work 4 rows even, end WS row. *Est patt:* (RS) Work 1 {0} st in St st (edge st), 85 (97, 109, 121) {61 (67, 75, 83)} sts in Polka Dot (Chart), beg and end where indicated for your size, 1 {0} st in St st (edge st). Work as est until piece meas 14" {8 (8½, 9, 9½)"} from beg, end WS row.

Shape armholes: (RS) BO 4 (5, 6, 7) {3 (4, 4, 5)} sts at beg of next 2 rows, 0 (2, 2, 3) {2 (2, 2, 3)} sts at beg of next 2 rows, then dec 1 st each side EOR 4 (6, 8, 9) {4 (4, 5, 6)} times— 71 (73, 79, 85) {43 (47, 53, 55)} sts rem. Work even until armhole meas 7½ (8, 8½, 9)" {5¼ (5½, 6¼, 6½)"} from beg of shaping, end WS row. *Shape shoulders:* (RS) BO 6 (6, 7, 8) {3 (4, 5, 5)} sts at beg of next 6 (4, 4, 4) {6 (4, 4, 6)} rows, 0 (7, 8, 9) {0 (3, 4, 0)} sts at beg of next 2 rows; and, **at the same time,** on the first row of shoulder shaping, work across to center 23 {19} sts, join second ball of yarn and BO center sts, work to end. Working both sides at same time, at each neck edge BO 3 {3} sts twice {once}.

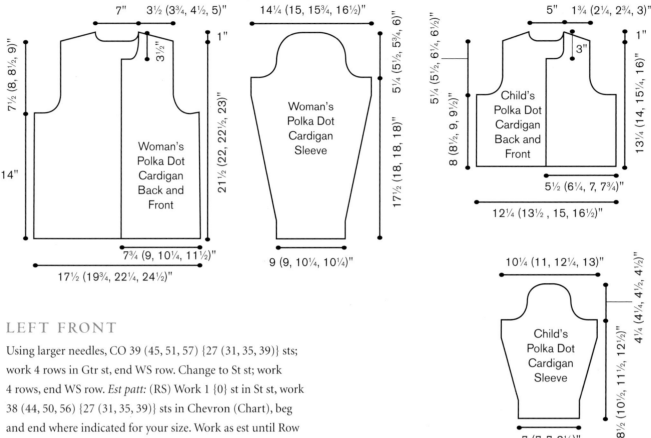

Woman's Polka Dot Cardigan Back and Front

7" 3½ (3¾, 4½, 5)" 3½" 1" 7½ (8, 8½, 9)" 21½ (22, 22½, 23)" 14" 7¾ (9, 10¼, 11½)" 17½ (19¾, 22¼, 24½)"

Woman's Polka Dot Cardigan Sleeve

14¼ (15, 15¾, 16½)" 5¼ (5½, 5¾, 6)" 17½ (18, 18, 18)" 9 (9, 10¼, 10¼)"

Child's Polka Dot Cardigan Back and Front

5" 1¾ (2¼, 2¾, 3)" 3" 1" 5¼ (5½, 6¼, 6½)" 8 (8½, 9, 9½)" 13¼ (14, 15¼, 16)" 5½ (6¼, 7, 7¾)" 12¼ (13½, 15, 16½)"

Child's Polka Dot Cardigan Sleeve

10¼ (11, 12¼, 13)" 4¼ (4¼, 4½, 4½)" 8½ (10½, 11½, 12½)" 7 (7, 7, 8¼)"

LEFT FRONT

Using larger needles, CO 39 (45, 51, 57) {27 (31, 35, 39)} sts; work 4 rows in Gtr st, end WS row. Change to St st; work 4 rows, end WS row. *Est patt:* (RS) Work 1 {0} st in St st, work 38 (44, 50, 56) {27 (31, 35, 39)} sts in Chevron (Chart), beg and end where indicated for your size. Work as est until Row 16 of Chevron Chart is complete. Change to St st; work 4 rows, end WS row. *Est patt:* (RS) Work 1 {0} st in St st, work 38 (44, 50, 56) {27 (31, 35, 39)} sts in Polka Dot (Chart), beg and end where indicated for your size. Work as est until piece meas same as back to armhole, end WS row. **Shape armhole** as for back at beg of RS rows only—31 (32, 35, 38) {18 (21, 24, 25)} sts rem. Cont as est until armhole meas 5 (5½, 6, 6½)" {3¼ (3½, 4¼, 4½)"} from beg of shaping, end RS row. **Shape neck:** (WS) At neck edge, BO 5 {4} sts once, 3 {2 (2, 3, 3)} sts once, 2 {0} sts once, then dec 1 st EOR 3 {3} times—18 (19, 22, 25) {9 (11, 14, 15)} sts rem for shoulder. Work even until armhole meas same as back to shoulder shaping, end WS row. **Shape shoulder** as for back at beg of RS rows only.

RIGHT FRONT

Using larger needles, CO 39 (45, 51, 57) {27 (31, 35, 39)} sts; work 4 rows in Gtr st, end WS row. Change to St st; work 4 rows, end WS row. *Est patt:* (RS) Work 38 (44, 50, 56) {27 (31, 35, 39)} sts in Chevron (Chart), beg and end where indicated for your size, 1 {0} st in St st (edge st). Work as est until Row 16 of Chevron Chart is complete. Change to St st; work 4 rows, end WS row. *Est patt:* (RS) Work 38 (44, 50, 54) {27 (31, 35, 39)} sts in Polka Dot (Chart), beg and end where indicated for your size, 1 {0} st in St st (edge st). Work as for left front,

rev all shaping by working armhole and shoulder shaping at beg of WS rows, and neck shaping at beg of RS rows.

SLEEVES

Using larger needles, CO 45 (45, 51, 51) {35 (35, 35, 41)} sts; work 4 rows in Gtr st, end WS row. Change to St st; work 4 rows, end WS row. *Est patt:* (RS) Work 1 {0} st in St st (edge st), 43 (43, 49, 49) {35 (35, 35, 41)} sts in Chevron (Chart), beg and end where indicated for your size, 1 {0} st in St st (edge st). Work as est until Row 16 of Chevron Chart is complete. Change to St st; work 4 rows, end WS row. *Est patt:* (RS) Work 1 {0} st in St st (edge st), 43 (43, 49, 49) {35 (35, 35, 41)} sts in Polka Dot (Chart), beg and end where indicated for your size, 1 {0} st in St st (edge st). Work 1 row as est. **Shape sleeve:** (RS) Inc 1 st each side this row, then every 4 rows 0 (0, 0, 1) {7 (6, 12, 8)} times, every 6 rows 7 (12, 8, 14) {0 (3, 0, 4)} times, every 8 rows 5 (2, 5, 0) {0} times, working inc sts in Polka Dot patt as they become available—71 (75, 79, 83) {51 (55, 61, 65)} sts. Work even until piece meas 17½ (18, 18, 18)" {8½ (10½, 11½, 12½)"} from beg, end WS row. **Shape cap:** (RS) BO 4 (5, 6, 7) {3 (4, 4, 5)} sts at beg of next 2 rows, 0 (2, 2, 3) {2 (2, 2, 3)} sts at beg of next 2 rows, then dec 1 st each side EOR 12

(12, 13, 14) {10} times—39 (37, 37, 35) {21 (23, 29, 29)} sts rem. BO 2 sts at beg of next 10 {6 (6, 8, 8)} rows—19 (17, 17, 15) sts rem. BO rem sts.

FINISHING

Block pieces to measurements. Sew shoulder seams. Set in sleeves; sew sleeve and side seams. **Button band:** With RS facing, using smaller needles, pick up and knit 95 (97, 99, 101) {57 (61, 65, 79)} sts evenly along left front edge. Work 3 rows in Gtr st, end WS row. Change to St st; work 4 rows, end WS row. Change to Gtr st; work 3 rows, end RS row. BO all sts. Pm for 7 {5} buttons, the first ¾" from lower edge, the last ¾" from neck edge, the rem 5 {3} evenly spaced bet. **Buttonhole band:** Work as for button band, working buttonholes opposite markers on second RS row of St st section as foll: [k2tog, yo] at

each marker. **Collar:** With WS of garment facing (RS of collar), using smaller needles, pick up and knit 77 {65} sts evenly around neck edge, beg and end in center of bands. *Est patt:* (WS of collar) Work 2 sts in Gtr st (edge sts), 73 {61} sts in St st, work 2 sts in Gtr st (edge sts). Work as est until collar meas 1" from pickup row, end WS row. *Est patt:* (RS of collar) Work 2 sts in Gtr st (edge sts), 73 {61} sts in Chevron (Chart), beg and end where indicated for your size, work 2 sts in Gtr st (edge sts). Work 1 row as est. Cont as est until Row 16 of Chevron Chart is complete; and, **at the same time, *shape sides:*** (RS of collar) Inc 1 st each side this row, then every 4 rows 3 times, working inc sts in Chevron patt as they become available— 85 {73} sts. *Est patt:* Work 2 sts in Gtr st, 81 {69} sts in St st, 2 sts in Gtr st (edge sts). Work 2 rows as est, end WS row. Change to Gtr st; work 3 rows, end RS row. BO all sts loosely.

◼ CHART A: CHEVRON

Multiple of 12 sts; 16-row rep

Beg Right Front Women's sizes S and L; Beg Back Child's size 6; st 12

End Left Front Child's size 6; Beg Right Front Child's size 6; st 11

Beg Sleeve Women's sizes S and M; Beg Back Child's size 4; st 10

Beg Back Child's size 8; st 9

End Left Front Women's sizes M and 1XL; st 8

End Left Front Child's size 4; Beg Right Front Child's size 4; st 7

Beg Right Front Women's sizes M and 1XL; st 6

End Back Child's size 8; st 5

Beg and end Back and Collar all Women's sizes; Beg Left Front, End Right Front all Women's sizes; Beg and end Sleeves Women's sizes L and 1XL; Beg and end Back Child's size 2; Beg Left Front all Child's sizes; End Right Front all Child's sizes; st 1

End Left Front Women's sizes S and L; End Back Child's size 6; st 2

End Left Front Child's sizes 2 and 8; Beg Right Front Child's sizes 2 and 8; st 3

End Sleeve Women's sizes S and M; End Back Child's size 4; st 4

☐ Knit on RS, purl on WS.
⊡ Purl on RS, knit on WS.

◼ CHART B: POLKA DOT

Multiple of 12 sts; 20-row rep

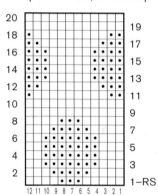

Beg Right Front Women's sizes S and L; Beg Back Child's size 6; st 12

End Left Front Child's size 6; Beg Right Front Child's size 6; st 11

Beg Sleeve Women's sizes S and M; Beg Back Child's size 4; st 10

Beg Back Child's size 8; st 9

End Left Front Women's sizes M and 1XL; st 8

End Left Front Child's size 4; Beg Right Front Child's size 4; st 7

Beg Right Front Women's sizes M and 1XL; st 6

End Back Child's size 8; st 5

Beg and end Back and Collar all Women's sizes; Beg Left Front and end Right Front all Women's sizes; Beg and end Sleeves Women's sizes L and 1XL; Beg and end Back Child's size 2; Beg Left Front all Child's sizes; End Right Front all Child's sizes; st 1

End Left Front Women's sizes S and L; End Back Child's size 6; st 2

End Left Front Child's sizes 2 and 8; Beg Right Front Child's sizes 2 and 8; st 3

End Sleeve Women's sizes S and M; End Back Child's size 4; st 4

WOOL-BAMBOO CABLED CARDIGAN

SIZES

Small (Medium, Large, 1X Large)

FINISHED MEASUREMENTS

37¼ (41½, 45, 49)", buttoned

MATERIALS

Classic Elite Yarns

Wool Bam Boo (50% wool, 50% bamboo; 50-g ball = approx 118 yd/108 m)

• 12 (12, 14, 15) balls 1660 Treasure

Equivalent yarn

Light worsted #3, 1416 (1416, 1652, 1770) yd

NEEDLES

• One pair size U.S. 6 (4 mm) or size to obtain gauge

• One crochet hook size U.S. E/4 (3.5 mm)

• One cable needle (cn)

Two large stitch holders

Stitch markers

Six ⅝" buttons

GAUGE

23 sts and 32 rows = 4" in Reverse Stockinette Stitch; 6 sts = approx 7/8" in Irregular Cable. Take time to save time, check your gauge.

SPECIAL TECHNIQUES

WRAP AND TURN

Bring yarn to front of work, sl 1p onto RH needle, bring yarn to back of work, sl same st back to LH needle, then turn work.

HIDE WRAPS

On knit row: Pick up wrap from front with RH needle and knit tog with st it wraps.

On purl row: Pick up wrap tbl with RH needle and purl tog with st it wraps.

PATTERN STITCHES

REVERSE STOCKINETTE STITCH (REV ST ST)

Purl on RS, knit on WS.

IRREGULAR CABLE (MULTIPLE OF 6 STS; 12-ROW REP)

See chart.

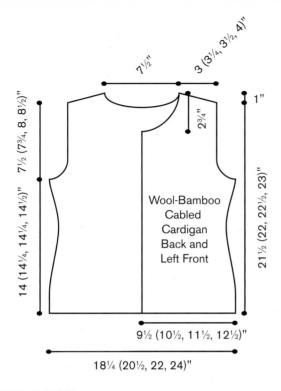

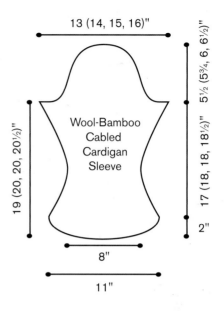

LEFT BACK

CO 57 (64, 69, 74) sts. *Est patt:* (RS) Work 5 sts in Rev St st, [6 sts Irregular Cable from chart, 10 sts Rev St st] 2 (3, 3, 3) times, 6 sts Irregular Cable from chart, 14 (5, 10, 15) sts Rev St st. Work even until piece meas 3" from beg, end WS row. Break yarn and place sts on holder.

RIGHT BACK

CO 57 (64, 69, 74) sts. Work as for left back, rev patt placement, until piece meas 3" from beg, end WS row. Do not break yarn.

BACK

Joining row: With RS facing, work as est across sts for right back; sl sts for left back to empty needle; work as est to end—114 (128, 138, 148) sts. Work 2 rows even, end RS row; and, **at the same time,** pms on last row as foll: Work 36 (43, 48, 53) sts, pm, *work 10 sts, pm, work 6 sts, pm; rep from * once, work 10 sts, pm, work to end. *Shape waist: Dec row:* (WS) Work to first marker, sl marker, *ssk, work to within 2 sts of next marker, k2tog, sl marker, work 6 sts, sl marker; rep from * once, ssk, work to within 2 sts of next marker, k2tog, sl marker, work to end—6 sts dec'd. Rep dec row every 6 rows 3 times, end WS row—90 (104, 114, 124) sts rem. Work 5 rows even, end RS row. *Dec row:* (WS) Work to first marker, *sl marker, ssk, sl marker, work 6 sts; rep from * once, sl marker, ssk, sl marker, work to end—87 (101, 111, 121) sts rem. Work even until piece meas 8½" from beg, end RS row. *Shape waist: Inc row:* (WS) Work to first marker, *sl marker, *m1, work to next marker, m1, sl marker, work 6 sts; rep from * once, sl marker,

m1, work to next marker, m1, sl marker, work to end—6 sts inc'd. Rep inc row every 10 rows 3 times, end WS row—111 (125, 135, 145) sts. Remove markers. Work even until piece meas 14 (14¼, 14½, 14½)" from beg, end WS row. *Shape armholes:* (RS) BO 3 (5, 5, 6) sts at beg of next 4 rows, then dec 1 st each side EOR 7 (9, 12, 13) times—85 (87, 91, 95) sts rem. Work even until armhole meas 7½ (7¾, 8, 8½)" from beg of shaping, end WS row. *Shape shoulders and neck:* (RS) BO 7 (7, 8, 9) sts at beg of next 4 (6, 4, 2) rows, then 6 (0, 7, 8) sts at beg of next 2 (0, 2, 4) rows; and, **at the same time,** on first row of shoulder shaping, work across to center 35 sts; join second ball of yarn and BO center sts, work to end. Working both sides at same time, at each neck edge BO 5 sts once.

LEFT FRONT

CO 61 (68, 73, 78) sts. *Est patt:* (RS) Work 14 (5, 10, 15) sts in Rev St st, [6 sts Irregular Cable from chart, 10 sts Rev St st] 2 (3, 3, 3) times, 6 sts Irregular Cable from chart, 9 sts Rev St st. Work even until piece meas 3" from beg, end RS row; and, **at the same time,** pm on last row as foll: Work 20 (27, 32, 37) sts, *pm, work 10 sts, pm, work 6 sts, pm, work 10 sts, pm, work to end. *Shape waist: Dec row:* (WS) Work to first marker, sl marker, ssk, work to within 2 sts of next marker, k2tog, sl marker, work 6 sts, sl marker, ssk, work to within 2 sts of next marker, k2tog, sl marker, work to end—4 sts dec'd. Rep dec row every 6 rows 3 times, end WS row—45 (52, 57, 62) sts rem. Work 5 rows even, end RS row. *Dec row:* (WS) Work to first marker, sl marker, ssk, sl marker, work 6 sts, sl marker, ssk, sl marker, work to end—43 (50, 55, 60) sts rem. Work

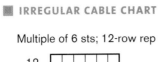
IRREGULAR CABLE CHART

Multiple of 6 sts; 12-row rep

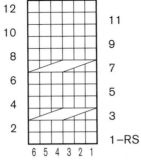

☐ Knit on RS,
   purl on WS.

⬜ Sl 3 sts to cn,
   hold in back;
   k3; k3 from cn.

even until piece meas 8½" from beg, end RS row. **Shape waist:** *Inc row:* (WS) Work to first marker, sl marker, m1, work 1 to next marker, m1, sl marker, work 6 sts, sl marker, m1, work to next marker, m1, sl marker, work to end—4 sts inc'd. Rep inc row every 10 rows 3 times, end WS row—59 (66, 71, 76) sts. Remove markers. Work even until piece meas 14 (14¼, 14½, 14½)" from beg, end WS row. **Shape armhole:** (RS) At armhole edge, BO 3 (5, 5, 6) sts twice, dec 1 st EOR 7 (9, 12, 13) times—46 (47, 49, 51) sts rem. Work even until armhole meas 5¾ (6, 6¼, 6¾)" from beg of shaping, end RS row. **Shape neck:** (WS) At neck edge, BO 6 sts once, 5 sts once, 4 sts once, 3 sts twice, then dec 1 st EOR 5 times; and, **at the same time,** when armhole meas same as back to shoulder shaping, end WS row. **Shape shoulder** as for back at beg of RS rows only. Pms for 6 buttons on left front, first 5½" from lower edge, last ½" from neck edge, rem 4 evenly spaced bet.

RIGHT FRONT

CO 61 (68, 73, 78) sts. Work as for left front, rev patt placement and all shaping by working armhole and shoulder shaping at beg of WS rows, and neck shaping at beg of RS rows; and, **at the same time,** work buttonholes opposite markers on left front as foll: (RS) Work 4 sts, [yo, p2tog] at each marker, work to end.

SLEEVES

CO 68 sts. *Est patt:* (RS) Work 15 sts in Rev St st, [6 sts Irregular Cable from chart, 10 sts Rev St st] twice, 6 sts Irregular Cable from chart, 15 sts Rev St st. Work 2 rows even, end WS row. **Shape lower sleeve:** as foll: *Row 1:* (RS) Work to last 2 sts, Wrap and Turn. *Row 2:* Work to last 2 sts, Wrap and Turn. *Row 3:* Work to last 3 sts, Wrap and Turn. *Row 4:* Work to last 3 sts, Wrap and Turn. *Row 5:* Work to last 4 sts, Wrap and Turn. *Row 6:* Work to last 4 sts, Wrap and Turn. Cont in this manner, working 1 less st before Wrap and Turn, until 8 sts at each side have been wrapped, end WS row. Work 2 rows even, hiding wraps, end WS row. Work 3 rows even, end RS row; and, **at the same time,** pms on last row as follows: Work 21 sts, pm, work 10 sts, pm, work 6 sts, pm, work 10 sts, pm, work to end. *Dec row:* (WS) Work to first marker, *sl marker, ssk, work to within 2 sts of next marker, k2tog, sl marker*, work 6 sts, sl marker, ssk, work to within 2 sts of next marker, k2tog, sl marker, work to end—4 sts dec'd. Rep dec row every 6 rows 3 times, end WS row, working dec sts as p2 tog—52 sts rem. **Shape sleeve:** (RS) Inc 1 st each side this row—54 sts. Work 4 rows even, end RS row. *Dec row:* (WS) Work to first marker, *sl marker, ssk, sl marker*, work 6 sts; rep from * to * once, work to end (2 sts dec'd)— 52 sts rem. Cont to shape sleeve each side every 6 rows 0 (0, 0, 9) times, every 8 rows 0 (0, 11, 5) times, every 10 rows 0 (4, 0, 0) times, every 12 rows 0 (4, 0, 0) times, every 16 rows 5 (0, 0, 0) times; and, **at the same time,** when 7 rows have been worked, inc bet markers as foll: (WS) Work to first marker, *sl marker, m1, work to next marker, m1, sl marker*, work 6 sts; rep from * to * once, work to end—4 sts inc'd bet markers. Rep inc row every 6 rows 3 times—16 sts inc'd bet markers. Remove markers. Cont to shape sleeve each side as est—78 (84, 90, 96) sts. Work even until piece meas 19 (20, 20, 20½)" from beg (meas down center of sleeve), end WS row. **Shape cap:** (RS) BO 3 (5, 5, 6) sts at beg of next 4 rows, then dec 1 st each side EOR 11 (8, 13, 13) times, every 4 rows 4 (6, 4, 5) times—36 sts rem. (RS) BO 5 sts at beg of next 4 rows—16 sts rem. BO rem sts.

FINISHING

Block pieces to measurements. Sew shoulder seams. Set in sleeves; sew side and sleeve seams. **Crochet edging:** With RS facing, using crochet hook and beg at lower right back seam, join yarn with a Sl st; ch 1 (does not count as st), work 1 rnd of sc evenly around bottom edge, front openings, neck edge, and back slit, working an even number of sts, end with Sl st to first sc. *Next rnd:* Ch 1 (does not count as st), sc in first sc, *ch 3, Sl st into same place as last sc, sc in next 2 sc; rep from * to last sc, end sc in last sc, Sl st to first sc. Fasten off. **Sleeve edging:** With RS facing, using crochet hook, beg at seam; join yarn with a Sl st and work crochet edging as for body. Sew on buttons.

LACE-PANEL VEST

SIZES
Extra Small (Small, Medium, Large)

FINISHED MEASUREMENTS
30¾, (34¾, 39, 43)"

MATERIALS
Classic Elite Yarns
Skye Tweed (100% wool; 50-g ball = approx 112 yd/103 m)
• 4 (4, 5, 5) balls 1232 Paisley Pink
Equivalent yarn
Worsted weight #4, 448 (448, 560, 560) yd
Needles
• One pair size U.S. 8 (5 mm) or size to obtain gauge
• One 16" circular size U.S. 6 (4 mm)
Two stitch holders
Stitch markers

GAUGE
16 sts and 24 rows = 4" in Stockinette Stitch; 15 sts and 24 rows = 4" in Back Lace Pattern; 17 sts = approx 3½" in Fish Scale Lace. Take time to save time, check your gauge.

PATTERN STITCHES

CIRCULAR 2 × 2 RIB (MULTIPLE FOR 4 STS)
Rnd 1 (RS): *K2, p2; rep from * across.
Rnd 2: Knit the knit sts and purl the purl sts as they face you.
Rep Rnd 2 for Circular 2 x 2 Rib.

4 × 4 RIB (MULTIPLE 8 STS + 2)
Note: Knit the first and last st throughout as edge sts.
Row 1: (RS) K1, p2 *k4, p4; rep from * across to last 7 sts, end k4, p2, k1.
Row 2: Maintaining first and last st as edge sts, knit the knit sts and purl the purl sts as they face you.
Rep Row 2 for 4 x 4 Rib.

BACK LACE PATTERN
(MULTIPLE OF 8 STS + 2; 2-ROW REP)
See Chart A. *Note:* While working shaping in Back Lace patt, to maintain accurate st count, do not work dec without compensating inc (yo).

FISH SCALE LACE (MULTIPLE OF 17 STS; 8-ROW REP)
See Chart B.

STOCKINETTE STITCH (ST ST)
Knit on RS, purl on WS.

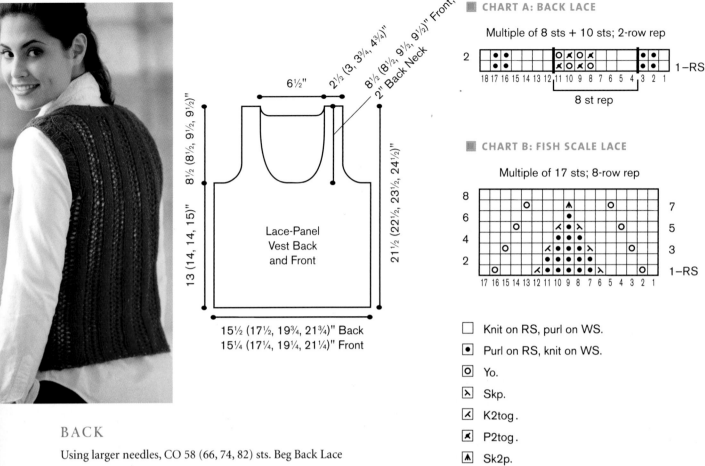

CHART A: BACK LACE

Multiple of 8 sts + 10 sts; 2-row rep

(chart grid)
Row labels: 2, 1–RS
Column numbers: 18 17 16 15 14 13 12 11 10 9 8 7 6 5 4 3 2 1
8 st rep

CHART B: FISH SCALE LACE

Multiple of 17 sts; 8-row rep

(chart grid)
Row labels: 8, 7, 6, 5, 4, 3, 2, 1–RS
Column numbers: 17 16 15 14 13 12 11 10 9 8 7 6 5 4 3 2 1

☐ Knit on RS, purl on WS.

• Purl on RS, knit on WS.

O Yo.

⟍ Skp.

⟋ K2tog.

⟋ P2tog.

⋀ Sk2p.

Schematic labels:
6½"
2½ (3, 3¾, 4¾)"
8½ (8½, 9½, 9½)" Front;
2" Back Neck
8½ (8½, 9½, 9½)"
13 (14, 14, 15)"
21½ (22½, 23½, 24½)"
Lace-Panel Vest Back and Front
15½ (17½, 19¾, 21¾)" Back
15¼ (17¼, 19¼, 21¼)" Front

BACK

Using larger needles, CO 58 (66, 74, 82) sts. Beg Back Lace patt; work even until piece meas 13 (14, 14, 15)" from beg, end WS row. **Shape armholes:** (RS) Cont in Back Lace patt as est, BO 4 (6, 6, 6) sts at beg of next 2 rows, 1 (1, 2, 2) sts at beg of next 2 rows. Dec 1 st each side every row twice, then EOR once—42 (46, 52, 60) sts rem. Work even until armhole meas 6½ (6½, 7½, 7½)" from beg of shaping, end WS row; pm each side of center 16 sts. **Shape neck:** (RS) Cont in Back Lace patt as est, work across to marker; join second ball of yarn and BO center sts, work to end—13 (15, 18, 22) sts rem each side. Working both sides at same time, at each neck edge, BO 2 sts once, then dec 1 st EOR twice—9 (11, 14, 18) sts rem each side for shoulder. Work even until armhole meas 8½ (8½, 9½, 9½)" from beg of shaping, end WS row. BO all sts.

FRONT

Using larger needles, CO 66 (74, 82, 90) sts. Beg 4 × 4 Rib, maintaining first and last st as edge sts; work even until piece meas 6 (7, 7, 7)" from beg, end WS row. **Est patt:** (RS) K1, k2tog, k22 (26, 30, 34) sts, pm; work Row 1 of Fish Scale Lace (see chart) across center 17 sts; pm, k24 (28, 32, 36) sts—65 (73, 81, 89) sts rem. Cont as est, maintaining edge sts, working sts each side of Fish Scale Lace in St st, until piece meas 13 (14, 14, 15)" from beg, end WS row. **Shape armholes**

and neck: (RS) BO 5 (6, 6, 6) sts at beg of next 2 rows for arm holes; and, **at the same time,** on first row of armhole shaping, knit across to marker, join second ball of yarn, BO center 17 sts for neck—19 (22, 26, 30) sts rem each side. Working both sides at same time, at each armhole edge BO 1 (1, 2, 2) sts once, then dec 1 st every row twice, EOR once; and **at same time,** at each neck edge, BO 2 sts EOR twice, then dec 1 st EOR 2 (3, 3, 3) times—9 (11, 14, 18) sts rem each side for shoulder. Work even until armhole meas 8½ (8½, 9½, 9½)" from beg of shaping, end WS row. BO all sts.

FINISHING

Block pieces to measurements. Sew shoulder and side seams. **Neckband:** With RS facing, using circular needle, beg at center of back neck, pick up and knit 112 (116, 120, 120) sts around the neck shaping; join, pm for beg of rnd. Beg Circular 2 × 2 Rib; work even until neckband meas 1" from pickup rnd. BO all sts in rib. **Armhole bands:** With RS facing, using circular needle, beg at underarm seam, pick up and knit 72 (76, 80, 80) sts around armhole; join, pm for beg of rnd. Beg Circular 2 × 2 Rib; work even until band meas ¾" from pickup rnd. BO all sts in rib.

DIAMOND YOKE PULLOVER

SIZES

Small (Medium, Large, 1X Large)

FINISHED MEASUREMENTS

38 (42, 46, 50)"

MATERIALS

Classic Elite Yarns

Wool Bam Boo (50% wool, 50% bamboo; 50-g ball = approx 18 yd/108 m)

• 10 (11, 11, 12) balls Main Color (MC)—1649 Blueberry

• 1 ball all sizes Color A—1660 Treasure

• 1 ball all sizes Color B—1681 Celery

• 1 ball all sizes Color C—1603 Flint

Equivalent yarn

Light worsted #3; MC: 1180 (1298, 1298, 1416) yd; Colors A, B, and C: 118 yd for all sizes

Needles

• One pair *each* size U.S. 4 (3.5 mm) and 6 (4 mm) or size to obtain gauge

• One 32" circular size U.S. 6 (4 mm) for yoke

• One 16" circular size U.S. 4 (3.5 mm) for neck finishing

Stitch holders

Stitch markers

GAUGE

20 sts and 29 rows = 4" in Stockinette Stitch, using larger needles. Take time to save time, check your gauge.

PATTERN STITCHES

4 × 4 RIB (MULTIPLE OF 8 STS)

Row 1 (RS): *K4, p4; rep from * across.

Row 2: Knit the knit sts and purl the purl sts as they face you.

Rep Row 2 for 4 x 4 Rib.

STOCKINETTE STITCH (ST ST)

Knit on RS, purl on WS.

CIRCULAR STOCKINETTE STITCH

Knit every rnd.

DIAMOND PATTERN (MULTIPLE OF 8 STS; 23-ROW)

See chart.

Multiple of 8 sts; 23-row rep

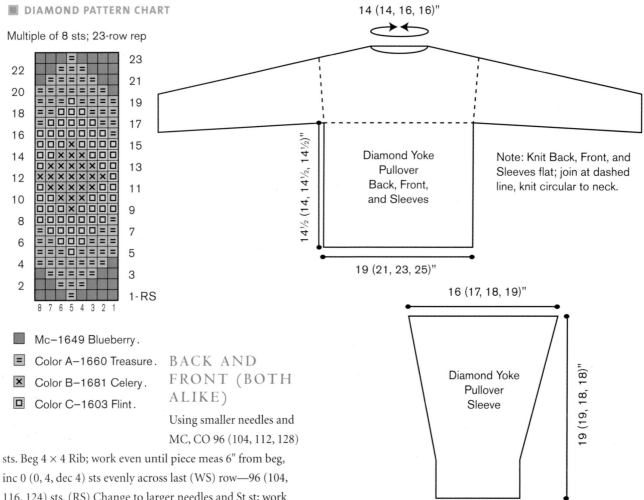

14 (14, 16, 16)"

Diamond Yoke Pullover
Back, Front,
and Sleeves

14½ (14, 14½, 14½)"

19 (21, 23, 25)"

Note: Knit Back, Front, and
Sleeves flat; join at dashed
line, knit circular to neck.

16 (17, 18, 19)"

Diamond Yoke
Pullover
Sleeve

19 (19, 18, 18)"

9 (9, 9½, 9½)"

Mc–1649 Blueberry.

Color A–1660 Treasure.

Color B–1681 Celery.

Color C–1603 Flint.

BACK AND FRONT (BOTH ALIKE)

Using smaller needles and MC, CO 96 (104, 112, 128) sts. Beg 4 × 4 Rib; work even until piece meas 6" from beg, inc 0 (0, 4, dec 4) sts evenly across last (WS) row—96 (104, 116, 124) sts. (RS) Change to larger needles and St st; work even until piece meas 14½ (14, 14½, 14½)" from beg, end WS row. **Shape underarm:** (RS) BO 5 sts at beg of next 2 rows—86 (94, 106, 114) sts rem; place rem sts on holder.

SLEEVES

Using smaller needles and MC, CO 48 (48, 56, 56) sts. Beg 4 × 4 Rib; work even until piece meas 4" from beg, end WS row. **Shape sleeve:** (RS) Beg this row, inc 1 st each side every 4 rows 0 (7, 8, 17) times, every 6 rows 16 (11, 9, 3) times and, **at the same time,** when piece meas 6" from beg, end WS row. Change to larger needles and St st; complete sleeve shaping—80 (84, 90, 96) sts. Work even until piece meas 19 (19, 18, 18)" from beg, end WS row. **Shape underarm:** (RS) BO 5 sts at beg of next 2 rows—70 (74, 80, 86) sts rem; place rem sts on holder.

YOKE

Joining rnd: Using larger circular needle and MC, knit across pieces in foll order: one sleeve (left), front, other sleeve (right), back; and, **at the same time,** dec 2 sts on each piece as foll: k2tog, knit across to last 2 sts, ssk, pm—8 sts total dec'd, 1 at beg and 1 at end of each piece (before and after markers)—

304 (328, 364, 392) sts rem. Join; pm for beg of rnd (bet back and left sleeve). **Shape armholes:** Cont in St st; dec 1 st each side of markers (in the same way as on joining rnd) EOR 12 times—208 (232, 268, 296) sts rem. *Setup rnd:* Cont with MC, work 1 rnd, dec 0 (0, 4, 0) sts evenly around—208 (232, 264, 296) sts rem. Beg Diamond Pattern (see chart): Changing colors as indicated, work Rows 1–23 of chart once. Change to MC only and **shape yoke:** *K2, k2tog; rep from * around—156 (174, 198, 222) sts. Work 1 rnd even. *Next rnd:* *K1, k2tog; rep from * around—104 (116, 132, 148) sts rem. Work 1 rnd even. *Next rnd:* *K2 (2, 1, 2), k2tog; rep from * around—78 (87, 88, 111) sts rem. Work 1 rnd even. **Shape neck:** Inc 2 (1, 0, 1) sts evenly around—80 (88, 88, 112) sts. Change to smaller needles and 4 × 4 Rib; work even until neck meas 6" from beg of rib. BO all sts loosely in rib.

FINISHING

Sew sleeve and side seams. Graft underarm sts tog. Block pieces to measurements.

ENTANGLED CABLE PULLOVER

SIZES
Small (Medium, Large, 1X Large)

FINISHED MEASUREMENTS
38 (42, 46, 50)"

MATERIALS
Classic Elite Yarn

Waterlily (100% extra fine merino; 50-g ball = approx 100 yd/91 m)

• 17 (18, 20, 21) balls 1972 Lily Pad

Equivalent yarn

Worsted weight #4; 1700 (1800, 2000, 2100) yd

Needles

• One pair *each* size U.S. 7 (4.5 mm) and 9 (5.5 mm) or size to obtain gauge

• One 16" circular size U.S. 7 (4.5 mm) for neck finishing

• One cable needle (cn)

Stitch holders

Stitch markers

Tapestry needle

GAUGE
18 sts and 24 rows = 4" in Reverse Stockinette Stitch, using larger needle. Take time to save time, check your gauge.
Note: Row gauge is important.

NOTE
Chart A is a panel of 37 sts that incs to 45 sts and then decs to 37 sts; all st counts given assume 37 sts for Chart A.

PATTERN STITCHES

REVERSE STOCKINETTE STITCH (REV ST ST)
Purl on RS, knit on WS.

BABY CABLE RIB (MULTIPLE OF 4 STS + 2)
Rows 1 and 3 (WS): K2 *p2, k2; rep from * across.

Row 2: P2, *k2tog, do not drop sts from LH needle, insert RH needle bet the 2 sts on LH needle and knit first st again, drop both sts from LH needle, p2; rep from * across.

Row 4: P2 *k2, p2; rep from * across.

Rep Rows 1–4 for Baby Cable Rib.

CABLES
See Charts A and B.

1 × 1 RIB (MULTIPLE OF 2 STS)
Row 1: *K1, p1; rep from * across.

Row 2: Knit the knit sts and purl the purl sts as they face you.

Rep Row 2 for 1 x 1 Rib.

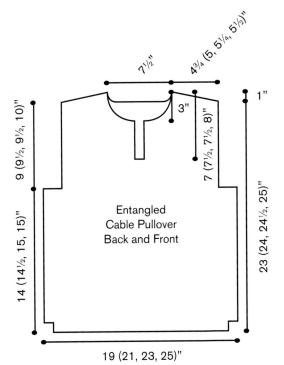

Entangled
Cable Pullover
Back and Front

7½" 4¾ (5, 5¼, 5½)"

3"

9 (9½, 9½, 10)"

7 (7½, 7 ½, 8)"

14 (14½, 15, 15)"

23 (24, 24½, 25)"

1"

19 (21, 23, 25)"

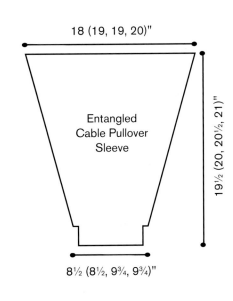

18 (19, 19, 20)"

Entangled
Cable Pullover
Sleeve

19½ (20, 20½, 21)"

8½ (8½, 9¾, 9¾)"

BACK

Using smaller needles, CO 90 (98, 106, 114) sts. Beg Baby Cable Rib; work even until piece meas 2" from beg, end Row 4. (WS) Work Row 1 of rib once more; and, **at the same time,** inc 10 sts evenly across, inc in knit stitches only and not in center 12 sts—100 (108, 116, 124) sts. Change to larger needles and *est patt:* (RS) Work 7 (11, 15, 19) sts in Rev St st, pm; beg Row 1 of charts, work Chart A across 37 sts, pm; work Chart B across 12 sts, pm; work Chart A across 37 sts, pm; work rem 7(11, 15, 19) sts in Rev St st. Work even as est until piece meas 14 (14½, 15, 15)" from beg, end WS row. *Shape armholes:* BO 6 (8, 10, 12) sts at the beg of next 2 rows— 88 (92, 96, 100) sts rem. Work even until armhole meas 9 (9½, 9½, 10)" from shaping, end (RS) Row 25 (1, 5, 9) of Chart A; pm each side of center 34 sts. *Shape shoulders* and discontinue inc and dec in Chart A: (WS): Cont as est, work across to marker; join second ball of yarn and BO center sts; work to end. Working both sides at same time, BO 9 (10, 10, 11) sts at beg of next 4 rows, 9 (9, 11, 11) sts at beg of next 2 rows.

FRONT

Work as for back until armhole meas 3" from beg of shaping, end WS row; pm each side of center 10 sts. *Shape front placket:* Cont in patt as est, work across to marker; join second ball of yarn and work center sts, place on holder for placket edging; work to end—39 (41, 43, 45) sts rem each side. Working both sides at same time, work even until armhole meas 7 (7½, 7 ½, 8)" from shaping, end WS row. *Note:* Do not turn cable closest to center neck on Row 17 after this point.

Shape neck: (RS) At each neck edge, BO 4 st once, then 2 sts once. Dec 1 st EOR 4 times. Work even until piece meas same as back to shoulder shaping, end WS row. *Shape shoulders* (RS) as for back.

SLEEVES

Using smaller needles, CO 42 (42, 46, 46) sts. Beg Baby Cable Rib; work even until piece meas 2 (2, 2½, 2½)" from beg, end Row 4. (WS) Work Row 1 of rib once more; and, **at the same time,** inc 15 (17, 15, 17) sts evenly across, inc in knit stitches only—57 (59, 61, 63) sts. Change to larger needles; work 10 (11, 12, 13) sts in Rev St st, pm; beg Row 1 of Chart A, work across 37 sts, pm; work to end in Rev St st. Work even as est for 3 rows. *Shape sleeve: Row 5:* (RS) Inc 1 st each side this row, then every 6 rows 17 (17, 18, 18) times, working inc sts in Rev St st— 91 (93, 97, 99) sts. Work even until piece meas 19½ (20, 20½, 21)" from beg, end WS row. (RS) BO all sts in patt.

RIGHT PLACKET EDGING

With WS facing, place sts from holder onto smaller needles. Beg 1 × 1 Rib; work even until piece, slightly stretched, meas same length as front neck slit; place sts on holder. Sew to right front neck slit.

LEFT PLACKET EDGING

With RS facing, using smaller needles, pick up and knit 10 sts behind Row 1 of right placket edging. Work as for right placket edging.

Panel of 37–45 sts; 28-row rep

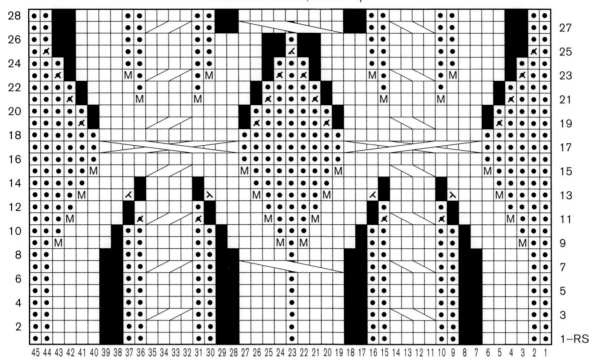

Knit on RS, purl on WS.

• Purl on RS, knit on WS.

M M1p.

⊼ P2tog.

⊼ P3tog.

⋋ Skp.

⊼ K2tog.

■ No st.

Sl 2 sts to cn, hold in back; k2; k2 from cn.

Sl 2 sts to cn, hold in front; k2; k2 from cn.

Sl 3 sts to cn, hold in front; k3; k3 from cn.

Sl 4 sts to cn, hold in front; (k4, p1) from LH needle; k4 from cn.

Sl 8 sts to cn, hold in back; k4 from LH needle, sl last 4 sts from cn to LH needle, knit these 4 sts, k4 from cn.

Sl 8 st to cn, hold in front; k4 from LH needle, sl last 4 sts from cn to LH needle, knit these 4 sts, k4 from cn.

FINISHING

Lightly block pieces, if necessary, being careful not to flatten texture. Sew shoulder seams. Set in sleeves; sew side and sleeve seams. **Collar:** With RS facing, using circular needle, work in 1 × 1 Rib as est across placket sts on holder; pick up and knit 79 sts around neck edge; work in 1 × 1 Rib as est across left placket sts on holder—99 sts. Beg 1 × 1 Rib on all sts; work even until collar meas 5½ (5½ , 6, 6)" from pickup row. BO all sts loosely in rib.

Multiple of 12 sts; 8-row rep

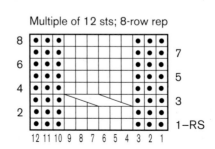

INTEGRATED SHRUG

SIZES

Small (Medium, Large, 1X Large)

FINISHED MEASUREMENTS

See schematic.

MATERIALS

Classic Elite Yarn

Waterlily (100% extra fine merino; 50-g ball = approx 100 yd/91 m)

• 13 (14, 16, 18) balls 1988 Goldfish

Equivalent yarn

Light worsted weight #3; 1300 (1400, 1600, 1800) yd

Needles

• One 29" circular size U.S. 7 (4.5 mm) or size to obtain gauge.

Split-ring stitch markers or waste yarn

GAUGE

29 sts and 24 rows = 4" in 1 x 1 Rib. Take time to save time, check your gauge.

NOTES

Shrug is worked in rows on circular needle to accommodate the large number of sts.

Shrug is worked in one piece; first and last 14 (15, 16, 17)" are worked in two sections, using a separate ball of yarn for each section, then joined into one piece. When setting up 1 x 1 Rib on first row, if first section ends with k1, beg second section with p1, so that pattern will be correct when sections are joined.

PATTERN STITCH

1 x 1 RIB (MULTIPLE OF 2 STS + 1)

Row 1: *K1, p1; rep from * across, end k1 if an odd number of sts.

Row 2: Knit the knit sts and purl the purl sts as they face you.

Rep Row 2 for 1 x 1 Rib.

SHRUG

Using first ball of yarn, CO 81 (81, 87, 88) sts. Using second ball of yarn, CO 50 (58, 58, 65) sts. Beg 1 × 1 Rib: Work both sections at the same time, using separate balls of yarn, until pieces meas 14 (15, 16, 17)" from beg. *Joining row:* Work across first section, pm; cont across rem section with same ball of yarn, break extra ball of yarn. Work even until piece meas 28 (30, 32, 34)" from joining row. *Dividing row:* Work across to marker; join second ball of yarn, work to end. *Note:* Sections are now divided as they were at the beg of piece. Work even until piece meas 14 (15, 16, 17)" from dividing row. BO all sts.

FINISHING

Sew tog foll assembly instructions in schematic.

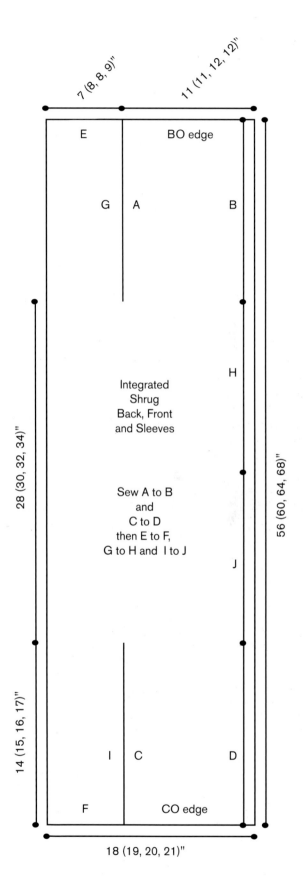

MEN'S KNITS

contents

ALPACA CABLE TURTLENECK

SIZES
Extra Small (Small, Medium, Large, 1X Large)

FINISHED MEASUREMENTS
37 (40, 44, 48, 52)"

MATERIALS
Classic Elite Yarn

Inca Alpaca (100% alpaca; 50-g hank = approx 109 yd/100 m)
• 16 (17, 18, 19, 20) hanks 1103 Amarino Grey

Equivalent yarn

Worsted weight #4, 1744 (1853, 1962, 2071, 2180) yd

Needles
• One pair *each* size U.S. 4 (3.5 mm) and 6 (4 mm)
  or size to obtain gauge
• One *each* 16" circular size U.S. 4 (3.5 mm) and 6 (4 mm)
• One cable needle (cn)

Stitch markers

GAUGE
20 sts and 26 rows = 4" in Reverse Stockinette Stitch, using larger needles; 74 sts = 8" in Cable Panel, using larger needles; 27 sts and 25 rows = 4" in 2 x 2 Rib, using larger needles. Take time to save time, check your gauge.

NOTES
Sl markers every row.

Work all incs and decs 1 st in from each edge.

While working shaping, if not enough sts rem to cont in cable, work in 2 x 2 Rib (knit the knit sts and purl the purl sts as they face you).

PATTERN STITCHES

2 × 2 RIB (MULTIPLE OF 4 STS + 2)
Row 1: (RS) K2, *p2, k2; rep from * across.

Row 2: Knit the knit sts and purl the purl sts as they face you.

Rep Row 2 for 2 x 2 Rib.

CIRCULAR 2 × 2 RIB (MULTIPLE OF 4 STS)
Rnd 1: *K2, p2; rep from * around.

Rnd 2: Knit the knit sts and purl the purl sts as they face you.

Rep Rnd 2 for Circular 2 x 2 Rib.

CABLE PANEL (MULTIPLE OF 48 STS + 26; 16-ROW REP)
See chart.

BACK
Using smaller needles, CO 170 (182, 194, 206, 218) sts. Beg 2 × 2 Rib; work even for 13 (15, 17, 17, 19) rows, end WS row. Change to larger needles. *Setup row:* (RS) Work 0 (6, 12, 18, 0) sts in 2 × 2 Rib as est, pm; beg Row 1 of Cable Panel (see chart), work 48-st rep 3 (3, 3, 3, 4) times, then 26 end sts of chart, pm; work rem 0 (6, 12, 18, 0) sts in 2 × 2 Rib as est. Work even until piece meas 15 (15¼, 15½, 15¾, 16)" from beg, end WS row. *Shape armholes:* (RS) BO 19 (22, 25, 28, 30) sts at beg of next 2 rows—132 (138, 144, 150, 158) sts rem. Work even until armhole meas 7½ (7¾, 8, 8¼, 8½)" from shaping, end WS row. *Shape neck and shoulders:* (RS) Work across 46 (49, 51, 54, 57) sts; join second ball of yarn and BO center 40 (40, 42, 42, 44) sts for neck, work to end. Cont as est, BO 5 sts each neck edge twice; and, **at the same time,** BO 12 (13, 14, 15, 16) sts each shoulder edge twice, then 12 (13, 13, 14, 15) sts once.

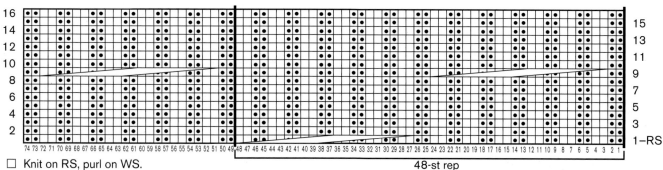

Multiple of 48 sts + 26; 16-row rep

48-st rep

☐ Knit on RS, purl on WS.

⊡ Purl on RS, knit on WS.

Sl 12 sts to cn, hold in back, k2, p2, k2, p2, k2; turn; p2, k2, p2, k2, p2; turn; k2, p2, k2, p2, k2; sl 2 p sts from cn to LH needle, purl these 2 sts; k2, p2, k2, p2, k2 from cn. (*Note:* 2 short rows are worked to minimize pull of large crossover.)

FRONT

Work as for back until armhole meas 5½ (5¾, 6, 6¼, 6½)" from shaping, end WS row—132 (138, 144, 150, 158) sts rem. ***Shape neck:*** (RS) Work across 50 (53, 55, 58, 61) sts, join second ball of yarn and BO center 32 (32, 34, 34, 36) sts for front neck, work to end. Working both sides at same time, BO 3 sts each neck edge twice, then 2 sts 4 times—36 (39, 41, 44, 47) sts rem each shoulder. When piece meas same as back to shoulder shaping, ***shape shoulders*** as for back.

SLEEVES

Using smaller needles, CO 74 (78, 82, 86, 90) sts. Beg 2 × 2 Rib; work even for 13 (15, 17, 17, 19) rows, end WS row. Change to larger needles. *Setup row:* (RS) Work 0 (2, 4, 6, 8) sts in 2 × 2 Rib as est, pm; beg Row 1 of Cable Panel (see chart), work 74 sts from chart, pm; work in 2 × 2 Rib as est to end. Cont as est, inc 1 st each side EOR 0 (0, 3, 0, 0) times, every 4 rows 23 (26, 22, 22, 24) times, then every 6 rows 2 (0, 0, 2, 0) times, working inc sts in 2 × 2 Rib—124 (130, 132, 134, 138) sts. Work even until piece meas 19½ (19¾, 20, 19½, 19)" from beg, end WS row. Pm for beg sleeve cap. Work even until piece meas 2 (2½, 3, 3½, 3¾)" from marker. BO all sts loosely in patt.

FINISHING

Block pieces lightly to measurements, being careful not to flatten texture. Join shoulder seams. ***Neckband:*** With RS facing, using smaller circular needle, beg at left shoulder, pick up and knit 104 (104, 108, 108, 112) sts evenly around neck shaping; pm for beg of rnd. Beg Circular 2 × 2 Rib; work even for 3". Change to larger circular needle; cont in rib as est for 4" more. BO all sts loosely in rib, using a larger needle,

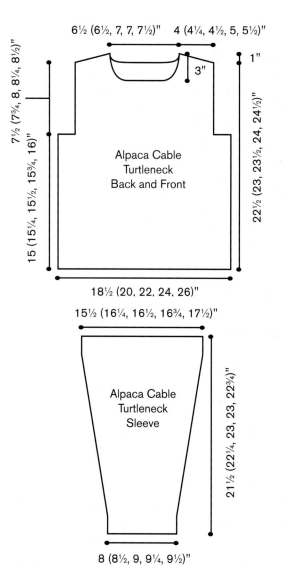

6½ (6½, 7, 7, 7½)"   4 (4¼, 4½, 5, 5½)"

1"

3"

7½ (7¾, 8, 8¼, 8½)"

Alpaca Cable Turtleneck Back and Front

22½ (23, 23½, 24, 24½)"

15 (15¼, 15½, 15¾, 16)"

18½ (20, 22, 24, 26)"

15½ (16¼, 16½, 16¾, 17½)"

Alpaca Cable Turtleneck Sleeve

21½ (22¼, 23, 23, 22¾)"

8 (8½, 9, 9¼, 9½)"

if necessary. Set in sleeves, matching marked points to beg of armhole shaping. Sew side and sleeve seams. Turn back neckband (as shown in photo).

STRIPED AND RIBBED UNISEX CREWNECK

SIZES

Small (Medium, Large, 1X Large)

FINISHED MEASUREMENTS

41½ (44, 49, 53½)"

MATERIALS

Classic Elite Yarns

Desert (100% wool; 50-g ball = approx 110 yd/101 m)

• 8 (9, 11, 12) balls 2058 Oasis

Equivalent yarn

Worsted weight #4; 880 (990, 1210, 1320) yd

Needles

• One pair size U.S. 7 (4.5 mm) or size to obtain gauge

• One 16" circular size U.S. 7 (4.5 mm)

Stitch holders

GAUGE

20 sts and 26 rows = 4" in Stockinette Stitch. Take time to save time check your gauge.

PATTERN STITCHES

4 × 2 RIB (MULTIPLE OF 6 STS + 2)

Row 1: (RS) *K4, p2; rep from * across to last 2 sts, end k2.

Row 2: Knit the purl sts and purl the knit sts as they face you.

Rep Row 2 for 4 x 2 Rib.

CIRCULAR 4 × 2 RIB (MULTIPLE OF 6 STS)

Rnd 1: (RS) *K4, p2; rep from * around.

Rnd 2: Knit the knit sts, and purl the purl sts as they face you.

Rep Rnd 2 for Circular 4 x 2 Rib.

BACK

CO 104 (110, 122, 134) sts. Beg 4 × 2 Rib; work even until piece meas 14 (15, 16, 17)" from beg, end WS row. ***Shape armholes:*** (RS) BO 9 (10, 12, 14) sts at beg of next 2 rows 86 (90, 98, 106) sts. Work even as est until armhole meas 8½ (9, 9½, 10)" from shaping, end WS row. BO all sts in rib.

FRONT

Work as for back until armhole meas 6½ (7, 7½, 8)" from shaping, end WS row. ***Shape neck:*** (RS) Work 30 (31, 34, 37) sts; place center 26 (28, 30, 32) sts on holder for neck; join second ball of yarn and work to end. Working both sides at same time, at each neck edge, dec 1 st EOR 5 times—25 (26, 29, 32) sts rem each shoulder. Work even until piece meas same as back to shoulder, end WS row. BO rem sts in rib.

SLEEVES

CO 44 (44, 50, 50) sts. Beg 4 × 2 Rib; work even for 3 rows, end WS row. ***Shape sleeve:*** (RS) Inc 1 st each side this row, then every 4 rows 21 (10, 4, 10) times, every 5 rows 0 (13, 19, 15) times—86 (90, 96, 100) sts. Work even until piece meas 19 (20, 21, 22)" from beg. BO all sts in rib.

FINISHING

Block pieces to measurements. Sew shoulder seams. Set in sleeves and sew sleeve and side seams. With RS facing, using circular needle, beg at left shoulder seam, pick up and knit 90 (90, 96, 96) sts evenly around neck edge. Beg Circular 4 × 2 Rib; work even for 1", end WS row. BO all sts loosely in rib.

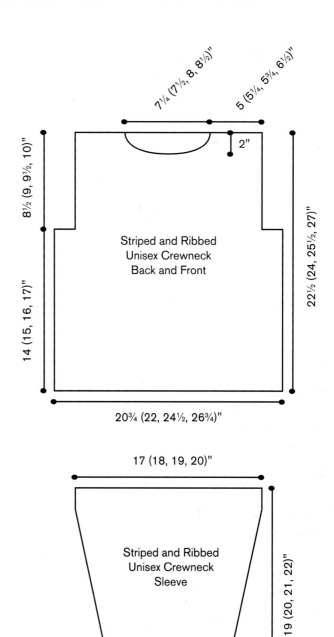

7¼ (7½, 8, 8½)"

5 (5¼, 5¾, 6½)"

2"

8½ (9, 9½, 10)"

22½ (24, 25½, 27)"

14 (15, 16, 17)"

Striped and Ribbed
Unisex Crewneck
Back and Front

20¾ (22, 24½, 26¾)"

17 (18, 19, 20)"

Striped and Ribbed
Unisex Crewneck
Sleeve

19 (20, 21, 22)"

8¾ (8¾, 10, 10)"

CABLE RIB V-NECK

SIZES
Small (Medium, Large, 1X Large)

FINISHED MEASUREMENTS
46 (49, 52, 55)"

MATERIALS
Classic Elite Yarns

Classic Silk (50% cotton, 30% silk, 20% nylon; 50-g ball = approx 135 yd/123 m)

• 12 (13, 15, 16) balls 6972 Moss

Equivalent yarn

Light worsted weight #3; 1620 (1755, 2025, 2160) yd

Needles

• One pair *each* size U.S. 5 (3.75 mm) and 7 (4.5 mm) or size to obtain gauge

• One cable needle (cn)

GAUGE
21 sts and 29 rows = 4" in 2 x 2 Rib, using larger needles; 10 sts = approx 1½" in Alternated Cable, using larger needles; 8 sts = approx 1⅜" in Right Twist or Left Twist, using larger needles. Take time to save time, check your gauge.

PATTERN STITCHES

2 × 2 RIB (MULTIPLE OF 4 STS + 2)
Row 1: (RS) *K2, p2; rep from * across, end k2.

Row 2: (WS) P2, *k2, p2; rep from * across.

Rep Rows 1–2 for 2 x 2 Rib.

RIGHT TWIST OR LEFT TWIST (MULTIPLE OF 8 STS)
Row 1: (RS) P2, k4, p2.

Row 2: (WS) K2, p4, k2.

Row 3: P2, C4B (for right twist) or C4F (for left twist), p2.

Row 4: K2, p4, k2.

Rep Rows 1–4 for Right Twist or Left Twist.

ALTERNATED CABLE (MULTIPLE OF 10 STS)
Row 1: (RS) P1, k8, p1.

Row 2: (WS) K1, p8, k1.

Row 3: P1, C4B, C4F, p1.

Row 4: K1, p2, k4, p2, k1.

Row 5: T3B, p4, T3F.

Rows 6, 8, and 10: P2, k6, p2.

Rows 7 and 9: K2, p6, k2.

Row 11: T3F, p4, T3B.

Row 12: K1, p2, k4, p2, k1.

Row 13: P1, C4F, C4B, p1.

Rows 14, 16, and 18: K1, p8, k1.

Rows 15 and 19: P1, C4B, C4F, p1.

Row 17: P1, k8, p1.

Row 20: K1, p8, k1.

Rep Rows 1–20 for Alternated Cable.

STOCKINETTE STITCH (ST ST)
Knit on RS, purl on WS.

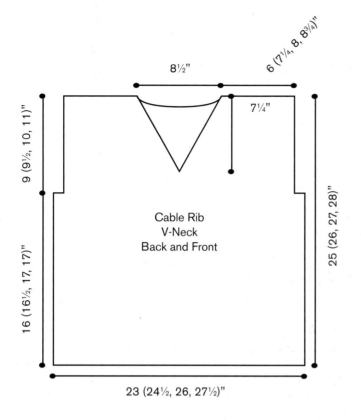

Cable Rib
V-Neck
Back and Front

8½"

6 (7¼, 8, 8¾)"

7¼"

9 (9½, 10, 11)"

16 (16½, 17, 17)"

25 (26, 27, 28)"

23 (24½, 26, 27½)"

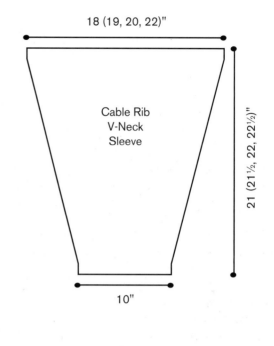

Cable Rib
V-Neck
Sleeve

18 (19, 20, 22)"

21 (21½, 22, 22½)"

10"

BACK

Using smaller needles, CO 134 (142, 150, 158) sts. *Est patt:* (RS) Work 18 (22, 26, 30) sts in 2 × 2 Rib, [8 sts Right Twist, 10 sts Alternated Cable, 8 sts Left Twist, 10 sts in 2 × 2 Rib] twice, 8 sts Right Twist, 10 sts Alternated Cable, 8 sts Left Twist, work 18 (22, 26, 30) sts in 2 × 2 Rib. Work as est until piece meas 1" from beg. Change to larger needles; work even until piece meas 16 (16½, 17, 17)" from beg, end WS row. *Shape armholes:* (RS) BO 7 sts at beg of next 2 rows— 120 (128, 136, 144) sts rem. Work even until armhole meas 8½, (9, 9½, 10½)" from beg of shaping, end WS row. *Shape neck:* (RS) Work 39 (43, 47, 51) sts, join second ball of yarn and BO center 42 sts, work to end. Working both sides at same time, at each neck edge BO 5 sts once—34 (38, 42, 46) sts rem each shoulder. Work even until armhole meas 9 (9½, 10, 11)" from beg of shaping, end WS row. BO all sts.

FRONT

Work as for back until armhole meas 1½, (2, 2½, 3½)" from beg of shaping, end WS row—120 (128, 136, 144) sts rem. *Shape V-neck:* (RS) Work 56 (60, 64, 68) sts, k2tog, k2; join second ball of yarn, k2, ssk, work to end. *Next row:* (WS) Work to last 3 sts on first side of neck, p3; on second side of neck, p3, work to end. Cont to dec as est EOR 25 times—34 (38, 42, 46)

sts rem each shoulder. Work even until armhole meas same as back to shoulders, end WS row. BO all sts.

SLEEVES

Using smaller needles, CO 54 sts. *Est patt:* (RS) Work 2 sts in St st, 8 sts Right Twist [6 sts in 2 × 2 Rib, 8 sts Right Twist] 3 times, work 2 sts in St st. Work as est until piece meas 1½" from beg, end WS row. Change to larger needles and *shape sleeve:* Inc 1 st each side this row, then every 4 rows 3 (10, 17, 30) times, every 6 rows 18 (14, 10, 2) times, working inc sts in 2 × 2 Rib—98 (104, 110, 120) sts. Work even until piece meas 21 (21½, 22, 22½)" from beg. BO all sts.

FINISHING

Block pieces to measurements. Sew right shoulder seam. *Neck edging:* With RS facing, using smaller needles, pick up and knit 133 sts evenly around neck edge; knit 1 row. BO all sts on next row purlwise. Sew left shoulder seam. Set in sleeves; sew sleeve and side seams.

WIDE-NECK STRIPED PULLOVERS

SIZES

Man's Small (Medium, Large, 1X Large) {Child's 4 (6, 8, 10)}

FINISHED MEASUREMENTS

44 (46½, 50, 53)" {26½ (30½, 33, 36)"}

Note: Men's directions are given first, and Child's directions appear in braces { }. If only one number is given, it applies to all sizes.

MATERIALS

Classic Elite Yarns

Renaissance (100% wool; 50-g hank = approx 110 yd/101 m)

- 7 (8, 8, 9) hanks Main Color (MC)—7110 Marine {3 (4, 5, 6) hanks MC—7157 Boticelli Blue}
- 2 hanks all sizes Color A—7147 September Sky {1 (1, 1, 2) hanks Color A—7115 Mountain Forest}
- 4 (4, 4, 5) hanks Color B—7173 Tuscan Field {2 (2, 2, 3) hanks Color B—7172 Green Pepper}

Equivalent yarn

Worsted weight #4, MC: 770 (880, 880, 990) {330 (440, 550, 660)} yd; Color A: 220 yd all sizes {110 (110, 110, 220) yd}; Color B: 440 (440, 440, 550) {220 (220, 220, 330) yd}

Needles

- One pair U.S. 7 (4.5 mm) or size needed to obtain gauge
- One pair U.S. 6 (4 mm) for neck finishing

Stitch holders

GAUGE

18 sts and 24 rows = 4" in Stockinette Stitch, using larger needles. Take time to save time, check your gauge.

PATTERN STITCHES

STOCKINETTE STITCH (ST ST)

Knit on RS, purl on WS.

FARROW RIB (MULTIPLE OF 3 STS)

Row 1: *K2, p1; rep from * to end.
Rep Row 1 for Farrow Rib.

STRIPE SEQUENCE

Rows 1–12: MC.
Row 13–14: Color A.
Row 15–20: Color B.
Rep Rows 1–20 for Stripe Sequence.

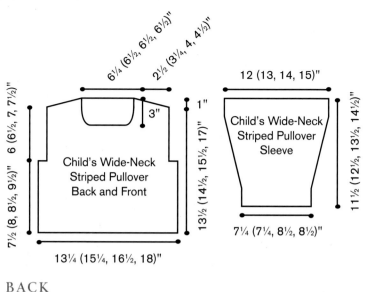

Child's Wide-Neck Striped Pullover Back and Front

6¼ (6½, 6½, 6½)"

2½ (3¼, 4, 4½)"

3"

1"

7½ (8, 8½, 9½)"

6 (6½, 7, 7½)"

13½ (14½, 15½, 17)"

13¼ (15¼, 16½, 18)"

Child's Wide-Neck Striped Pullover Sleeve

12 (13, 14, 15)"

11½ (12½, 13½, 14½)"

7¼ (7¼, 8½, 8½)"

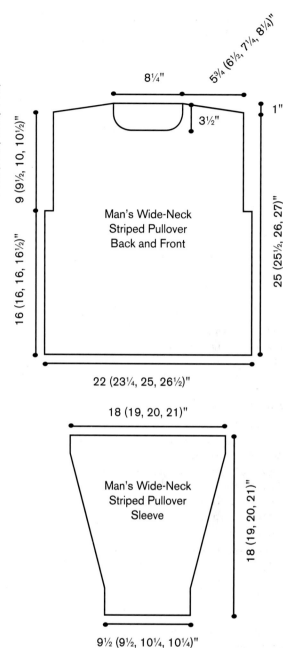

Man's Wide-Neck Striped Pullover Back and Front

8¼"

5¾ (6½, 7¼, 8¼)"

3½"

1"

9 (9½, 10, 10½)"

16 (16, 16, 16½)"

25 (25½, 26, 27)"

22 (23¼, 25, 26½)"

Man's Wide-Neck Striped Pullover Sleeve

18 (19, 20, 21)"

18 (19, 20, 21)"

9½ (9½, 10¼, 10¼)"

BACK

Using MC, CO 99 (105, 113, 121) {60 (69, 75, 81)} sts; work 12 rows in Farrow Rib and Stripe Sequence, end WS row. Change to St st and cont Stripe Sequence; work even until piece meas 16 (16, 16, 16½)" {7½ (8, 8½, 9½)"} from beg, end WS row. **Shape armholes:** (RS) BO 5 {4 (5, 5, 5)} sts at beg of next 2 rows—89 (95, 103, 111) {52 (59, 65, 71)} sts rem. Work even until armhole meas 9 (9½, 10, 10½)" {6 (6½, 7, 7½)"} from beg, end WS row. **Shape shoulders and neck:** (RS) BO 9 (10, 11, 12) {4 (5, 6, 7)} sts at the beg of next 4 (4, 6, 4) {6} rows, 8 (9, 0, 13) {0} sts at beg of next 2 rows—37 {28 (29, 29, 29)} sts rem. Place rem sts on holder.

FRONT

Work as for back until armhole meas 6½ (7, 7½ , 8)" {4 (4½, 5, 5½)"} from shaping, end WS row—89 (95, 103, 111) {52 (59, 65, 71)} sts rem. **Shape neck:** (RS) Work 34 (37, 41, 45) {18 (21, 24, 27)} sts, join second ball of yarn, work center 21 {16 (17, 17, 17)} sts and place on holder, work to end. Working both sides at same time, at each neck edge, BO 3 {2} sts once, 2 {0} sts once, then dec 1 st EOR 3 {4} times—26 (29, 33, 37) {12 (15, 18, 21)} sts rem each shoulder. Work even until piece meas same as back to shoulders. **Shape shoulders** as for back.

SLEEVES

Using MC, CO 42 (42, 46, 46) {33 (33, 39, 39)} sts; work 12 rows in Farrow Rib and Stripe Sequence, end WS row {inc 1 (0, 0, 0) sts on last WS row}—42 (42, 46, 46) {34 (33, 39, 39)} sts. Change to St st and cont Stripe Sequence; work even until piece meas 2½" from beg, end WS row. **Shape sleeve:** (RS) Inc 1 st each side this row, then every 4 rows 16 (20, 14, 17) {4 (10, 4, 7)} times, every 6 rows 3 (1, 7, 6) {5 (2, 7, 6)} times—82 (86, 90, 94) {54 (59, 63, 67)} sts. Work even until piece meas 18 (19, 20, 21)" {11½ (12½, 13½, 14½)"} from beg. BO all sts.

FINISHING

Block pieces to measurements. Sew left shoulder seam. **Neckband:** With RS facing, using smaller needles and MC, work 37 {28 (29, 29, 29)} sts from holder for back neck, pick up and knit 16 {11} sts along left neck edge, work 21 {16 (17, 17, 17)} sts from holder for front neck, pick up and knit 16 {11} sts along right neck edge—90 {66 (68, 68, 68)} sts. Purl 1 row, {inc 0 (1, 1, 1) sts in center back of band}—90 {66 (69, 69, 69)} sts. Work in Farrow Rib until band meas 1" from pickup row. BO all sts loosely in patt. Sew up neck seam. Sew right shoulder seam. Set in sleeves; sew sleeve and side seams.

DIAMOND TEXTURED PULLOVER

SIZES
Small (Medium, Large, 1X Large)

FINISHED MEASUREMENTS
43 (46, 49, 53)"

MATERIALS
Classic Elite Yarns
Provence (100% mercerized Egyptian cotton, 100-g hank = approx 205 yd/187 m)
• 8 (9, 9, 10) hanks 2647 Delft Blue
Equivalent yarn
Light worsted weight #3, 1640 (1845, 1845, 2050) yd
Needles
• One pair size U.S. 6 (4 mm) or size to obtain gauge
• One 16" circular size U.S. 5 (3.75 mm) for neck finishing
Stitch marker

GAUGE
22 sts and 28 rows = 4" in Diamond Rib Pattern, using larger needles. Take time to save time, check your gauge.

PATTERN STITCHES

DIAMOND RIB PATTERN
(MULTIPLE OF 18 STS + 1; 24-ROW REP)
See chart.

CIRCULAR 1 × 1 RIB (MULTIPLE OF 2 STS)
Rnd 1: *K1, p1; rep from * around.
Rep Rnd 1 for Circular 1 × 1 Rib.

BACK
CO 119 (127, 135, 145) sts; work Rows 1 and 2 in Diamond Rib Pattern (see chart) 3 times, beg and end where indicated for your size. *Next row:* (RS) Cont from chart, beg with Row 1 and work Diamond Rib Pattern; work even until piece meas 15 (15½, 16, 16½)" from beg, end WS row. *Shape armholes:* BO 10 (10, 10, 11) sts at beg of next 2 rows—99 (107, 115, 123)

sts rem. Work even until armhole meas 9 (9½, 10, 10½)" from shaping, end WS row. PM each side of center 33 (35, 37, 39) sts. *Shape shoulders and neck:* (RS) BO 9 (10, 11, 12) sts at beg of next 6 rows; and, **at the same time,** on first row of shoulder shaping, work across to marker, join second ball of yarn, BO center sts, work to end. Working both sides at same time, at each neck edge, BO 3 sts twice.

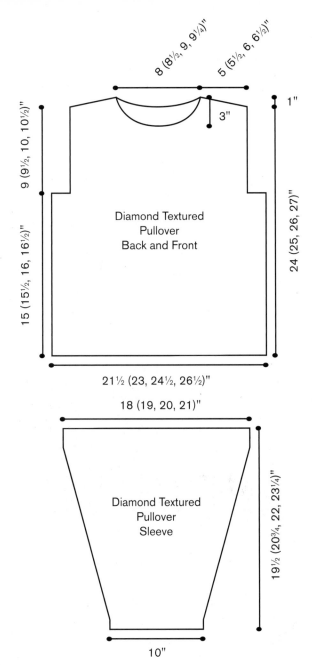

Diamond Textured
Pullover
Back and Front

8 (8½, 9, 9¼)"

5 (5½, 6, 6½)"

1"

3"

9 (9½, 10, 10½)"

15 (15½, 16, 16½)"

24 (25, 26, 27)"

21½ (23, 24½, 26½)"

18 (19, 20, 21)"

Diamond Textured
Pullover
Sleeve

19½ (20¾, 22, 23¼)"

10"

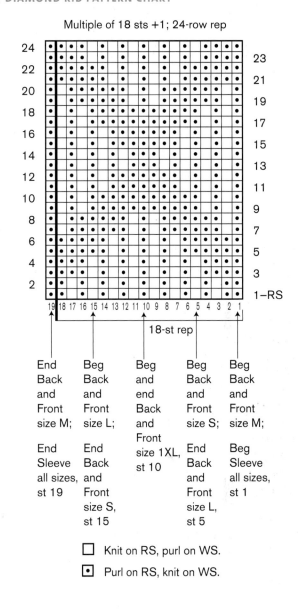

Multiple of 18 sts +1; 24-row rep

18-st rep

End Back and Front size M; End Sleeve all sizes, st 19

Beg Back and Front size L; End Back and Front size S, st 15

Beg and end Back and Front size 1XL, st 10

Beg Back and Front size S; End Back and Front size L, st 5

Beg Back and Front size M; Beg Sleeve all sizes, st 1

☐ Knit on RS, purl on WS.

⊡ Purl on RS, knit on WS.

FRONT

Work as for back until armhole meas 7 (7½, 8, 8½)" from beg of shaping, end WS row—99 (107, 115, 123) sts. *Shape neck:* (RS) Work 42 (45, 49, 52) sts, join second ball of yarn and BO center 15 (17, 17, 19) sts, work to end. Working both sides at same time, at each neck edge BO 4 sts once, 3 sts twice, then dec 1 st EOR 5 (5, 6, 6) times; and, **at the same time,** when piece meas same as back to shoulders, *shape shoulders* as for back.

SLEEVES

CO 55 sts; work Rows 1 and 2 from Diamond Rib Pattern (see chart) 3 times, beg and end where indicated for your size. *Next row:* (RS) Cont from chart, beg with Row 1 and work

Diamond Rib Pattern; work even until piece meas 2½" from beg, end WS row. *Shape sleeve:* Inc 1 st each side this row, then every 4 rows 10 (16, 17, 24) times, every 6 rows 11 (8, 9, 5) times, working inc sts in Diamond Rib Pattern—99 (105, 109, 115) sts. Work even until piece meas 19½ (20¾, 22, 23¼)" from beg. BO all sts.

FINISHING

Block pieces to measurements. Sew shoulder seams. Set in sleeves; sew sleeve and side seams. *Neckband:* With RS facing, using circular needle, pick up and knit 106 (110, 112, 116) sts evenly around neck edge, pm for beg of rnd. Work in Circular 1 × 1 Rib until band meas 1" from pickup row. BO all sts loosely in patt.

TRAVELING RIB PULLOVER

SIZES

Small (Medium, Large, 1X Large, 2X Large)

FINISHED MEASUREMENTS

41 (43, 46, 49, 51)"

MATERIALS

Classic Elite Yarns

Inca Alpaca (100% alpaca, 50-g hank = approx 109 yd/100 m)

• 16 (17, 18, 19, 21) hanks 1155 Harvest Bounty

Equivalent yarns

Light worsted weight #3 or worsted weight #4; 1744 (1853, 1962, 2071, 2289) yd

Needles

• One pair size U.S. 6 (4 mm) or size to obtain gauge

• One cable needle (cn)

GAUGE

24 sts and 30 rows = 4" in Traveling Garter Rib. Take time to save time, check your gauge.

PATTERN STITCHES

**TRAVELING GARTER RIB
(MULTIPLE OF 24 STS; 20-ROW REP)**

See chart.

K2, P2 RIB (MULTIPLE OF 4 STS)

Row 1: K2, p2; rep from * to end.

Row 2: Knit the knit sts and purl the purl sts as they face you,

Rep Rows 1–2 for K2, P2 Rib.

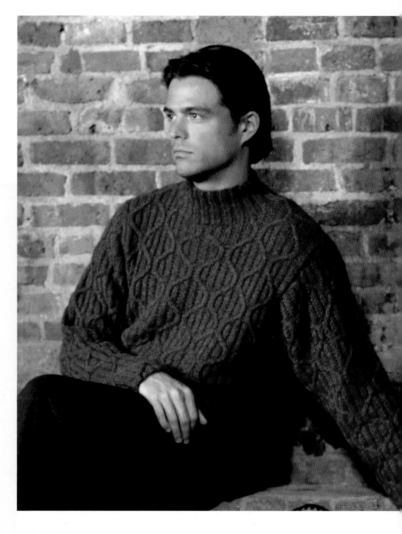

BACK

CO 122 (130, 138, 146, 154) sts; work Traveling Garter Rib (see chart), beg and end where indicated for your size; work even until piece meas 15" from beg, end WS row. *Shape armholes:* (RS) BO 12 (16, 16, 20, 20) sts at beg of next 2 rows—98 (98, 106, 106, 114) sts rem. Work even until piece meas 23½ (24, 24½, 25, 25½)" from beg, end WS row. *Shape shoulders:* (RS) BO 9 (9, 10, 10, 11) sts at beg of next 4 (4, 6, 6, 6) rows, 10 (10, 0, 0, 0) sts at beg of next 2 rows—42 (42, 46, 46, 48) sts rem. BO rem sts.

FRONT

Work as for back until piece meas 21½ (22, 22½, 23, 23½)" from beg, end WS row. *Shape neck:* (RS) Work 40 (40, 42, 42, 45) sts; join second ball of yarn, BO center 18 (18, 22, 22, 24) sts, work to end. Working both sides at same time, at each neck edge, BO 3 sts once, 2 sts twice, then dec 1 st every row 5 times—28 (28, 30, 30, 33) sts rem each shoulder. Work even until piece meas same as back to shoulders; *shape shoulders* as for back.

Multiple of 24 sts; 20-row rep

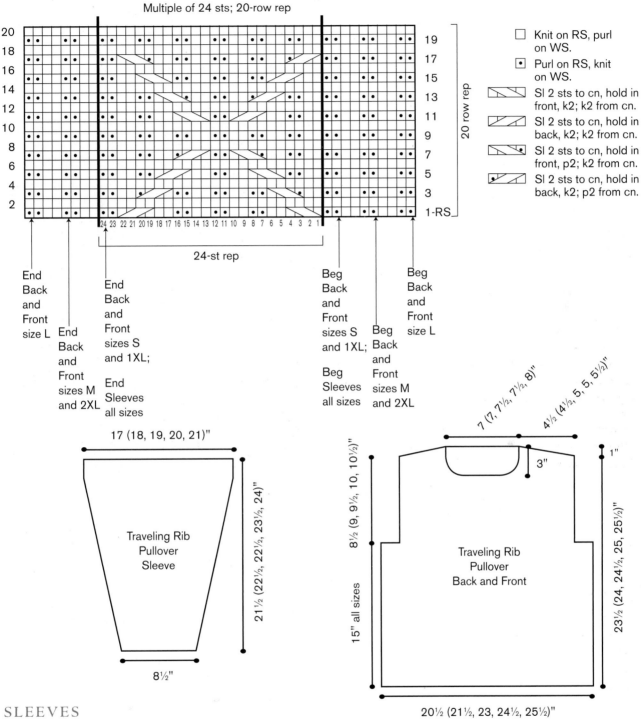

	Knit on RS, purl on WS.
	Purl on RS, knit on WS.
	Sl 2 sts to cn, hold in front, k2; k2 from cn.
	Sl 2 sts to cn, hold in back, k2; k2 from cn.
	Sl 2 sts to cn, hold in front, p2; k2 from cn.
	Sl 2 sts to cn, hold in back, k2; p2 from cn.

24-st rep

End Back and Front size L

End Back and Front sizes M and 2XL

End Back and Front sizes S and 1XL; End Sleeves all sizes

Beg Back and Front sizes S and 1XL; Beg Sleeves all sizes

Beg Back and Front sizes M and 2XL

Beg Back and Front size L

17 (18, 19, 20, 21)"

Traveling Rib Pullover Sleeve

21½ (22½, 22½, 23½, 24)"

8½"

7 (7, 7½, 7½, 8)"

4½ (4½, 5, 5, 5½)"

8½ (9, 9½, 10, 10½)"

3"

1"

Traveling Rib Pullover Back and Front

15" all sizes

23½ (24, 24½, 25, 25½)"

20½ (21½, 23, 24½, 25½)"

SLEEVES

CO 50 sts; work Traveling Garter Rib (see chart), beg and end where indicated for your size. Work even until piece meas 1" from beg, end WS row. *Shape sleeve:* Inc 1 st each side this row, then EOR 0 (0, 0, 0, 3) times, every 4 rows 8 (15, 24, 33, 34) times, every 6 rows 17 (13, 7, 1, 0) times, working inc sts in Traveling Garter Rib as they become available—102 (108, 114, 120, 126) sts. Work even until piece meas 21½ (22½, 22½, 23½, 24)" from beg. BO all sts.

FINISHING

Block pieces to measurements. Sew left shoulder seam. *Neckband:* With RS facing, pick up and knit 96 (96, 104, 104, 108) sts evenly around neck edge; work in 2x2 Rib until band meas 3½" from pickup row. BO all sts loosely in patt. Sew right shoulder seam, including neckband. Set in sleeves; sew sleeve and side seams.

TRIANGLE PATTERN V-NECK

SIZES
Small (Medium, Large, 1X Large)

FINISHED MEASUREMENTS
44 (47, 51, 54)"

MATERIALS
Classic Elite Yarns

Provence (100% mercerized Egyptian cotton, 100-g hank = approx 205 yd/187 m)

• 9 (10, 11, 12) hanks 2682 Asparagus

Equivalent yarn

Light worsted weight #3, 1845 (2050, 2255, 2460) yd

Needles

• One pair *each* size U.S. 5 (3.75 mm) and 6 (4 mm) or size to obtain gauge

• One cable needle (cn)

GAUGE
24 sts and 30 rows = 4" in Textured Pattern, using larger needles. Take time to save time, check your gauge.

PATTERN STITCHES

2 × 3 RIB (MULTIPLE OF 5 STS + 2)
Row 1: (RS) *K2, p3; rep from * across to last 2 sts, k2.

Row 2: Knit the knit sts and purl the purl sts as they face you.

Repeat Row 2 for 2 x 3 Rib.

TEXTURED PATTERN (MULTIPLE OF 10 STS; 10-ROW REP)
See chart.

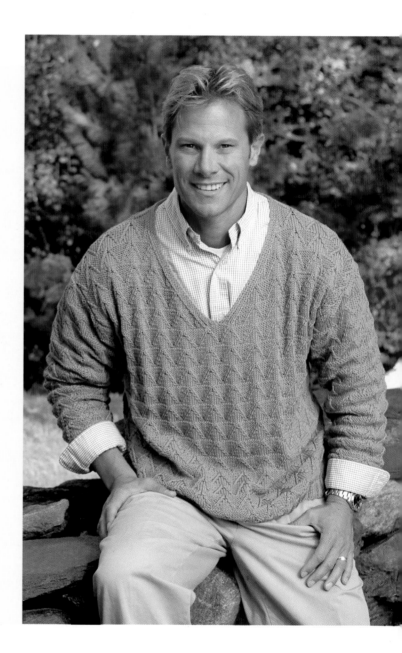

BACK

With smaller needles, CO 132 (142, 152, 162) sts; work 2 × 3 Rib until piece meas 1½" from beg, end WS row. Change to larger needles and Textured Pattern (see chart), beg and end where indicated for your size. Work as est until piece meas 15" from beg, end WS row. **Shape armholes:** (RS) BO 10 sts at beg of next 2 rows—112 (122, 132, 142) sts rem. Work even until armhole meas 8½ (9, 9½, 10)" from beg of shaping, end WS row. **Shape neck:** (RS) Work 28 (33, 38, 43) sts, join second ball of yarn, BO center 56 sts, work to end. Working both sides at the same time, work even until armhole meas 9 (9½, 10, 10½)" from beg of shaping, end WS row. **Shape shoulders:** (RS) BO 7 (8, 10, 11) sts at beg of next 6 rows, then 7 (9, 8, 10) sts at beg of next 2 rows.

Multiple of 10 sts; 10-row rep

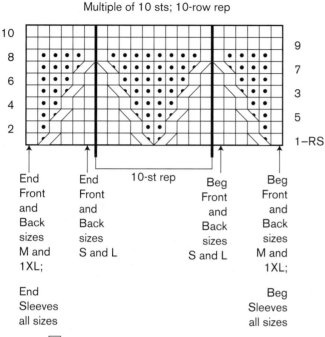

End
Front
and
Back
sizes
M and
1XL;

End
Sleeves
all sizes

End
Front
and
Back
sizes
S and L

10-st rep

Beg
Front
and
Back
sizes
S and L

Beg
Front
and
Back
sizes
M and
1XL;

Beg
Sleeves
all sizes

☐　Knit on RS, purl on WS.

▣　Purl on RS, knit on WS.

▨　Sl 1 st to cn, hold in front; p1, k1 from cn.

▨　Sl 1 st to cn, hold in back; k1, p1 from cn.

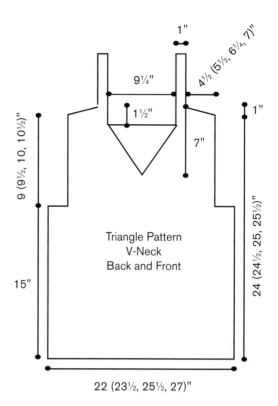

Triangle Pattern
V-Neck
Back and Front

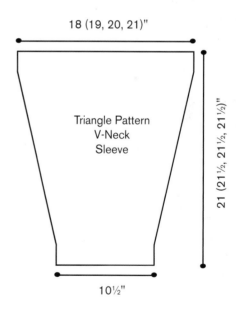

Triangle Pattern
V-Neck
Sleeve

FRONT

Work as for back until armhole meas approx 3 (3½, 4, 4½)"
from beg, end Row 10 of Textured Pattern. **Shape neck:** (RS)
Cont in Textured Pattern as est, for left side of neck, work
49 (54, 59, 64) sts, k2tog, [p1, k1] twice, p1; for right side of
neck, join second ball of yarn, [p1, k1] twice, p1, ssk, work
to end. Working both sides at same time, work 1 row even in
Textured Pattern as est, and k1, p1 rib over 6 sts at each neck
edge. *Dec row:* (RS) For left side of neck, work as est to last
7 sts, k2tog, [p1, k1] twice, p1; for right side of neck, [p1, k1]
twice, p1, ssk, work as est to end. Work dec row EOR 20 times,
then every 4 rows once—34 (39, 44, 49) sts rem each shoulder.
Work even until armhole meas same as back to shoulder
shaping. **Shape shoulders** as for back—6 sts rem each side.
Neckband: Cont as est on these 6 sts until bands meet at center
back when slightly stretched. BO rem sts.

SLEEVES

Using smaller needles, CO 62 sts. Work 2 × 3 Rib until piece
meas 2" from beg, end WS row. Change to larger needles,
Textured Pattern (see chart), beg and end where indicated for

your size, and **shape sleeve:** (RS) Inc 1 st each side this
row, then every 4 rows 4 (11, 20, 29) times, then every 6 rows
18 (14, 8, 2) times, working inc sts in Textured Pattern as they
become available—108 (114, 120, 126) sts. Work even until
piece meas 21 (21½, 21½, 21½)" from beg. BO all sts.

FINISHING

Block pieces to measurements. Sew shoulder seams. Sew side
edges of neckbands to back neck edge; sew bands tog at center
back. Set in sleeves; sew sleeve and side seams.

PRINT PULLOVER

SIZES
Small (Medium, Large, 1X Large)

FINISHED MEASUREMENTS
40 (43, 46, 49)"

MATERIALS
Classic Elite Yarns
Inca Print (100% alpaca; 50-g hank = approx 109 yd/100 m)
• 12 (13, 13, 14) hanks 4678 Peat Moss
Equivalent yarns
Worsted weight #4; 1308 (1417, 1417, 1526) yd
Needles
• One pair size U.S. 6 (4 mm) or size to obtain gauge
• One 16" circular size U.S. 6 (4 mm)
Stitch markers

GAUGE
20 sts and 30 rows = 4" in Garter Ridge Pattern. Take time to save time, check your gauge.

PATTERN STITCHES

STOCKINETTE STITCH (ST ST)
Knit on RS, purl on WS.

REVERSE STOCKINETTE STITCH (REV ST ST)
Purl on RS, knit on WS.

1 × 1 RIB (MULTIPLE OF 2 STS + 1)
Row 1: K1, *p1, k1; rep from * across.
Row 2: Knit the knit sts, and purl the purl sts as they face you.
Rep Row 2 for 1 x 1 Rib.

CIRCULAR 1 × 1 RIB (MULTIPLE OF 2 STS)
Rnd 1: *P1, k1; rep from * around.
Rnd 2: Purl the purl sts, knit the knit sts as they face you.
Rep Rnd 2 for Circular 1 x 1 Rib.

GARTER RIDGE PATTERN (ANY NUMBER OF STS)
Rows 1–4: Work in St st.
Row 5: Work in Rev St st.
Rep Rows 1–5 for Garter Ridge Pattern.

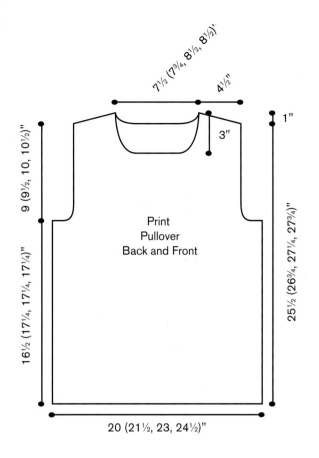

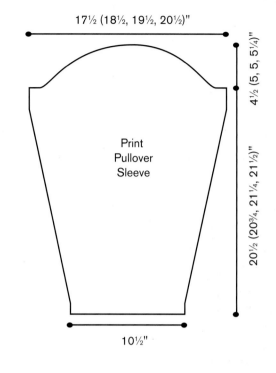

BACK

CO 101 (107, 115, 123) sts. Beg 1 × 1 Rib; work even until piece meas 1" from beg, end WS row. Change to Garter Ridge Pattern; work even until piece meas 16½ (17¼, 17¼, 17¼)" from beg, end WS row. **Shape armholes:** (RS) BO 7 sts at beg of next 2 rows—87 (93, 101, 109) sts rem. Dec 1 st each side every row 3 (5, 7, 11) times—81 (83, 87, 87) sts rem. Work even until armhole meas 9 (9½, 10, 10½)" from beg of shaping, end RS row; pm each side of center 23 (25, 29, 29) sts. **Shape neck:** (WS) Work across to marker; join second ball of yarn and BO center sts, work to end—29 sts rem each shoulder. **Shape shoulders and neck:** At armhole edge, BO 8 sts at beg of next 2 rows, then 7 sts at beg of next 4 rows; and, **at the same time,** on first row of shoulder shaping, at each neck edge, BO 3 sts once, 2 sts twice.

FRONT

Work as for back until armhole meas 7 (7½, 8, 8½)" from beg of shaping, end WS row; pm each side of center 23 (25, 29, 29) sts. **Shape neck:** (WS) Work across to marker; join second ball of yarn and BO center sts, work to end—29 sts rem each side. At each neck edge, BO 3 sts once, 2 sts twice—22 sts rem each shoulder. Work even until piece meas same as back to shoulder shaping. **Shape shoulders** as for back.

SLEEVES

CO 53 sts. Beg 1 × 1 Rib; work even until piece meas 1" from beg, end WS row. Change to Garter Ridge Pattern; work even for 6 (6, 6, 4) rows, end WS row. **Shape sleeve:** (RS) Inc 1 st each side this row and then every 6 (6, 6, 4) rows 2 (9, 19, 1) times, then every 8 (8, 8, 6) rows 15 (10, 3, 23) times—89 (93, 99, 103) sts, end WS row. **Shape cap:** (RS) BO 7 sts at the beg of next 2 rows—75 (79, 85, 89) sts rem. Dec 1 st each side every row 26 (26, 32, 34) times, then EOR 1 (3, 0, 0) times— 21 sts rem. BO 4 sts at the beg of next 2 rows—13 sts rem. BO rem sts.

FINISHING

Block pieces to measurements, being careful not to flatten texture. Sew shoulder seams. Set in sleeves; sew side and sleeve seams. **Neckband:** With RS facing, and circular needle, pick up and knit 104 (108, 116, 116) sts evenly around neck; pm for beg of rnd. Beg Circular 1 × 1 Rib; work even until band meas 1" from pickup row. BO all sts loosely in rib.

CRISS-CROSS PULLOVER

SIZES

Extra Small (Small, Medium, Large, 1X Large, 2X Large)

FINISHED MEASUREMENTS

38½ (41, 43, 48, 53, 56½)"

MATERIALS

Classic Elite Yarns

Wings (55% alpaca, 23% silk, 22% wool, hollow core, 50-g hank = approx 109 yd/100 m)

• 16 (17, 18, 18, 19, 20) hanks 2346 Larkspur

Equivalent yarns

Worsted weight #4, 1744 (1853, 1962, 1962, 2071, 2180) yd

Needles

• One pair size U.S. 7 (4.5 mm) or size to obtain gauge

• One 16" circular size U.S. 6 (4 mm) for neck finishing

• One cable needle (cn)

Stitch marker

GAUGE

26 sts and 30 rows = 4" in Criss Cross Cable. Take time to save time, check your gauge.

PATTERN STITCHES

STOCKINETTE STITCH (ST ST)

Knit on RS, purl on WS.

2 × 2 RIB (MULTIPLE OF 4 STS + 2)

Row 1: K2, *p2, k2; rep from * across.

Row 2: Knit the knit sts and purl the purl sts as they face you.

Rep Row 2 for 2 x 2 Rib.

CRISS-CROSS CABLE (MULTIPLE OF 8 STS + 2)

See chart.

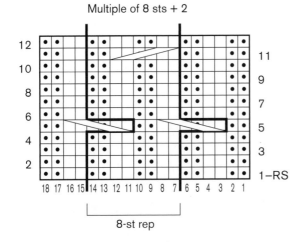

Multiple of 8 sts + 2

8-st rep

☐ Knit on RS, purl on WS.

⊡ Purl on RS, knit on WS.

▱ SI 2 sts to cn, hold in front;
k2, p2; k2 from cn.

▱ SI 4 sts to cn, hold in back;
k2; p2, k2 from cn.

BACK

CO 126 (134, 142, 158, 174, 186) sts; work in 2 × 2 Rib until piece meas 1½" from beg, end WS row. *Est patt:* (RS) Work 2 (2, 2, 2, 2, 0) sts in St st, 122 (130, 138, 154, 170, 186) sts in Criss-Cross Cable (see chart), 2 (2, 2, 2, 2, 0) sts in St st. Cont in patt as est; work even until piece meas 13 (14, 15, 16, 17, 17)" from beg, end WS row. **Shape armholes:** (RS) BO 8 sts at beg of next 2 rows, then dec 1 st each side EOR 4 times—102 (110, 118, 134, 150, 158) sts rem. Work even until armholes meas 7¾ (8, 8¼, 8½, 9½, 10)" from beg of shaping. BO all sts.

FRONT

Work as for back until armholes meas 4¾ (5, 5¼, 5½, 6½, 7)" from beg of shaping, end WS row. **Shape neck:** (RS) Work 38 (41, 44, 52, 59, 65) sts, join second ball of yarn, BO center 26 (28, 30, 30, 32, 32) sts, work to end. Working both sides at same time, at each neck edge, BO 3 sts once, 2 sts once, then dec 1 st EOR 3 times—30 (33, 36, 44, 51, 55) sts rem each shoulder. Work even until armholes meas same as back to shoulders. BO all sts.

SLEEVES

CO 54 (54, 54, 62, 62, 62) sts; work in 2 × 2 Rib until piece meas 1½" from beg, end WS row. *Est patt:* (RS) Work 2 sts in St st, 50 (50, 50, 58, 58, 58) sts in Criss-Cross Cable (see chart), 2 sts in St st. Work even until piece meas 2" from beg, end WS row. **Shape**

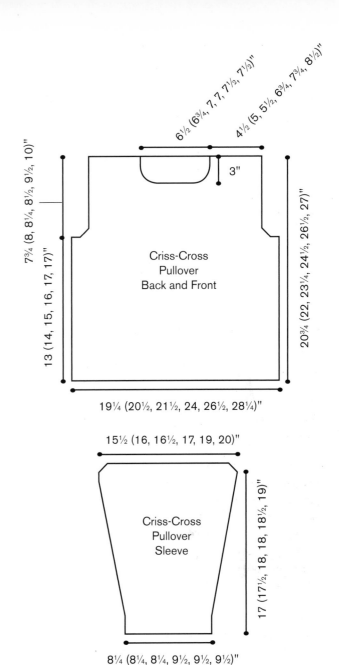

Criss-Cross
Pullover
Back and Front

Criss-Cross
Pullover
Sleeve

sleeve: (RS) Inc 1 st each side this row, then every 4 rows 16 (20, 24, 14, 28, 27) times, every 6 (6, 6, 6, 2, 2) rows 6 (4, 2, 9, 2, 6) times—100 (104, 108, 110, 124, 130) sts. Work even until piece meas 17 (17½, 18, 18, 18½, 19)" from beg, end WS row. **Shape cap:** BO 8 sts at beg of next 2 rows, then dec 1 st each side EOR 4 times—76 (80, 84, 86, 100, 106) sts rem. BO rem sts.

FINISHING

Block pieces to measurements. Sew shoulder seams. Set in sleeves; sew sleeve and side seams. **Neckband:** With RS facing, using circular needle, pick up and knit 96 (100, 104, 104, 108, 108) sts evenly around neck edge; pm for beg of rnd. Work in St st until neckband meas 1½" from pickup row. BO all sts loosely.

STRIPES AND SEEDS PULLOVER

SIZES
Small (Medium, Large, 1X Large)

FINISHED MEASUREMENTS
42 (45, 49½, 54)"

MATERIALS
Classic Elite Yarns

Montera (50% llama, 50% wool; 100-g hank = approx 127 yd/116 m)
• 8 (9, 10, 11) hanks 3823 Spring Leaf

Equivalent yarns

Worsted weight #4, 1016 (1143, 1270, 1397) yd

Needles
• One pair *each* size U.S. 8 (5 mm) and 9 (5.5 mm) or size to obtain gauge
• One 16" circular size U.S. 8 (5 mm)

Stitch markers

GAUGE
14½ sts and 20 rows = 4" in Seed Stitch and Stockinette Stitch, using larger needles. Take time to save time, check your gauge.

PATTERN STITCHES

STOCKINETTE STITCH (ST ST)
Knit on RS, purl on WS.

SEED STITCH (MULTIPLE OF 2 STS)
Row 1: (RS) *K1, p1; rep from * across.
Row 2: Purl the knit sts and knit the purl sts as they face you.
Rep Row 2 for Seed Stitch.

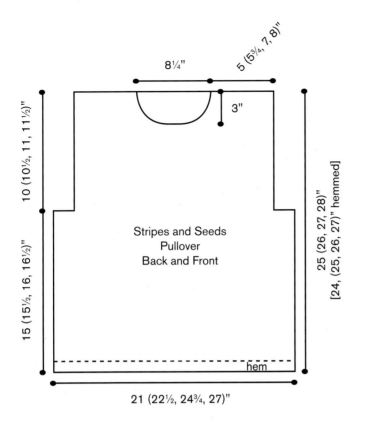

8¼"

5 (5¾, 7, 8)"

3"

10 (10½, 11, 11½)"

15 (15½, 16, 16½)"

Stripes and Seeds
Pullover
Back and Front

25 (26, 27, 28)"
[24, (25, 26, 27)" hemmed]

hem

21 (22½, 24¾, 27)"

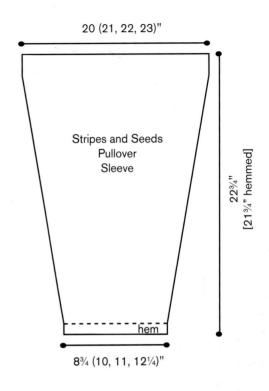

20 (21, 22, 23)"

Stripes and Seeds
Pullover
Sleeve

22¾"
[21¾" hemmed]

hem

8¾ (10, 11, 12¼)"

BACK

Hem: Using smaller needles, CO 76 (82, 90, 98) sts. Work 4 rows in St st, end WS row. Change to larger needles and *est patt:* (RS) Work 5 (8, 12, 16) sts in St st, *14 sts in Seed st, 12 sts in St st; rep from * to last 19 (22, 26, 30) sts, work 14 sts in Seed st, 5 (8, 12, 16) sts in St st. Work as est until piece meas 15 (15½ , 16, 16½)" from beg, end WS row. **Shape armholes:** (RS) BO 5 sts at beg of next 2 rows—66 (72, 80, 88) sts rem. Work even until armhole meas 10 (10½, 11, 11½)" from beg of shaping, end WS row. BO all sts.

FRONT

Work as for back until armhole meas 7 (7½, 8, 8½)" from beg of shaping, end WS row—66 (72, 80, 88) sts rem. **Shape neck:** (RS) Work 25 (28, 32, 36) sts, join second ball of yarn, BO center 16 sts, work to end. Working both sides at same time, dec 1 st at neck edge EOR 7 times—18 (21, 25, 29) sts rem each shoulder. Work even until armhole meas same as back to shoulders, end WS row. BO all sts.

SLEEVES

Hem: Using smaller needles, CO 32 (36, 40, 44) sts. Work Work 4 rows in St st, end WS row. Change to larger needles and *est patt:* (RS) Work 9 (11, 13, 15) sts in St st, 14 sts in Seed st, 9 (11, 13, 15) sts in St st. Cont in patt est; work 3 rows even, end WS row. **Shape sleeve:** Inc 1 st each side this row, then every 4 rows 9 times, every 6 rows 10 times, working inc sts in patt as for body as sts become available—72 (76, 80, 84) sts. Work even until piece meas 22¾" from beg, end WS row. BO all sts.

FINISHING

Block pieces to measurements. Sew shoulder seams. Set in sleeves; sew sleeve and side seams. Fold up hems and sew to WS. **Neckband:** With RS facing, using circular needle, pick up and knit 30 sts along back neck, 13 sts along left neck edge, 16 sts along front neck, 13 sts along right neck edge—72 sts; pm for beg of rnd. *Est patt:* *Work 6 sts in Seed st, 6 sts in St st; rep from * around. Work even until band and meas 2½" from pickup row; BO all sts in patt.

UNISEX STRIPED V-NECK PULLOVER

[SKILL LEVEL: INTERMEDIATE]

Note: See p. 148 for matching Children's sweater and p. 150 for matching stocking cap.

SIZES

Extra Small (Small, Medium, Large, 1X Large)

FINISHED MEASUREMENTS

36 (40, 44, 48, 52)"

MATERIALS

Classic Elite Yarns

Montera (50% llama, 50% wool, 100-g hank = approx 127 yd/116 m)

• 4 (4, 5, 5, 5) hanks Main Color (MC)—3803 Falcon Grey
• 1 hank all sizes Color A—3888 Magenta
• 1 hank all sizes Color B—3827 Cochineal
• 1 (1, 1, 2, 2) hanks Color C—3893 Ch'ulla Blue
• 1 (1, 1, 2, 2) hanks Color D—3887 Pear
• 1 hank all sizes Color E—3883 Strawfield
• 1 hank all sizes Color F—3885 Bolsita Orange
• 1 (1, 1, 2, 2) hanks Color G—3856 Majolica Blue

Equivalent yarn

Worsted weight #4, MC: 508 (508, 635, 635, 635) yd; Colors A, B, E, and F: 127 yd all sizes; Colors C, D, and G: 127 (127, 127, 254, 254) yd

Needles

• One 24" circular size U.S. 9 (5.5 mm) or size needed to obtain gauge
• One 16" circular size U.S. 8 (5 mm) for neck finishing

Stitch holders

Stitch markers

GAUGE

16 sts and 20 rows = 4" in Stockinette Stitch, using larger needles. Take time to save time, check your gauge.

NOTES

The Stripe Sequence is worked using eight colors. Some of the colors are worked in single-row stripes. The pieces are worked flat but are worked on circular needles to eliminate cutting and rejoining colors, leaving ends to weave in later. Simply slide the sts to the end where the next color to be used was left and work the next row (RS or WS) in patt st.

Work Stripe Sequence in order once; rep Stripe Sequence in rev order, beg with Row 47 once; then rep Stripe Sequence in order, beg with Row 9.

PATTERN STITCHES

STOCKINETTE STITCH (ST ST)

Knit on RS, purl on WS.

HURDLE RIB (MULTIPLE OF 2 STS +1)

Rows 1 and 2: Knit.

Row 3: *K1, p1; rep from * across to last st, k1.

Row 4: P1, *k1, p1; rep from * across.

Rep Rows 1–4 for Hurdle Rib.

CIRCULAR HURDLE RIB (MULTIPLE OF 2 STS)

Rnd 1: Purl.

Rnds 2, 3, 6, and 7: *K1, p1; rep from * around.

Rnd 4: Knit.

Rnd 5: Purl.

Rnd 8: Knit.

Work Rnds 1–8 for Circular Hurdle Rib.

STRIPE SEQUENCE

Rows 1–9: MC.

Row 10: Color E.

Row 11: MC.

Rows 12–14: Color B.

Row 15: MC.

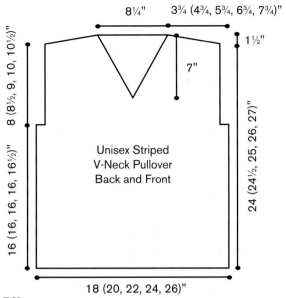

BACK

Using MC and larger needles, CO 73 (81, 89, 97, 105) sts. Work Hurdle Rib and Stripe Sequence for 8 rows, end WS row. Change to St st and cont Stripe Sequence, beg with Row 9; work even until piece meas 16 (16, 16, 16, 16½)" from beg, end WS row. *Shape armhole:* BO 5 sts at the beg of the next 2 rows—63 (71, 79, 87, 95) sts rem. Work even until piece meas 24 (24½, 25, 26, 27)" from beg, end WS row. *Shape shoulders and neck:* (RS) BO 5 (7, 7, 9, 11) sts at the

beg of the next 2 rows, BO 5 (6, 8, 9, 10) sts at the beg of the next 4 rows—33 sts rem. Place rem sts on holder for neck.

FRONT

Work as for back until piece meas 18 (18½, 19, 20, 21)" from beg, end WS row. *Shape neck:* (RS) Work 31 (35, 39, 43, 47) sts, join second ball of yarn, work center st and place on holder for V-neck, work to end. Working both sides at same time, dec 1 st each neck edge EOR 16 times—15 (19, 23, 27, 31) sts rem each shoulder. Work even until piece meas same as back to shoulders. *Shape shoulders* as for back.

SLEEVES

Using MC and larger needles , CO 35 (37, 37, 39, 41) sts; work Hurdle Rib and Stripe Sequence for 8 rows, end WS row. Change to St st, cont Stripe Sequence beg with Row 9; and, **at the same time,** *shape sleeves:* Inc 1 st each side this row, then every 4 rows 6 (8, 12, 19, 21) times, then every 6 rows 8 (7, 5, 1, 0) times—65 (69, 73, 81, 85) sts. Work even until piece meas 18 (18½, 19½, 20, 20½)" from beg. BO all sts.

FINISHING

Block pieces to measurements. Sew shoulder seams. Set in sleeves; sew side and sleeve seams. *Neckband:* With RS facing, using smaller circular needle and MC, k33 sts from holder for back neck, pick up and knit 28 sts along left front neck edge, pm, k1 from holder for V-neck, pm, pick up and knit 28 sts along right front neck edge, pm for beg of rnd—90 sts. Work Circular Hurdle Rib for 1 rnd. *Dec rnd:* *Cont in patt as est, work to 2 sts before marker, ssk, k1 [center st], k2 tog, work to end of rnd; rep from * 6 times—76 sts rem. BO rem sts purlwise.

Rows 16 and 18: *Work 1 st using MC, 1 st using Color C; rep from * across.
Row 17: *Work 1 st using Color C, 1 st using MC; rep from * across.
Row 19: MC.
Row 20: Color D.
Row 21: Color C.
Row 22: Color D.
Rows 23 and 24: Color G.
Row 25: Color D.
Row 26: Color C.
Row 27: Color D.
Rows 28–32: MC.
Rows 33 and 34: Color C.
Rows 35–37: MC.
Row 38: Color F.
Row 39: *Work 1 st using Color F, 1 st using Color E; rep from * across.
Rows 40 and 41: Color F.
Row 42: MC.
Rows 43 and 44: Color G.
Row 45: Color A.
Row 46: Color G.
Row 47: Color D.
Rows 48 and 49: MC.

CABLED MOCK TURTLENECK PULLOVER

SKILL LEVEL: BEGINNER

Note: See p. 168 for Children's sweater.

SIZES
Small (Medium, Large, 1X Large)

FINISHED MEASUREMENTS
42½ (45, 49, 53)"

MATERIALS
Classic Elite Yarns
Two.Two (100% Highland wool, 50-g hank = approx 55 yd/50 m)
• 15 (16, 17, 18) hanks 1575 Heather Zinc
Equivalent yarn
Bulky weight #5, 825 (880, 935, 990) yd
Needles
• One pair size U.S. 11 (8 mm) or size to obtain gauge
• One 16" circular size U.S. 10 (6 mm)
• One cable needle (cn)
Stitch markers

GAUGE
12 sts and 16 rows = 4" in Cable pattern, using larger needles.
Take time to save time, check your gauge.

PATTERN STITCHES

CABLE (MULTIPLE OF 10 STS + 4; 8-ROW REP)
Row 1: (RS) K4, *p1, k4, p1, k4; rep from * across.
Row 2 and all WS rows: *P4, k1, p4, p1; rep from * across to last 4 sts, p4.
Row 3: K4, *p1, sl 2 sts to cn, hold in front, k2, k2 from cn, p1, k4; rep from * across.
Rows 5 and 7: Rep Row 1.
Row 8: Rep Row 2.
Rep Rows 1–8 for Cable.

CIRCULAR CABLE (MULTIPLE OF 10 STS; 8-ROW REP)
Rnds 1 and 2: K4, p1, k4, p1; rep from * around.
Rnd 3: *K4, p1, sl 2 sts to cn, hold in front, k2, k2 from cn, p1; rep from * around.
Rnds 4–8: Rep Rnd 1.
Rep Rnds 1–8 for Circular Cable.

BACK

CO 64 (68, 74, 80) sts. *Est patt:* (RS) Work 0 (2, 0, 3) sts in St st, work 64 (64, 74, 74) sts in Cable patt, 0 (2, 0, 3) sts in St st. Cont in patt as est; work even until piece meas 24 (25, 26, 27)" from beg. BO all sts.

FRONT

Work as for back until piece meas 21 (22, 23, 24)" from beg, end WS row. *Shape neck:* Work 26 (28, 30, 33) sts, join second ball of yarn, BO center 12 (12, 14, 14) sts, work to end. Working both sides at the same time, at each neck edge, dec 1 st EOR 5 times—21 (23, 25, 28) sts rem each shoulder. Work even until piece meas same as back. BO rem sts.

SLEEVES

CO 24 (24, 24, 28) sts. *Est patt:* (RS) Work 0 (0, 0, 2) sts in St st; work 24 sts in Cable patt; work 0 (0, 0, 2) sts in St st. Cont in patt as est; work even until piece meas 1" from beg, end WS row. *Shape sleeve:* Inc 1 st each side this row, then every 4 rows 12 (11, 14, 11) times, every 6 rows 2 (3, 2, 4) times, working inc sts in Cable patt as they become available— 54 (54, 58, 60) sts. Work even until piece meas 17 (18, 19, 20)" from beg. BO all sts.

FINISHING

Block pieces to measurements. Sew shoulder seams. Meas down 9 (9, 9½, 10)" from shoulders on back and front, pm. Sew sleeves bet markers. Sew sleeve and side seams. *Mock turtleneck:* With RS facing and circular needle, pick up and knit 60 sts evenly around neck edge; pm for beg of rnd. Work Circular Cable patt until turtleneck meas 5" from beg. BO all sts loosely in patt.

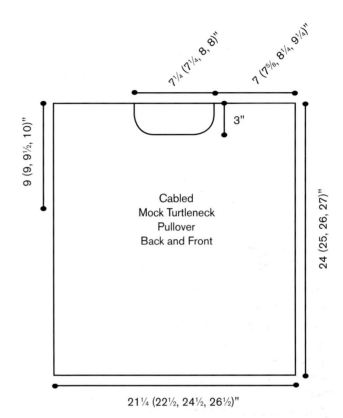

7¼ (7¼, 8, 8)" 7 (7⅝, 8¼, 9¼)"

3"

9 (9, 9½, 10)"

Cabled Mock Turtleneck Pullover Back and Front

24 (25, 26, 27)"

21¼ (22½, 24½, 26½)"

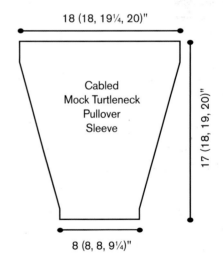

18 (18, 19¼, 20)"

Cabled Mock Turtleneck Pullover Sleeve

17 (18, 19, 20)"

8 (8, 8, 9¼)"

BLUE WATER PULLOVER

[SKILL LEVEL: INTERMEDIATE]

Note: See p. 179 for Children's sweater.

SIZES
Small (Medium, Large, 1X Large)

FINISHED MEASUREMENTS
40 (44, 48, 52)"
Note: Measurements given are for lightly blocked piece; choose size accordingly.

MATERIALS
Classic Elite Yarns
Waterlily (100% extra-fine merino; 50-g ball = approx 100 yd/91 m)
• 16 (17, 18, 21) balls 1948 Inlet
Equivalent yarn
Worsted weight #4, 1600 (1700, 1800, 2100) yd
Needles
• One pair *each* size U.S. 7 (4.4 mm) and 8 (5 mm) or size to obtain gauge
• One 16" circular size U.S. 7 (4.5 mm)
• One cable needle (cn)
Stitch markers

GAUGE
24 sts and 26 rows = 4" in 1 x 1 Rib unblocked, using smaller needles; 22 sts = 4" in Cable Rib lightly blocked, using larger needles. Take time to save time, check your gauge.

NOTE
Work sleeve incs 2 sts in from each side.

PATTERN STITCHES

1 × 1 RIB (MULTIPLE OF 2 STS + 1)
Row 1: (RS) K1, * p1, k1; rep from * across.
Row 2: Knit the knit sts and purl the purl sts as they face you.
Rep Row 2 for 1 x 1 Rib.

CIRCULAR 1 × 1 RIB (MULTIPLE OF 2 STS)
Rnd 1: * K1, p1; rep from * around.
Rep Rnd 1 for Circular 1 x 1 Rib.

CABLE RIB (MULTIPLE OF 22 STS + 5; 6-ROW REP + 6)
See chart.

REVERSE STOCKINETTE STITCH (REV ST ST)
Purl on RS, knit on WS.

BACK

Using larger needles, CO 103 (111, 123, 131) sts. Change to smaller needles and beg 1 × 1 Rib; work even until piece meas 2" from beg, end RS row. (WS) Knit 1 row (Garter ridge); pm each side of center 85 (105, 105, 125) sts. *Est patt:* *Row 1:* (RS) [K2, p1] 3 (1, 3, 1) times, sl marker; beg Row 1 of Cable Rib (see chart) work across sts bet markers as foll: *[K2, p1] twice, k2, m1, k1, [p1, k2] 3 times, m1, k1, p1; rep from * across to 5 sts before second marker, k2, p1, k2; sl marker, [p1, k2] 3 (1, 3, 1) times—111 (121, 133, 143) sts. *Row 2:* (WS) Change to larger needles. Work Row 2 of Cable Rib over all sts. Work even, cont 6-row rep of Cable Rib on center sts and keeping sts each side of markers in rib as est until piece meas 18½" from beg, end WS row. **Shape armholes:** (RS) BO 5 (5, 7, 7) sts at beg of next 2 rows, 0 (2, 3, 6) sts at beg of next 2 rows, then dec 1 st each side EOR 6 (6, 7, 8) times—89 (95, 99, 101) sts rem. Work even until armhole meas 8½ (9, 9½, 10)" from beg of shaping, end WS row; pm each side of center 35 (35, 37, 39) sts. **Shape shoulders:** (RS) BO 8 (9, 10, 10) sts at beg of next 2 rows, 7 (8, 8, 8) sts at beg of next 4 rows; and, **at the same time,** on the first row of shoulder shaping, work across to center sts; join second ball of yarn and BO center sts; work to end. Working both sides at same time, at each neck edge BO 3 sts once, 2 sts once.

FRONT

Work as for back until armhole meas 6 (6½, 7, 7½)" from beg of shaping, end WS row—89 (95, 99, 101) sts rem; pm each side of center 27 (27, 29, 31) sts. **Shape neck:** (RS) Work across to center sts; join second ball of yarn, BO center sts; work to end. Working both sides at same time, at each neck edge BO 2 sts 3 times, then 1 st each side EOR 3 times—22 (25, 26, 26) sts rem each shoulder. Work even until piece meas same as back to shoulder shaping. **Shape shoulders** as for back.

SLEEVES

Using larger needles, CO 55 (57, 57, 59) sts. Change to smaller needles and beg 1 × 1 Rib; work even until piece meas 3" from beg, end RS row. (WS) Knit 1 row, (Garter ridge); pm each side of center 45 sts. *Est patt:* (RS) K2 (0, 0, 1) [k2, p1] 1 (2, 2, 2) times, sl marker; beg Row 1 of Cable Rib (see chart) work across 45 sts bet markers as foll: *[K2, p1] twice, k2, m1, k1, [p1, k2] 3 times, m1, k1, p1; rep from * across to 5 sts before second marker, k2, p1, k2; sl marker, [p1, k2] 1 (2, 2, 2) times, k2 (0, 0, 1)—59 (61, 61, 63) sts. *Row 2:* Change to larger needles. Work Row 2 of Cable Rib over all sts. Work even for 4 rows, working Rows 3–6 of Cable Rib on center sts and

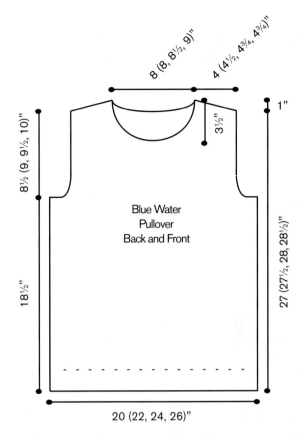

8 (8, 8½, 9)"

4 (4½, 4¾, 4¾)"

1"

3½"

8½ (9, 9½, 10)"

18½"

27 (27½, 28, 28½)"

Blue Water
Pullover
Back and Front

20 (22, 24, 26)"

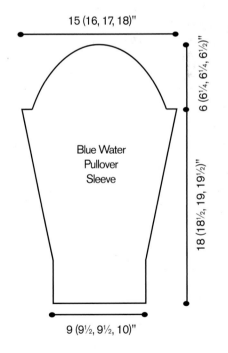

15 (16, 17, 18)"

6 (6¼, 6¼, 6½)"

18 (18½, 19, 19½)"

Blue Water
Pullover
Sleeve

9 (9½, 9½, 10)"

keeping sts each side of markers in rib as est, end WS row.
Shape sleeve: (RS) Cont as est, working 6-row rep of Cable Rib on center sts, inc 1 st each side this row, then every 8 rows 9 (5, 0, 0) times, every 6 rows 2 (8, 14, 13) times, every 4 rows 0 (0, 2, 4) times, working inc sts in Cable Rib as they become available—83 (89, 95, 99) sts. Work even until piece meas 18 (18½, 19, 19½)" from beg, end WS row. ***Shape cap:*** BO 5 (5, 7, 7) sts at beg of next 2 rows, 0 (2, 3, 6) sts at beg of next 2 rows—73 (75, 75, 73) sts rem. Dec 1 st each side EOR 15 times—43 (45, 45, 43) sts rem. Dec 2 (2, 2, 1) sts every row 8 (8, 8, 10) times—27 (29, 29, 33) sts rem. BO rem sts.

FINISHING

Lightly block pieces to measurements. Sew shoulder seams. Set in sleeves; sew side and sleeve seams. ***Neckband:*** With RS facing, using circular needle, pick up and knit 140 (140, 144, 148) sts evenly around neck edge. Join; pm for beg of rnd. Purl 1 rnd (Garter Ridge). Beg Circular 1 × 1 Rib; work even until band meas 1" from pickup rnd. BO all sts loosely in rib.

▇ **CABLE RIB CHART**

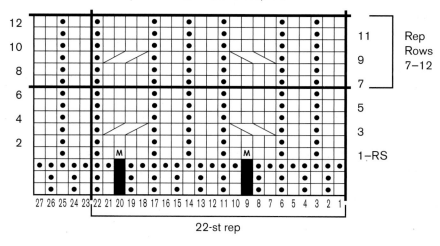

Multiple of 22 sts + 5; 6-row rep + 6

□ Knit on RS, purl on WS.

⊡ Purl on RS, knit on WS.

■ No st.

Ⓜ M1.

◺ Sl 2 sts to cn, hold in front, k2; k2 from cn.

◿ Sl 2 sts from cn, hold in back, k2; k2 from cn.

ROPE CABLE CREWNECK

SIZES

Small (Medium, Large, 1X Large)

FINISHED MEASUREMENTS

42½ (46½, 51½, 55½)"

MATERIALS

Classic Elite Yarns

Bazic (100% superwash wool; 50-g ball = approx 65 yd/59 m)

• 22 (25, 28, 32) balls 2993 Trojan Blue

Equivalent yarn

Worsted weight #4, 1430 (1625, 1820, 2080) yd

Needles

• One pair *each* size U.S. 7 (4.5 mm) and 9 (5.5 mm) or size to obtain gauge

• One 16" circular size U.S. 7 (4.5 mm)

• One cable needle (cn)

Stitch markers

Stitch holder

GAUGE

16 sts and 23 rows = 4" in Reverse Stockinette Stitch, using larger needles; 15 sts = 2¼" in Large and Mini Rope Cables (Charts B and C), using larger needles; 3 sts = ¾" in Mini Rope Cable (Charts A and D), using larger needles; 21 sts = 3¼" in Double-Mirrored Rope Cable (Chart E), using larger needles. Take time to save time, check your gauge.

NOTE

If there are not enough sts to complete a cable, work in St st until enough sts are present.

PATTERN STITCHES

REVERSE STOCKINETTE STITCH (REV ST ST)

Purl on RS, knit on WS.

MINI ROPE CABLE (MULTIPLE OF 3 STS; 4-ROW REP)

See Charts A and D.

LARGE AND MINI ROPE CABLES (MULTIPLE OF 15 STS; 8-ROW REP)

See Charts B and C.

DOUBLE-MIRRORED ROPE CABLE (MULTIPLE OF 21 STS; 8-ROW REP)

See Chart E.

CIRCULAR 2 × 2 RIB (MULTIPLE OF 4 STS)

All rnds: *P2, k2; rep from * around.

BACK

Using smaller needles, CO 141 (151, 171, 181) sts. *Setup row:* (WS) Work 0 (2, 0, 2) sts Rev St st; p 0 (3, 0, 3); pm; [k3, p2, k2, p2, k3, p3] 4 (4, 5, 5) times; pm; [k3, p2, k2, p2] twice, k3, pm; [p3, k3, p2, k2, p2, k3] 4 (4, 5, 5) times; pm; p 0 (3, 0, 3) times, work 0 (2, 0, 2) sts in Rev St st. *Est rib patt: Row 1:* (RS) Work 0 (2, 0, 2) sts Rev St st; k0 (3, 0, 3); pm; [p3, k2, p2, k2, p3, k3] 4 (4, 5, 5) times; pm; [p3, k2, p2, k2] twice, p3, pm;

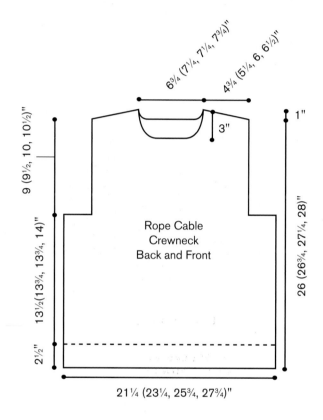

13½ (13¾, 13¾, 14)"

2½"

9 (9½, 10, 10½)"

6¾ (7¼, 7¼, 7¾)"

4¾ (5¼, 6, 6½)"

3"

1"

26 (26¾, 27¼, 28)"

Rope Cable
Crewneck
Back and Front

21¼ (23¼, 25¾, 27¾)"

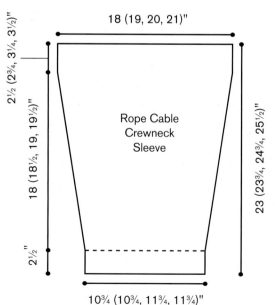

18 (19, 20, 21)"

2½ (2¾, 3¼, 3½)"

18 (18½, 19, 19½)"

2½"

23 (23¾, 24¾, 25½)"

Rope Cable
Crewneck
Sleeve

10¾ (10¾, 11¾, 11¾)"

[k3, p3, k2, p2, k2, p3] 4 (4, 5, 5) times; pm; k 0 (3, 0, 3) times, work 0 (2, 0, 2) sts Rev St st. *Row 2 and all WS rows:* Work sts as they appear, knit the knit sts, purl the purl sts as they face you. *Rows 3, 7, and 11:* Work 0 (2, 0, 2) sts Rev St st, ½ RC 0 (1, 0, 1) time; [p3, k2, p2, k2, p3, ½ RC] 4 (4, 5, 5) times; [p3, k2, p2, k2] twice, p3; [½ LC, p3, k2, p2, k2, p3] 4 (4, 5, 5) times; pm; ½ LC 0 (1, 0, 1) time, 0 (2, 0, 2) sts Rev St st. *Rows 5, 9, and 13:* Work as Row 1. Change to larger needles and *est patt:* (RS) Beg with Row 1 of cables, work 0 (2, 0, 2) sts Rev St st; Mini Rope Right Cross (Chart A) 0 (1, 0, 1) time; Large and Mini Rope Cables Right Cross (Chart B) 4 (4, 5, 5) times; Double-Mirrored Rope Cable (Chart E); Large and Mini Rope Cables Left Cross (Chart C) 4 (4, 5, 5) times, Mini Rope Cable Left Cross (Chart D) 0 (1, 0, 1) time; 0 (2, 0, 2) sts in Rev St st. Work even as est until piece meas 16 (16¼, 16¼, 16½)" from beg, end WS row. *Shape armholes:* (RS) BO 17 (19, 22, 24) sts at beg next 2 rows—107 (113, 127, 133) sts rem. Work even as est until armhole meas 9 (9½, 10, 10½)" from beg of shaping, end WS row. *Shape shoulders and neck:* (RS) BO 10 (11, 13, 13) sts at beg of next 4 rows, 10 (10, 13, 14) sts at beg of next 2 rows; and, **at the same time,** on the first row of shoulder shaping, work across to center 32 (34, 34, 34) sts; join second ball of yarn, BO 15 (16, 16, 16) sts, k2tog, BO 15 (16, 16, 16) sts, work to end. Working both sides at same time, at each neck edge, BO 4 (4, 4, 5) sts twice.

FRONT

Work as for back until armhole meas 7 (7½, 8, 8½)" from shaping, end WS row. *Shape neck:* Work 41 (44, 51, 53) sts; join second ball of yarn, BO 12 (12, 12, 13) sts, k2tog, BO 12 (12, 12, 13) sts, work to end. Working both sides at same time, at each neck edge, BO 3 sts 1 (2, 2, 2) times, 2 sts 3 (2, 2, 2) times, then 1 st 2 (2, 2, 3) times—30 (32, 39, 40) sts rem each shoulder. Work even as est until armhole meas same as back to shoulder shaping; *Shape shoulders* as for back.

SLEEVES

Using smaller needles, CO 63 (63, 69, 69) sts. *Setup row:* (WS) [K1, p2] 0 (0, 1, 1) times, k3, p3, k3, p2, k2, p2, k3, p3; pm; [k3, p2, k2, p2] twice, k3; pm; p3, k3, p2, k2, p2, k3, p3, k3, [p2, k1] 0 (0, 1, 1) time. *Est rib patt: Row 1:* (RS) [P1, k2] 0 (0, 1, 1) time, p3, k3, p3, k2, p2, k2, p3, k3; pm; [p3, k2, p2, k2] twice, p3; pm; k3, p3, k2, p2, k2, p3, k3, p3, [k2, p1] 0 (0, 1, 1) time. *Row 2 and all WS rows:* Work sts as they appear, knit the knit sts and purl the purl sts as they face you. *Rows 3, 7, and 11:* [P1, k2] 0 (0, 1, 1) time; p3, ½ RC, p3, k2, p2, k2, p3, ½ RC, [p3, k2, p2, k2] twice, p3, ½ LC, p3, k2, p2, k2, p3, ½ LC, p3, [k2, p1] 0 (0, 1, 1) time. *Rows 5, 9, and 13:* Work as Row 1.

Change to larger needles and *est patt*: (RS) Beg with Row 1 of cables, beg with st 10 (10, 7, 7) of Large and Mini Rope Cables Right Cross (Chart B) and work 21 (21, 24, 24) sts; work 21 sts Double-Mirrored Rope Cable (Chart E); work 21 (21, 24, 24) sts Large and Mini Rope Cables Left Cross (Chart C), end with st 6 (6, 9, 9). Work 1 row even as est. *Shape sleeve:* (RS) Inc 1 st at each side EOR 3 (5, 3, 8) times, every 4 rows 16 (23, 25, 23) times, then every 6 rows 5 (0, 0, 0) times, working all new sts in patt from Large and Mini Rope Cables Right Cross as est to right of center Double-Mirrored Rope Cable and in patt from Large and Mini Rope Cables Left Cross as est to left of center Double-Mirrored Rope Cable—111 (119, 125, 131) sts. Work

even until piece meas 23 (23¾, 24¾, 25½)". BO all sts loosely in patt.

FINISHING

Block pieces to measurements. Sew shoulder seams. Set in sleeves; sew side and sleeve seams. *Neckband:* With RS facing, using circular needle, beg at left shoulder, pick up and knit 14 sts along left front neck edge; 24 (24, 24, 26) sts across front neck, 14 sts along right front neck, 48 (52, 52, 52) sts across back neck, pm for beg of rnd—100 (104, 104, 108) sts. Work in Circular 2 × 2 Rib until band meas 1" from pickup row. BO all sts loosely in patt.

■ CHART A: MINI ROPE CABLE RIGHT CROSS

Multiple of 3 sts; 4-row rep

■ CHART B: LARGE AND MINI ROPE CABLES RIGHT CROSS

Multiple of 15 sts; 8-row rep

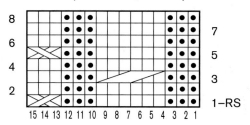

■ CHART C: LARGE AND MINI ROPE CABLES LEFT CROSS

Multiple of 15 sts; 8-row rep

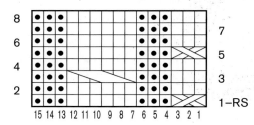

■ CHART D: MINI ROPE CABLE LEFT CROSS

Multiple of 3 sts; 4row rep

☐   Knit on RS, purl on WS.

⊡   Purl on RS, knit on WS.

⧓   Sl 2 sts to cn, hold in back, k1, sl next st on cn to LH needle, k1, k1 from cn.

⧓   Sl 1 st to cn, hold in front, k2, k1 from cn.

⬲   Sl 3 sts to cn, hold in back, k3, k3 from cn.

⬱   Sl 3 sts to cn, hold in front, k3, k3 from cn.

■ CHART E: DOUBLE-MIRRORED ROPE CABLE

Multiple of 21 sts; 8-row rep

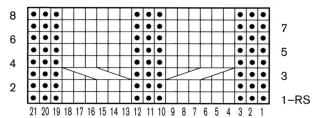

SEED RIB CREWNECK

SIZES
Small (Medium, Large, 1X Large)

FINISHED MEASUREMENTS
41½ (44, 48½, 53)"

MATERIALS
Classic Elite Yarns

Montera (50% llama, 50% wool; 100-g hank = approx 127 yd)

• 7 (8, 9, 10) hanks 3843 Coffee Bean

Equivalent yarns

Worsted weight #4, 889 (1016, 1143, 1270) yd

Needles

• One pair size U.S. 10 (6 mm) or size to obtain gauge

• One 16" circular size U.S. 10 (6 mm) for neck finishing

Stitch markers

GAUGE
14 sts and 22 rows = 4" in Seed Rib. Take time to save time, check your gauge.

PATTERN STITCHES

1 x 1 RIB (MULTIPLE OF 2 STS + 1)

Row 1: (RS) K1, *p1, k1; rep from * across.

Row 2: Knit the knit sts and purl the purl sts as they face you.

Rep Row 2 for 1 x 1 Rib.

SEED RIB (MULTIPLE OF 4 STS + 1; 2-ROW REP)

See chart.

BACK

CO 73 (77, 85, 93) sts. Beg 1 × 1 Rib; work even until piece meas 2½" from beg, end WS row. Change to Seed Rib (see chart); work even until piece meas 14 (15, 16, 17)" from beg, end WS row. *Shape armholes:* BO 5 (6, 8, 9) sts at beg of the next 2 rows—63 (65, 69, 75) sts rem. Work even until armhole meas 8½ (9, 9½, 10)" from shaping, end on WS row. BO all sts in patt.

FRONT

Work as for back until armhole meas 6½ (7, 7½, 8)" from shaping, end WS row; pm each side of center 17 (19, 21, 23) sts. *Shape neck:* (RS) Work across to marker; join second ball of yarn and BO center sts, work to end—23 (23, 24, 26) sts rem each side. Working both sides at same time, at each neck edge, dec 1 st EOR 4 times—19 (19, 20, 22) sts rem each shoulder. Work even until piece meas same as back to shoulders, end on WS row. BO all sts in patt.

SLEEVES

CO 29 (33, 37, 37) sts. Beg 1 × 1 Rib; work even until piece meas 2" from beg, end WS row. Change to Seed Rib (see chart); (RS) work even for 4 rows, end WS row. *Shape sleeve:* Inc 1 st each side this row, then every 4 rows 0 (14, 0, 0) times, every 5 rows 6 (0, 0, 0) times, then every 6 rows 8 (0, 14, 16) times—59 (63, 67, 71) sts. Work even until piece meas 19 (20, 22, 23)" from beg, end WS row. BO all sts in patt.

FINISHING

Block pieces to measurements. Sew shoulder seams. *Neckband:* With RS facing, using circular needle and beg at left shoulder seam, pick up and knit 64 (68, 72, 76) sts evenly around neck edge, pm for beg of rnd. Beg Seed Rib (see chart), aligning sts with front and back neck where possible; work even for 1". BO all sts loosely in patt. Set in sleeves; sew sleeve and side seams.

Multiple of 4 sts + 1; 2-row rep

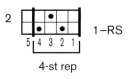

4-st rep

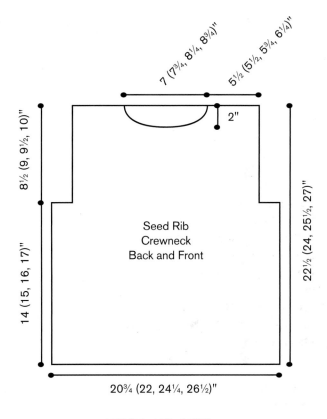

7 (7¾, 8¼, 8¾)"   5½ (5½, 5¾, 6¼)"

2"

8½ (9, 9½, 10)"

14 (15, 16, 17)"

22½ (24, 25½, 27)"

Seed Rib
Crewneck
Back and Front

20¾ (22, 24¼, 26½)"

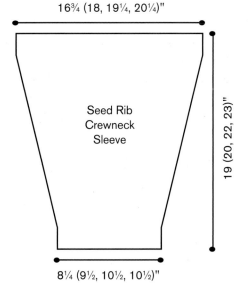

16¾ (18, 19¼, 20¼)"

Seed Rib
Crewneck
Sleeve

19 (20, 22, 23)"

8¼ (9½, 10½, 10½)"

CHILDREN'S KNITS

contents

FLOWER VEST

SIZES

2 (4, 6, 8)

FINISHED MEASUREMENTS

24½ (28, 32, 35½)"

MATERIALS

Classic Elite yarns

Bubbles (50% cotton, 30% nylon, 20% acrylic; 50-g ball = approx 61 yd/56 m)

• 4 (5, 5, 6) balls Color A—2485 Orange Fizz

• 1 (1, 1, 2) balls Color B—2454 Grape Nehi

• 1 ball all sizes Color C—2435 Mountain Dew

Equivalent yarn

Bulky weight #5, Color A: 244 (305, 305, 366) yd; Color B: 61 (61, 61, 122) yd; Color C: 61 yd all sizes

Needles

• One pair *each* size U.S. 9 (5.5 mm) and 10½ (6.5 mm) or size to obtain gauge

One ¾" pin back for flower

Stitch markers

GAUGE

13 sts and 20 rows = 4" in Stockinette Stitch, using larger needles. Take time to save time, check your gauge.

PATTERN STITCHES

GARTER STITCH (GTR ST)

Knit every row.

2 x 2 RIB (MULTIPLE OF 4 STS)

Row 1: (WS) *P2, k2; rep from * across.

Row 2: Knit the knit sts and purl the purl sts as they face you.

Rep Row 2 for 2 x 2 Rib

STOCKINETTE STITCH (ST ST)

Knit on RS, purl on WS.

BACK

Using larger needles and Color B, CO 40 (46, 52, 58) sts. Beg Gtr st; work even for 3 rows, end WS row. Change to St st and Color A. Work even in St st until piece meas 5½ (6, 6½, 7)" from beg, end WS row. *Shape armholes:* BO 3 (4, 4, 5) sts at beg of next 2 rows—34 (38, 44, 48) sts rem. Dec 1 st each side EOR twice—30 (34, 40, 44) sts rem. Work even until armhole meas 5½ (6, 6, 6½)" from beg of shaping, end WS row; pm each side of center 14 (16, 18, 20) sts. *Shape shoulders and neck:* BO 4 (4, 5, 6) sts at beg of next 2 rows, 3 (4, 5, 5) sts at beg of next 2 rows; and, **at the same time,** on first row of shoulder shaping, work across to marker; join second ball of yarn and BO center sts, work to end. Working both sides at same time, at each neck edge, dec 1 st once. *Next RS row:* BO rem sts.

LEFT FRONT

Using larger needles and Color B, CO 19 (22, 24, 27) sts. Work as for back until armhole meas 1" from beg of shaping, end WS row—14 (16, 18, 20) sts rem. *Shape neck:* (RS) Cont in St st, at neck edge, dec 1 st every 4 rows 7 (8, 8, 9) times as foll: Knit across to last 2 sts, sl 1, k1, psso—7 (8, 10, 11) sts rem for shoulders; and, **at the same time,** when armhole meas same as back to shoulder shaping, *shape shoulder* as for back.

RIGHT FRONT

Work as for left front, rev all shaping by working armhole and shoulder shaping at the beg of WS rows, neck shaping at beg of RS rows as foll: K2tog, work to end.

FINISHING

Block pieces to measurements. Sew shoulder seams. *Armhole edging:* With RS facing, using smaller needles and Color B, pick up and knit 44 (48, 52, 56) sts around armhole shaping. Beg 2 × 2 Rib; work even for 2 rows. BO all sts loosely in rib. *Front and neck edging:* With RS facing, using smaller needles and Color B, beg at lower right front edge, pick up and knit 29 (32, 35, 38) sts along right front to beg of neck shaping, 18 (20, 20, 22) sts along neck edge to shoulder, 20 (22, 24, 26) sts across back neck, 18 (20, 20, 22) sts along left front neck shaping, and 29 (32, 35, 38) sts along left front to lower edge—114 (126, 134, 146) sts. Beg 2 × 2 Rib, beg and end p2; work even for 2 rows. BO all sts loosely in rib. Sew side seams.

FLOWER PETALS (MAKE 5)

Using larger needles and Color A, CO 2 sts. *Row 1:* K1-f/b of both sts—4 sts. *Row 2:* Purl. *Row 3:* K1-f/b of each st—8 sts. *Row 4:* Sl 1 purlwise, purl to end. *Row 5:* Sl 1 knitwise, BO 2 sts, knit to end—6 sts. *Row 6:* Sl 1 purlwise, BO 2 sts, purl to end—4 sts. *Row 7:* Sl 1 knitwise, BO rem sts. Join petals in circle, overlapping the RH side over the LH side of the previous petal (see photo).

FLOWER CENTER

Using larger needles and Color B, CO 4 sts. Beg St st; work even for 3 rows. BO all sts. Gather all 4 corners tog and pull them through the center of the flower petals. Weave in ends to secure center.

LEAF (MAKE 1)

Using larger needles and Color C; *CO 18 sts. *Row 1:* BO 5 sts, knit to end—13 sts. *Row 2:* Purl across to last st, sl last st. *Row 3:* BO 5 sts, knit to end—8 sts. *Row 4:* Purl across to last st, sl last st. *Row 5:* BO 4 sts, knit to end—4 sts. *Row 6:* Purl across to last st, sl last st. *Row 7:* BO rem sts. Do *not* end off. Rep from * once. Attach leaf to underside of petals (see photo). Sew pin back onto WS of flower. Weave in ends.

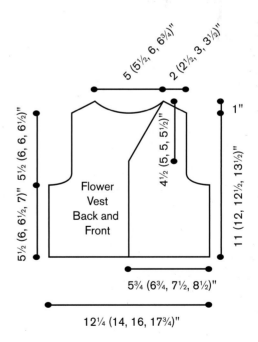

LADDER-RIB PULLOVER

SIZES

2 (4, 6, 8)

FINISHED MEASUREMENTS

28 (31, 34, 37)"

MATERIALS

Classic Elite Yarns

Beatrice (100% merino wool; 50-g hank = approx 63 yd/58 m)

• 8 (9, 11, 12) hanks 3257 Seurat's Pond

Equivalent yarn

Bulky weight #5, 504 (567, 693, 756) yd

Needles

• One pair size U.S. 10 (6 mm) or size to obtain gauge

• One 16" circular size U.S. 9 (5.5 mm) for neck

Stitch holders

Stitch markers

GAUGE

16 sts and 24 rows = 4" in Stockinette Stitch, using larger needles; 17 sts and 24 rows = 4" in Ladder Rib, using larger needles. Take time to save time, check your gauge.

PATTERN STITCHES

STOCKINETTE STITCH (ST ST)

Knit on RS, purl on WS.

GARTER STITCH (GTR ST)

Knit every row.

LADDER RIB (MULTIPLE OF 12 STS +7)

Rows 1 and 3: *P3, k1, p3, k5; rep from * across to last 7 sts, p3, k1, p3.

Row 2: K3, p1, k3, *p5, k3, p1, k3; rep from * across.

Row 4: Knit.

Rep Rows 1–4 rows for Ladder Rib.

CIRCULAR LADDER RIB (MULTIPLE OF 10 STS)

Rnds 1–3: *P3, k1, p3, k3; rep from * around.

Rnd 4: Purl.

Work Rnds 1–4 for Circular Ladder Rib.

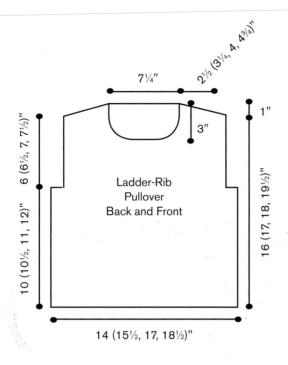

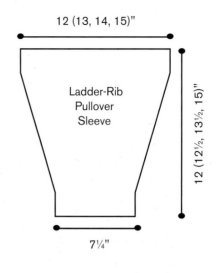

BACK

Using larger needles, CO 61 (67, 73, 79) sts. *Est patt:* (RS) Work 3 (0, 3, 0) sts in St st, 55 (67, 67, 79) sts in Ladder Rib, 3 (0, 3, 0) sts in St st. Work even as est until piece meas 5 (5½, 6, 7)" from beg, end WS row. Change to Gtr st; and, **at the same time,** dec 4 sts evenly across row—57 (63, 69, 75) sts. Work 2 rows even, end RS row. (WS) Change to St st; work even until piece meas 10 (10½, 11, 12)" from beg, end WS row. *Shape armholes:* (RS) BO 4 sts at beg of next 2 rows— 49 (55, 61, 67) sts rem. Work even until armhole meas 6 (6½, 7, 7½)" from shaping, end WS row. *Shape shoulders and neck:* (RS) BO 3 (4, 5, 6) sts at beg of next 4 rows, then 4 (5, 6, 7) sts at beg of next 2 rows—29 sts rem. Place rem sts on holder for neck.

FRONT

Work as for back until armhole meas 4 (4½, 5, 5½)" from shaping, end WS row—49 (55, 61, 67) sts rem. *Shape neck:* (RS) Work 17 (20, 23, 26) sts, join second ball of yarn, work center 15 sts and place on a holder for neck, work to end. Working both sides at same time, at each neck edge, BO 2 sts once, then dec 1 st EOR 5 times—10 (13, 16, 19) sts rem each shoulder. Work even until armhole meas same as back to shoulder shaping, end WS row. *Shape shoulders* as for back.

SLEEVES

Using larger needles, CO 31 sts; work even in Ladder Rib patt until piece meas 2" from beg, end WS row. *Est patt:* (RS) Work 6 sts in Gtr st, 19 sts in Ladder Rib as est, work to end in Gtr st. Work 2 rows as est, end RS row. *Est patt:* (WS) Work 6 sts in St st, 19 sts as est, work in St st to end. *Shape sleeve:* (RS) Cont as est, inc 1 st each side this row, then every 4 rows 8 (10, 12, 14) times, working inc sts in St st as they become available—49 (53, 57, 61) sts. Work even until piece meas 12 (12½, 13½, 15)" from beg, end WS row. BO all sts.

FINISHING

Block pieces to measurements. Sew shoulder seams. Set in sleeves; sew side and sleeve seams. *Neckband:* With RS facing, using smaller circular needle, work 29 sts from holder for back neck, pick up and knit 8 sts along left front neck edge, work 15 sts from holder for front neck, pick up and knit 8 sts along right front neck edge, pm for beg of rnd—60 sts. Work 4 rnds in Circular Ladder Rib for neckband. BO all sts purlwise.

ZIP-UP SWEATER

SIZES
4 (6, 8, 10)

FINISHED MEASUREMENTS
29 (30½, 32½, 35)"

MATERIALS
Classic Elite yarns

Flash (100% mercerized cotton; 50-g hank = approx 93 yd/85 m)
- 4 (4, 5, 6) hanks Main Color (MC)—6193 Electric Blue
- 1 hank all sizes Color A—6104 Thistle
- 1 hank all sizes Color B—6140 Red Rose
- 1 hank all sizes Color C—6146 Lily Pad
- 2 (2, 2, 3) hanks Color D—6168 Tangerine
- 1 hank all sizes Color E—6106 Off White

Equivalent yarns

Worsted weight #4, MC: 372 (372, 465, 558) yd; Colors A, B, C, and E: 93 yd all sizes; Color D: 186 (186, 186, 279) yd

Needles
- One 24" circular size U.S. 7 (4.5 mm) or size to obtain gauge

12 (14, 14, 16)" separating zipper in color to match MC

GAUGE
19 sts and 24 rows = 4" in Stockinette Stitch. Take time to save time, check your gauge.

NOTE
Stripe Sequence is worked using six colors. Some of the colors are worked in single-row stripes. The pieces are worked flat but are worked on circular needles to eliminate cutting and rejoining colors, leaving ends to weave in later. Simply slide the sts to the end where the next color to be used was left and work the next row (RS or WS) in patt.

PATTERN STITCHES

STOCKINETTE STITCH (ST ST)
Knit on RS, purl on WS.

1 x 1 RIB (MULTIPLE OF 2 STS + 1)
Row 1: *K1, p1; rep from * across to last st, k1.

Row 2: Purl the purl sts and knit the knit sts as they face you.

Rep Rows 1–2 for 1 x 1 Rib.

LEFT FRONT ZIPPER EDGING (3 STS)
Row 1: (RS) P1, k2.

Row 2: (WS) Sl 1, p1, k1.

Rep Rows 1–2 for Left Front Zipper Edging.

RIGHT FRONT ZIPPER EDGING (3 STS)
Row 1: (RS) Sl 1, k1, p1.

Row 2: (WS) K1, p2.

Rep Rows 1–2 for Right Front Zipper Edging.

LEFT SLEEVE STRIPE SEQUENCE

Rows 1–3: Color D.

Rows 4–6: Color B.

Rows 7–9: MC.

Rows 10–12: Color B.

Rows 13 and 14: Color E.

Rows 15 and 16: Color B.

Rows 17 and 18: Color D.

Rows 19–22: Color A.

Rows 23–25: Color C.

Rows 26–28: Color E.

Rows 29–31: Color B.

Row 32: Color E.

Row 33: Color B.

Row 34: Color E.

Row 35: Color B.

Row 36: Color E.

Row 37: Color B.

Rows 38–40: Color E.

Row 41: MC.

Rows 42 and 43: Color B.

Rows 44–50: Color A.

Rows 51–53: Color B.

Rows 54–59: Color E.

Rows 60–62: Color A.

Rows 63–65: MC.

Rows 66–68: Color A.

Rows 69–71: MC.

Rows 72–80: Color D.

RIGHT SLEEVE STRIPE SEQUENCE

Rows 1 and 2: Color B.

Rows 3 and 4: Color E.

Rows 5 and 6: Color B.

Rows 7 and 8: Color D.

Rows 9–12: Color A.

Rows 13–15: Color C.

Rows 16–18: Color E.

Rows 19–21: Color B.

BACK

Using MC, CO 69 (73, 77, 83) sts; work 4 rows in 1 × 1 Rib, end WS row. Change to St st; work even until piece meas 7" from beg, end WS row. Change to Color A; work 4 rows, end WS row. (RS) Change to Color B; work even until piece meas 8 (9¼, 9¼, 11)" from beg, end WS row. **Shape armholes:** (RS) BO 7 sts at beg of next 2 rows—55 (59, 63, 69) sts. Work even until piece meas 10½ (10½, 11, 11½)" from beg, end WS row. Change to Color C; work 4 rows, end WS row. (RS) Change to Color D; work even until piece meas 13½ (15½, 15½, 17½)" from beg, end WS row. **Shape shoulders:** (RS) BO 4 (4, 5, 6) sts at beg of next 4 rows, then BO 3 (5, 5, 6) sts at beg of next 2 rows—33 sts rem. BO rem sts.

LEFT FRONT

Using MC, CO 34 (36, 38, 42) sts. *Est patt:* (RS) Work 31 (33, 35, 39) sts in 1 × 1 Rib, 3 sts in Left Front Zipper Edging. Work 4 rows as est, end WS row. *Est patt:* (RS) Work 31 (33, 35, 39) sts in St st, 3 sts in Left Front Zipper Edging. Cont as est; work even until piece meas 7" from beg, end WS row. (RS) Change to Color A; work 4 rows, end WS row. (RS) Change to Color B; work even until piece meas 8 (9¼, 9¼, 11)" from beg, end WS row. **Shape armhole:** (RS) BO 7 sts at beg of this row—27 (29, 31, 35) sts. Work even until piece meas 10½ (10½ , 11, 11½)" from beg, end WS row. (RS) Change to Color C; work 4 rows, end WS row. (RS) Change to Color D; work even until piece meas 12 (14, 14, 16)" from beg, end RS row. **Shape neck:** (WS) At neck edge, BO 10 sts once, 3 (3, 3, 4) sts once, then dec 1 st EOR 3 times—11 (13, 15, 18) sts; and, **at the same time,** when piece meas 13½ (15½, 15½, 17½)" from beg, end WS row and **shape shoulder:** (RS) At armhole edge, BO 4 (4, 5, 6) sts twice, 3 (5, 5, 6) sts once.

RIGHT FRONT

Using MC, CO 34 (36, 38, 42) sts. *Est patt:* (RS) Work 3 sts in Right Front Zipper Edging, 31 (33, 35, 39) sts in 1 × 1 Rib. Work 4 rows as est, end WS row. *Est patt:* (RS) Work 3 sts in Right Front Zipper Edging, 31 (33, 35, 39) sts in St st. Cont as est; work even until piece meas 7" from beg, end RS row. (WS) Change to Color A; work 4 rows, end RS row. (WS) Change to Color B; work even until piece meas 8 (9¼, 9¼, 11)" from beg, end RS row. **Shape armhole:** (WS) BO 7 sts at beg of this row—27 (29, 31, 35) sts. Work even until piece meas 10½ (10 ½, 11, 11½)" from beg, end RS row. (WS) Change to Color C; work 4 rows, end RS row. (WS) Change to Color D; work even until piece meas 12 (14, 14, 16)" from beg, end WS row. **Shape neck:** (RS) At neck edge, BO 10 sts once, 3 (3, 3, 4) sts once, then dec 1 st EOR 3 times—11 (13, 15, 18) sts; and, **at the same time,** when piece meas 13½ (15½, 15½, 17½)" from beg, end RS row and **shape shoulder:** (WS) At armhole edge, BO 4 (4, 5, 6) sts twice, 3 (5, 5, 6) sts once.

LEFT SLEEVE

Using MC, CO 33 (35, 35, 37) sts; work 4 rows in 1 × 1 Rib and Left Sleeve Stripe Sequence. Cont Stripe Sequence and change to St st; work even until piece meas 1" from beg, end WS row. **Shape sleeve:** (RS) Inc 1 st, each side this row, then every 6 rows 4 (9, 11, 9) times, every 8 (4, 8, 8) rows 5 (2, 0, 2) times—53 (59, 59, 61) sts. Work even until piece meas 12 (12½, 13, 14)" from beg, end WS row. BO all sts.

RIGHT SLEEVE

Using MC, CO 33 (35, 35, 37) sts; work 4 rows in 1 × 1 Rib. Change to St st; work even until piece meas 1" from beg, end WS row. **Shape sleeve** as for left sleeve; and, at the same time, when piece meas 4" from beg, work Right Sleeve Stripe Sequence once. Change to MC; work even until piece meas same as left sleeve, end WS row. BO all sts.

FINISHING

Block pieces to measurements. Sew shoulders seams. Set in sleeves; sew side and sleeve seams. Sew in zipper. **Neckband:** With RS facing, using Color D, pick up and knit 73 sts evenly around neck edge. Work in 1 × 1 Rib, working 1 row using Color D, 1 row using Color C, 1 row using Color B, 1 row using Color A. Change to MC; BO all sts loosely in patt.

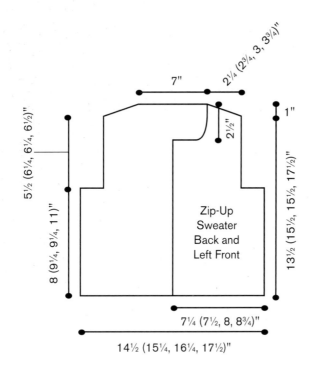

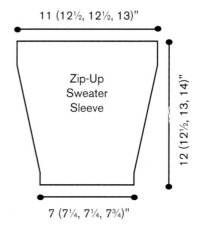

RIB CARDIGAN AND
RIB PULLOVER

SIZES
2 (4, 6, 8, 10)

FINISHED MEASUREMENTS
26 (28, 30, 32, 34)"

MATERIALS
Classic Elite Yarns
Bazic (100% wool, 50-g ball = approx 65 yd/59 m)
• 8 (9, 10, 11, 12) balls 2961 Carnation for cardigan
• 8 (9, 10, 11, 12) balls 2960 Grove for pullover
Equivalent yarn
Worsted weight #4, 520 (585, 650, 715, 780) yd
Needles
• One pair size U.S. 9 (5.5 mm) or size to obtain gauge
• Two double-pointed needles (dpn) size U.S. 9 (5.5 mm)
  for cardigan only
Stitch markers
Five 1" buttons, for cardigan only

GAUGE
16 sts and 22 rows = 4" in Stockinette Stitch. Take time to save time,
check your gauge.

PATTERN STITCHES

STOCKINETTE STITCH (ST ST)
Knit on RS, purl on WS.

CIRCULAR STOCKINETTE STITCH
Knit every rnd.

1 × 1 RIB (MULTIPLE OF 2 STS + 1)
Row 1: (RS) *K1, p1; rep from * across, [end k1 if an odd number of sts].
Row 2: Knit the knit sts and purl the purl sts as they face you.
Rep Rows 1–2 for 1 x 1 Rib.

I-CORD
Using dpn, CO 3 sts; *knit 1 row. Without turning the work, sl sts back
to beg of row (RH side of needle), pull yarn tightly from end of row;
rep from * until cord is of desired length.

BACK
(FOR CARDIGAN AND PULLOVER)

CO 53 (57, 61, 65, 69) sts. (RS) Beg St st; work even until piece meas 8 (8, 9, 9, 10)" from beg, end WS row. Change to 1 × 1 Rib; work even until piece meas 13 (14, 15, 16, 17)" from beg; BO all sts.

FRONT
(FOR PULLOVER ONLY)

CO 53 (57, 61, 65, 69) sts. (RS) Beg St st; work even until piece meas 8 (8, 9, 9, 10)" from beg, end WS row. Change to 1 × 1 Rib; work even until piece meas 11 (12, 13, 14)" from beg, end WS row. **Shape neck:** (RS) Work 19 (21, 23, 24, 26) sts; join second ball of yarn and BO center 15 (15, 15, 17, 17) sts, work to end. Working both sides at same time, at each neck edge, BO 3 sts once, 2 sts once, then dec 1 st EOR 3 times—11 (13, 15, 16, 18) sts rem each shoulder. Cont in patt as est; work even until piece meas same as back to shoulders. BO all sts.

LEFT FRONT
(FOR CARDIGAN ONLY)

CO 31 (33, 35, 37, 39) sts. *Est patt:* (RS) Work 26 (28, 30, 32, 34) sts in St st, 5 sts in 1 × 1 Rib for button band. Cont in patt as est; work even until piece meas 8 (8, 9, 9, 10)" from beg,

end WS row. (RS) Change to 1 × 1 Rib; work even until piece meas 10 (11, 12, 13, 14)" from beg, end RS row. **Shape neck:** (WS) At neck edge, BO 10 (10, 10, 11, 11) sts once, 3 sts once, 2 sts twice, then dec 1 st EOR 3 times—11 (13, 15, 16, 18) sts rem. Cont in patt as est; work even until piece meas same as back to shoulders. BO all sts. Pm for 5 buttons, first ½" from lower edge, last ½" before beg of neck shaping, rem 3 evenly spaced bet.

RIGHT FRONT
(FOR CARDIGAN ONLY)

CO 31 (33, 35, 37, 39) sts. *Est patt:* Work 5 sts in 1 × 1 Rib for buttonhole band, 26 (28, 30, 32, 34) sts in St st. Work as for left front, rev shaping by working neck shaping at beg of RS rows; and, **at the same time,** working buttonholes in buttonhole band opposite markers on left front as foll: (RS) K1, p1, [yo, p2tog], k1, work to end in St st. *Next row:* work yo in patt as est.

SLEEVES
(FOR CARDIGAN AND PULLOVER)

CO 24 (26, 29, 29, 33) sts. (RS) Beg St st; work even until piece meas ½" from beg, end WS row. **Shape sleeve:** Inc 1 st each side this row, then every 4 rows 1 (2, 0, 0, 0) times, every 6 rows

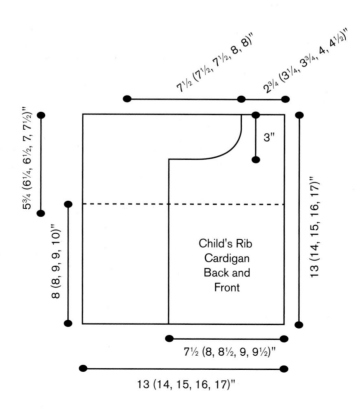

7½ (7½, 7½, 8, 8)"

2¾ (3¼, 3¾, 4, 4½)"

3"

5¾ (6¼, 6½, 7, 7½)"

8 (8, 9, 9, 10)"

13 (14, 15, 16, 17)"

Child's Rib
Cardigan
Back and
Front

7½ (8, 8½, 9, 9½)"

13 (14, 15, 16, 17)"

9 (9, 11, 13, 13) times—46 (50, 53, 57, 61) sts. Work even until piece meas 12 (13, 14, 15, 16)" from beg. BO all sts.

FINISHING

Block pieces to measurements. Sew shoulder seams. Meas down 5¾ (6¼, 6½, 7, 7½)" from shoulders on front and back, pm; sew sleeves bet markers. Sew sleeve and side seams. **CARDIGAN ONLY:** *Neckband:* With RS facing, beg at right front, pick up and knit 76 (76, 76, 78, 78) sts evenly around neck edge. Work 2" in St st; BO all sts. *Tie:* Using dpn, CO 3 sts; work I-cord until piece meas 52 (56, 60, 64, 68)" from beg. BO all sts. Lace I-cord through sweater just below the 1 × 1 Rib, beg at right front edge and end at left front edge. *Pompoms (optional):* Make two pompoms; attach one pompom to each end of I-cord. Sew on buttons. **PULLOVER ONLY** *Neckband:* With RS facing, using circular needle, beg at right shoulder, pick up and knit 66 (66, 66, 70, 70) sts evenly around neck edge; pm for beg of rnd. Work 2" in St st. BO all sts.

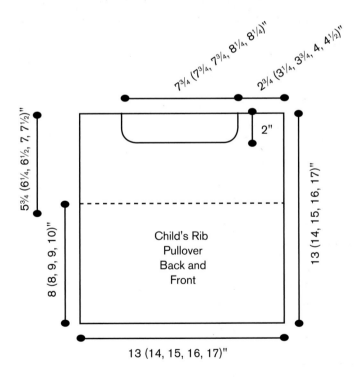

7¾ (7¾, 7¾, 8¼, 8¼)"

2¾ (3¼, 3¾, 4, 4½)"

2"

5¾ (6¼, 6½, 7, 7½)"

8 (8, 9, 9, 10)"

13 (14, 15, 16, 17)"

Child's Rib
Pullover
Back and
Front

13 (14, 15, 16, 17)"

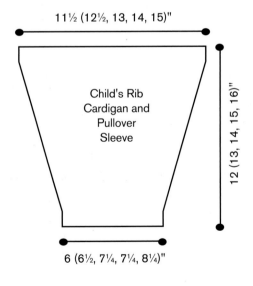

11½ (12½, 13, 14, 15)"

12 (13, 14, 15, 16)"

Child's Rib
Cardigan and
Pullover
Sleeve

6 (6½, 7¼, 7¼, 8¼)"

MULTI-STRIPED V-NECK PULLOVER

Note: See p. 150 for matching stocking cap and p. 124 for matching Men's sweater.

SIZES
4 (6, 8, 10)

FINISHED MEASUREMENTS
30 (32, 34, 36)"

MATERIALS
Classic Elite Yarns

Montera (50% llama, 50% wool; 100g hank = approx 127 yd/116 m)

- 2 (3, 3, 3) hanks Main Color (MC)—3856 Majolica Blue
- 1 hank all sizes Color A—3888 Magenta
- 1 hank all sizes Color B—3827 Cochineal
- 1 hank all sizes Color C—3893 Ch'ulla Blue
- 1 hank all sizes Color D—3887 Pear
- 1 hank all sizes Color E—3883 Strawfield
- 1 hank all sizes Color F—3883 Bolsita Orange
- 1 hank all sizes Color G—3803 Falcon Grey

Equivalent yarn

Worsted weight #4, MC: 254 (381, 381, 381) yd; Colors A–G: 127 yd all sizes

Needles
- One 24" circular size U.S. 9 (5.5 mm) or size to obtain gauge
- One 16" circular size U.S. 8 (5 mm)

Stitch holders
Stitch markers

GAUGE
16 sts and 20 rows = 4" in Stockinette Stitch, using larger needles. Take time to save time, check your gauge.

NOTES
The Stripe Sequence is worked using eight colors. Some of the colors are worked in single-row stripes. The pieces are worked flat but are worked on circular needles to eliminate cutting and rejoining colors, leaving ends to weave in later. Simply slide the sts to the end where the next color to be used was left and work the next row (RS or WS) in patt st.

Work Stripe Sequence in order once; rep Stripe Sequence in rev order, beg with Row 47.

PATTERN STITCHES

STOCKINETTE STITCH (ST ST)
Knit on RS, purl on WS.

HURDLE RIB (MULTIPLE OF 2 STS + 1)
Row 1 and 2: Knit.

Row 3: *K1, p1; rep from * across to last st, k1.

Row 4: P1 *k1, p1; rep from * across.

Rep Rows 1–4 for Hurdle Rib.

CIRCULAR HURDLE RIB (MULTIPLE OF 2 STS)
Rnd 1: Purl.

Rnd 2, 3, 6, 7: *K1, p1; rep from * around.

Rnd 4, 5, and 8: Knit.

Rep Rnds 1–8 for Circular Hurdle Rib.

BACK

Using MC and larger needle, CO 61 (65, 69, 73) sts; work Hurdle Rib and Stripe Sequence for 8 rows, end WS row. Change to St st; cont Stripe Sequence, beg with Row 9; work even until piece meas 15 (15½, 16, 17)" from beg, end WS row. **Shape shoulders and neck:** BO 8 (9, 10, 11) sts at the beg of next 4 rows—29 sts rem. Place rem sts on holder for neck.

FRONT

Work as for back until piece meas 10 (10½, 11, 12)" from beg, end WS row. **Shape neck:** Work 30 (32, 34, 36) sts, join second ball of yarn, work center st and place on holder for V-neck, work to end. Working both sides at same time, dec 1 st each neck edge EOR 14 times—16 (18, 20, 22) sts rem each shoulder. Work even until piece meas same as back to shoulders. **Shape shoulders** as for back.

SLEEVES

Using MC and larger needle , CO 31 (33, 33, 33, 33) sts; work Hurdle Rib and Stripe Sequence for 8 rows, end WS row. Change to St st; cont Stripe Sequence, beg with Row 9; and, **at the same time,** *shape sleeve:* Inc 1 st each side every 4 rows 7 (8, 11, 14) times, then every 6 rows 2 (2, 1, 0) times—49 (53, 57, 61) sts. Work even until piece meas 12 (12½, 13½, 15)" from beg. BO all sts.

FINISHING

Block pieces to measurements. Sew shoulder seams. Meas down 6 (6½, 7, 7½)" from shoulders, on back and front; pm. Sew sleeves bet markers; sew side and sleeve seams. **Neckband:** With RS facing, using smaller circular needle and MC, beg at right shoulders work 29 sts from holder for neck, pick up and knit 24 sts along left front neck edge, pm, work 1 st from holder for V-neck, pm, 24 sts along right front neck edge, pm for beg of rnd—78 sts. Work Circular Hurdle Rib for 1 rnd. *Dec rnd:* *Cont in est patt, work to 2 sts before marker, ssk, k1, k2tog, work to end of rnd; rep from * 6 times—64 sts rem. BO rem sts purlwise.

STRIPE SEQUENCE

Rows 1–9: MC.
Row 10: Color E.
Row 11: MC.
Rows 12–14: Color B.
Row 15: MC.
Row 16: *Work 1 st using MC, 1 st using Color C; rep from * across.
Row 17: *Work 1 st using Color C, 1 st using MC; rep from * across.
Row 18: *Work 1 st using MC, 1 st using Color C; rep from * across.
Row 19: MC.
Row 20: Color D.
Row 21: Color C.
Row 22: Color D.
Rows 23–24: Color G.
Row 25: Color D.
Row 26: Color C.
Row 27: Color D.
Rows 28–32: MC.
Rows 33–34: Color C.
Rows 35–37: MC.
Row 38: Color F.
Row 39: *Work 1 st using Color F, 1 st using Color E; rep from * across.
Rows 40 and 41: Color F.
Row 42: MC.
Rows 43 and 44: Color G.
Row 45: Color A.
Row 46: Color G.
Row 47: Color D.
Row 48 and 49: MC.

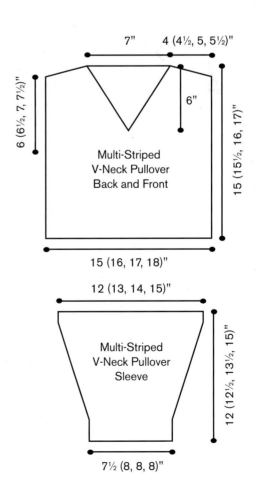

CHILD'S AND ADULT'S STRIPED STOCKING CAP

Note: Cap is shown in photos on p. 124 and p. 148.

SIZES

Child's (Woman's, Man's)

FINISHED MEASUREMENTS

18½ (20½, 22½)"

MATERIALS

Classic Elite Yarns

Montera (50% llama, 50% wool; 100-g hank = approx 127 yd/ 116 m)

• 1 hank Main Color (MC)— 3856 Majolica Blue

• 1 hank all sizes Color A— 3888 Magenta

• 1 hank all sizes Color B— 3827 Cochineal

• 1 hank all sizes Color C— 3893 Ch'ulla Blue

• 1 hank all sizes Color D— 3887 Pear

• 1 hank all sizes Color E— 3883 Strawfield

• 1 hank all sizes Color F— 3885 Bolsita Orange

• 1 hank all sizes Color G— 3803 Falcon Grey

Equivalent yarn

Worsted weight #4, MC: 127 yd all sizes; Colors A–G: 127 yd all sizes

Needles

• One 24" circular size U.S. 9 (5.5 mm) or size to obtain gauge

• Two double-pointed needles (dpn) size U.S. 9 (5.5 mm)

GAUGE

16 sts and 20 rows = 4" in Stockinette Stitch. Take time to save time, check your gauge.

NOTES

The Stripe Sequence is worked using eight colors. Some of the colors are worked in single-row stripes. The pieces are worked flat but are worked on circular needles to eliminate cutting and rejoining colors, leaving ends to weave in later. Simply slide the sts to the end where the next color to be used was left and work the next row (RS or WS) in patt st.

Work Stripe Sequence in order once; rep Stripe Sequence in rev order, beg with Row 47 once; then rep Stripe Sequence in order, beg with Row 9 until you have worked to desired length of hat.

PATTERN STITCHES

STOCKINETTE STITCH (ST ST)

Knit on RS, purl on WS.

HURDLE RIB (MULTIPLE OF 2 STS + 1)

Row 1 and 2 Knit.

Row 3: *K1, p1; rep from * across to last st, k1.

Row 4: P1 *k1, p1; rep from * across.

Rep Rows 1–4 for Hurdle Rib.

I-CORD

Using dpn, CO 4 sts; *knit 1 row. Without turning work, sl sts back to beg of row (RH side of needle), pull yarn tightly from end of row; rep from * until desired length of cord.

STRIPE SEQUENCE

Rows 1–9: MC.

Row 10: Color E.

Row 11: MC.

Rows 12–14: Color B.

Row 15: MC.

Row 16: *Work 1 st using MC, 1 st using Color C; rep from * across.

Row 17: *Work 1 st using Color C, 1 st using MC; rep from * across.

Row 18: *Work 1 st using MC, 1 st using Color C; rep from * across.

Row 19: MC.

Row 20: Color D.

Row 21: Color C.

Row 22: Color D.

Rows 23–24: Color G.

Row 25: Color D.

Row 26: Color C.

Row 27: Color D.

Rows 28–32: MC.

Rows 33–34: Color C.

Rows 35–37: MC.

Row 38: Color F.

Row 39: *Work 1 st using Color F, 1 st using Color E; rep from * across.

Rows 40 and 41: Color F.

Row 42: MC.

Rows 43 and 44: Color G.

Row 45: Color A.

Row 46: Color G.

Row 47: Color D.

Row 48 and 49: MC.

HAT

Using MC, CO 75 (81, 90) sts, work 8 rows in Hurdle Rib, end WS row. Change to St st and cont Stripe Sequence, beg with Row 9; work even until piece meas 3½" from beg, end WS row. **Shape crown:** (RS) Dec 1 st each side this row, then every 4 rows 10 (6, 3) times, EOR 23 (30, 37) times—7 (7, 8) sts rem. Work even until piece meas 21" from beg, end WS row. Leave rem sts on needle; break yarn leaving 12" tail and draw tail through rem sts.

FINISHING

Block piece lightly. Sew back seam. ***I-cord tassel:*** Using Color A; work I-Cord until piece meas 3" from beg. BO all sts. Using Colors B through G, work 6 more I-Cords. Attach I-Cords to top of hat for tassel.

WAVY LINE PULLOVER

{ SKILL LEVEL: INTERMEDIATE }

Note See p. 42 for the matching Women's sweater.

SIZES

4 (6, 8, 10)

FINISHED MEASUREMENTS

30 (32, 34, 36)"

MATERIALS

Classic Elite Yarns

Four Seasons (70% cotton, 30% wool, 50-g hank = approx 103 yd/94 m)

• 7 (8, 9, 10) hanks Main Color (MC)—7696 Spring Green
• 1 (1, 2, 2) hanks Color A—7691 Aegean Sea
• 1 (1, 2, 2) hanks Color B—7693 Everblue
• 1 (1, 2, 2) hanks Color C—7655 Orange Peel
• 1 (1, 2, 2) hanks Color D—7685 Burnt Orange

Equivalent yarn

Worsted weight #4, MC: 721 (824, 927, 1030) yd; Color A: 103 (103, 206, 206) yd; Color B: 103 (103, 206, 206) yd; Color C: 103 (103, 206, 206) yd; Color D: 103 (103, 206, 206) yd

Needles

• One pair *each* size U.S. 6 (4 mm) and 7 (4.5 mm) or size to obtain gauge
• One 16" circular size U.S. 6 (4.5 mm) for neck finishing

GAUGE

18 sts and 28 rows = 4" in Stockinette Stitch, using larger needles. Take time to save time, check your gauge.

PATTERN STITCHES

STOCKINETTE STITCH (ST ST)

Knit on RS, purl on WS.

GARTER STITCH (GTR ST)

Knit every row.

GARTER STRIPE SEQUENCE (WORKED IN GTR ST)

Rows 1–4: Color B.
Rows 5 and 6: MC.

Rows 7–10: Color C.
Rows 11–14: Color A.
Rows 15 and 16: Color D.
Work Rows 1–16 for Garter Stripe Sequence.

GARTER ACCENT

See chart.

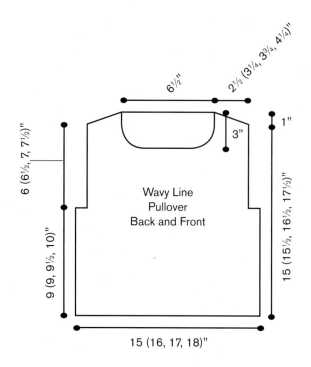

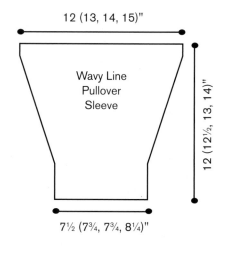

BACK

Using MC, CO 68 (72, 76, 82) sts, work 16 rows in Garter Stripe Sequence. Change to larger needles, MC and Garter Accent (see chart), beg and end where indicated for your size. Work even until piece meas 9 (9, 9½, 10)" from beg, end WS row. *Shape armhole:* (RS) BO 6 sts at beg of next 2 rows—56 (60, 64, 70) sts. Work even until piece meas 15 (15½, 16½, 17½)" from beg, end WS row. *Shape shoulders:* BO 4 (5, 6, 7) sts at beg of next 4 rows, 5 (5, 5, 6) sts at beg of next 2 rows—30 sts rem. BO rem sts.

FRONT

Work as for back until piece meas 13 (13½, 14½, 15½)", from beg, end WS row—56 (60, 64, 70) sts. *Shape neck:* (RS) Work 21 (23, 25, 28) sts, join second ball of yarn, BO 14 center sts, work to end. Working both sides at same time, at each neck edge, BO 3 sts once, 2 sts once, then dec 1 st EOR 3 times—13 (15, 17, 20) sts rem for shoulder; and **at the same time,** when piece meas same as back to shoulders, *shape shoulders* as for back.

SLEEVES

Using MC, CO 34 (36, 36, 38) sts; work 16 rows in Garter Stripe Sequence. Change to larger needles, MC and Garter Accent (see chart), beg and end where indicated for your size. Work 2 rows, end WS row. *Shape sleeve:* (RS) Cont Garter Accent, inc 1 st each side this row, then every 4 rows 9 (10, 13, 14) times, working inc sts in St st as they become available—54 (58, 64, 68) sts. Work even until piece meas 12 (12½, 13, 14)" from beg. BO all sts.

FINISHING

Block pieces to measurements. Sew left shoulder seam. *Neckband:* With RS facing, using circular needle and Color A, beg at back neck, pick up and knit 70 sts evenly around neck edge. Work in Gtr st; 1 row in Color A. Change to Color C; work 2 rows. Change to Color B; work 1 row, then BO all sts loosely. Sew right shoulder seam and neckband seam. Set in sleeves; sew sleeve and side seams.

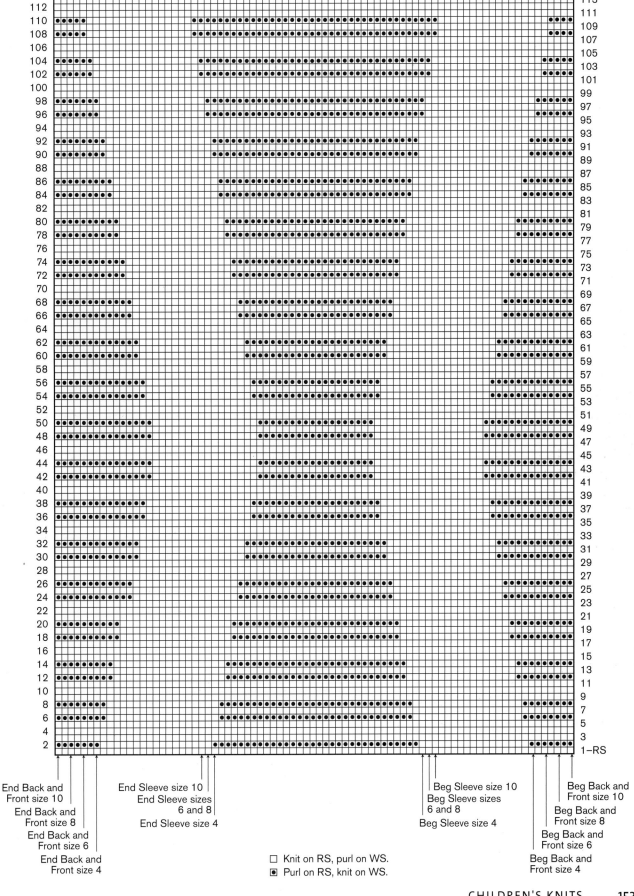

End Back and
Front size 10

End Back and
Front size 8

End Back and
Front size 6

End Back and
Front size 4

End Sleeve size 10
End Sleeve sizes
6 and 8
End Sleeve size 4

Beg Sleeve size 10
Beg Sleeve sizes
6 and 8
Beg Sleeve size 4

Beg Back and
Front size 10

Beg Back and
Front size 8

Beg Back and
Front size 6

Beg Back and
Front size 4

☐ Knit on RS, purl on WS.
▣ Purl on RS, knit on WS.

COLOR-FLECKED RIB CARDIGAN

SIZES
4 (6, 8, 10)

FINISHED MEASUREMENTS
27½ (29, 31, 33)"

MATERIALS
Classic Elite Yarns

Bubbles (70% viscose, 15% nylon, 50-g ball = approx 94 yd/86 m)
• 7 (8, 9, 10) balls Main Color (MC)—2435 Mountain Dew
• 1 ball Contrast Color (CC)—2431 Gulfstream

Equivalent yarn

Bulky weight #5, MC: 427 (488, 549, 610) yd; CC: 61 yd all sizes

NEEDLES
• One pair size U.S. 10½ (6.5 mm) or size to obtain gauge

Five 1" buttons

Stitch holders

Stitch markers

GAUGE
13 sts and 24 rows = 4" in 3 x 3 Rib. Take time to save time, check your gauge.

PATTERN STITCHES

3 × 3 RIB (MULTIPLE OF 6 STS + 3)
Row 1: (RS) K3, *p3, k3; rep from * across.
Row 2: *P3, k3; rep from * across to last 3 sts, p3.
Rep Rows 1–2 for 3 x 3 Rib.

GARTER STITCH (GTR ST)
Knit every row.

STOCKINETTE STITCH (ST ST)
Knit on RS, purl on WS.

REVERSE STOCKINETTE STITCH (REV ST ST)
Purl on RS, knit on WS.

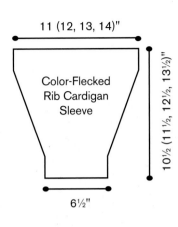

11 (12, 13, 14)"

Color-Flecked Rib Cardigan Sleeve

10½ (11½, 12½, 13½)"

6½"

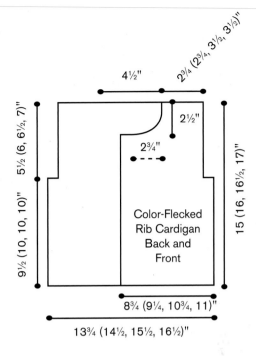

4½"

2¾ (2¾, 3½, 3½)"

2½"

2¾"

5½ (6, 6½, 7)"

9½ (10, 10, 10)"

Color-Flecked Rib Cardigan Back and Front

15 (16, 16½, 17)"

8¾ (9¼, 10¾, 11)"

13¾ (14½, 15½, 16½)"

BACK

Using MC, CO 45 (47, 51, 53) sts. *Est patt:* (RS) Work 0 (1, 0, 1) st in St st, 45 (45, 51, 51) sts in 3 × 3 Rib, 0 (1, 0, 1) in St st. Cont in patt as est; work even until piece meas 2" from beg, end WS row. Change to CC and Gtr st; work 2 rows. Change to MC; work 1 row. *Est patt:* (WS) Work 0 (1, 0, 1) st in St st, 45 (45, 51, 51) sts in 3 × 3 Rib, 0 (1, 0, 1) in St st. Work even until piece meas 9½ (10, 10, 10)" from beg, end WS row. *Shape armholes:* BO 6 (7, 6, 7) sts at the beg of next 2 rows—33 (33, 39, 39) sts. Cont in patt as est; work even until armhole meas 5½ (6, 6½, 7)" from beg, end WS row. *Shape shoulders:* BO 9 (9, 12, 12) sts at beg of next 2 rows—15 sts rem. Place rem sts on holder for back neck.

LEFT FRONT

Using MC, CO 29 (30, 35, 36) sts. *Est patt:* (RS) Work 0 (1, 0, 1) st in St st, 21 (21, 27, 27) sts in 3 × 3 Rib, 3 sts in Rev St st, 5 sts in St st [button band]. Cont in patt as est; work even until piece meas 2" from beg, end WS row. Change to CC and Gtr st; work 2 rows. Change to MC; work 1 row. *Est patt:* (WS) Work 5 sts in St st [button band], 3 sts Rev St st, 21 (21, 27, 27) sts in 3 × 3 Rib, 0 (1, 0, 1) st in St st. Work even until piece meas same as back to armhole, end WS row. *Shape armhole:* (RS) BO 6 (7, 6, 7) sts beg of this row—23 (23, 29, 29) sts rem. Cont in patt as est; work even until armhole meas 3 (3½, 4, 4½)" from beg of shaping, end RS row. *Shape neck:* (WS) At neck edge, BO 4 sts once, 3 sts twice, 2 sts once, then dec 1 st every row 2 (2, 5, 5) times—9 (9, 12, 12) sts rem for shoulder. Work even until armhole meas same as back to shoulder; BO rem sts. Pm for 5 buttons, first ¾" from lower edge, last ¾" from beg of neck shaping, rem 3 evenly spaced bet.

RIGHT FRONT

Using MC, CO 29 (30, 35, 36) sts. *Est patt:* (RS) Work 5 sts in St st [buttonhole band], 3 sts Rev St st, 21 (21, 27, 27) sts 3 × 3 Rib, 0 (1, 0, 1) st in St st. Cont in patt as est; work as for left front, omitting pocket, rev all shaping, working armhole shaping at beg of WS rows, and neck shaping at beg of RS rows; and, **at the same time,** working buttonholes in buttonhole band opposite markers on left front as foll: Work 2 sts, [yo, k2tog] at each marker, work to end.

SLEEVES

Using MC, CO 21 sts; work 3 × 3 Rib until piece meas 2" from beg, end WS row. Change to CC and Gtr st; work 2 rows. Change to MC; work 1 row. (WS) Change to 3 × 3 Rib; and, **at the same time,** *shape sleeve:* Inc 1 st each side this row, then every 4 rows 7 (8, 10, 11) times, working inc sts in 3 × 3 Rib as they become available—37 (39, 43, 45) sts. Work even until piece meas 10½ (11½, 12½, 13½)" from beg, end WS row. BO all sts.

FINISHING

Block pieces to measurements. Sew shoulders tog. Set in sleeves; sew sleeve and side seams. *Right front edging:* With RS facing using MC, pick up and knit 58 (60, 62, 64) sts along right front edge. BO all sts. *Left front edging:* Work as for right front edging. *Neckband:* Using CC, pick up and knit 59 (59, 67, 67) sts evenly around neck edge; work 2 rows in Gtr st. BO all sts. Sew on buttons.

STRIPED ROLL-NECK PULLOVER

SIZES

2 (4, 6, 8)

FINISHED MEASUREMENTS

28 (30½, 32, 34)"

MATERIALS

Classic Elite Yarns

Flash (100% mercerized marled cotton, 50-g hank = approx 93 yd/85 m)

• 3 (4, 4, 5) hanks Color A—6192 Lapis

• 3 (3, 4, 4) hanks Color B—6147 Cool Mix

Equivalent yarn

Worsted weight #4, Color A: 279 (372, 372, 465) yd; Color B: 279 (279, 372, 372) yd

Needles

• One pair size U.S. 7 (4.5 mm) or size needed to obtain gauge

• One 16" circular size U.S. 7 (4.5 mm) for neck finishing

Stitch holders

GAUGE

21 sts and 26 rows = 4" in Reverse Stockinette Stitch. Take time to save time, check your gauge.

PATTERN STITCHES

GARTER STITCH (GTR ST)

Knit every row.

REVERSE STOCKINETTE STITCH (REV ST ST)

Purl on RS, knit on WS.

CIRCULAR REVERSE STOCKINETTE STITCH

Purl every rnd.

STOCKINETTE STITCH (ST ST)

Knit on RS, purl on WS.

CENTER RIB (MULTIPLE OF 22 STS)

Row 1: K5, p3, k6, p3, k5.

Row 2: P5, k3, p6, k3, p5.

Rep Rows 1–2 for Center Rib.

STRIPE SEQUENCE (ANY NUMBER OF STS)

Rows 1–10: Color A.

Rows 11–20: Color B.

Rows 21–24: Color A.

Rows 25–28: Color B.

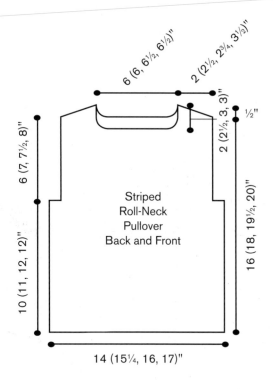

6 (6, 6½, 6½)"   2 (2½, 2¾, 3½)"

2 (2½, 3, 3)"   ½"

10 (11, 12, 12)"

6 (7, 7½, 8)"

16 (18, 19½, 20)"

Striped
Roll-Neck
Pullover
Back and Front

14 (15¼, 16, 17)"

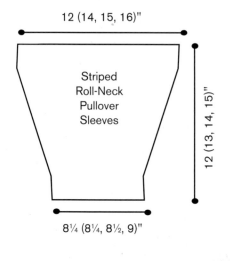

12 (14, 15, 16)"

Striped
Roll-Neck
Pullover
Sleeves

12 (13, 14, 15)"

8¼ (8¼, 8½, 9)"

BACK

Using Color A, CO 74 (80, 84, 90) sts; work 1" in Gtr st, end WS row. Change to Rev St st and beg Stripe Sequence; work even until piece meas 10 (11, 12, 12)" from beg, end WS row. **Shape armholes:** BO 10 sts at beg of next 2 rows—54 (60, 64, 70) sts. Cont in patt as est; work even until armhole meas 5½ (6 ½, 7, 7 1/2)" from shaping, end WS row. **Shape shoulders and neck:** BO 5 (7, 7, 9) sts at beg of next 2 (4, 2, 4) rows, then 6 (0, 8, 0) sts at beg of next 2 rows; and, **at same time,** on first row of shoulder shaping, work across to center 32 (32, 34, 34) sts, join second ball of yarn, work center sts and place on holder for back neck, work to end.

FRONT

Using Color A, CO 74 (80, 84, 90) sts. Work 1" in Gtr st, end WS row. *Est patt:* Beg Stripe Sequence; and, **at the same time,** work 26 (29, 31, 34) sts in Rev St st, 22 sts Center Rib, work to end in Rev St st. Cont in patt as est; work even until piece meas 10 (11, 12, 12)" from beg, end WS row. **Shape armholes:** BO 10 sts at beg of next 2 rows—54 (60, 64, 70) sts. Cont in patt as est, work even until armhole meas 4½ (5, 5, 5)" from shaping, end WS row. **Shape neck:** Work 19 (22, 23, 26) sts, join second ball of yarn, BO center 16 (16, 18, 18) sts and place rem sts on holder for front neck, work to end. Working both sides at

same time, at each neck edge, dec 1 st every row 8 times—11 (14, 15, 18) sts rem each shoulder. Cont in patt as est; work even until piece meas same as back to shoulders. Shape shoulders as for back.

SLEEVES

Using Color A, CO 43 (43, 45, 47) sts; work 1" in Gtr st, end WS row. *Est patt:* Work 20 (20, 21, 22) sts in Rev St st, 3 sts in St st, work to end in Rev St st. Cont in patt as est; work even until piece meas 2" from beg, end WS row. **Shape sleeve:** Inc 1 st this row each side, then every 6 (4, 4, 4) rows 9 (14, 16, 18) times—63 (73, 79, 85) sts. Cont in patt as est, work even until piece meas 12 (13, 14, 15)" from beg. BO all sts.

FINISHING

Block pieces to measurements. Sew shoulder seams. Set in sleeves; sew sleeve and side seams. **Neckband:** With RS facing, using circular needle and Color B, work 32 (32, 34, 34) sts from holder for back neck, pick up and knit 16 (16, 17, 17) sts along left front neck edge, work 16 (16, 18, 18) sts from holder for front neck, pick up and knit 16 (16, 17, 17) sts along right front neck edge—80 (80, 86, 86) sts. Work 6 rnds in Circular Rev St st. BO all sts.

BASKET-WEAVE PULLOVER

SIZES

2 (4, 6, 8)

FINISHED MEASUREMENTS

27 (30, 32, 35)"

MATERIALS

Classic Elite Yarns

Provence (100% mercerized Egyptian cotton, 100-g hank = approx 205 yd/187 m)

• 3 (4, 4, 5) hanks 2647 Delft Blue

Equivalent yarn

Light worsted weight #3, 615 (820, 820, 1025) yd

Needles

• One pair *each* size U.S. 5 (3.75 mm) and 6 (4 mm) or size to obtain gauge
• One 16" circular size U.S. 4 (3.5 mm)

Stitch holders

Stitch markers

GAUGE

21 sts and 32 rows = 4" in Garter Basket Weave, using larger needles; 22 sts and 28 rows = 4" in Beaded Rib, using larger needles.
Take time to save time, check your gauge.

SPECIAL TECHNIQUE

THREE-NEEDLE BIND-OFF METHOD

Sl sts from holders onto separate needles, with needles pointing in same direction and held parallel. Hold WS of garment pieces tog (to form ridge on outside). With a third needle, knit first st of front and back needles tog, *knit next st from each needle tog (2 sts on RH needle), BO 1 st; rep from * until all sts are bound off.

PATTERN STITCHES

BEADED RIB (MULTIPLE OF 5 STS + 2)

Row 1: (RS) P2, *k1, p1, k1, p2; rep from * to end.
Row 2: (WS) K2, *p3, k2; rep from * to end.
Rep Rows 1–2 for Beaded Rib.

CIRCULAR BEADED RIB (MULTIPLE OF 5 STS)

Rnd 1: *P2, k1, p1, k1; rep from * across.
Rnd 2: *P2, k3; rep from * across.
Rep Rnds 1–2 for Beaded Rib.

GARTER BASKET WEAVE (MULTIPLE OF 7 STS + 1)

See chart.

GARTER STITCH (GTR ST)

Knit every row.

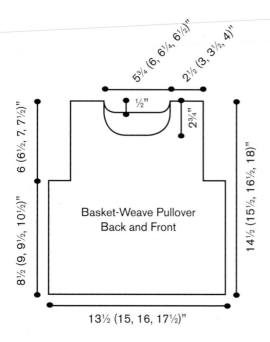

5¾ (6, 6¼, 6½)"

2½ (3, 3½, 4)"

½"

2¾"

6 (6½, 7, 7½)"

14½ (15½, 16½, 18)"

8½ (9, 9½, 10½)"

Basket-Weave Pullover
Back and Front

13½ (15, 16, 17½)"

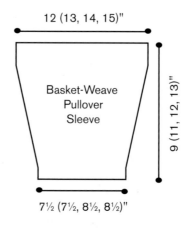

12 (13, 14, 15)"

Basket-Weave
Pullover
Sleeve

9 (11, 12, 13)"

7½ (7½, 8½, 8½)"

▪ GARTER BASKET WEAVE CHART

Multiple of 7 sts + 1; 18 row repeat

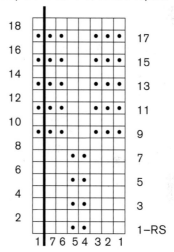

☐ Knit on RS, purl on WS.

⊡ Purl on RS, knit on WS.

BACK

Using smaller needles, CO 72 (77, 87, 92) sts; work 2½ (2½, 3, 3)" in Beaded Rib, end RS row. Knit 1 row on WS, dec 1 (inc 1, dec 2, 0) sts across—71 (78, 85, 92) sts rem. *Next row:* (RS) BO all sts. *Next row:* (WS) Pick up 71 (78, 85, 92) sts. Change to larger needles and Garter Basket Weave; work even until piece meas 8½ (9, 9½, 10½)" from beg, end WS row. **Shape armholes:** BO 7 sts at beg of next 2 rows—57 (64, 71, 78) sts rem. Work even until armhole meas 5½ (6, 6½, 7)" from beg, end WS row. **Shape neck:** (RS) Work 17 (20, 23, 26) sts, join second ball of yarn, BO center 23 (24, 25, 26) sts, work to end. Working both sides at same time, BO 4 sts at each neck edge once—13 (16, 19, 22) sts rem each shoulder. Work even until armhole meas 6 (6½, 7, 7½)" from shaping; place sts on holder.

FRONT

Work as for back until armhole meas 3¼ (3¾, 4¼, 4¾)" from shaping, end WS row—57 (64, 71, 78) sts rem. **Shape neck:** (RS) Work 22 (25, 28, 31) sts, join second ball of yarn, BO 13 (14, 15, 16) center sts, work to end. Working both sides at same time, at each neck edge, BO 3 sts once, 2 sts once, then dec 1 st EOR 4 times—13 (16, 19, 22) sts rem each shoulder. Work even until piece meas same as back to shoulders; place sts on holder.

SLEEVES

Using larger needles, CO 42 (42, 47, 47) sts; work in Beaded Rib for 1", end WS row. **Shape sleeve:** (RS) Inc 1 st each side this row, then every 4 rows 11 (14, 14, 15) times, every 6 rows 0 (0, 0, 2) times—66 (72, 77, 83) sts. Work even until piece meas 8½ (10½, 11½, 12½)" from beg, end RS row; work 5 rows in Gtr st, dec 3 (4, 4, 5) sts evenly on first row—63 (68, 73, 78) sts. BO rem sts.

FINISHING

Block pieces to measurements. With WS facing, join shoulder seams using Three-Needle Bind-Off Method. Set in sleeves; sew sleeve and side seams. **Neckband:** With RS facing, using circular needle, pick up and knit 100 (100, 105, 105) sts evenly around neck edge; pm for beg of rnd. Purl 1 rnd, then work 8 rnds in Circular Beaded Rib. BO all sts loosely purlwise.

CAT SWEATER

SKILL LEVEL: INTERMEDIATE

Note: See p. 162 for Mouse Skirt and p. 164 for matching socks.

SIZES
2 (4, 6)

FINISHED MEASUREMENTS
24 (26, 28)"

MATERIALS
Classic Elite yarns

Star (99% cotton, 1% Lycra; 50-g hank = approx 112 yd/102 m)

• 4 (5, 6) hanks Main Color (MC)—5189 Norwich Pink or 5150 Bittersweet

• 1 hank all sizes 5101 Bleach (for embroidery)

Dazzle (100% nylon; 50-g ball = approx 94 yd/86 m)

• 1 ball all sizes Contrast Color (CC)— 1830 Tickled Pink or 1885 Gorgeous Orange

Equivalent yarn

Worsted weight #4, MC: 448 (560, 672) yd; embroidery color: 112 yd; worsted weight #4 to bulky #5, CC: 94 yd all sizes

Needles

• One pair size U.S. 11 (8 mm) or size to obtain gauge

• One 16" circular size U.S. 11 (8 mm)

Three ⅝" buttons for cat's face

Tapestry needle

GAUGE
16 sts and 26 rows = 4" in Stockinette Stitch, using MC with 2 strands of yarn held tog. Take time to save time, check your gauge.

PATTERN STITCHES

REVERSE STOCKINETTE STITCH (REV ST ST)
Purl on RS, knit on WS.

STOCKINETTE STITCH (ST ST)
Knit on RS, purl on WS.

CAT EMBROIDERY
See Cat Embroidery Diagram.

Note: Embroidery diagram is not shown full size.

6"

1¾ (2, 2¼)"

2½ (2½, 2¾)"

5 (5½, 6)"

½ (½, ¾)"

12 (13, 14)"

Cat Sweater
Back and Front

7 (7½, 8)"

12 (13, 14)"

10 (11, 12)"

2¾ (3, 3½)"

Cat Sweater
Sleeve

9½ (10½, 11½)"

8 (8½, 9)"

Buttons

Chain Stitch

A
B

A
B

Backstitch

BACK

Using 2 strands of CC held tog, CO 48 (52, 56) sts; work
3 rows in Rev St st, end RS row. (WS) Change to MC with
2 strands of yarn held tog, and St st; work 4 rows, end RS
row. Knit 1 WS row. (RS) Change to St st; work even until
piece meas 7 (7½, 8)" from beg, end WS row. *Shape armholes:*
(RS) BO 2 (3, 3) sts at beg of next 2 rows, then dec 1 st each
side EOR 3 (3, 4) times—38 (40, 42) sts rem. Work even until
armhole meas 5 (5½, 6)" from beg of shaping, end WS row.
Shape shoulders and neck: (RS) BO 3 (4, 3) sts at beg of next
2 (4, 6) rows, then 4 (0, 0) sts at beg of next 2 rows; and, **at the
same time,** on the first row of shoulder shaping, work across
to center 16 sts, join second ball of yarn and BO center sts,
work to end. Working both sides at same time, BO 4 sts at each
neck edge once.

FRONT

Work as for back until armhole meas 3 (3½, 4)" from beg of
shaping, end WS row—38 (40, 42) sts. *Shape neck:* (RS) Work
15 (16, 17) sts; join second ball of yarn, BO center 8 sts, work
to end. Working both sides at same time, at each neck edge,
BO 3 sts once, 2 sts once, then dec 1 st EOR 3 times—7 (8, 9)

sts rem each shoulder. Work even until armhole meas same as
back to shoulders. *Shape shoulders* as for back.

SLEEVES

Using 2 strands of CC held tog, CO 32 (34, 36) sts; work
3 rows in Rev St st, end RS row. (WS) Change to MC with
2 strands of yarn held tog, and St st; work 4 rows, end RS
row. Knit 1 WS row. (RS) Change to St st; work 3 rows, end
RS row. Knit 1 WS row. (RS) Change to St st; work even until
piece meas 9½ (10½, 11½)" from beg, end WS row. *Shape
cap:* (RS) BO 2 (3, 3) sts at beg of next 2 rows, then dec 1 st
each side EOR 6 (6, 6) times—16 (16, 18) sts. BO 2 sts at beg
of next 2 (2, 2) rows—12 (12, 14) sts rem. BO rem sts.

FINISHING

Block pieces to measurements. Sew shoulder seams. Set in
sleeves; sew sleeve and side seams. *Neckband:* With RS facing,
using circular needle and 2 strands of MC held tog, pick up
and knit 60 sts evenly around neck edge. BO all sts purlwise.
Embroider cat on front of garment as shown in the photo and
Cat Embroidery Diagram.

MOUSE SKIRT

Note: See p. 160 for Cat Sweater and p. 164 for matching socks.

SIZES

2 (4, 6)

FINISHED MEASUREMENTS

Waist: 22 (23, 24)"

Length: 9½ (10½ , 11½)"

MATERIALS

Classic Elite yarns

Star (99% cotton, 1% Lycra; 50-g hank = approx 112 yd/102 m)

- 4 (5, 6) hanks Main Color (MC)—5189 Norwich Pink
  or 5150 Bittersweet
- 1 hank all sizes 5101 Bleach (for pocket openings and embroidery)

Dazzle (100% nylon, 50-g ball = approx 94 yd/86 m)

- 2 balls all sizes Contrast Color (CC)—1830 Tickled Pink
  or 1885 Gorgeous Orange

Equivalent yarn

Worsted weight #4, MC: 448 (560, 672) yd; embroidery and pocket trim color: 112 yd all sizes; worsted weight #4 to bulky #5, CC: 188 yd all sizes

Needles

- One 16" circular size U.S. 11 (8 mm) or size to obtain gauge

Stitch markers

¾ yd ¾"-wide elastic for waistband

Tapestry needle

GAUGE

16 sts and 26 rows = 4" in Stockinette Stitch, using MC with 2 strands of yarn held tog. Take time to save time, check your gauge.

PATTERN STITCHES

REVERSE STOCKINETTE STITCH (REV ST ST)

Purl every rnd.

STOCKINETTE STITCH (ST ST)

Knit on RS, purl on WS.

CIRCULAR STOCKINETTE STITCH (ST ST)

Knit every rnd.

GARTER STITCH (GTR ST)

Knit every row.

CIRCULAR GARTER STITCH (GTR ST)

Rnd 1: Knit.

Rnd 2: Purl.

Rep Rnds 1–2 for Garter Stitch.

MOUSE EMBROIDERY

See Mouse Embroidery Diagram.

Note: Embroidery diagram is not shown full size.

SKIRT

Using MC with 2 strands of yarn held tog, CO 112 (116, 120) sts; join, taking care not to twist sts and pm for beg of rnd. *Est patt:* Work 1 st in Rev St st, work 111 (115, 119) sts in St st. *Work 2 rnds as est. Purl 1 rnd. Rep from * once. Cont as est; work even until piece meas 4 (4½, 5)" from beg. **Pocket openings:** Work 38 (42, 46) sts as est, return last 20 sts just worked to left side of needle and work them with waste yarn, with MC work 56 (60, 64) sts, return last 20 sts just worked to left side of needle and work them with waste yarn, work to end. Cont as est; work even until piece meas 6 (7, 8)" from beg. *Est patt:* Work 1 st in Rev St st, 53 (55, 57) sts in St st, 5 sts in Gtr st, 53 (55, 57) sts in St st. Cont as est until piece meas 6½ (7½, 8½)" from beg; and, **at the same time,** pm on last rnd as foll: work 14 (15, 15) sts, pm, [work 28 (29, 30) sts, pm] 3 times, work to end. **Shape waist:** *Dec rnd:* Work to 2 sts before first marker, k2tog, work to second marker, ssk after marker, work to 2 sts before third marker, k2tog, work to fourth marker, ssk after marker—108 (112, 116) sts rem. Rep dec rnd EOR 5 times—88 (92, 96) sts rem. Work even until piece meas 9½ (10½, 11½)" from beg. **Waistband Turning Row:** Purl 1 rnd. Change to St st; work back and forth until band meas 1" from purl rnd; BO all sts.

FINISHING

Block piece to measurements. Fold down waistband and sew to WS of garment. Insert elastic into waistband. Adjust elastic to size, sew ends tog, and trim. Sew opening closed. **Pocket linings:** Carefully remove waste yarn, placing lower sts on one needle for pocket bands and upper sts on another needle for lining. Turn piece upside down and work lining in St st. Work even until piece meas 3½ (4, 4½)" from opening. BO all sts. Embroider mouse on outside of pocket, as shown in the photo and Mouse Embroidery Diagram. Sew linings neatly to WS. **Pocket bands:** Using CC, work lower sts in Gtr st; work 4 rows even. BO all sts. Sew side edges of pocket bands neatly to RS.

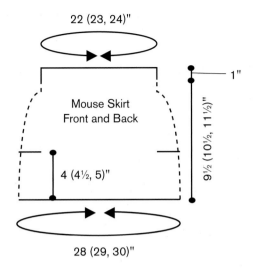

22 (23, 24)"

Mouse Skirt
Front and Back

1"

9½ (10½, 11½)"

4 (4½, 5)"

28 (29, 30)"

■ **MOUSE EMBROIDERY DIAGRAM**

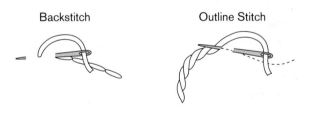

Backstitch

Outline Stitch

French Knot

TRIMMED SOCKS

{ SKILL LEVEL: INTERMEDIATE }

SIZES

2 (4, 6, 8, 10)

FINISHED MEASUREMENTS (FOOT LENGTH)

4½ (5½, 6½, 7½, 8)"

MATERIALS

Classic Elite Yarns

Star (99% cotton, 1% Lycra; 50-g hank = approx 112 yd/122 m)

• 2 (2, 3, 3, 4) hanks Main Color (MC)—5189 Norwich Pink
or 5150 Bittersweet

Dazzle (100% nylon; 50-g ball = approx 94 yd/102 m)

• 1 ball all sizes Contrast Color (CC) 1830 Tickled Pink
or 1885 Gorgeous Orange

Equivalent yarn

Worsted weight #4, MC: 224 (224, 336, 336, 448) yd; worsted weight
#4 to bulky #5, CC: 94 yd all sizes

Needles

• One set of 5 doubled-pointed needles (dpn) size U.S. 8 (5 mm)
or size to obtain gauge

Stitch markers

Tapestry needle

GAUGE

22 sts and 32 rows = 4" in Stockinette Stitch. Take time to save time,
check your gauge.

PATTERN STITCHES

GARTER STITCH (GTR ST)

Rnd 1: Knit.

Rnd 2: Purl.

Rep Rnds 1–2 for Garter Stitch

STOCKINETTE STITCH (ST ST)

Knit every rnd.

LEG

Using CC, CO 36 (36, 40, 40, 44) sts loosely. Divide sts evenly on four needles—9 (9, 10, 10, 11) sts on each needle. Join, taking care not to twist sts; pm for beg of rnd. Work in Gtr st until piece meas ½" from beg. Change to MC and St st; work even until piece meas 3½ (4, 4, 4½, 4½)" from beg.

HEEL FLAP

Knit 9 (9, 10, 10, 11) sts across first needle. Turn and, on a single needle, sl 1 st, p17 (17, 19, 19, 21) sts. Work back and forth on 18 (18, 20, 20, 22) sts for heel. *Row 1:* (RS) *Sl 1, k1; rep from * across. *Row 2:* Sl 1, purl to end. Rep Rows 1 and 2 until heel flap meas 1¾ (1¾, 2, 2, 2½)" from beg of ribbing, end WS row.

TURN HEEL

Row 1: (RS) Knit 9 (9, 10, 10, 11) sts across to center of heel, k4 sts, ssk, turn. *Row 2:* Sl 1 st, p8, p2tog, turn. *Row 3:* Sl 1 st, k8, ssk, turn. *Row 4:* Sl 1 st, p8, p2tog, turn. Rep Rows 3 and 4 until all side sts have been worked, end WS row—10 sts rem. *Next row:* K5 sts [center of row].

HEEL GUSSET

Using another needle, k5 sts and, with the same needle, pick up and knit 9 (9, 10, 10, 11) sts along right side of heel; work across instep sts, keeping them on 2 needles; then, with fifth needle, pick up and knit 9 (9, 10, 10, 11) sts along left side of heel and work across the rem 5 heel sts—14 (14, 15, 15, 16) sts on first needle, 9 (9, 10, 10, 11) sts on second and third needles, 14 (14, 15, 15, 16) sts on fourth needle—46 (46, 50, 50, 54) sts total.

SHAPE GUSSET

Pm in center of heel; rnds beg at center of heel. *Rnd 1:* Work to last 3 sts on first needle, k2tog, k1; work across second and third needles (instep sts); at beg of fourth needle, k1, ssk, work to end. *Rnd 2:* Knit all sts. Rep Rnds 1 and 2, dec at end of first needle and beg of fourth needle, until 36 (36, 40, 40, 44) sts rem. Cont on these sts until piece meas 2 (3, 4, 5, 6)" from beg of heel gusset.

SHAPE TOE

Rnd 1: Knit to last 3 sts on first needle, k2tog, k1; at beg of second needle k1, ssk, knit to end of needle; on third needle, knit to last 3 sts, k2tog, k1; on fourth needle, k1, ssk, knit to end—32 (32, 36, 36, 40) sts rem. *Rnd 2:* Knit all sts. Rep Rnds 1 and 2 until 20 sts rem, then rep Rnd 1 only until 8 sts rem. Thread yarn onto tapestry needle, pass yarn through rem 8 sts; pull tight and secure.

SIDEWAYS CABLE PULLOVER

SIZES

4 (6, 8, 10)

FINISHED MEASUREMENTS

28 (30, 32, 34)"

MATERIALS

Classic Elite Yarns

Paintbox (100% merino wool; 100-g = 110 yd/101 m)

• 4 (5, 6, 7, 8) balls 6857 French Ultramarine

Equivalent yarn

Bulky weight #5, 440 (550, 660, 770, 880) yd

Needles

• One pair size U.S. 10 (6 mm) or size to obtain gauge

• One 16" circular size U.S. 9 (5.5 mm)

• One cable needle (cn)

Stitch markers

GAUGE

14 sts and 18 rows = 4" in Reverse Stockinette Stitch, using larger needle. Take time to save time, check your gauge.

NOTE

The back, front, and sleeves of this sweater are worked from side to side.

PATTERN STITCHES

REVERSE STOCKINETTE STITCH (REV ST ST)

Purl on RS, knit on WS.

CIRCULAR STOCKINETTE STITCH (STS T)

Knit every rnd.

CABLE PANEL (MULTIPLE OF 16 STS)

Rows 1, 3, 7: (RS) K6, p4, k6.

Rows 2, 4, 6: P6, k4, p6.

Row 5: C6B, p4, C6B.

Row 8: P6, k4, p6.

Rep Rows 1–8 for Cable Panel.

BACK

Using larger needles, CO 51 (58, 63, 67) sts. *Est patt:* (RS) Work 35 (42, 47, 51) sts in Rev St st, work 16 sts Cable Panel, beg with Row 1 (3, 1, 3) of patt. Work 15 (17, 19, 21) rows as est, end WS row. **Shape neck:** (RS) Dec 1 st at beg of this row [neck edge], then dec 1 st at neck edge every row twice— 48 (55, 60, 64) sts rem. Work 26 rows even, end RS row. **Shape neck:** (WS) Inc 1 st at neck edge every row 3 times—51 (58, 63, 67) sts. Work 16 (18, 20, 22) rows as est. BO all sts loosely.

FRONT

Work as for back to beg of neck shaping, end WS row. **Shape neck:** (RS) Dec 1 st at beg of this row [neck edge], then dec 1 st at neck edge every row 10 times—40 (47, 52, 56) sts rem. Work 10 rows even, end RS row. **Shape neck:** (WS) Inc 1 st at neck edge every row 11 times—51 (58, 63, 67) sts. Work even for 16 (18, 20, 22) rows. BO all sts loosely.

SLEEVES

Using larger needles, CO 3 sts; knit 1 (WS) row. **Shape sleeve:** (RS) CO 5 sts—8 sts. Work 2 rows in Rev St st, end WS row. (RS) CO 5 sts at beg of this row, then EOR 4 (6, 6, 7) times, then 4 sts EOR 3 (1, 1, 2) times, then 3 sts 0 (0, 1, 0) time— 35 (37, 40, 46) sts. Work 2 rows even, end WS row. (RS) CO 16 sts—51 (53, 56, 62) sts. Work 1 row. *Est patt:* (WS) Work 35 (37, 40, 46) sts as est, 16 sts Cable Panel, beg with Row 4. Work as est for 32 more rows, end WS row. **Shape sleeve:** (RS) BO 16 sts, work to end—35 (37, 40, 46) sts rem. Work 1 row even. BO 3 sts at beg of this row 0 (0, 1, 0) time, then 4 sts 3 (1, 1, 2) times, then 5 sts 4 (6, 6, 7) times—3 sts rem. Work 1 row even. BO all sts loosely.

FINISHING

Block pieces to measurements. Sew shoulder seams. Meas down 7 (7, 7½, 8)" from shoulder seam on front and back, pm. Sew sleeves bet markers. Sew side and sleeve seams. **Neckband:** With RS facing, using circular needle, pick up and knit 62 sts evenly around neck edge, pm for beg of rnd. Work in St st until band meas 1¾" from pickup row; BO all sts loosely.

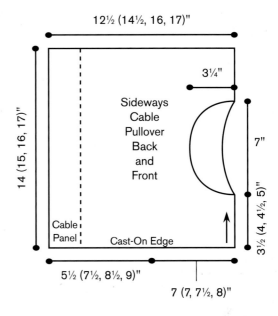

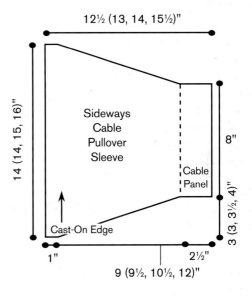

RIB POCKET HOODIE

Note: see p. 126 for Men's sweater.

SIZES
(4, 6, 8, 10)

FINISHED MEASUREMENTS
25 (28, 30½, 32½, 36)"

MATERIALS
Classic Elite Yarns
Two.Two (100% Highland wool, 50-g hank = approx 55 yd/50 m)
• 8 (9, 10, 11, 13) hanks 1558 Barn Red
Equivalent yarn
Bulky weight #5, 440 (495, 550, 605, 715) yd
Needles
• One pair size U.S. 11 (8 mm) or size to obtain gauge
• One 16" circular size U.S. 11 (8 mm) for hood
Stitch markers

GAUGE
12 sts and 17 rows = 4" in Stockinette Stitch. Take time to save time, check your gauge.

PATTERN STITCHES

2 × 2 RIB (MULTIPLE OF 4 STS + 2)
Row 1: K2, *p2, k2; rep from * across.
Row 2: Knit the knit sts and purl the purl sts as they face you.
Rep Rows 1–2 for 2 x 2 Rib.

STOCKINETTE STITCH (ST ST)
Knit on RS, purl on WS.

BACK

CO 38 (42, 46, 50, 54) sts; work in 2 × 2 Rib until piece meas 2" from beg, end WS row. Change to St st; work even until piece meas 13 (14, 15, 16, 17)" from beg. BO all sts; pm each side of center 22 (22, 22, 24, 24) sts for neck.

FRONT

Work as for back until piece meas 11 (12, 13, 14, 15)" from beg, end WS row. *Shape neck:* Work 13 (15, 17, 18, 20) sts, join second ball of yarn, BO center 12 (12, 12, 14, 14) sts, work to end. Working both sides at the same time, dec 1 st each neck edge every row 5 times—8 (10, 12, 13, 15) sts rem each shoulder. Work even until piece meas same as back to shoulders. BO rem sts.

SLEEVES

CO 22 (22, 22, 26, 26) sts; work in 2 × 2 Rib until piece meas 2" from beg, end WS row. Change to St st and *shape sleeve:* (RS) Inc 1 st each side this row, then every 4 rows 0 (6, 5, 10, 0) times, then every 6 rows 6 (2, 4, 0, 10) times—38 (40, 42, 48, 48) sts. Work even until piece meas 12 (13, 14, 15, 16)" from beg. BO all sts.

POCKET

CO 18 sts; work in 2 × 2 Rib until piece meas 6 (7, 7, 8, 8)" from beg. BO all sts.

FINISHING

Block pieces to measurements. Sew shoulder seams. Meas down 6¼ (6½, 7, 8, 8)" from shoulder seams on back and front, pm. Sew sleeves bet markers; sew sleeve and side seams. Sew pocket to front of garment, 1" above rib. *Hood:* With RS facing, using circular needle, beg and end 2" out from center front, pick up and knit 6 sts evenly along right front neck edge, 22 (22, 22, 24, 24) sts across back neck, and 6 sts along left front neck edge—34 (34, 34, 36, 36) sts. Work in St st until hood meas 10 (11, 11, 12, 12)" from pickup row. BO all sts. Fold hood in half at center back; sew hood seam. *Hood band:* With RS facing, beg at right front edge, pick up and knit 62 (66, 66, 70, 70) sts evenly around hood edge. Work in 2 × 2 Rib until band meas 2" from pickup row. BO all sts. Sew short edges of hood band to center front of garment.

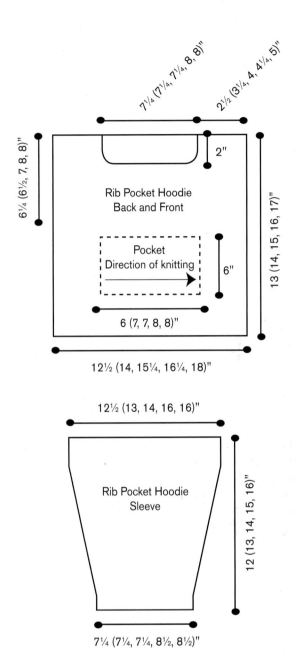

7¼ (7½, 7½, 8, 8)"   2½ (3¼, 4, 4¼, 5)"

6¼ (6½, 7, 8, 8)"

2"

Rib Pocket Hoodie Back and Front

Pocket Direction of knitting

6"

13 (14, 15, 16, 17)"

6 (7, 7, 8, 8)"

12½ (14, 15¼, 16¼, 18)"

12½ (13, 14, 16, 16)"

Rib Pocket Hoodie Sleeve

12 (13, 14, 15, 16)"

7¼ (7¼, 7¼, 8½, 8½)"

LARGE FLOWER PATTERN CARDIGAN

Note: See p. 173 for matching hat and p. 65 for matching Women's sweater.

SIZES

Girl's 4 (6, 8, 10)

FINISHED MEASUREMENTS

28 (30, 32, 34)"

MATERIALS

Classic Elite Yarns

Provence (100% mercerized Egyptian cotton; 100-g hank = approx 205 yd/187 m)

• 3 (3, 4, 4) hanks Main Color (MC)—2632 Mad Magenta

• 2 (2, 2, 3) hanks Color A—2695 Watermelon

• 1 hank all sizes Color B—2698 Orange Peel

• 1 hank all sizes Color C—2625 Rosa Rugosa

Equivalent yarn

Light worsted weight #3 or worsted weight #4, MC: 615 (615, 820, 820) yd; Color A: 410 (410, 410, 615) yd; Colors B and C: 205 yd each all sizes

Needles

• One pair *each* size U.S. 4 (3.5 mm) and 6 (4 mm) or size to obtain gauge

Six ¾" buttons

GAUGE

20 sts and 28 rows = 4" in Stockinette Stitch, using larger needles. Take time to save time, check your gauge.

PATTERN STITCHES

GARTER STITCH (GTR ST)

Knit every row.

FLORAL PATTERN

See chart.

BACK

Using smaller needles and MC, CO 70 (74, 80, 84) sts, beg Gtr st. Work 2 rows, end WS row. Change to Color A; work 3 rows. Change to MC; work 1 row, end WS row. Change to larger needles and Floral Pattern (see chart), beg and end where indicated for your size. Work as est until piece meas 9½ (10, 10, 10½)" from beg, end WS row. *Shape armholes:* (RS) Dec 1 st each side this row, then EOR 4 times—60 (64, 70, 74) sts rem. Work even until armhole meas 5 (5½, 6½, 7)" from beg, end WS row. *Shape neck:* (RS) Work 18 (19, 21, 23), join second ball of yarn, BO 24 (26, 28, 28) sts, work to end. Working both sides at same time, dec 1 st each neck edge once—17 (18, 20, 22) sts rem each shoulder. Work as est until armhole meas 5½ (6, 7, 7½)" from beg of shaping. BO rem sts.

LEFT FRONT

Using smaller needles and MC, CO 35 (37, 40, 42) sts, beg Gtr st. Work 2 rows, end WS row. Change to Color A; work 3 rows. Change to MC; work 1 row, end WS row. Change to larger needles and Floral Pattern (see chart), beg and end where indicated for your size. Work as est until piece meas 9½ (10, 10, 10½)" from beg, end WS row. *Shape armhole:* (RS) Dec 1 st at armhole edge EOR 5 times—30 (32, 35, 37) sts rem. Work as est until armhole meas 3½ (4, 5, 5½)" from beg of shaping, end RS row. *Shape neck:* (WS) At neck edge, BO 5 (5, 5, 6) sts once, 4 sts once, 3 sts once, 1 (2, 3, 2) sts once—17 (18, 20, 22) sts rem. Work as est until armhole meas 5½ (6, 7, 7½)" from beg of shaping. BO rem sts.

RIGHT FRONT

Work as for left front rev all shaping and placing Floral Pattern as indicated on chart.

SLEEVES

Using smaller needles and MC, CO 36 (36, 40, 40) sts, beg Gtr st. Work 2 rows, end WS row. Change to Color A; work 3 rows. Change to MC; work 1 row, end WS row. Change to larger needles and beg working Floral Pattern (see chart), beg and end where indicated for your size; and, **at the same time,** inc 1 st each side every 4 rows 10 (12, 15, 18) times—56 (60, 70, 76) sts. Work even until piece meas 10 (11, 12, 13)" from beg, end WS row. *Shape cap:* (RS) Dec 1 st each side EOR 5 times—46 (50, 60, 66) sts rem. BO rem sts.

FINISHING

Block pieces to measurements. Sew shoulder seams. Set in sleeves; sew side and sleeve seams. *Neckband:* With RS facing, using smaller needles and MC, pick up and knit 58 (60, 62, 64) sts evenly around neck edge. Beg Gtr st; work 1 row. Change to Color A; work 3 rows. Change to MC; work 1 row. BO all sts. *Button band:* With RS facing, using smaller needles and MC, pick up 65 (70, 76, 80) sts evenly along left front center edge. Beg Gtr st; work 1 row. Change to Color A; work 3 rows. Change to MC; work 1 row. BO all sts. *Buttonhole band:* With RS facing, using smaller needles and MC, pick up and knit 65 (70, 76, 80) sts evenly along right front center edge. Beg Gtr st; work 1 row. Change to Color A and work buttonhole row as foll: Work 4 (4, 3, 3) sts, *BO 2 sts, k12 (13, 15, 16); rep from * 4 times, BO 2 sts, work to end. *Next row:* Work in Gtr st and CO 2 sts over BO sts of previous row. Change to MC; work 1 row. BO all sts. Sew on buttons.

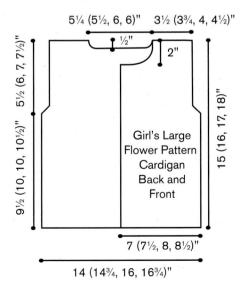

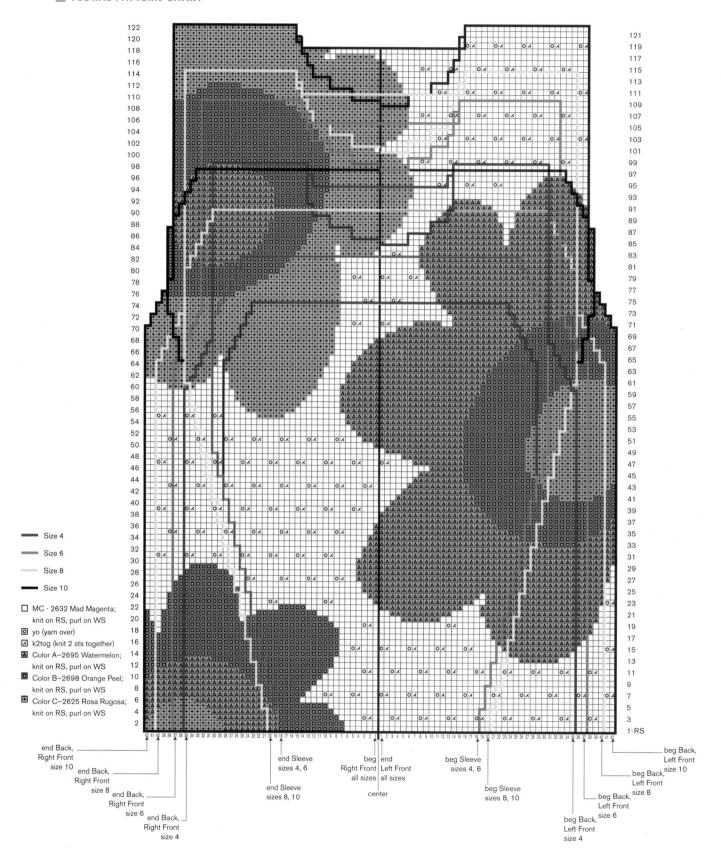

Size 4
Size 6
Size 8
Size 10

☐ MC - 2632 Mad Magenta;
  knit on RS, purl on WS
◙ yo (yarn over)
◪ k2tog (knit 2 sts together)
▲ Color A–2695 Watermelon;
  knit on RS, purl on WS
◙ Color B–2698 Orange Peel;
  knit on RS, purl on WS
✚ Color C–2625 Rosa Rugosa;
  knit on RS, purl on WS

end Back,
Right Front
size 10

end Back,
Right Front
size 8

end Back,
Right Front
size 6

end Back,
Right Front
size 4

end Sleeve
sizes 4, 6

end Sleeve
sizes 8, 10

beg   end
Right Front Left Front
all sizes all sizes

center

beg Sleeve
sizes 4, 6

beg Sleeve
sizes 8, 10

beg Back,
Left Front
size 10

beg Back,
Left Front
size 8

beg Back,
Left Front
size 6

beg Back,
Left Front
size 4

HAT WITH FLOWER

SIZES

Small (Large)

FINISHED MEASUREMENTS

Circumference: 18 (21)"

MATERIALS

Classic Elite Yarns

Provence (100% mercerized Egyptian cotton; 100-g hank = approx 205 yd/187 m)

- 1 hank both sizes Main Color (MC)—2632 Mad Magenta
- 1 hank both sizes Color A—2695 Watermelon
- 1 hank both sizes Color B—2698 Orange Peel
- 1 hank both sizes Color C—2625 Rosa Rugosa

Equivalent yarn

Light worsted weight #3, MC: 205 yd both sizes; Colors A–C: 205 yd both sizes

Needles

- One pair *each* size U.S. 6 (4 mm) and 8 (5 mm) or size to obtain gauge
- Two double-pointed needles (dpn) size U.S. 8 (5 mm)

GAUGE

14 sts and 28 rows = 4" in Stockinette Stitch using 2 strands of yarn held tog and larger needles. Take time to save time, check your gauge.

PATTERN STITCHES

GARTER STITCH (GTR ST)

Knit every row.

STOCKINETTE STITCH (ST ST)

Knit on RS, purl on WS.

I-CORD

Using dpn, *knit 1 row. Without turning the work, sl sts back to beg of row (RH side of needle), pull yarn tightly from end of row; rep from * until desired length of cord.

BRIM

Using larger needle, Color A, and 2 strands held tog, CO 120 (132) sts; beg Gtr st. Work 1 row. *Row 1:* (RS) *K8 (9), k2tog; rep from * across—108 (120) sts rem. *Row 2 and all WS rows:* Knit. *Row 3:* *K7 (8), k2tog; rep from * across—96 (108) sts rem. *Row 5:* *K6 (7), k2tog; rep from * across—84 (96) sts rem. *Row 7:* *K5 (6), k2tog; rep from * across—72 (84) sts rem. *Row 9: size Small only:* *[K4, k2tog] twice, k6; rep from * across—64 sts. *Row 9: size Large only:* *K5, k2tog; rep from * across—72 sts rem. *All sizes:* Change to MC, using 2 strands held tog, work 1 WS row in Gtr st. Change to St st; work even until piece meas 4 (5½)" from beg, end RS row. Change to Color B, using 2 strands held tog, work 1 WS row in Gtr st.

CROWN

Row 1: (RS) *K6, k2tog; rep from * across—56 (63) sts rem. *Row 2 and all WS rows:* Purl. Row 3: *K5 (7), k2tog; rep from * across—48 (56) sts rem. *Row 5:* *K4 (6), k2tog; rep from * across—40 (49) sts rem. *Row 7:* *K3 (5), k2tog; rep from * across—32 (42) sts rem. *Row 9:* *K2 (4), k2tog; rep from * across—24 (35) sts rem. *Row 11:* *K1 (3), k2tog; rep from * across—16 (28) sts rem. *Row 12:* Purl. *Size Small only:* Cut yarn, leaving approx 12" tail. Thread tail through rem sts. *Row 13: size Large only:* *K2, k2tog; rep from * across—21 sts rem. *Row 15:* *K1, k2tog; rep from * across—14 sts rem. *Row 17:* *K2tog; rep from * across—7sts rem. Cut yarn, leaving approx 12" tail. Thread tail through rem sts.

FINISHING

Sew center back seam.

LARGE FLOWER (OPTIONAL)

Center: Using smaller needles, Color B, and 1 strand, CO 45 sts; knit 1 row. *Shape center: Row 1:* (RS) *K3, k2tog; rep from * across—36 sts rem. *Row 2:* Purl. *Row 3:* *K2, k2tog; rep from * across—27 sts rem. *Row 4:* Change to Color A, using 1 strand, knit. *Row 5:* *K1, k2tog; rep from * across—18 sts rem. *Row 6:* Purl. *Row 7:* *K2tog; rep from * across—9 sts rem. Cut yarn, leaving approx 12" tail. Thread tail through rem sts. *Petal:* With RS facing, using Color C and 1 strand, pick up and knit 9 sts from CO row; work 3 rows in St st, end WS row. *Shape petal:* (RS) K2tog, k5, ssk—7 sts rem. Purl 1 WS row. Cont to dec 1 st each side EOR until 3 sts rem. Cut yarn, leaving approx 12" tail. Thread tail through rem sts. Work 4 more petals across CO row. Sew side edges tog, forming a circle. Using MC and 1 strand, work running stitch embroidery around Color B band on flower. Sew flower to side of small hat.

SMALL FLOWER (OPTIONAL)

Using larger needles, Color B, and 2 strands held tog, CO 60 sts; knit 1 row. *Next row:* (RS) *K1, BO 10 sts, k1; rep from * across—10 sts rem. *Next row:* (WS) *P2tog 5 times—5 sts rem. *Next row:* (RS): K2tog, k3—4 sts rem. Change to dpn needles and 2 strands of Color A; purl 1 row. Change to I-Cord; work even until cord meas 2½" from beg. Cut yarn and thread tail through all sts. Tie I-cord in overhand knot, forming the flower center. Sew flower to side of large hat.

SMOCKED JACKET

SIZES
(4, 6, 8)

FINISHED MEASUREMENTS
26 (28½, 31, 33)"

MATERIALS
Classic Elite Yarns

Montera (50% llama, 50% wool; 50-g hank = approx 127 yd/116 m)
- 4 (5, 6, 7) hanks Main Color (MC)—3862 Kingfisher Blue
- 1 (1, 1, 2) hanks Contrast Color (CC)—3823 Spring Leaf

Equivalent yarn

Worsted weight #4, MC: 508 (635, 762, 889) yd; CC: 127 (127, 127, 254) yd

Needles
- One pair *each* size U.S. 7 (4.5 mm) and 9 (5.5mm) or size to obtain gauge

Three (3, 4, 4) ¾" buttons

Stitch markers

GAUGE
16 sts and 21 rows = 4" in Stockinette Stitch, using larger needles; 26 sts and 21 rows = 4" in Smocking Pattern, using larger needles. Take time to save time, check your gauge.

PATTERN STITCHES

GARTER ST (GTR ST)
Knit every row.

STOCKINETTE ST (ST ST)
Knit on RS, purl on WS.

SMOCKING PATTERN (MULTIPLE OF 8 STS + 2)
Rows 1, 3, 5, and 7: (WS) K2, *p2, k2; rep from * across.

Rows 2 and 6: *P2, k2; rep from * across to last 2 sts, p2.

Row 4: *P2, insert RH needle from front bet sixth and seventh sts on LH needle and draw up a loop; sl this loop to LH needle and knit it tog with first st on LH needle; k1, p2, k2; rep from * across to last 2 sts, p2.

Row 8: *P2, k2, p2, insert RH needle from front bet sixth and seventh sts on LH needle and draw up a loop; sl this loop to LH needle and knit it tog with first st on LH needle, k1; rep from * across to last 10 sts, [p2, k2] twice, p2.

Rep Rows 1–8 for Smocking Pattern.

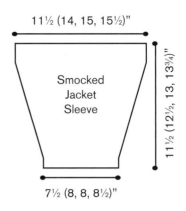

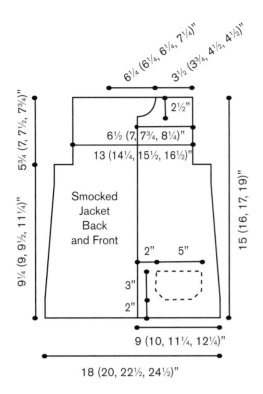

BACK

Using smaller needles and CC, CO 72 (80, 90, 98) sts; work
1" in Gtr st, end WS row. Change to larger needles, MC and St
st; work even until piece meas 6½ (6½, 6, 6)" from beg, end
WS row. **Shape sides:** (RS) Dec 1 st each side this row, then
every 4 rows 0 (0, 1, 1) time—70 (78, 86, 94) sts rem. Work
even until piece meas 9¼ (9, 9½, 11¼)" from beg, end WS row.
Inc row: (RS) K3 (7, 4, 8), m1, [k5 (5, 6, 6), m1] 13 times, k2
(6, 4, 8)—84 (92, 100, 108) sts. *Est patt:* (WS) Work 1 st in St
st, 82 (90, 98, 106) sts in Smocking Pattern, 1 st in St st. Work
as est until piece meas 15 (16, 17, 19)" from beg, end WS row.
BO all sts.

LEFT FRONT

Using smaller needles and CC, CO 36 (40, 45, 49) sts; work
1" in Gtr st, end WS row. Change to larger needles, MC, and
St st; work even until piece meas 6½ (6½, 6, 6)" from beg,
end WS row. **Shape side:** (RS) Dec 1 st beg of this row, then
every 4 rows 0 (0, 1, 1) time—35 (39, 43, 47) sts. Work even
until piece meas 9¼ (9, 9½, 11¼)" from beg, end WS row. *Inc
row:* (RS) K3 (5, 4, 6), m1, [k5 (5, 6, 6), m1] 6 times, k2 (4,
3, 5)—42 (46, 50, 54) sts. *Est patt:* (WS) Work 0 (2, 0, 2) sts in
St st, 42 (42, 50, 50) sts in Smocking Pattern, 0 (2, 0, 2) sts in St
st. Work as est until piece meas 12½ (13½, 14½, 16½)" from
beg, end RS row. **Shape neck:** (WS) At neck edge, BO 8 sts
twice, then 4 sts 0 (0, 0, 1) time, then dec 1 st EOR 4 times—
22 (26, 30, 30) sts rem. Work even until piece meas same as
back to shoulders, end WS row. BO all sts.

RIGHT FRONT

Work as for left front rev all shaping by working side shaping
at end of RS rows, and neck shaping at beg of RS rows.

SLEEVES

Using smaller needles and CC, CO 30 (32, 32, 34) sts; work
1" in Gtr st, end WS row. Change to larger needles, MC, St st
and *shape sleeve:* (RS) Inc 1 st each side this row, then every
4 rows 0 (9, 13, 12) times, every 6 rows 7 (2, 0, 1) times—
46 (56, 60, 62) sts. Work even until piece meas 11½ (12½,
13, 13¾)" from beg, end WS row. BO all sts.

POCKETS (MAKE 2)

Using larger needles and MC, CO 14 sts; work 1 row in St st.
Shape sides: (RS) Cont in St st and inc 1 st each side this row,
then EOR twice—20 sts. Work even until piece meas 2½" from
beg, end WS row. Change to smaller needles, CC, and Gtr st;
dec 3 sts evenly across first row—17 sts. Work even until piece
meas 3" from beg; BO all sts loosely.

FINISHING

Block pieces to measurements. Pm 3½ (4, 4½, 4½)" in from
armhole edge on back. Sew shoulder seams from armhole
edge to marker. Set in sleeves; sew sleeve and side seams.
Sew pockets to front of garment as indicated on schematic.
Neckband: With RS facing, using smaller needles and CC, pick
up and knit 65 (65, 65, 71) sts evenly around neck edge. Work
in Gtr st until band meas 1" from pickup row, end WS row.
BO all sts loosely. **Button band:** With RS facing, using smaller
needles and CC, pick up and knit 55 (59, 63, 70) sts evenly
along left front edge. Work in Gtr st until band meas 1" from
pickup row; BO all sts loosely. Pm for 3 (3, 4, 4) buttons, first
½" from beg of Smocking Pattern, last ½" from neck edge, rem
1 (1, 2, 2) evenly spaced bet. **Buttonhole band:** Work as for
button band, working buttonholes opposite markers on second
RS row as foll: [k2tog, yo] at each marker. Sew on buttons.

COTTON GUERNSEY

SIZES

2 (4, 6, 8, 10)

FINISHED MEASUREMENTS

28 (30, 32, 34, 36)"

MATERIALS

Classic Elite Yarns

Provence (100% mercerized cotton; 100-g hank = approx 205 yd/187 m)

3 (4, 4, 5, 5) hanks 2616 Natural

Equivalent yarn

Light worsted weight #3, 615 (820, 820, 1025, 1025) yd

Needles

• One pair size U.S. 6 (4 mm) or size to obtain gauge

• One 16" circular size U.S. 5 (3.75 mm) for neck finishing

Stitch holders

GAUGE

20 sts and 28 rows = 4" in Stockinette Stitch, using larger needles. Take time to save time, check your gauge.

PATTERN STITCHES

STOCKINETTE STITCH (ST ST)

Knit on RS, purl on WS.

CIRCULAR STOCKINETTE STITCH (ST ST)

Knit every rnd.

REVERSE STOCKINETTE STITCH (REV ST ST)

Purl on RS, knit on WS.

2 × 2 RIB (MULTIPLE OF 4 STS)

Row 1: *K2, p2; rep from * across [end k2 if odd number of ribs].

Row 2: Knit the knit sts and purl the purl sts as they face you.

Rep Row 2 for 2 x 2 Rib.

CIRCULAR 2 × 2 RIB (MULTIPLE OF 4 STS)

Rnd 1: *K2, p2; rep from * around, [end k2 if odd number of ribs].

Rnd 2: Knit the knit sts and purl the purl sts as they face you.

Rep Rnd 2 for Circular 2 x 2 Rib.

RIDGE STITCH (ANY NUMBER OF STS)

Rows 1, 3, and 5: (RS) Knit.

Rows 2, 4, and 6: Purl.

Row 7: Purl.

Row 8: Knit.

Rep Rows 1–8 for Ridge Stitch.

RIB PANEL (MULTIPLE OF 10 STS)

Row 1: (RS) Knit all sts.

Row 2: Purl all sts.

Row 3: K2, p2, k2, p2, k2.

Row 4: P2, k2, p2, k2, p2.

Rep Rows 1–4 for Rib Panel.

DIAMOND PANEL (MULTIPLE OF 15 STS)

Rows 1, 3, and 17: (RS) Knit all sts.

Rows 2, 4, 16, and 18: P7, k1, p7.

Rows 5 and 15: K6, p1, k1, p1, k6.

Rows 6 and 14: P5, [k1, p1] twice, k1, p5.

Rows 7 and 13: K4, [p1, k1] 3 times, p1, k4.

Rows 8 and 12: P3, [k1, p1] 4 times, k1, p3.

Rows 9 and 11: K2, [p1, k1] 5 times, p1, k2.

Row 10: [P1, k1] 7 times, p1.

Rep Rows 1–18 for Diamond Panel.

BACK

CO 70 (74, 82, 86, 90) sts. Work 3 rows in St st. Change to 2 × 2 Rib; work even until piece meas 1½" from beg, inc (inc, dec, dec, inc) 1 st on last WS row—71 (75, 81, 85, 91) sts. Change to St st; work even until piece meas 8 (9, 10, 11, 12)" from beg, end WS row. Change to Rev St st; work 2 rows. *Est patt:* (RS) Work 18 (20, 23, 25, 28) sts in Ridge Stitch, 10 sts in Rib Panel, 15 sts in Diamond Panel, 10 sts in Rib Panel, 18 (20, 23, 25, 28) sts in Ridge Stitch. Cont in patt as est; work even until piece meas 15 (16, 17, 18, 19)" from beg, end WS row. BO all sts.

FRONT

Work as for back until piece meas 13 (14, 15, 16, 17)" from beg. **Shape neck:** Cont in patt as est; work 28 (29, 30, 32, 35) sts, place center 15 (17, 21, 21, 21) sts on holder, join second ball of yarn, work to end. Working both sides at same time, at neck edge, BO 1 st EOR 5 times—23 (24, 25, 27, 30) sts rem each shoulder. Work even until piece meas same as back to shoulders. BO all sts.

SLEEVES

CO 34 (38, 42, 46, 46) sts. Work 3 rows in St st. Change to 2 × 2 Rib; work even until piece meas 1½" from beg, inc 1 st on last WS row—35 (39, 43, 47, 47) sts. Change to St st. **Shape sleeve:** Inc 1 st each side this row, then every 4 rows 14 (12, 9, 8, 11) times, every 6 rows 0 (3, 6, 8, 7) times, working inc sts in patt as they become available—65 (71, 75, 81, 85) sts; and, **at the same time,** when piece meas 6½ (7½, 8½, 9½, 10½)" from beg, end WS row. Change to Rev St st; work 2 rows. Pm each side of center 35 sts. *Est patt:* Work Ridge Stitch across to first marker, work 10 sts in Rib Panel, 15 sts in Diamond panel, 10 sts in Rib Panel, work Ridge Stitch to end. Cont in patt as est; work even until piece meas 12 (13, 14, 15, 16)" from beg. BO all sts.

FINISHING

Block pieces to measurements. Sew shoulder seams. Meas down 6½ (7, 7½, 8, 8½)" from shoulders on back and front, pm. Sew sleeves bet markers; sew sleeve and side seams. *Neckband:* With RS facing and circular needle, pick up and knit 72 (76, 80, 80, 80) sts evenly around neck edge; pm for beg of rnd. Work 2" in Circular 2 × 2 Rib. Change to Circular St st; work for 3 rnds. BO all sts.

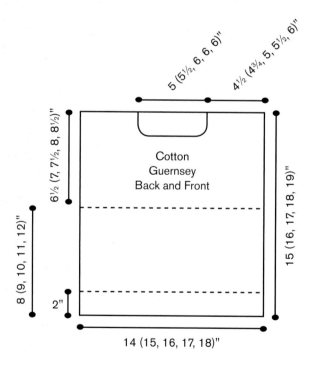

5 (5½, 6, 6, 6)"   4½ (4¾, 5, 5½, 6)"

6½ (7, 7½, 8, 8½)"

Cotton Guernsey Back and Front

15 (16, 17, 18, 19)"

8 (9, 10, 11, 12)"

2"

14 (15, 16, 17, 18)"

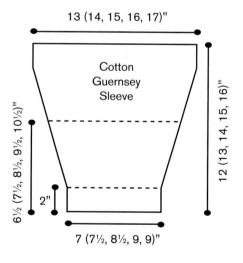

13 (14, 15, 16, 17)"

Cotton Guernsey Sleeve

6½ (7½, 8½, 9½, 10½)"

2"

12 (13, 14, 15, 16)"

7 (7½, 8½, 9, 9)"

BLUE WATER PULLOVER

SKILL LEVEL: EASY

Note: See p. 128 for matching Men's sweater.

SIZES

4 (6, 8)

FINISHED MEASUREMENTS

25 (26½, 28)"

Note: Measurements given are for lightly blocked piece; choose size accordingly.

MATERIALS

Classic Elite Yarns

Waterlily (100% extra fine merino; 50-g ball = approx 100 yd/109 m)

• 5 (7, 8) balls 1948 Inlet

Equivalent yarn

Worsted weight #4, 500 (700, 800) yd

Needles

• One pair *each* size U.S. 7 (4.5 mm) and 8 (5mm) or size to obtain gauge

• One 16" circular size U.S. 7 (4.5 mm)

• One cable needle (cn)

Stitch markers

GAUGE

24 sts and 26 rows = 4" in 1 x 1 Rib unblocked, using smaller needles; 22 sts = 4" in Cable Rib lightly blocked, larger needles. Take time to save time check your gauge.

NOTE

Work sleeve incs 2 sts in from each side.

PATTERN STITCHES

1 x 1 RIB (MULTIPLE OF 2 STS + 1)

Row 1 (RS): K1, * p1, k1; rep from * across.

Row 2: Knit the knit sts and purl the purl sts as they face you.

Rep Row 2 for 1 x 1 Rib.

CIRCULAR 1 x 1 RIB (MULTIPLE OF 2 STS)

Rnd 1: * K1, p1; rep from * around.

Rep Rnd 1 for Circular 1 x 1 Rib.

CABLE RIB (MULTIPLE OF 22 STS + 5; 6-ROW REP)

See chart on p. 130.

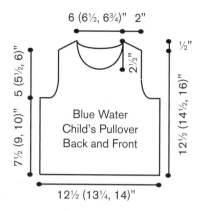

6 (6½, 6¾)" 2"

7½ (9, 10)" 5 (5½, 6)" ½"

2½"

Blue Water
Child's Pullover
Back and Front

12½ (14½, 16)"

12½ (13¼, 14)"

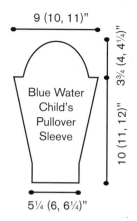

9 (10, 11)"

3¾ (4, 4¼)"

Blue Water
Child's
Pullover
Sleeve

10 (11, 12)"

5¼ (6, 6¼)"

BACK

Using larger needles, CO 65 (69, 73) sts. Change to smaller needles and beg 1 × 1 Rib; work even until piece meas 1¼ (1½, 1½)" from beg, end RS row. (WS) Knit 1 row (Garter ridge); pm each side of center 45 (45, 65) sts. *Est patt: Row 1:* (RS) K1 (0, 1) [k2, p1] 3 (4, 1) times, sl marker; beg Cable Rib (see chart) across sts bet markers as foll: *[K2, p1] twice, k2, m1, k1, [p1, k2] 3 times, m1, k1, p1; rep from * across to 5 sts before second marker, k2, p1, k2; sl marker, [p1, k2] 3 (4, 1) times, k1 (0, 1)—69 (73, 79) sts. *Row 2:* (WS) Change to larger needles. Work Row 2 of Cable Rib over all sts. Work even, cont 6-row rep of Cable Rib on center sts and keeping sts each side of markers in rib as est until piece meas 7½ (9, 10)" from beg, end WS row. **Shape armholes:** (RS) BO 4 (5, 6) sts at beg of next 2 rows, then dec 1 st each side EOR 3 (3, 4) times—55 (57, 59) sts rem. Work even until armhole meas 5 (5½, 6)" from beg of shaping, end WS row; pm each side of center 27 (29, 31) sts. **Shape shoulders:** (RS) BO 6 sts at beg of next 2 rows, 5 sts at beg of next 2 rows; and, **at the same time,** on the first row of shoulder shaping, work across to center sts; join second ball of yarn and BO center sts; work to end. Working both sides at same time, at each neck edge BO 3 sts once.

FRONT

Work as for back until armhole meas 3 (3½, 4)" from beg of shaping, end WS row—55 (57, 59) sts rem; pm each side of center 23 (25, 27) sts. **Shape neck:** (RS) Work across to center sts; join second ball of yarn, BO center sts, work to end. Working both sides at same time, at each neck edge BO 2 sts once, then 1 st each side EOR 3 times—11 sts rem each shoulder. Work even until piece meas same as back to shoulder shaping. **Shape shoulders** as for back.

SLEEVES

Using larger needles, CO 31 (35, 37) sts. Change to smaller needles and beg 1 × 1 Rib; work even until piece meas 2" from beg, end RS row. (WS) Knit 1 row, (Garter ridge); pm each side

■ SAILBOAT CHART

Multiple of 22 sts + 5; 6-row rep + 6

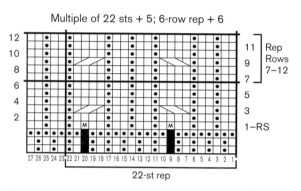

12
10
8
6
4
2

11 Rep
9   Rows
7   7–12
5
3
1–RS

27 26 25 24 23 22 21 20 19 18 17 16 15 14 13 12 11 10 9 8 7 6 5 4 3 2 1

22-st rep

☐ Knit on RS, purl on WS.
⊡ Purl on RS, knit on WS.
■ No s.

M M1.

⬚ Sl 2 sts to cn, hold in front, k2; k2 from cn.

⬚ Sl 2 sts from cn, hold in back, k2; k2 from cn.

of center 25 sts. *Est patt: Row 1:* (RS) K0 (2 ,0), [k2, p1] 1 (1, 2) times, sl marker; work Cable Rib (see chart) across 25 sts bet markers as foll: *[K2, p1] twice, k2, m1, k1, [p1, k2] 3 times, m1, k1, p1, k2, p1, k2; sl marker, [p1, k2] 1 (1, 2) times, k0 (2, 0)—33 (37, 39) sts. *Row 2:* (WS) Change to larger needles. Work Row 2 of Cable Rib over all sts. **Shape sleeve:** (RS) Cont as est, working 6-row rep of Cable Rib on center sts, inc 1 st each side this row, then every 4 rows 2 (1, 4) times; every 6 rows 5 (7, 6) times, working inc sts in rib as they become available—49 (55, 61) sts. Work even until piece meas 10 (11, 12)" from beg, end WS row. **Shape cap:** (RS) BO 4 (5, 6) sts at beg of next 2 rows, then dec 1 st each side EOR 10 (11, 12) times—21 (23, 25) sts rem. BO 3 sts at beg of next 2 rows—15 (17, 19) sts rem. BO rem sts.

FINISHING

Lightly block pieces to measurements, if desired. Sew shoulder seams. Set in sleeves; sew side and sleeve seams. **Neckband:** With RS facing, using circular needle, pick up and knit 66 (70, 74) sts evenly around neck edge; pm for beg of rnd. Purl 1 rnd (Garter Ridge). Beg Circular 1 × 1 Rib; work even until band meas 1" from pickup rnd. BO all sts loosely in rib.

SEASIDE HOODIE

SIZE
(4, 6, 8)

FINISHED MEASUREMENTS
26 (28, 30, 33)"

MATERIALS
Classic Elite Yarns

Star (99% cotton, 1% Lycra; 50-g hank = approx 112 yd/10 2m)

• 7 (8, 9, 10) hanks Main Color (MC)—5149 Indigo Bunting
• 1 hank all sizes Color A—5172 Lime Sherbet
• 1 hank all sizes Color B—5117 Mineral Water
• 1 hank all sizes Color C—5102 Arizona Sun
• 1 hank all sizes Color D—5101 Bleach

Equivalent yarn

Light worsted weight #3, MC: 784 (896, 1008, 1120) yd; Colors A–D: 112 yd for all sizes

Needles

• One pair *each* sizes U.S. 6 (4 mm), 7 (4.5 mm), and 8 (5 mm) or size to obtain gauge
• One additional size U.S. 6 (4 mm) needle or dpn for binding off
• One 24" circular size U.S. 6 (4 mm) for finishing

Stitch markers

GAUGE
22 sts and 32 rows = 4" in Stockinette Stitch, using medium needles; 22 sts and 32 rows = 4" in Fish, Wave, and Sailboat patterns, using larger needles. Take time to save time, check your gauge.

SPECIAL TECHNIQUE

THREE-NEEDLE BIND-OFF METHOD
With needles pointing in same direction and held parallel, hold RS of garment pieces tog (to form ridge on inside). With a third needle, knit first st of front and back needles tog, *knit next st from each needle tog (2 sts on RH needle), BO 1 st; rep from * until all sts are bound off.

PATTERN STITCHES

GARTER STITCH (GTR ST)
Knit every row.

STOCKINETTE STITCH (ST ST)
Knit on RS, purl on WS.

FISH (MULTIPLE OF 14 STS)
See chart.

WAVE (MULTIPLE OF 20 STS)
See chart.

SAILBOAT (MULTIPLE OF 20 STS)
See chart.

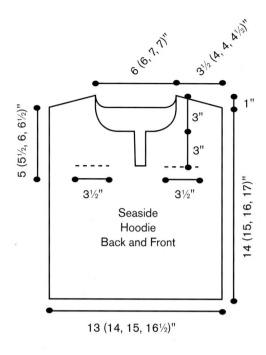

6 (6, 7, 7)"   3½ (4, 4, 4½)"

5 (5½, 6, 6½)"

1"

3"

3"

3½"   3½"

Seaside
Hoodie
Back and Front

14 (15, 16, 17)"

13 (14, 15, 16½)"

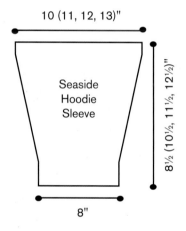

10 (11, 12, 13)"

Seaside
Hoodie
Sleeve

8½ (10½, 11½, 12½)"

8"

BACK

Using smallest needles and MC, CO 72 (78, 84, 90) sts; work 6 rows in Gtr st, end WS row. Change to medium needles and St st; work 4 rows, end WS row. Change to largest needles and *est Fish patt (see chart):* (RS) Work 1 (4, 0, 3) sts in St st, 70 (70, 84, 84) sts in Fish patt, beg and end where indicated for your size, 1 (4, 0, 3) sts in St st. Work even until Fish chart is complete. Change to medium needles and cont in St st; work 3 rows, end WS row. Change to Gtr st; work 2 rows, end WS row. Change to St st; work 2 rows, end WS row. Change to largest needles and *est Wave patt (see chart):* (RS) Work 6 (9, 2, 5) sts in St st, 60 (60, 80, 80) sts in Wave patt, beg and end where indicated for your size, 6 (9, 2, 5) sts in St st. Work even until Wave chart is complete. Change to medium needles and cont in St st; work 3 rows, end WS row. Change to Gtr st; work

2 rows, end WS row. Change to St st; work 2 rows, end WS row. Change to largest needles and *est Sailboat patt (see chart):* (RS) Work 7 (0, 3, 6) sts in St st, 58 (78, 78, 78) sts in Sailboat patt, beg and end where indicated for your size, 7 (0, 3, 6) sts in St st. Work even until Sailboat chart is complete. Change to medium needles and cont in St st. Work even until piece meas 14 (15, 16, 17)" from beg, end WS row. ***Shape shoulders and neck:*** (RS) BO 5 (6, 6, 7) sts at beg of next 6 (4, 6, 4) rows, 4 (5, 5, 6) sts at beg of next 2 (4, 2, 4) rows; and, **at the same time,** on the first row of shoulder shaping, work across to center 16 (16, 20, 20) sts; join second ball of yarn, BO center sts, work to end. Working both sides at same time, at each neck edge BO 3 sts 3 times.

FRONT

Work as for back until piece meas 9 (10, 11, 12)" from beg, end WS row. ***Make pocket openings and divide for neck:*** (RS) Work 24 (27, 30, 33) sts, return last 19 sts to LH needle, and knit them with waste yarn, work 8 sts; join second ball of yarn, BO center 8 sts; work 27 sts, return last 19 sts to LH needle, and knit them with waste yarn, work last 5 (8, 11, 14) sts—32 (35, 38, 41) sts each side. Working both sides at same time, work even until piece meas 12 (13, 14, 15)" from beg, end WS row. ***Shape neck:*** (RS) At each neck edge, BO 5 (5, 6, 6) sts once, 3 (3, 4, 4) sts once, 2 sts once, then dec 1 st EOR 3 times—19 (22, 23, 26) sts rem each shoulder. Work even until piece meas same as back to shoulder shaping, end WS row. ***Shape shoulders*** as for back. ***Pocket linings:*** Carefully remove waste yarn, placing lower sts on one medium needle and upper sts on another medium needle. Work lower sts in Gtr st for pocket edging. Turning piece upside down using MC, work 3 rows even; BO all sts. Work upper sts in St st for pocket lining. Using MC, work even until lining meas 4" from pocket opening; BO all sts.

SLEEVES

Using smallest needles and MC, CO 43 sts; work 6 rows in Gtr st, end WS row. Change to medium needles and St st; work 4 rows, end WS row. Change to largest needles and *est patt:* (RS) Work 1 st in St st, work 42 sts in Fish patt (see chart), beg and end where indicated for your size. Work even as est until Fish chart is complete. Change to medium needles, cont in St st; work 3 rows even, end WS row. Change to Gtr st, work 2 rows, end WS row. Change to St st and ***shape sleeve:*** (RS) Inc 1 st each side this row, then every 6 rows 3 (7, 7, 7) times, every 8 (8, 4, 4) rows 2 (1, 4, 6) times—55 (61, 67, 71) sts. Work even until piece meas 8½ (10½, 11½, 12½)" from beg. BO all sts.

Multiple of 20 sts

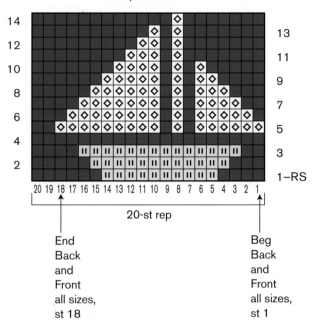

20-st rep

End
Back
and
Front
all sizes,
st 18

Beg
Back
and
Front
all sizes,
st 1

■ MC–5149 Indigo Bunting.

▲ Color A–5172 Lime Sherbet.

☒ Color B–5117 Mineral Water.

ΙΙ Color C–5102 Arizona Sun.

◇ Color D–5101 Bleach.

Multiple of 20 sts

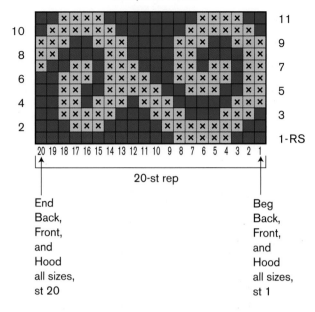

20-st rep

End
Back,
Front,
and
Hood
all sizes,
st 20

Beg
Back,
Front,
and
Hood
all sizes,
st 1

Multiple of 14 sts

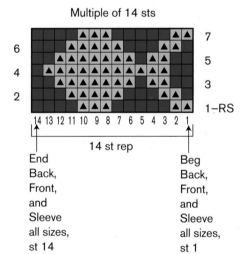

14 st rep

End
Back,
Front,
and
Sleeve
all sizes,
st 14

Beg
Back,
Front,
and
Sleeve
all sizes,
st 1

FINISHING

Block pieces to measurements. Sew shoulder seams. Meas down 5 (5½, 6, 6½)" from shoulders on front and back, pm. Sew sleeves bet markers. Sew sleeve and side seams. Sew pocket linings neatly to WS of garment. ***Hood:*** With RS facing, using smallest needles and MC, pick up and knit 80 (80, 84, 84) sts evenly around neck edge. Work in St st until hood meas 10 (10½, 11, 11½)" from pickup row, end WS row. Work 40 (40, 42, 42) sts; fold hood in half and work Three-Needle Bind-Off Method. ***Hood edging:*** With RS facing, using circular needle and MC pick up and knit 16 sts evenly along right front neck edge, 110 (116, 122, 128) sts evenly around hood edge,

16 sts evenly along left front neck edge—142 (148, 154, 160) sts. Knit 1 WS row. Work 2 rows in St st, end WS row. *Est Wave patt (see chart):* (RS) Work 1 (4, 7, 0) sts in St st, 140 (140, 140, 160) sts in Wave patt, 1 (4, 7, 0) sts in St st. Work even as est until Wave chart is complete. (WS) Change to St st; work 2 rows, end RS row. Knit 1 WS row (turning ridge). Change to St st; work 15 rows even. BO all sts. Fold hood edging to inside of hood at turning ridge, forming a facing; sew BO edge to pickup row. Tack down side edges of hood edging to 8 BO sts at center front neck, overlapping the right side edge over the left side edge.

MOTHER AND DAUGHTER ALPACA PONCHOS

SIZES

Child's 4–6 (8–10) {Woman's Small–Medium (Large–2X Large)}

FINISHED MEASUREMENTS

• Height (without fringe) 12 (15)" {17½ (19½)"}
• Length (from edge to edge, without fringe) 36 (44)" {54 (60)"}

Note: Child's directions are given first, and Woman's directions appear in braces { }.

MATERIALS

Classic Elite Yarns

Inca Alpaca (100% alpaca; 50-g hank = approx 109 yd/100 m)

• 4 (7), {9 (11)} hanks 1132 Mojave Magenta {1135 Cala Cala Moss}

Equivalent yarn

Worsted weight #4, 436 (763) yd {981, (1199) yd}

Needles

• One pair size U.S. 5 (3.75 mm) or size to obtain gauge
• One crochet hook size U.S. E/4 (3.5 mm)

GAUGE

22 sts and 31 rows = 4", in Lace Pattern after blocking. Take time to save time, check your gauge.

PATTERN STITCH

LACE PATTERN (MULTIPLE OF 6 STS + 5; 12-ROW REP)

Rows 1, 3, and 5: (RS) K1, *skp, k2, yo, k2, rep from * to 4 sts rem, k1, yo, p2tog, k1.

Row 2 and all WS rows: Sl 1p, yo, p2tog, purl to end.

Rows 7, 9, and 11: K4, *yo, k2, k2tog, k2, rep from * to 7 sts rem, yo, k2, k2tog, yo, p2tog, k1.

Rep Rows 1–12 for Lace Pattern.

BODY

CO 65 (83) {95 (107)} sts. *Est patt:* (WS) Sl 1p, *yo, p2tog, rep from * to end. *Next row:* (RS) Beg with Row 1, work Lace Pattern until piece meas 36 (44)" {54 (60)"} from beg, end Row 6 of Lace Pattern. *Next row:* (RS) K1, *yo, p2tog, rep from * across. *Next row:* (WS) Loosely BO all sts purlwise.

FINISHING

Steam block piece to measurements. ***Fringe:*** Cut fringe 8 (9)" {10 (11)"} long. Using 3 pieces of yarn, attach fringe in every second yo along long edge and every yo along CO and BO edges as foll: Insert crochet hook through yo and over 3 pieces of folded yarn. Pull through, making a loop, then draw ends through loop and tighten. Trim yarn ends. ***Assembly:*** *As shown for Child's version:* Fold in half, and seam along non-fringed edges to within 9 (10)" {12 (12)"} of fold line (for neck opening). Steam press seam. *As shown for Women's version:* Turn so one short, fringed edge sits along non-fringed edge, leaving approx 24 (29)" {36 (40)"} circle open at upper edge. Sew short fringed edge over non-fringed edge.

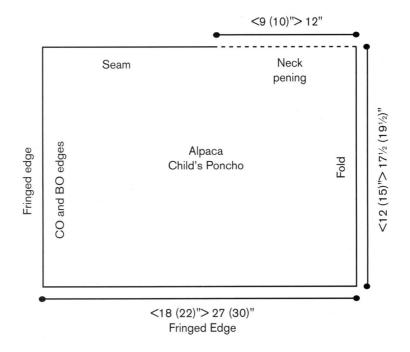

<9 (10)"> 12"

Seam

Neck opening

Alpaca Child's Poncho

Fold

Fringed edge

CO and BO edges

<12 (15)"> 17½ (19½)"

<18 (22)"> 27 (30)"
Fringed Edge

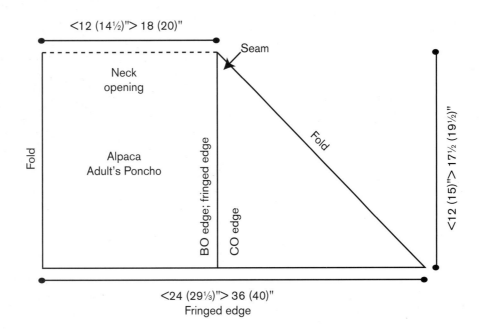

<12 (14½)"> 18 (20)"

Neck opening

Seam

Alpaca Adult's Poncho

Fold

BO edge; fringed edge

CO edge

Fold

<12 (15)"> 17½ (19½)"

<24 (29⅓)"> 36 (40)"
Fringed edge

STARFISH SWEATER

SIZES

2 (4, 6, 8, 10)

FINISHED MEASUREMENTS

29 (31, 33, 35, 37)"

MATERIALS

Classic Elite Yarns

Flash (100% mercerized cotton, 50-g hank = approx 93 yd/85 m)

• 7 (8, 9, 11, 12) hanks 6146 Lily Pad

Equivalent yarn

Worsted weight #4, 651 (744, 837, 1023, 1116) yd

Needles

• One pair size U.S. 7 (4.5 mm) or size to obtain gauge
• One 16" circular size U.S. 7 (4.5 mm) for neck finishing

Stitch holders

Stitch markers

GAUGE

20 sts and 28 rows = 4" in Stockinette Stitch. Take time to save time check your gauge.

PATTERN STITCHES

STOCKINETTE STITCH (ST ST)

Knit on RS, purl on WS.

SEED STITCH (MULTIPLE OF 2 STS)

Row 1: K1, *p1, k1; rep from * across.

Row 2: Purl the knit sts and knit the purl sts as they face you.

Rep Row 2 for Seed Stitch.

CIRCULAR SEED STITCH (MULTIPLE OF 2 STS)

All Rnds: *K1, p1; rep from * to end.

SEED STITCH RIB (MULTIPLE OF 5 STS + 2)

Row 1: (RS) K2, *p1, k1, p1, k2; rep from * across.

Row 2: *P2, p1, k1, p1; rep from * across to last 2 sts, p2.

Rep Rows 1–2 for Seed Stitch Rib.

CIRCULAR SEED STITCH RIB (MULTIPLE OF 5 STS)

Rnd 1: *K2, p1, k1, p1; rep from * around.

Rnd 2: *K2, k1, p1, k1; rep from * around.

Rep Rnds 1–2 for Circular Seed Stitch Rib.

STARFISH

See chart.

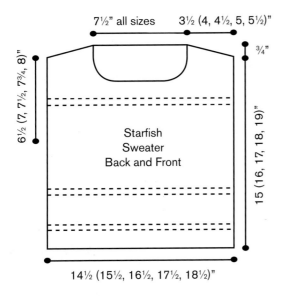

7½" all sizes   3½ (4, 4½, 5, 5½)"

¾"

6½ (7, 7½, 7¾, 8)"

Starfish
Sweater
Back and Front

15 (16, 17, 18, 19)"

14½ (15½, 16½, 17½, 18½)"

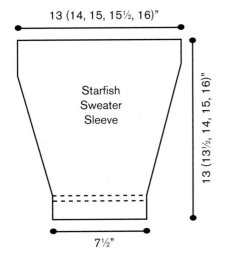

13 (14, 15, 15½, 16)"

Starfish
Sweater
Sleeve

13 (13½, 14, 15, 16)"

7½"

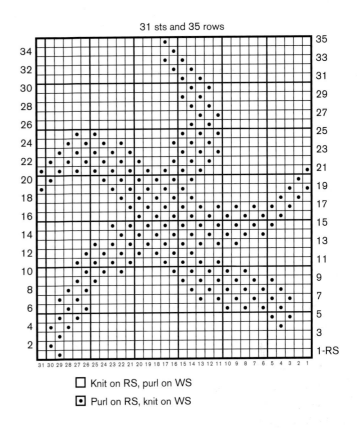

31 sts and 35 rows

☐ Knit on RS, purl on WS
⊡ Purl on RS, knit on WS

BACK

CO 73 (77, 83, 87, 93) sts; work in Seed Stitch Rib until piece meas 1" from beg, end WS row. Change to Seed st; work 4 rows. Change to St st; work even until piece meas 3 (4, 5, 6, 7)" from beg, end WS row. Change to Seed st; work 4 rows. Change to St st; work 52 rows. Change to Seed st; work 4 rows. Change to St st; work even until piece meas 15 (16, 17, 18, 19)" from beg, end WS row. **Shape shoulders:** BO 6 (7, 8, 8, 9) sts at beg of next 6 (4, 4, 4, 4) rows, 0 (6, 7, 9, 10) sts at beg of next 2 rows—37 sts rem. Place rem sts on holder for neck.

FRONT

Work as for back until piece meas 3 (4, 5, 6, 7)" from beg, end WS row. Change to Seed st; work 4 rows. Change to St st; work 8 rows, end WS row. *Est patt:* Work 21 (23, 26, 28, 31) sts in St st, work Row 1 of Starfish pattern across 31 sts, work to end in St st. Cont in patt as est, working Rows 2–35 of Starfish pattern. Change to St st; work 9 rows. Change to Seed St; work

4 rows. Change to St st; work even until piece meas 13 (14, 15, 16, 17)" from beg, end WS row. **Shape neck:** Work 30 (32, 35, 37, 40) sts, join second ball of yarn and work 13 center sts, place on holder for neck, work to end. Working both sides at same time, work 1 row even. At each neck edge, BO 4 sts once, 3 sts once, 2 sts once, then dec 1 st EOR 3 times—18 (20, 23, 25, 28) sts rem each shoulder. Work even until piece meas same as back to shoulders. **Shape shoulders** as for back.

SLEEVES

CO 37 sts; work in Seed Stitch Rib until piece meas 1" from beg, end WS row. Change to Seed st; work 4 rows. Change to St st; and, **at the same time, *shape sleeve:*** Inc 1 st each side this row, then every 4 rows 2 (10, 12, 12, 16) times, every 6 rows 11 (6, 6, 7, 5) times—65 (71, 75, 77, 81) sts. Work even until piece meas 13 (13½, 14, 15, 16)" from beg. BO all sts.

FINISHING

Block pieces to measurements. Sew shoulder seams. Meas down 6½ (7, 7½, 7¾, 8)" from shoulders on back and front; pm. Sew sleeves bet markers. Sew sleeve and side seams. ***Neckband:*** With RS facing and circular needle, pick up and knit 80 sts evenly around neck edge; pm for beg of rnd. Work 4 rnds in Circular Seed st. Change to Circular Seed Stitch Rib; work 4 rnds. BO all sts loosely in patt.

V-CABLE PULLOVER

Note: See p. 73 for matching Women's sweater.

SIZES
4 (6, 8, 10)

FINISHED MEASUREMENTS
28 (31, 32½, 34½)"

MATERIALS
Classic Elite Yarns
Skye Tweed (100% wool; 50-g ball = approx 112 yd/103 m)
• 5 (6, 8, 9) balls 1258 Tartan Red
Equivalent yarn
Worsted weight #4, 560 (672, 896, 1008) yd
Needles
• One pair *each* size U.S. 4 (3.5 mm) and U.S. 6 (4 mm)
  or size to obtain gauge
• 16" circular needle U.S. size 4 (3.5 mm) for neck finishing
• One cable needle (cn)
Stitch holders
Stitch markers

GAUGE
16 sts and 24 rows = 4" in Stockinette Stitch, using larger needles.
Take time to save time, check your gauge.

PATTERN STITCHES

TWISTED RIB (MULTIPLE OF 4 STS + 2)
Row 1: (RS) [K1b] twice, *p2, [k1b] twice; rep from * across.
Row 2: *[P1b] twice, k2; rep from * across to last 2 sts, [p1b] twice.
Rep Rows 1–2 for Twisted Rib.

CIRCULAR TWISTED RIB (MULTIPLE OF 4 STS)
All rnds: *[K1b] twice, p2; rep from * around.

STOCKINETTE STITCH (ST ST)
Knit on RS, purl on WS.

REVERSE STOCKINETTE STITCH (REV ST ST)
Purl on RS, knit on WS.

LEFT O-CABLE (MULTIPLE OF 6 STS; 4-ROW REP)
See Chart A on p. 75.

RIGHT O-CABLE (MULTIPLE OF 6 STS; 4-ROW REP)
See Chart B on p. 75.

V-CABLE (MULTIPLE OF 26 STS; 12-ROW REP)
See Chart C on p. 75.

BACK

Using smaller needles, CO 62 (66, 70, 74) sts; work in Twisted Rib until piece meas 1 (1, 1½ , 1½)" from beg, end WS row. Change to larger needles and purl 1 row, inc 8 (10, 12, 12) sts evenly across row—70 (76, 82, 86) sts. *Est patt:* (WS) Work 10 (13, 10, 12) sts in St st, 12 (12, 18, 18) sts Left O-Cable (Chart A), 26 sts V-Cable (Chart C), 12 (12, 18, 18) sts Right O-Cable (Chart B), 10 (13, 10, 12) sts in St st. Work as est until piece meas 8 (9, 10, 10½)" from beg, end WS row. **Shape armholes:** (RS) BO 7 (8, 9, 11) sts at beg of next 2 rows, then dec 1 st each side EOR 3 (3, 4, 3) times—50 (54, 56, 58) sts rem. Cont as est until armhole meas 5½ (6, 6½, 7)" from beg of shaping, end WS row. **Shape neck:** BO 15 (16, 16, 16) sts, work center 20 (22, 24, 26) sts and place on holder for neck. BO rem 15 (16, 16, 16) sts.

FRONT

Work as for back until armhole meas 3½ (4, 4, 4½)" from beg of shaping, end WS row—50 (54, 56, 58) sts rem. **Shape neck:** (RS) Work 17 (18, 18, 18) sts, join second ball of yarn, work center 16 (18, 20, 22) sts and place on holder for neck, work to end. Working both sides at same time, at each neck edge, dec 1 st EOR twice—15 (16, 16, 16) sts rem each shoulder. Work even until armhole meas same as back to shoulders. BO rem sts.

SLEEVES

Using smaller needles, CO 30 (34, 38, 38) sts; work in Twisted Rib until piece meas 1½" from beg, end WS row. Change to larger needles and purl 1 row, inc 4 (4, 6, 8) sts evenly across row—34 (38, 44, 46) sts. *Est patt:* (WS) Work 7 (9, 12, 13) sts in St st, 18 sts Left O-Cable (Chart A), 2 sts in Rev St st, 7 (9, 12, 13) in St st. Work as est until piece meas 2" from beg, end WS row. **Shape sleeve:** (RS) Inc 1 st each side this row, then every 8 rows 4 (5, 1, 3) times, every 6 (6, 10, 10) rows 3 (2, 5, 4) times, working inc sts in St st—50 (54, 58, 62) sts. Work even until piece meas 10½ (11½, 12½, 13½)" from beg, end WS row. **Shape cap:** BO 7 (8, 9, 11) sts at beg of next 2 rows, then dec 1 st each side EOR 6 (7, 8, 8) times—24 sts rem. BO 1 st at beg of next 6 rows—18 sts rem. BO rem sts.

FINISHING

Block pieces to measurements. Sew shoulder seams. Set in sleeves; sew sleeve and side seams. *Neckband:* With RS facing, using circular needle, work 20 (22, 24, 26) sts from holder for back neck, pick up and knit 8 sts along left neck edge, work 16 (18, 20, 22) sts from holder for front neck, pick up and knit 8 sts along right neck edge, pm for beg of rnd—52 (56, 60, 64) sts. Work Circular Twisted Rib until band meas 1 (1, 1½, 1½)" from pickup row; BO all sts loosely in patt.

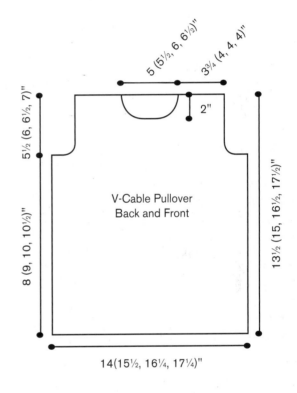

V-Cable Pullover
Back and Front

5 (5½, 6, 6½)"

3¾ (4, 4, 4)"

2"

5½ (6, 6½, 7)"

8 (9, 10, 10½)"

13½ (15, 16½, 17½)"

14 (15½, 16¼, 17¼)"

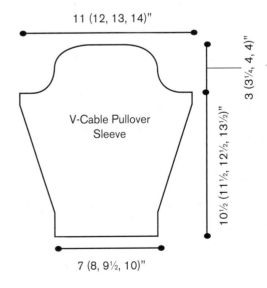

V-Cable Pullover
Sleeve

11 (12, 13, 14)"

3 (3¼, 4, 4)"

10½ (11½, 12½, 13½)"

7 (8, 9½, 10)"

ACCESSORIES

contents

RAINBOW SCARF

SIZE
One size

FINISHED MEASUREMENT
6½ " wide x 76" long (without fringe)

MATERIALS
Classic Elite Yarns
La Gran (76 1/2% mohair, 17 1/2% wool, 6% nylon;
42-g ball = approx 90 yd/82 m)

• 1 ball Color A—6572 Underappreciated Green
• 1 ball Color B—6546 Azure
• 1 ball Color C—6593 Electric Blue
• 1 ball Color D—6579 European Plum
• 1 ball Color E—6555 Infra Red
• 1 ball Color F—6585 Pumpkin

Equivalent yarn
Bulky weight #5, Colors A–F: 90 yd

Needles
• One pair U.S. 11 (8 mm) or size to obtain gauge
• Crochet hook U.S. size G (4 mm) for fringe

GAUGE
12 sts and 15 rows = 4" in Garter Stitch and Stockinette Stitch.
Take time to save time, check your gauge.

PATTERN STITCHES

GARTER STITCH (GTR ST)
Knit every row.

STOCKINETTE STITCH (ST ST)
Knit on RS, purl on WS.

COLOR SEQUENCE
Color A.
Color B.
Color C.
Color D.
Color E.
Color F.

SCARF

Using Color A, CO 20 sts and work as foll: *Rows 1–8:* Work in Gtr st. *Rows 9–15:* Work in St st. Cont in patt as est, changing colors every 15 rows; work Color Sequence three times. BO all sts.

FRINGE

Using a 7" piece of cardboard and Color A, wind yarn around cardboard 20 times. Cut one end of yarn and set aside. Rep using Color F.

FINISHING

Attach fringe evenly spaced across each end of scarf as foll: RS facing, *insert crochet hook from back to front through scarf and over 2 pieces of folded yarn. Pull through, making a loop, then draw ends through loop and tighten up; rep from * at both ends of scarf. Trim yarn ends.

RIBBED COWL NECK WARMER

{ SKILL LEVEL: BEGINNER }

SIZE
One size

FINISHED MEASUREMENTS
12" wide x 58" long

MATERIALS
Classic Elite Yarns
MarL La (100% wool; 100-g hank = approx 57 yd/52 m)
• 4 hanks 8588 Warm Mix
Equivalent yarns
Super bulky weight #6, 228 yd
Needles
• One pair size U.S. 17 (12.75 mm) or size to obtain gauge

GAUGE
8 sts and 8 rows = 4" in 2 fk 2 Rib. Take time to save time, check your gauge.

PATTERN STITCH

2 × 2 RIB (MULTIPLE OF 4 STS + 2)
Row 1: (RS) K2, *p2, k2; rep from * across.
Row 2: Knit the knit sts and purl the purl sts as they face you.
Rep Row 2 for 2 x 2 Rib.

SCARF
CO 26 sts. Beg 2 × 2 Rib; work even until piece meas 58" from beg, end WS row. BO all sts loosely in rib.

FINISHING
Block piece to measurements. Fold scarf in half; sew CO and BO edges tog.

RAISED-ROSE SCARF

{ SKILL LEVEL: INTERMEDIATE }

SIZE

One size

FINISHED MEASUREMENTS

4¾" wide x 62" long

MATERIALS

Classic Elite yarns

Duchess (40% merino, 28% viscose, 10% cashmere, 7% angora, 15% nylon; 50-g ball = approx 75 yd/69 m)

• 4 balls Main Color (MC)—1016 Natural

• 1 ball Color A—1058 Royal Red

• 1 ball Color B—1015 Superior Spruce

Equivalent yarn

Bulky weight #5, Main Color (MC): 300 yd; Colors A and B: 75 yd

Crochet hook

• One size U.S. G/6 (4.25 mm) or size to obtain gauge

Tapestry needle

GAUGE

14 sts and 7 rows = 4" in Double Crochet. Take time to save time, check your gauge.

SCARF

Using MC, ch 19. *Row 1:* Dc into fourth ch from hook and in each ch across; turn—17 dc. *Row 2:* Ch 3 (counts as dc), dc in next st and in each st across; turn. Rep Row 2 until piece meas 62".

ROSE

Using Color A, ch 5; Sl st into first ch to form a ring. *Rnd 1:* *Ch 7, Sl st into ring; rep from * 5 times, join with a Sl st into Sl st that formed ring—6 ch-7 spaces. *Rnd 2:* Ch 1; *work 7 dc into ch-7 space, Sl st into Sl st; rep from * 5 times. *Note:* For rem rnds, work into same Rnd 1 Sl sts for each rnd. *Rnd 3:* *Ch 5, Sl st into next Rnd 1 Sl st; rep from * 5 times. *Rnd 4:* Ch 1, *work 6 dc in ch-5 space; Sl st into Sl st; rep from * 5 times. *Rnd 5:* *Ch 3, Sl st into next Sl st; rep from * 5 times; Sl st into Sl st. *Rnd 6:* Ch 1, *work 4 dc in ch-3 space; *Sl st into next Sl st; rep from * 5 times. Fasten off, leaving an 18" tail for sewing onto scarf.

LEAF (MAKE 2)

Using Color B, ch 5. Sl st in second ch from hook, sc in next st, dc in next st, work 2 tr into next st, work 2 dc in next st; *do not turn.* Working along opposite side of beg ch-5, work 2 tr in next st, dc in next st, sc in next st, join with a Sl st in beg Sl st. Fasten off, leaving an 18" tail for sewing onto scarf.

STEM

Using Color B, ch 35. Sl st in second ch from hook and in each ch across. Fasten off, leaving an 18" tail for sewing onto scarf.

FINISHING

With RS facing, sew stem, leaves, and rose onto scarf as shown in photo, being careful that ends do not show on WS. Block piece to measurements.

PATTERN STITCHES

CHAIN (CH)
Beg by making a sl knot on hook. Yo hook and draw it through loop on hook to form first ch. Rep this step as many times as instructed. (Loop on hook is never included when counting number of chains.)

DOUBLE CROCHET (DC)
Yo hook, insert hook into indicated st, yo and pull up a loop; (yo and draw through 2 loops on hook) twice.

SINGLE CROCHET (SC)
Insert hook in indicated st, yo and pull up a loop; yo and draw through both loops on hook.

SLIP STITCH (SL ST)
Insert hook in indicated st, yo and draw through both st and loop on hook.

TREBLE CROCHET (TR)
Yo hook two times, insert hook in indicated st, yo and pull up a loop; (yo and draw through 2 loops on hook) three times.

RECTANGLE WRAP

SIZE
One size

FINISHED MEASUREMENTS
20" wide x 60" long (without fringe)

MATERIALS
Classic Elite Yarns
Imagine (53% cotton, 47% rayon, 50-g hank = approx 93 yd/85 m)
• 12 hanks 9217 Flower Market
Equivalent yarn
Worsted weight #4; 1116 yd
Needles
One pair size U.S. 6 (4 mm) or size to obtain gauge
One crochet hook, any size, for attaching fringe

GAUGE
21 sts and 27 rows = 4" in Stockinette Stitch. Take time to save time, check your gauge.

WRAP

CO 100 sts. *Row 1 and all WS rows* K5, p90, k5. *Row 2:* K5, *[yo, ssk] twice, k2; rep from * to last 5 sts, k5. *Row 4:* K5, *k1, [yo, ssk] twice, k1; rep from * to last 5 sts, k5. *Row 6:* K5, *k2, [yo, ssk] twice; rep from * to last 5 sts, k5. *Row 8:* K6, *k2, [yo, ssk] twice; rep from * to last 10 sts, k2, yo, ssk, k6. *Row 10:* K5, *yo, ssk, k2, yo, ssk; rep from * to last 5 sts, k5. *Row 12:* K6, *yo, ssk, k2, yo, ssk; rep from * to last 10 sts, yo, ssk, k8. Rep Rows 1–12 until piece meas approx 60" from beg, end Row 12. BO all sts loosely.

FINISHING

Lightly block piece to measurements. ***Fringe:*** Wrap yarn around a 7½" piece of cardboard. Cut one end of yarn. Attach 3 ends of fringe to every other st at each end of wrap. Trim fringe evenly.

EASY SHAWL

Note: See p. 71 for matching sweater.

SIZE
One size

FINISHED MEASUREMENTS
16" wide x 72" long

MATERIALS
Classic Elite Yarns
Princess (40% merino, 28% viscose, 10% cashmere, 7% angora, 15% nylon; 50-g ball = approx 150 yd/137 m)
• 6 balls 3458 Royal Red
Equivalent yarn
Worsted weight #4, 900 yd
Needles
One pair size U.S. 7 (4.5 mm) or size to obtain gauge

GAUGE
20 sts and 28 rows = 4" in Stockinette Stitch. Take time to save time, check your gauge.

PATTERN STITCHES

STOCKINETTE STITCH (ST ST)
Knit on RS, purl on WS.

REVERSE STOCKINETTE STITCH (REV ST ST)
Purl on RS, knit on WS.

2 × 2 RIB (MULTIPLE OF 4 STS)
Row 1: (RS) *K2, p2; rep from * across.
Row 2: Knit the knit sts and purl the purl sts as they face you.
Rep Row 2 for 2 × 2 Rib.

SHAWL

CO 85 sts. *Est patt:* (RS) Work 12 sts in 2 × 2 Rib, *11 sts in St st, 2 sts in Rev St st, 12 sts in 2 × 2 Rib; rep from * once, work 11 sts in St st, 2 sts in Rev St st, 8 sts in 2 × 2 Rib, 2 sts in St st. Work even as est until piece meas 72" from beg, end WS row. BO all sts in patt.

FINISHING

Block piece to measurements.

LOOPED HAT, SCARF, AND WRISTLET SET

{ SKILL LEVEL: INTERMEDIATE }

SIZE
One size for all pieces

FINISHED MEASUREMENTS
Hat: 22" around

Scarf: 5 ¾" wide x 88" long

Wristlets: 7¼" around x 3¾" long

MATERIALS
Classic Elite Yarns

Princess (40% merino wool, 28% viscose, 10% cashmere, 7% angora, 15% nylon; 50-g ball = 150 yd/137 m)

- 2 balls Color A—3495 Privileged Plum
- 2 balls Color B—3432 Majesty's Magenta
- 2 balls Color C—3497 Ladylike Leaf
- 2 balls Color D—3431 Top Turq

Duchess (40% merino wool, 28% viscose, 10% cashmere, 7% angora, 15% nylon; 50-g ball = 75 yd/69 m) for embroidery and tassel on hat

- 1 ball Color E—1095 Privileged Plum
- 1 ball Color F—1032 Majesty's Magenta
- 1 ball Color G—1097 Ladylike Leaf
- 1 ball Color H—1031 Top Turq

Equivalent yarn

Worsted weight #4, Colors A–D: 300 yd; bulky weight #5, Colors E–H: 75 yd

Needles

- Hat: One 16" circular size U.S. 5 (3.75 mm) or size to obtain gauge
- Hat and Wristlets: One set dpn size U.S. 5 (3.75 mm) or size to obtain gauge
- Scarf: One pair size U.S. 5 (3.75 mm) or size to obtain gauge

Stitch markers (Hat)

Tapestry needle with eye large enough to fit a double strand of Duchess yarn

GAUGE
20 sts and 32 rows = 4" in Seed stitch, using thinner yarn. Take time to save time, check your gauge.

PATTERN STITCHES

STOCKINETTE STITCH (ST ST)
Knit on RS, purl on WS.

CIRCULAR STOCKINETTE STITCH (ST ST)
Knit every rnd.

SEED STITCH (MULTIPLE OF 2 STS)
Row/Rnd 1: (RS) *K1, p1; rep from * across/around.

Row/Rnd 2: Knit the purl sts and purl the knit sts as they face you.

Rep Row/Rnd 2 for Seed Stitch.

DETACHED LOOP BACKSTITCH
See Embroidery Diagram.

HAT

Using circular needle and Color A, CO 110 sts, pm for beg of rnd and join, being careful to not twist sts. Knit 1 rnd, pm every 22 sts. *Est patt:* *Work 2 sts in St st, work 20 sts in Seed st; rep from * around. Work as est until piece meas ¾" from beg. Change to Color B; work as est until piece meas 2¾" from beg. Change to Color C; work even until piece meas 3½" from beg. Change to Color D; work even until piece meas 4 ½" from beg. **Shape crown:** *Dec rnd:* *Work 1 st in St st, ssk, work to marker in Seed st; rep from * around. *Next rnd:* Work 2 sts in St st, work to marker in Seed st; rep from * around. Rep dec rnd this rnd, then EOR twice— 90 sts rem. Change to Color B; work dec rnd every rnd 16 times, changing to dpn when needed—10 sts rem. Break yarn and thread through rem sts. **Embroidery:** With RS facing, using 1 strand Color G and 1 strand Color H, work Detached Loop Backstitch (see Embroidery Diagram) around lower edge of hat. Work another rnd of Detached Loop Backstitch, using Colors A and C, at the lower edge of Color C stripe. **Tassel:** Using Colors E, F, G, and H wrap yarn around 6" piece of cardboard, leaving 12" strand loose at either end. With a yarn needle, knot both sides to first loop and run loose strand under wrapped strands. Pull tightly and tie at top. Cut lower edge of tassel and, holding tassel, about ¾" from the top, wind top strands (one clockwise and one counterclockwise) around tassel. Thread 2 strands onto needle and insert them through top of the tassel. Sew tassel to top of hat.

SCARF

Using straight needles and Color A, CO 29 sts; work 48 rows in Seed st. Change to Color B; work 6 rows. Change to Color C; work 32 rows. Change to Color D; work 6 rows. Change to Color C; work 40 rows. Change to Color D; work 6 rows. Change to Color B; work 56 rows. Change to Color A; work 6 rows. Change to Color D; work 40 rows Change to Color C; work 6 rows. Change to Color D; work 32 rows. Change to Color C; work 6 rows. Change to Color A; work 72 rows. Change to Color C; work 72 rows. Change to Color A; work 6 rows. Change to Color B; work 32 rows. Change to Color A; work 6 rows. Change to Color B; work 40 rows. Change to Color C; work 6 rows. Change to Color D; work 56 rows. Change to Color B; work 6 rows. Change to Color A; work 40 rows. Change to Color B; work 6 rows. Change to Color A; work 32 rows. Change to Color D; work 6 rows. Change to Color C; work 48 rows. BO all sts. **Embroidery:** With RS facing, using one strand of Color E and one strand of Color F, work Detached Loop Backstitch (see Embroidery Diagram) at lower edge of every Color C and Color D 6-row stripe, and at the BO edge of scarf; using 1 strand of Color G and 1 strand of Color H work Detached Loop Backstitch at lower edge of Color A and Color B 6-row stripes and CO edge of scarf.

WRISTLETS

Using dpn and Color D, CO 36 sts; pm for beg of rnd and join, being careful to not twist sts. Work 6 rnds in Seed st. Change to Color C; work 24 rnds; BO all sts. **Embroidery:** Using 1 strand of Color E and 1 strand of Color F, work Detached Loop Backstitch (see Embroidery Diagram) around CO edge of wristlet. Work second wristlet as for first wristlet, using Color B, changing to Color A, then working embroidery using Colors G and H.

■ **DETACHED LOOP BACKSTITCH EMBROIDERY DIAGRAM**

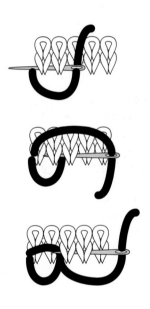

SIZE
One size

FINISHED MEASUREMENTS
Circumference: 8"
Length 10 ½" (with a 3" cuff)

MATERIALS
Classic Elite Yarn
Inca Print (100% alpaca; 50-g hank = approx 109 yd/100 m)
• 2 hanks Main Color (MC)—4652 Orchard
Inca Alpaca (100% alpaca; 50-g hank = approx 109 yd/100 m)
• 1 hank Contrast Color (CC)—1127 Cochineal
Equivalent yarn
Worsted weight #4, MC: 218 yd; CC: 109 yd
Needles
• One set *each* of 4 double-pointed needles (dpn)
  size U.S. 5 (3.75 mm) and 6 (4 mm)
• One pair size U.S. 5 (3.75 mm) or size to obtain gauge
• Crochet hook size U.S. G/6 (4 mm)
Safety pin
Stitch markers
Stitch holders

GAUGE
21 sts and 28 rows = 4" in Stockinette Stitch, using larger needles.
Take time to save time, check your gauge.

NOTE
To avoid color pooling, alternate skeins of Inca Print every 2 rnds.

SPECIAL TECHNIQUE

PROVISIONAL CAST-ON
Using crochet hook and CC, make a loose ch of 4 sts more than you
need to CO. Using dpn and MC, and beg 2 sts from end of ch, pick
up and knit 1 st through back loop of each crochet ch st for desired
number of sts. Work piece as desired; when ready to work in opposite
direction, gently pull out crochet ch to expose live sts.

PATTERN STITCHES

1 × 1 RIB (MULTIPLE OF 2 STS)
All Rnds/Rows: K1, p1; rep from around/across.

CIRCULAR STOCKINETTE STITCH (ST ST)
Knit every rnd.

CHAIN (CH):
Make a sl knot on hook. Wrap yarn around hook and draw it through
loop on hook to form first ch. Rep from this step as many times as
instructed.

MITTEN

Cuff: Using CC and Provisional Cast-On, ch 46 sts. Using smaller dpn and MC, pick up and knit 42 sts, divide sts evenly onto 3 dpn. Place safety pin on first st of needle 1 to mark beg of rnd; join for working in rnd, being careful not to twist sts. Work in 1 × 1 Rib until piece meas 3" from beg. Change to St st and work 1 rnd. Change to larger dpn and **shape thumb gusset:** *Inc rnd:* k1-f/b, pm, work to last st of rnd, pm, k1-f/b (4 sts bet markers)—44 sts. Work 1 rnd even. Cont to inc EOR 1 st before first marker and 1 st after second marker 4 times (12 sts bet markers)—52 sts. Cont as est, work even until piece meas 3" from end of cuff. *Next rnd:* Work to first gusset marker, sl these 6 sts from needle 1 onto holder along with last 6 sts from needle 3 (12 gusset sts on holder), work to end of rnd. Remove markers. *Next rnd:* CO 2 sts; join rnd and pm bet the 2 CO sts for beg of rnd—42 sts. Cont as est, work even until piece meas 6½" from end of cuff. *Next rnd, Dec rnd 1:* K1, k2tog, k15, k2tog, k2, k2tog, k15, k2tog, k1—38 sts rem. Work 1 rnd even. *Dec Rnd 2:* K1, k2tog, k13, k2tog, k2, k2tog, k13, k2tog, k1—34 sts rem. Work 1 rnd even. *Dec Rnd 3:* K1, k2tog, k11, k2tog, k2, k2tog, k11, k2tog, k1—30 sts rem. *Dec Rnd 4:* K1, k2tog, k9, k2tog, k2, k2tog, k9, k2tog, k1—26 sts rem. *Dec Rnd 5:* K2tog around—13 sts rem. Break yarn, leaving 6" tail and draw through rem sts. **Thumb:** Place 12 gusset sts from holder onto 2 dpn with RS facing. Join MC, work 12 sts, with third needle pick up and knit 2 sts from the base of CO on the palm—14 sts. Pm for beg of rnd, join and work even in St st until thumb meas 2". *Next rnd:* K2tog around—7 sts rem. Break yarn, leaving 3" tail and draw through rem sts.

SCARF

Carefully remove Provisional Cast-On, and place 42 sts on smaller dpn. Join MC and work 18 sts, then BO rem 24 sts. With RS facing, using smaller needles and CC; work in 1 × 1 Rib on rem 18 sts until piece meas 57" from pickup row, end WS row.

MITTEN

With RS facing, using smaller dpn and MC, work 18 sts; CO 24 sts and pm for beg of rnd. Work as for first mitten.

COLOR BLOCKS
HAT AND NECK WRAP

SIZES
One size

FINISHED MEASUREMENTS
Circumference: 21"

MATERIALS
Classic Elite Yarns
Bazic (100% superwash wool; 50-g ball = approx 65 yd/59 m)
Hat
• 2 balls Main Color (MC)—2957 Basic Blue
• 1 ball Color A—2921 Nile Green
• 1 ball Color B—2925 Sunflower
• 1 ball Color C—2993 Trojan Blue
• 1 ball Color D—2960 Grove
• 1 ball Color E—2985 Marigold
• 1 ball Color F—2904 Ancient Mariner
Neck wrap
• 2 balls Main Color (MC)—2958 Barn Red
• 1 ball Color A—2985 Marigold
• 1 ball Color B—2953 Magenta
• 1 ball Color C—2904 Ancient Mariner
• 1 ball Color D—2925 Sunflower
• 1 ball Color E—2935 Citrine
• 1 ball Color F—2908 Azure Stone
Equivalent yarn
Worsted weight #4, Hat—MC: 130 yd; Colors A–F: 65 yd; Neck
Wrap—MC: 130 yd; Colors A–F: 65 yd.
Needles
• One pair *each* size U.S. 8 (5 mm) and 9 (5.5 mm) or size to
  obtain gauge

GAUGE
16 sts and 20 rows = 4" in Stockinette Stitch and Block Pattern.
Take time to save time, check your gauge.

NOTE

When working Block Pattern, the yarns must be twisted around each
other at each color change to prevent holes in the work. Drop the
first color and pick up next color from under the first color and work
to the next color change.

PATTERN STITCHES

GARTER STITCH (GTR ST)
Knit every row.

STOCKINETTE STITCH (ST ST)
Knit on RS, purl on WS.

BLOCK PATTERN (MULTIPLE OF 42 STS; 20-ROW REP)
See chart.

Multiple of 42 sts; 20-row rep

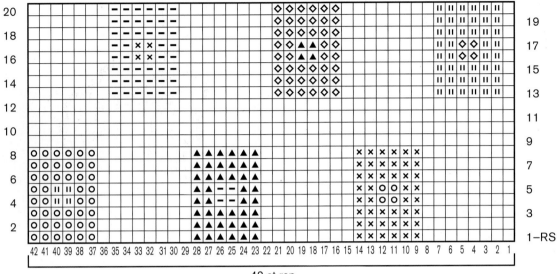

42-st rep

Hat Colors

☐	MC–2957 Basic Blue
☒	Color A–2921 Nile Green
⊙	Color B–2925 Sunflower
▲	Color C–2993 Trojan Blue
−	Color D–2960 Grove
‖	Color E–2985 Marigold
◇	Color F–2904 Ancient Mariner

Neck Wrap Colors

☐	MC–2958 Barn Red
☒	Color A–2985 Marigold
⊙	Color B–2953 Magenta
▲	Color C–2904 Ancient Mariner
−	Color D–2925 Sunflower
‖	Color E–2935 Citrine
◇	Color F–2908 Azure Stone

HAT

Using smaller needles and MC, CO 84 sts; work 7 rows in Gtr st, end WS row. Change to larger needles and St st; work 2 rows even, end WS row. Cont in St st and work Block Pattern (see chart); work until chart is complete, end WS row. Using MC only, cont in St st; work 2 rows even, end WS row. **Shape crown:** *Dec row:* (RS) *Work 19 sts, k2tog; rep from * across—80 sts rem. Purl 1 row. *Dec row:* (RS) *Work 8 sts, k2tog; rep from across—72 sts rem. Purl 1 row. *Dec row:* (RS) *Work 7 sts, k2tog; rep from * across—64 sts rem. Purl 1 row. Cont to dec in this manner, EOR, working 1 less st bet decs until 8 sts rem. Break yarn, pull tail through rem sts.

NECK WRAP

Using smaller needles and MC, CO 84 sts; work 3 rows in Gtr st, end WS row. Change to larger needles and St st; work 2 rows even, end WS row. Cont in St st and work Block Pattern (see chart); work until chart is complete, end WS row. Using MC only, cont in St st; work 2 rows even, end WS row. Change to smaller needles and Gtr st; work 3 rows; BO all sts.

FINISHING

Block neck wrap to measurements. Sew center back seam.

EARFLAP CAP

SIZES
Small (Medium, Large)

FINISHED MEASUREMENTS
Circumference: 17¾ (21, 25)"

MATERIALS
Classic Elite Yarns

Beatrice (100% merino wool, 50-g ball = approx 63 yd/58 m)

• 3 balls 3253 Sugar Maple

Equivalent yarn

Bulky #5, 189 yd

Needles

• One 16" circular needle size U.S. 9 (5.5 mm) or size to obtain gauge

• One set double-pointed needles (dpn) size U.S. 9 (5.5 mm)

Stitch holders

Stitch markers

Tapestry needle

GAUGE
18 sts and 22 rows = 4" in K2, P2 Rib, slightly stretched. Take time to save time, check your gauge.

SPECIAL TECHNIQUES

I-CORD BIND-OFF METHOD
CO 3 sts at beg of row, k2, k2tog. Sl 3 sts from RH needle back to LH needle, pull yarn taut across back of work; rep from * across until all sts are bound off; k3tog.

WRAP AND TURN
On knit row: Bring yarn to front of work, sl 1p onto RH needle, bring yarn to back of work, sl same st back to LH needle, then turn work.

On purl row: Sl 1p onto RH needle, bring yarn to back of work, sl same st to LH needle, bring yarn to front of work, then turn work.

HIDING WRAPS
On knit row: Pick up wrap from front with RH needle and knit tog with st it wraps.

On purl row: Pick up wrap tbl with RH needle and purl tog with st it wraps.

PATTERN STITCHES

DOUBLE-KNIT SLIPPED-STITCH EDGE
Row 1: (RS) K1, sl 1p, k1, work to last 3 sts, k1, sl 1p, k1.

Row 2: Sl 1p, p1, sl 1p, work to last 3 sts, sl 1p, p1, sl 1p.

Rep Rows 1–2 for Double-Knit Slipped-Stitch Edge.

I-CORD
Using dpn, CO 3 sts; *knit 1 row. Without turning work, sl sts back to beg of row (RH side of needle), pull yarn tightly from end of row; rep from * until cord meas desired length.

I-CORD LOOPS (MAKE 5)

With dpn, CO 1 st; inc 2 sts in 1 st—3 sts. Work I-cord until piece meas 3" from beg. *Next row:* K1, sl CO st onto LH needle, k2tog, k1; place 3 sts on holder. Repeat for four more I-cord loops. Distribute 15 sts on three dpn.

CROWN

Rnd 1: K1, *k2tog, k1; rep to * to last 2 sts, k1, pm for beg of rnd [back of cap], join sts by knitting last st tog with first st, being careful not to twist sts—10 sts. *Rnd 2:* K all sts, inc 2 sts evenly around—12 sts. *Rnd 3:* K1, *p1, k2; rep from * end last rep k1. *Rnd 4:* K1, *p1, m1p, k2; rep from * end last rep k1—16 sts. *Rnd 5:* K1, *p1, m1p, p1, k2: rep from * end last rep k1—20 sts. *Rnd 6:* K1, *p2, m1p, p1, k2; rep from * end last rep k1—24 sts. *Rnd 7:* K1, *p2, m1k, p2, k2; rep from * end last rep k1—28 sts. *Rnd 8:* K1, *p2, k1, m1k, p2, k2; rep from * end last rep k1—32 sts. *Rnd 9 and all odd numbered rnds:* Work in patt as est. *Rnd 10:* Rep Rnd 5—40 sts. *Rnd 12:* Rep Rnd 6—48 sts. *Rnd 14:* Rep Rnd 7—56 sts. *Rnd 16:* Rep Rnd 8—64 sts. *Rnd 18:* Rep Rnd 5—80 sts (end here for size Small). *Rnd 20:* Rep Rnd 6—96 sts (end here for size Medium). *Rnd 22:* K1, *p2, m1p, p2, k2; rep from * around to last st, k1—112 sts (end here for size Large). Change to circular needle. *Next rnd, all sizes:* K1, *p3 (4, 5), k2; rep from * end last rep k1—80 (96, 112) sts. Working rib patt as est, work even until piece meas 5 (6½, 8)" from beg, pm on last rnd as foll: work 21 (25, 29) sts, pm, work 38 (46, 54) sts, pm, work to end of rnd.

SHAPE RIGHT SIDE

Shape right side by short rows as foll: Work 33 (40, 47) sts, Wrap and Turn. Work 31 (37, 43) sts, Wrap and Turn. Work 28 (34, 40) sts, Wrap and Turn. Work 26 (31, 36) sts, Wrap and Turn. Work 23 (28, 33) sts, Wrap and Turn. Work 21 (25, 29) sts, Wrap and Turn. Work to marker, turn.

RIGHT TIE

Next row Small only: (WS) P2, k3, p2. Place all sts except for last 7 worked on holder. *Next row Medium only:* (WS) p2, k1, k2tog, k1, p2. Place all sts except for last 7 worked on holder. *Next row Large only:* (WS) p2, k2tog, k1, k2tog, p2—7 sts. Place all sts except for last 7 worked on holder. *Next row All Sizes:* (RS) K1, m1k, k1, p3, k1, m1k, k1; mark this row—9 sts. Work Double-Knit Slipped Stitch Edge, beg with Row 2; work even until tie meas 10" from marker, end WS row.

I-CORD LOOPS

(RS) Place first 3 sts on dpn [6 sts rem on circular needle]. Using dpn, work 3 sts in I-cord until piece meas 4½" from beg; k3tog—1 st rem. Place rem st on circular needle; p2tog, p2, k3—6 sts rem. (WS) Place first 3 sts on dpn [3 sts rem on circular needle]. Using dpn, work 3 sts in I-cord until loop meas 4½" from beg; k3tog—1 st rem. Place rem st on circular needle; k2tog, k2—3 sts rem. (RS) Place 3 rem sts on dpn; work I-cord until loop meas 4½" from beg; k3tog—1 st rem. Break yarn leaving a 12" tail and pull through last st. Using tapestry needle, sew end of last I-cord to end of tie to form loop, do not break yarn. Draw yarn tail through the center of each I-cord loop, creating 6 smaller loops, and sew to end of tie.

SHAPE LEFT SIDE

Shape left side by short rows as foll: Attach yarn to front edge of right tie, place sts on needle and work as est to marker at back of cap, Hiding Wraps. Turn [WS of cap facing] and beg short row shaping: Work 33 (40, 47) sts, Wrap and Turn. Work 31 (37, 43) sts, Wrap and Turn. Work 28 (34, 40) sts, Wrap and Turn. Work 26 (31, 36) sts, Wrap and Turn. Work 23 (28, 33) sts, Wrap and Turn. Work 21 (25, 29) sts, *do not wrap st*, turn. Work to marker, turn.

LEFT TIE

(RS) K1, m1k, k1, p3, k1, m1k—9 sts; place rem sts on holder. Work as for right tie, including I-cord loops.

EDGINGS

Front edging: Join yarn to lower edge of cap in front of right tie. Work I-Cord Bind-Off Method from edge of right tie to edge of left tie. Sew ends of I-Cord Bind-Off to side edge of ties. *Back edging:* Join yarn to lower edge of cap in back of left tie. Work I-Cord Bind-Off Method from edge of left tie to edge of right tie. Sew ends of I-Cord Bind-Off to side edge of ties.

FINISHING

With CO tails, secure 5 loops at top of cap evenly and close hole.

QUICK HAT
AND MITTEN SET

SIZE

One size

FINISHED MEASUREMENTS

Hat: 20" circumference

Mittens: approx 9½" long

MATERIALS

Classic Elite Yarns:

Tigress (100% wool; 200-g hank = approx 181 yd/166 m)

• 1 hank 7095 Party Cat for both projects

Equivalent yarns

Super Bulky #6, 181 yd

Needles

• One set of 5 double-pointed needles (dpn) size U.S. 11 (8 mm) or size to obtain gauge

Stitch markers

Three safety pins or two small stitch holders and one safety pin

GAUGE

12 sts and 16 rows = 4" in Circular Stockinette Stitch. Take time to save time, check your gauge.

PATTERN STITCH

Circular Stockinette Stitch (St st)

Knit every rnd.

TOP-DOWN HAT

Using dpn, CO 4 sts. *Rnd 1:* Knit. *Rnds 2–3:* Without turning the needle, slide sts to other end of needle, pulling yarn tightly across back, and knit sts. *Rnd 4:* Using one dpn, k1, m1; *using another dpn, k1, m1; rep from * 2 times—8 sts, distributed on 4 needles. Pm for beg of rnd and join, being careful not to twist sts. *Rnd 5:* Knit. *Rnd 6:* *K1, m1, k1; rep from * around—12 sts. *Rnd 7:* Knit. *Rnd 8:* *K1, m1, k1, m1, k1; rep from * around—20 sts. *Rnd 9:* Knit. *Rnd 10:* *K1, m1, k3, m1, k1; rep from * around—28 sts. *Rnd 11:* Knit. *Rnd 12:* *K1, m1, k5, m1, k1; rep from * around—36 sts. *Rnds 13 and 14:* Knit. *Rnd 15:* *K1, m1, k7, m1, k1; rep from * around—44 sts. *Rnds 16–18:* Knit. *Rnd 19:* *K1, m1, k9, m1, k1; rep from * around—52 sts. *Rnds 20–23:* Knit. *Rnd 24:* *K1, m1, k11, m1, k1; rep from * around—60 sts. *Rnds 25–27:* Purl. *Rnds 28–45:* Knit. BO all sts loosely.

TOP-DOWN MITTENS

Using dpn, CO 4 sts. Knit 1 row. Hold piece with CO edge up. Using a second dpn, pick up and knit 4 sts along the CO edge—8 sts. *Rnd 1:* Using one dpn, k1, m1, k1; *using another dpn, k1, m1, k1; rep from * 2 times—12 sts, distributed on 4 needles. *Note:* The first two dpn form one side of the hand, the last two dpns form the other side of the hand. Pm for beg of rnd and join, being careful not to twist sts. *Rnd 2:* Knit. *Rnd 3:* *K1, m1, k4, m1, k1; rep from * once—16 sts [4 sts on each dpn]. *Rnd 4:* Knit. *Rnd 5:* *K1, m1, k6, m1, k1; rep from * once—20 sts [5 sts on each dpn]. *Rnds 6–38:* Work even in Circular St st, placing last 2 sts on stitch holder (piece meas approx 6½" from beg). *Rnd 39:* Work 2 sts and place on holder, work around to end, CO 3 sts—19 sts. *Rnd 40:* CO 3 sts; work around to end—22 sts [6 sts on first dpn, 5 sts on second and third dpn, 6 sts on last dpn]. *Rnds 41–43:* Knit. *Rnd 44:* K2, ssk, k14, k2tog, k2—20 sts rem. *Rnds 45–47:* Purl. *Rnds 48–60:* Knit. BO all sts loosely. **Thumb:** Place sts from holders on dpn; join yarn and pick up and knit 5 sts along left edge of thumb opening, pm, pick up and knit 5 sts along right edge of thumb opening—14 sts. Distribute sts on 3 dpns (5 sts on first needle, 4 sts on second needle, 5 sts on third needle); join, being careful not to twist sts. *Rnd 1:* K3, ssk, work around to end, and transfer last st from last dpn to first dpn—13 sts rem. *Rnd 2:* K2tog, work around to end—12 sts rem. *Rnds 3–6:* Knit. *Rnd 7:* *K2tog, k2; rep from * around—9 sts rem. *Rnds 8–11:* Knit. *Rnd 9:* *K2tog, k1; rep from * around—6 sts rem. *Rnd 10:* *K2tog; rep from * around—3 sts rem. Break yarn leaving a 6" tail; draw tail through rem sts, and pull tight.

FELTED HAT WITH FLOWER

SIZES
Medium (Large)

FINISHED MEASUREMENTS
21 (23)" in circumference, after felting

MATERIALS
Classic Elite Yarns
Paintbox (100% merino wool, 100-g ball =
approx 110 yd/101 m)
• 2 balls 6832 Winsor Violet for hat
• 1 ball 6832 Winsor Violet for flower
Equivalent yarn
Bulky weight #5: 330 yd for both sizes (*Note:* Must shrink when
felted.)
Needles
• One set of 4 double-pointed needles (dpn) U.S. 11 (8 mm)
• One 16" circular needle size U.S. 11 (8 mm) or size to obtain gauge
Stitch marker
Tapestry needle

GAUGE
12 sts and 16 rows = 4" in Stockinette Stitch. Take time to save time,
check your gauge.

PATTERN STITCH

CIRCULAR STOCKINETTE STITCH (ST ST)
Knit every rnd.

HAT

Crown: Using dpn, CO 12 sts; pm for beg of rnd. Divide sts
evenly on three needles. *Rnd 1 and all odd rnds:* Knit. *Rnd
2:* *K1, m1; rep from * around. *Rnd 4:* *K2, m1; rep from *
around. *Rnd 6:* *K3, m1; rep from * around. Cont to work in
this manner, adding an additional knit st before each m1 until
you have 66 (72) sts. Change to circular needles. Work even in
St st until piece meas 8 (8½)" from top of crown. **Brim:** *Rnd 1:*
*K2, m1; rep from * around. Work 4" in St st. BO all sts loosely.

FINISHING

To felt the hat, see "Felting Instructions" on p. 3.

FLOWER ADORNMENT
(NOT FELTED)

Using circular needle, CO 25 sts. *Row 1:* Knit. *Row 2:* Purl.
Row 3: *K1, L1; rep from * around. *Row 4:* Purl. *Row 5:* Purl.
Row 6: *K2, L1; rep from * around. *Row 7:* Purl. *Row 8:* Knit.
Row 9: Purl. *Row 10:* BO all sts, leaving a 12" tail. Roll piece to
form a flower. Using tapestry needle, thread BO tail through BO
sts to secure base of flower, and pull tightly. Sew flower to hat.

FELTED STRIPED SCARF

Note: See p. 210 for matching purse.

SIZE
One size

FINISHED MEASUREMENTS
6½" wide x 51" long, after felting

MATERIALS
Classic Elite Yarns
Inca Alpaca (100% alpaca, 50-g hank = approx 109 yd/100 m)
1 hank Color A—1107 Camacho Blue
1 hank Color B—1197 Canyon Green
1 hank Color C—1179 Santos Grape

1 hank Color D—1135 Cala Cala Moss
1 hank Color E—1127 Cochineal
Equivalent yarn
Worsted weight #4, Colors A–E: 109 yd (*Note:* Must shrink when felted.)
Needles
• One pair size U.S. 9 (5.5 mm) or size to obtain gauge

GAUGE
14 sts and 24 rows = 4" in Stockinette Stitch before felting. Take time to save time, check your gauge.

NOTE

Sl 1k at beg of every row.

PATTERN STITCHES

GARTER STITCH (GTR ST)
Knit every row.

STOCKINETTE STITCH (ST ST)
Knit on RS, purl on WS.

STRIPE SEQUENCE
Rows 1–16: Color A.
Rows 17–32: Color B.
Rows 33–48: Color C.
Rows 49–64: Color D.
Rows 65–80: Color E.
Rep Rows 1–80 for Stripe Sequence.

SCARF

Using Color A, CO 30 sts; beg Gtr st. Work 4 rows, end WS row. (RS) Change to St st and Stripe Sequence; work even until piece meas 67½" from beg, end WS row. Change to Color A; work 3 rows in Gtr st; BO all sts.

FINISHING

To felt the scarf, see "Felting Instructions" on p. 3.

FLOWERED
AND FELTED BAG

Note: See p. 209 for scarf.

SIZE

One size

FINISHED MEASUREMENTS

15" wide x 13" high, after felting

MATERIALS

Classic Elite yarns

Montera (50% llama, 50% wool, 100-g hank = approx 127 yd/116 m)

• 3 hanks Main Color (MC)—3887 Pear
• 1 hank Color A—3893 Ch'ulla Blue
• 1 hank Color B—3832 Puma Magenta
• 1 hank Color C—3856 Majolica Blue
• 1 hank Color D—3885 Bolsita Orange
• 1 hank Color E—3840 Tuscan Hills

Equivalent yarn

Worsted weight #4, MC: 381 yd; Colors A–E: 127 yd (*Note:* Must shrink when felted.)

Needles

• One pair size U.S. 10½ (6.5 mm) for bag and pocket
• One pair size U.S. 9 (5.5 mm) for strap or size to obtain gauge

GAUGE

14 sts and 20 rows = 4" in Stockinette Stitch, using larger needles, before felting. Take time to save time, check your gauge.

PATTERN STITCHES

STOCKINETTE STITCH (ST ST)

Knit on RS, purl on WS.

GARTER STITCH (GTR ST)

Knit every row.

EMBROIDERY

See Embroidery Diagram.

BAG

Using larger needles and MC, CO 62 sts; work in St st until piece meas 35½" from beg; BO all sts.

POCKET

Using larger needles and MC, CO 40 sts; work in St st until piece meas 9" from beg, end WS row. Change to Color B and Gtr st; work 4 rows in St st. BO all sts.

STRAPS (MAKE 2)

Using smaller needles and Color A, CO 8 sts; work in Gtr st until piece meas 38½" from beg. BO all sts.

FINISHING

Sew ends of straps to inside of bag 3" from side edges and 1½" below upper edge of bag. With right sides tog, fold bag in half and sew side seams. Do not sew pocket to bag; felt it separately. To felt the bag and pocket, see "Felting Instructions" on p. 3. When felting is complete and the bag and pocket are dry, work embroidery as indicated on diagram and shown in photo. Sew pocket to bag using cross stitch.

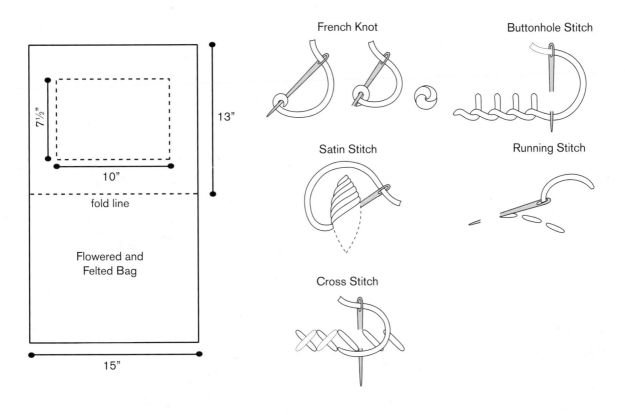

French Knot

Buttonhole Stitch

Satin Stitch

Running Stitch

Cross Stitch

7½"

10"

13"

fold line

Flowered and
Felted Bag

15"

Embroidery Detail

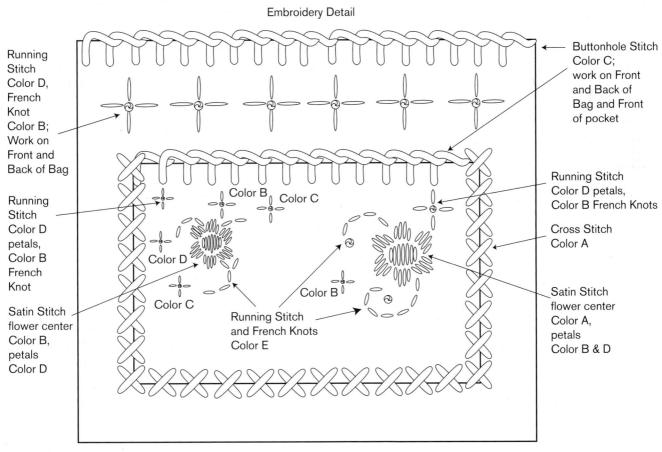

Running
Stitch
Color D,
French
Knot
Color B;
Work on
Front and
Back of Bag

Running
Stitch
Color D
petals,
Color B
French
Knot

Satin Stitch
flower center
Color B,
petals
Color D

Color B   Color C

Color D

Color C

Running Stitch
and French Knots
Color E

Color B

Buttonhole Stitch
Color C;
work on Front
and Back of
Bag and Front
of pocket

Running Stitch
Color D petals,
Color B French Knots

Cross Stitch
Color A

Satin Stitch
flower center
Color A,
petals
Color B & D

CABLED PURSE

SIZE

One size

FINISHED MEASUREMENTS

11" wide x 8" high x 2" deep

MATERIALS

Classic Elite Yarns

Montera (50% llama, 50% wool; 100-g hank = approx 127 yd/116 m)

• 3 hanks 3818 Bittersweet

Equivalent yarn

Worsted weight #4, 381 yd

Needles

• One pair size U.S. 9 (5.5 mm) or size to obtain gauge

• Two double-pointed needles (dpn), size U.S. 7 (4.5 mm)

• One cable needle (cn)

Stitch markers

Tapestry needle

1 snap for purse closure

1 pair 6"-high x 9½"-wide bamboo handles from MJ Trimming (www.mjtrim.com), or equivalent

GAUGE

27 sts = 4 ¾" in Chart A or C, using larger needles; 8 sts = 1 ½" in Chart B, using larger needles; 64 sts = 11" in combined charts, using larger needles; 23 rows = 4" in combined charts, using larger needles; 14 sts and 10 rows = 2" in Linen Stitch, using larger needles. Take time to save time, check your gauge.

NOTE

Sl markers every row.

PATTERN STITCHES

CABLE PANELS

See Charts A (multiple of 27 sts; 8-row rep), B (multiple of 8 sts; 20-row rep), and C (multiple of 27 sts; 8-row rep).

PATTERN SETUP FOR FLAP

See Chart D.

GARTER STITCH (GTR ST)

Knit every row.

LINEN STITCH (EVEN NUMBER OF STITCHES)

Row 1: *K1; with yarn in back, sl 1p; rep from * across.

Row 2: Take yarn to back of work, *k1, sl 1p; rep from * across.

Rep Rows 1–2 for Linen Stitch.

FLAP

Using larger needles, CO 20 sts. Beg working from Pattern Setup for Flap (Chart D) or from text for curved section of flap. *Foundation row:* (WS) K2, p2, k2, pm; p8, pm; k2, p2, k2; CO 7 sts—27 sts. *Row 1:* (RS) P1, k6, p2, 1/1 LC, p2, k8, p2, 1/1 RC, p2; CO 7 sts—34 sts. *Row 2:* K1, p6, k2, p2, k2, p8, k2, p2, k2, p6, k1; CO 6 sts—40 sts. *Row 3:* K1, p2, 1/1 LC, p2, k6, p2, 1/1 RC, p2, 2/2 RC, 2/2 LC, p2, 1/1 LC, p2, k6, p1; CO 6 sts—46 sts. *Row 4:* P1, k2, p2, k2, p6, k2, p2, k2, p8, k2, p2, k2, p6, k2, p2, k2, p1; CO 6 sts—52 sts. *Row 5:* K7, p2, 1/1 RC, p2, k6, p2, 1/1 LC, p2, k8, p2, 1/1 RC, p2, k6, p2, 1/1 LC, p2, k1; CO 6 sts—58 sts. *Row 6:* P7; k2, p2, k2, p6, k2, p2, k2, p8, k2, p2, k2, p6, k2, p2, k2, p7; CO 3 sts—61 sts.

PURSE BODY

Beg with Row 1 of charts; K1 (Gtr edge st), work across 27 sts Chart A, 8 sts Chart B, first 25 sts from Chart C, CO 3 sts [this completes the 27 sts of Chart C, plus 1 edge st]—64 sts. Cont as est, maintaining Gtr edge sts and charts as est. Work even until piece meas 24" from beg. BO all sts in patt.

SIDE GUSSETS (MAKE 2)

Using larger needles, CO 14 sts. Work in Linen Stitch until piece meas 8" from beg, end WS row. BO all sts.

FLAP EDGING (ATTACHED I-CORD)

With WS facing, using dpn, beg at RH side of work approx 4" from beg of flap, CO 4 sts to dpn. *Slide sts to opposite end of needle; k3, sl 1p, insert needle into purse 1 st in from edge, pull up a loop to make a st, psso this new st. Rep from *, attaching cord into each space along edge to CO edge. Work I-cord for 3 rows without attaching to round corner of flap. Rep from *, attaching I-cord into every CO st along curved flap edge. Work I-cord for 3 rows without attaching to round corner of flap. Rep from * until cord length matches opposite end. *Next row:* [K2tog] twice, slide sts to opposite end of dpn, k2tog to end off. Break yarn.

FINISHING

With RS facing and beg at BO edge of purse, sew gusset along side edge for 8", sew 2" short end of gusset to bottom of purse, sew gusset along edge of purse for 8". Rep with second gusset along opposite edge. Attach handles to top of gussets. Sew snaps in place to underside of flap and right side of purse body (see schematic for placement) and fold flap of purse over.

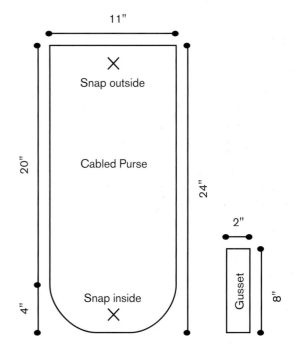

◼ CHART A: CABLE PANEL

Multiple of 27 sts; 8-row rep

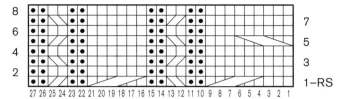

◼ CHART B: CABLE PANEL

Multiple of 8 sts; 20-row rep

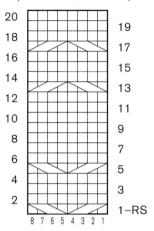

◼ CHART C: CABLE PANEL

Multiple of 27 sts; 8-row rep

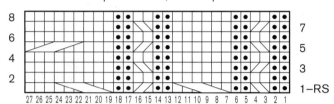

◼ CHART D: PATTERN SETUP FOR FLAP

Multiple of 64 sts; 7-row rep

Beg attached I-Cord

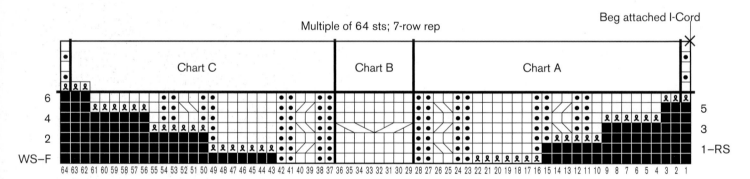

ꝝ	CO.
◼	No st.
☐	Knit on RS, purl on WS.
☐•	Purl on RS, knit on WS.
⧄	Sl 1 st to cn, hold in back, k1; k1 from cn.
⧅	Sl 1 st to cn, hold in front, k1; k1 from cn.
⧄	Sl 2 sts to cn, hold in back, k2; k2 from cn.
⧅	Sl 2 sts to cn, hold in front, k2; k2 from cn.
⧄	Sl 3 sts to cn, hold in back, k3; k3 from cn.
⧅	Sl 3 sts to cn, hold in front, k3; k3 from cn.

FELTED SHOULDER BAG

SIZE

One size

FINISHED MEASUREMENTS

Panels: 12½" wide x 16¾" high, before felting; 10" wide x 14" high, after felting

Strap: 4½" wide x 77" long, before felting; 3" wide x 71" long, after felting

MATERIALS

Classic Elite Yarns

Montera (50% llama, 50% wool; 100-g hank = approx 127 yd/116 m)

• 3 hanks Color A—3846 Maquito Teal

Desert (100% wool; 50-g hank = approx 110 yd/101 m)

• 4 hanks Color B—2093 Endless Sky

Equivalent yarn

Worsted weight #4, Color A: 381 yd; Color B: 440 yd (*Note:* Must shrink when felted.)

Needles

• One pair size U.S. 11 (8 mm) or size to obtain gauge

• Two double-pointed needles (dpn) size U.S. 7 (4.5 mm) for I-Cord.

One 1¼" button

GAUGE

11 sts and 22 rows = 4" in Garter Stitch using 1 strand each of Color A and Color B held tog; 11 sts and 16 rows = 4" in Stockinette Stitch using 1 strand each of Color A and Color B held tog. Take time to save time, check your gauge.

PATTERN STITCHES

GARTER STITCH (GTR ST)

Knit every row.

STOCKINETTE STITCH (ST ST)

Knit on RS, purl on WS.

I-CORD

Using dpn, CO 4 sts; *knit 1 row. Without turning work, sl sts back to beg of row (RH side of needle), pull yarn tightly from end of row; rep from * until cord meas desired length.

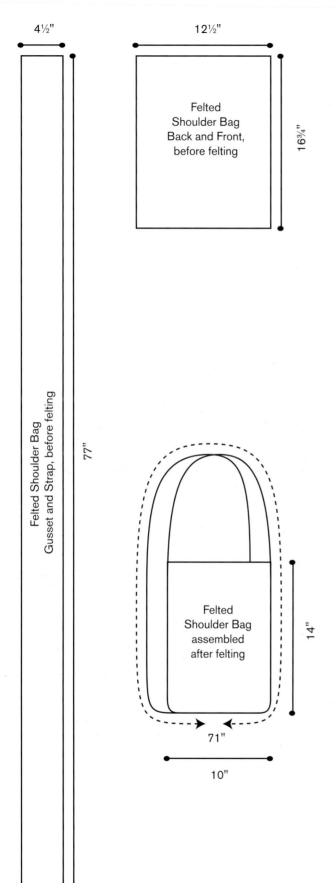

4½"   **12½"**

Felted
Shoulder Bag
Back and Front,
before felting

16¾"

Felted Shoulder Bag
Gusset and Strap, before felting

77"

Felted
Shoulder Bag
assembled
after felting

14"

71"

10"

GUSSET AND STRAP

Using 1 strand each Color A and Color B held tog, CO 12 sts. Beg Gtr st; work even until piece meas 77" from beg. BO all sts.

PANELS (MAKE 2)

Using 1 strand each Color A and Color B held tog, CO 46 sts. Beg Gtr st; work even for 3 rows. Est patt as follows: *Row 1:* (RS) Knit. *Row 2:* K3, p40, k3. Cont as est, working 3 sts each side in Gtr st, center sts in St st, until piece meas 12" from beg, end RS row. Change to Gtr st; work even for 3 rows. BO all sts.

FINISHING

Sew strap around 3 sides of panels, joining pieces into a bag; join ends of strap (see diagram). To felt the bag, see "Felting Instructions" on p. 3; shape bag to finished measurements, stuff with plastic bags if desired to help bag hold its shape, and allow to dry. **Button loop:** Using 1 strand color of choice, work a piece of I-Cord 5" long; attach to center of one panel at the upper edge; sew button opposite button loop.

Designers

Index

Note: **Bold** page numbers indicate a photo, and *italicized* page numbers indicate an illustration or pattern. (When only one number of a page range is **bold** or *italicized*, a photo or illustration appears on one or more of the pages.) Unless noted, all projects are for women.